CLASHING AGENDAS

To Andrew, Emily and Juliet

David Freud

CLASHING AGENDAS

Inside the Welfare Trap

NINE ELMS BOOKS 2021

Published in 2021 by
Nine Elms Books Ltd
Unit 6B, Clapham North Arts Centre
26–32 Voltaire Road,
London SW4 6DH
E info@nineelmsbooks.co.uk
W *www.nineelmsbooks.co.uk*

ISBN print 978-1-910533-52-9
ISBN e-book 978-1-910533-53-6

Jacket illustration by Alamy Stock Photo
Jacket portrait of author by Anna Freud
Jacket and text design, typesetting and layout
by Lyn Davies at *www.lyndaviesdesign.com*
Printed and bound in the UK by Clays Ltd

Contents

PROLOGUE: REFORM

An unplanned journey   I

AMBUSH

1. *The Welfare Trap*   9
2. *Blunting the Salami-slicer*   24

MANOEUVRES

3. *Change of Regime*   37
4. *Inside the Department*   46
5. *The Conservatives Pounce*   53

OPPOSITION

6. *Get Britain Working*   61
7. *Lords and Legislation*   70
8. *Enter Iain Duncan Smith*   76
9. *Moment of Serendipity*   82

PERSUASION

10. *Minister for Welfare Reform*   89
11. *What's the Catch?*   99
12. *Reform for Cuts*   106

PRIVILEGE

13. *Holding the Line*   123
14. *The Lords' Den*   137

AGILE

15. *Digital by Default*   157
16. *Timetable under Pressure*   173

WRITE-OFF

17. *Poacher turns Gamekeeper*   193
18. *The Twin Track*   207

WORTH

19. *Yet another Vacuum*   229
20. *Problems to Solve*   236
21. *UC at Work*   245
22. *Ed Miliband strikes*   251

CUTS

23. *The Pressure Mounts*   263
24. *Tax Credit Volte-face*   273
25. *An Explosive Resignation*   289

VISION

26. *Exit and Future*   297

ADDENDUM: REFORM

Lessons for Government Projects   323

Acknowledgements   337
Dramatis Personæ   338
Glossary of terms   343
Notes   350
Index   356

An Unplanned Journey

"I don't want to do the job," I told the new Conservative Prime Minister. "It's not what I came in to do. I came in to do welfare reform."

"That's exactly what we want you to do," David Cameron assured me. We were on the phone in May 2010. It was two days after he had been invited by the Queen to form a Government in coalition with the Liberal Democrat Party. I had been offered the junior Ministerial job of Parliamentary Undersecretary of State in the Department for Work and Pensions. This was a step down from Minister of State and I was concerned that I wouldn't have the authority to carry out the reforms I was keen to put in hand.

A year earlier David Cameron had put me in the House of Lords to be the Conservative Party's spokesman there on welfare. I was well aware that most junior Ministers in the Lords passed their time putting legislation through the House, not creating and implementing policy. "I spent last summer sorting out a Conservative welfare reform strategy and that is what I wanted to make sure was put into effect," I explained. "I don't particularly want to be a legislative jockey in the Lords."

"That's exactly what IDS wants you to do. The job description is much more important than anything else. He is going to be a chairman figure, so you will be in charge." IDS was shorthand for Iain Duncan Smith, a previous leader of the party and a surprise appointment the previous day to the Cabinet role of Secretary of State at the Department.

"Can I be called Minister for Welfare Reform?"

"Yes, and you can have access to me."

After a little more dickering, I folded. "Well on the basis of the title of Minister for Welfare Reform and access I'm pleased to accept the offer."

My journey to this point had been both unconventional and completely unplanned. Its origins go back to the rivalry between Tony Blair, Labour Prime Minister for 10 years, and his Chancellor and successor, Gordon Brown. By late 2006 Brown had succeeded in forcing his rival to declare his retirement and Blair, somewhat forlornly, wanted to put some control on the policies his putative heir would pursue. With time running out, I was chosen to produce a report on how to get people off welfare into work. This was based less on my background in welfare economics, which was non-existent, and more on my twofold reputation as a problem solver in the investment banking world and as a former journalist who could write quickly.

My report was entitled *Reducing dependency, increasing opportunity: options for the future of welfare to work.*[1] It was published in March 2007 after vigorous battles with Gordon Brown, just three months before he became Prime Minister. Wrangling in semi-public with Gordon Brown was always a sound career move. More importantly, my report found the balance between Right and Left in British politics by increasing the obligation to find work (Right) and designing a funded structure to help people make the move (Left). It was endorsed by all three of the major parties in Parliament. As a result I became, for a time, a symbol of radical welfare reform.

Given this reputation, when James Purnell was appointed by Gordon Brown to take over at the Department for Work and Pensions in early 2008, he thought it made sense to re-appoint me as an independent adviser, rather than leave the opportunity open to the Conservatives. He made the offer without asking Gordon Brown, who I heard later was furious.

The Conservatives did not give up and, as my year with the Department came to an end, they made me an offer to become their welfare spokesman in the House of Lords. The prospect of implementing the welfare changes I was keen on, rather than just advising on them, was irresistible. While I was called a turncoat by Labour, in reality the change I made was from apolitical (albeit Conservative-voting) adviser to front-line politician. In the 15 months till the following election I busied myself designing the Conservative approach to boosting employment as the country struggled to recover from the financial meltdown of 2008. I also helped develop a way of rebuilding the structure of the benefits system itself. This latter challenge was the central reason I accepted David Cameron's offer to be the Minister for Welfare Reform in May 2010.

I was in my 60th year when I entered Ministerial office and my background was as unconventional as my journey. My father was the grandson of Sigmund Freud, the inventor of psychoanalysis, and he made sure I was conversant with our family traditions. Indeed, I was to find an awareness of psychological complexities valuable many years later when addressing welfare issues. Nevertheless, I avoided the family trade and became a journalist. I spent eight years at the *Financial Times*, which was where I first began to explore the nature of the UK welfare system. From here I was head-hunted into the City, where I spent the greater part of my career as an investment banker. I retired from banking in 2003 and was working for a charitable foundation by the time I was approached to look into the welfare system.

I stayed in my role as Minister for Welfare Reform for six-and-a-half years. Indeed, when I retired, at the end of 2016, I was the only member of the Government doing the same substantial portfolio as at the outset in May 2010. My role spanned a number of functions. I was responsible for creating the policy for reforming the welfare system and in particular the Universal Credit centrepiece. I needed to justify those policies in public and, as the process of implementation became more and more problematic, found myself sucked into detailed project implementation. Through all this I was driven by a determination to end the trap for those on welfare – the trap that made it difficult for people to free themselves from dependency on the state. Iain Duncan Smith, my Secretary of State for most of the period, proved anything but a hands-off chairman figure and threw himself wholeheartedly into the reform strategy. We formed a close and effective working relationship and he let me push ahead with all the interrelated projects with minimal interference. After he resigned in an explosion of rage in March 2016, he told me: "I couldn't have done it without you and you couldn't have done it without me." This is a typically succinct summary of our mutual dependence and, not surprisingly, Iain is a major figure in this account.

I found the language of politics the most difficult to adjust to. Businessmen survive by seeing the world for what it is and adapting to those realities. This is doubly the case for those operating in financial markets, where dramatic and rapid value swings reflect developments in the real world with great immediacy. These imperatives do not exist in politics, where language is deliberately opaque to avoid giving offence and often aspires to describe what the world should be like or, indeed, might be like in the future. My boss, Iain Duncan Smith, was a past master of this use of language – privately and publicly. Occasionally I caught him looking at me in despair as I described the reality as I saw it. In truth I had a difficult hand to play here. I was trying to reform the system and help implement that reform. This needed an analytic approach, and straight talking about the real issues, not confusing myself with hoped-for outcomes. In the event, I was only caught a handful of times making an inappropriate (and sometimes over-colourful) observation, although some of the episodes were quite painful.

The story of how difficult it proved to achieve major reform in welfare turns into tragedy in the later chapters of this book, after the Conservatives won an outright majority in 2015. Two agendas clashed violently; the systemic reform that Iain and I were promoting from the Department and the determination of the Chancellor, George Osborne, to take a substantial and immediate bite out of the welfare budget. I had accepted the need for earlier rounds of cuts as the Chancellor battled to reduce the alarming deficit generated after the 2008 crash. However, I was fundamentally opposed to the bulk of the cuts imposed from 2015 by the Chancellor's enforcer, the Treasury, even though I had to carry many of them out. I had found the welfare system to be driven by a complex interplay of skills, expectations and disability. Crude cuts in one area risked demand springing up elsewhere, as indeed the Government discovered when the demand for disability payments rose. Real cost reductions, in my view, could only be achieved by sophisticated restructuring.

My objections in 2015 were based on a view that austerity had been conducted in a partial way. It had focused on targets such as students, Local Authorities and welfare recipients. Pensioners were untouched, despite as a group owning the majority of assets. By 2015, the spending cuts had shrunk the gap between the amount the Government was spending and the tax it was raising. As the deficit closed in on the 3 percent of GDP generally found unproblematic, I believed that it was time to move to a more balanced approach. The Chancellor, however, doubled down on his welfare strategy. The struggle left the country with a new, streamlined welfare system at the cost of real hardship for many benefit recipients. In subsequent years many of the cuts were to be reversed, particularly under the pressure of responding to the Covid 19 crisis. The system itself, meanwhile, stood up to the dramatic increase in claimant volumes.

The book closes with two sections which reflect my experience. Chapter 26 incorporates my views on how the welfare system can be developed and improved in the decades to come. The final chapter takes a broader theme. It examines why it was so difficult to implement an endeavour of the scale of Universal Credit and explores improvements in Governance to allow future projects a smoother path.

Clashing Agendas takes the whole 10-year period of my involvement in welfare, from the Independent Report of 2007 to my retirement at the end of 2016. It is not intended as a definitive history of welfare reform over this tumultuous period. Rather it aims to describe my own experience, albeit, since I was one of the major actors, capturing much of the process. In the main, I have stuck to what I saw and heard with my own eyes and ears. Events are described as they appeared to me at the time, though I have occasionally incorporated afterthoughts, reflecting information I learned later. I have not attempted to do much interpretation of people's motives, allowing their actions to speak for them whenever I can. I have also endeavoured to allow all the actors their own space – whatever my own standpoint and reactions might have been at the time.

I have written for the general reader, albeit one interested in how Government actually works. In particular, I have illustrated the interaction between the political system and the permanent civil service. I have relied heavily on direct speech through the book, not least to maintain the immediacy of the experience. While I was ferociously busy for the period, every week or fortnight I would jot down the key bits of dialogue that had occurred in the interim. At crunch meetings I was sometimes able to write an absolutely contemporaneous note in the shorthand I had learned as a journalist. So, while the quotes may not always contain the exact phraseology, I was recording them soon enough to capture their substance and spirit.

My goal has been to capture the pell-mell process of transforming the British welfare system. This is a structure that, I believe, will be one of the foundation stones of our society for many decades to come. Others will be able to assemble the formal history (with the Institute of Government having already made a start).[2] Here, I aim to capture the personalities and battles in what proved a monumental task.

May 2021

PART I

AMBUSH

November 2006 – March 2007

CHAPTER I

The Welfare Trap

"The folk round at Work and Pensions are looking for someone to write a paper on what to do with welfare. I told them you were just the man for it. Do you have any spare capacity at the moment? It shouldn't be too onerous: two or three days a week for a couple of months."

It was late November 2006 and I was looking at an email from Tim Stone, a former banking colleague from S.G. Warburg. He was now an adviser at the corporate finance arm of the giant accountancy firm KPMG and evidently had been engaged by the Department for Work and Pensions. I was instantly attracted to the prospect. Many years earlier, as deputy to the economics correspondent of the *Financial Times*, I had written a mainstream feature on how the welfare system was trapping people in poverty. "The relationship between the means-tested benefits and the tax system has also led to the development of the so-called poverty trap, in which net earnings can fall with increased wages. People in the trap lose more in benefits than they gain in wages after tax is taken into account." [3] My casual observation over the years since I wrote in 1979 suggested a substantial further deterioration in the way the system demotivated and trapped people within it. Most invidiously, the number of disabled claimants, prohibited from normal working under the rules of their benefit, had soared to 2.7 million over the period.

As to my spare capacity, I had plenty. I had retired from investment banking at the end of 2003 and two years later had taken up a role running the Portland Trust, a foundation operating in the Middle East. The Trust's approach was to encourage the peace process between Israelis and Palestinians through economic development on both sides. With the violent Hamas take-over of Gaza raging, all relevant activity in the region was at a standstill. I was twiddling my thumbs.

A couple of days later I turned up at Richmond House, with its neo-Tudor façade opposite the Foreign Office on Whitehall, to meet John Williams, Special Adviser to the Secretary of State. Unknown to me, he had been working up a concept of using payment by results to incentivise contractors to deal with hard employment cases.

I laid out my stall. "We're wasting an enormous amount of money paying people to do nothing when we could be investing in getting them into the world of work and making sure they are securely placed there."

He tested me: "How could we afford that? The Treasury won't let us have any funding."

"We use the savings that the state makes when people go back to work. It doesn't matter that the Treasury won't let us have the money upfront. We'll get the funding from the private sector. They'll invest their money to get people into work and the state can reimburse them from the actual savings when it doesn't have to pay out the benefits."

"Will the private sector want to take the risk?"

"I'm sure it will. It will be an attractive new business area."

Fortuitously I had focused on exactly the issues that interested John. He was immediately interested in this mechanism for ramping up the numbers getting back into work. He had previously spent several years as director of public services at the Confederation of British Industry (CBI), so was fully conversant with business dynamics. He had become John Hutton's Special Adviser less than two years earlier when he was Cabinet Office Minister and had followed him to the Department later in 2005. He was confident, clever and good company. Now he filled me in on the background to the project.

"Tony's setting up these six reviews to shape policy after he's gone," he told me. [4] 'Tony' was a familiar reference to the Prime Minister, Tony Blair. He went on: "One of them is on economic efficiency. So a couple of months ago John asked him whether he wanted anything on welfare to go into that policy review. Tony practically bit his hand off. Of course, Gordon's being difficult. But at the moment he's on board. We need this report bloody fast. Tony's likely to go in the summer but it could be before. Could you be ready by early March?"

That left me three months.

"If I need to be."

"And don't expect an easy ride. This Department has always been a fiefdom of the Treasury. Under John Hutton it's become much more independent. So you can expect quite a lot of resistance."

It was the key interview. Shortly afterwards I was back at Richmond House, this time to meet John Hutton, alongside John Williams and Leigh Lewis, the Department's Permanent Secretary. John Hutton and I sat on two armchairs, facing each other. Originally a law lecturer, he had secured his first cabinet post less than a year earlier at the Department. His delivery, while relaxed, was somewhat clipped. He had clearly mastered his brief, and we focused on the issues in some detail, spending most of the time going over the way private sector funding could be used to get people back to work.

"The Treasury will resist, you know. They have rigid rules about not allowing benefit spending to be mixed with our Departmental budget."

"The Treasury have a lot of dysfunctional rules. When they come under pressure, they usually manage to find a justification to change them. That's what I found when we rescued the Channel Tunnel Rail Link." This 1998 restructuring had been my responsibility while I was a banker.

John Williams and Leigh Lewis left the office as we moved on to the sharp end of the meeting. John Hutton said: "We would like to employ you to write this Independent Report for the Department. We don't think it will take too much of your time; a few days a week for the next two or three months. We'll provide a strong team to support you, meaning you'll have a largely supervisory role. So if we can agree terms..."

"Oh, I don't want to be paid," I interrupted. He looked genuinely shocked. There was a long pause. "Well in that case, if you are agreeable, it is my pleasure to confirm your appointment. It'll be a few weeks before we announce it publicly – just to give you time to get going."

As simply as that I was given the enormous task of reviewing the ramshackle structure of UK welfare, grown piecemeal over generations in response to conflicting imperatives till it was incomprehensible and incoherent. The role could only have gone to such an outsider as me in the peculiar political circumstances of the time. The coup against Tony Blair during the previous September had forced him to announce a rough departure time-table which in turn created pressure for rapid output before anything else. My experience in public/private financing as an investment banker had clearly been a plus-point in favour of my appointment; but equally important was my background as a journalist accustomed to tight deadlines.

As for my refusal of payment, when I retired from banking three years earlier, I had decided that I would only do things that interested me and not allow financial considerations to influence the selection. I was also deeply suspicious of the political process and did not wish to feel owned by anyone. I continued to resist payment subsequently and it probably proved a key factor in saving my career when it hung by a thread many years later – although at the time I never remotely envisaged such a consequence.

I didn't get out of the building unscathed. As I walked down the corridor, Leigh Lewis, the Permanent Secretary, took me firmly to one side. He left me in no doubt as to his position.

"I need to warn you, David, against contracting all the employment services out from Jobcentre Plus. I have spent years putting benefits delivery together with employment services and I am simply not prepared to see that torn apart again. Do you understand me?"

Leigh had passed virtually his whole civil service career in DWP and its predecessor departments. Ironically, this first encounter was the only time I was to see him lose the calm, supportive presence that was his norm. In the months to come I would find myself seeking – and following – his advice on a number of occasions. He told me later that he was reacting to some of the 'glib' suggestions in the meeting that Jobcentre Plus (commonly referred to as JCP) should simply be split up and sold off in whole or part to the private sector.

I left the building under no illusions that, if I recommended the contracting out of all employment services from JCP, my report would never see the light of day and if it did, then none of it would be enacted.

Here was the outsider's first lesson in weaving a path through the requirements of the key actors. Leigh Lewis had been responsible for creating JCP, putting the old Jobcentre employment services together with the Benefits Agency, which made payments to the disabled, single mothers, unemployed and others. That process had only been completed earlier in the year, after a five-year roll-out costing £1.9 billion and involving the closure of nearly half the offices of the two arms.[5]

"The private sector spend should be on top of current activity, not replace it," I said weakly. Our encounter made one decision straight-forward. The Permanent Secretary sent two prospective team leaders for me to choose between. The clincher for the selection of Isobel Stephen was the fact that she had been deeply involved in JCP implementation. If I wanted to side-step one particular battle, having someone Leigh Lewis trusted at my side could do no harm.

She proved extremely quick at absorbing and then internalising new concepts. At our first meeting she looked shocked at some of the ideas I threw at her – particularly around the contracting model. Within a week she was saying: "There's nothing so special about this approach, David. It's all pretty obvious, isn't it?" She was to recruit a formidable team, with Tony Wilson working on the drafts and Phill Wells analysing the data and throwing it into a series of graphs and tables. Pete Searle, back from a secondment in Australia, created a section of international comparisons.

There was one further key meeting as I got under way. John Williams took me to see Gareth Davies, Blair's senior policy adviser on welfare. In his early thirties, he was fresh-faced and welcoming. His original career had been as a consultant at the accountants Price Waterhouse Coopers, where he worked on privatisation and regulation, the cross-over between the public and private sectors.

"We need to do something radical, like they did in the US," he told me. "John Hutton and I travelled over there in the summer and what they've done is genuinely impressive."

John Williams had more advice for me: "You need to create a 'burning platform', David." I must have looked puzzled. "You've got to make this issue urgent, so that inaction isn't an option," he explained.

"Why don't you tell us how much extra economic activity there will be if we get all these extra people into work?" Gareth proposed.

Now I had a mountain of material to absorb and Isobel set about collecting it for me and making sure I saw the relevant Departmental experts. Coincidentally in early December I was attending a conference in Washington and took the opportunity to meet one of the principal architects of US welfare reform, Ron Haskins. [6]

We met in his office at the Brookings Institution. I had read his account of the battle to reform welfare in the US with fascination. In the flesh, he was jovial and knowledgeable, peering over his brown-framed glasses with an academic's enthusiasm for pinning down the implications of key measures.

"It was important to put a five-year limit on the time people can receive welfare," he told me. "But the mechanical process was secondary. Much more key was that we changed the dynamic, the expectation that people have of welfare provision. And once you've set up the expectations, you've got to work the caseload." This was the most valuable advice I got from the interview. However, the US reform had been focused on limiting the support for lone parents and did nothing to help people with disabilities back into the work-place. On this issue, I would have to look elsewhere for solutions.

Back in London I asked Isobel: "Didn't I read a newspaper article a few months ago saying they had proved work is good for you?"

"Oh yes. That was one of our pieces of research. I'll get it for you."

Gordon Waddell and Kim Burton's *Is Work Good For Your Health and Wellbeing?* had been published in September and was an eye-opener. It was a thorough review of all the evidence and its conclusions were unequivocal.

"Work is central to individual identity, social roles and social status," it found. "Work is generally good for physical and mental health and well-being." The converse held: "There is strong evidence that unemployment is generally harmful to health." Most significantly, the findings applied to the sick and disabled. "When their health condition permits, sick and disabled people (particularly those with 'common health problems') should be encouraged to remain in or to (re)-enter work as soon as possible." [7]

Why then, I thought, as I examined the report, did we have a welfare system that protected many people from work, as if it was a necessary evil which only the fittest could undertake? The findings meant that my review could focus unrelentingly on work as an outcome for all, losing the ambiguity that was present in the system as it stood. One of the earliest conclusions I wrote in my review as a consequence was: "This corpus of evidence stands traditional Government policy on its head. Far from being reluctant to engage, the Government could on this evidence be accused of dereliction if it were to fail to do so." It was a sentence that survived intact through all the drafting and re-drafting that was to follow.

By mid-December Isobel's intensive regime of internal meetings was in full swing and she was filling a storage crate with papers and documents which needed reading. Department officials were unburdening themselves to me. "Our regime for lone parents is the kindest in the world," one of them told me. "There is no requirement for them to work until their youngest child is 16 years old. Their only obligation to the state is to show up for an interview at JCP every six months." She showed me a table of international comparisons, with the Netherlands at five years, France and Germany at three, and the US below one year. "If they worked for just 16 hours a week, most of these parents would get out of poverty."

The senior labour analyst I met was scathing about the Government's existing programmes to help people back to work, branded the New Deal. "The bottom line is that most of these programmes cost much more than the Exchequer got back from them." The only exception was the New Deal for those aged 50-plus. This analysis ignored any potential upside from the wider social benefit of providing work for the unemployed. Nevertheless, it represented a highly unwelcome finding.

The New Deal programmes were the Chancellor's personal brainchild. Gordon Brown had spent a significant portion of his time in Opposition developing his ideas on how to move people from welfare benefits into paid employment. His plans emerged as a prominent part of the Labour campaign for the 1997 General Election, and he explicitly funded them with a £5.2 billion windfall tax on the privatised utilities. There were individual New Deal programmes for young people, the long term unemployed and lone parents. There was even a New Deal for musicians. Although the programmes had been contracted out, they were heavily specified and paid the contractors mainly on the basis of completing the requirements. I was not surprised they performed poorly on a crude value for money basis. After all, how could the state successfully lay down a set of common steps to be followed, when people's problems in finding work were so varied?

The full realisation of how sensitive was the ground on which I would be stepping came to me as I went through the table of outcomes. John

Hutton had been careful to incorporate a favourable nod to the New Deal in the terms of reference for my appointment, where I would explore "how the Government can build on its success in using policies such as the New Deal to continue to reduce inactivity..." Nevertheless, I would need to be extremely careful how I expressed myself and should anticipate outright hostility from a Chancellor notoriously sensitive to encroachment on his territory.

Usefully, one of the smaller elements within the New Deal programme did show promise. The Department had experimented with contracting out in 13 areas, called Employment Zones. In these the long-term unemployed were referred to private providers for a period of 30 weeks, with largely outcome related payments based on the contractor's ability to place the client in work and keep them there for at least 13 weeks. They were put on this programme rather than the standard one for this age group, called the New Deal 25 Plus. A detailed comparative study found that "the Zones were substantially more effective in helping participants into work than we estimate would have occurred if the programme operating had been the New Deal 25 Plus."[8] The increased flexibility was seen as the main reason for this relative success.

A week before Christmas, John Hutton announced my appointment, which allowed me to be seen out and about. His speech talked about "whether and how we should strengthen incentives to work; and whether there is a role for greater conditionality in the system." He also foreshadowed my contracting structure, asking: "How can we build a more effective market in the provision of employment services?"[9]

On the Thursday three days later, the last full working day of the year, Isobel took me down to see the Croydon JCP. The evocative scene of the dole office in the comedy film *The Full Monty*, showing long queues up to a counter protected by grills, could not have been more historic. Claimants were seen by appointment and would move down a series of desks if they needed to see a particular expert – a specialist in benefit entitlement first, perhaps, then an employment specialist. It was a slick, high volume operation. And that realisation gave me a solution to the warning shot from the Permanent Secretary four weeks earlier. The Jobcentres could continue to deal with the volumes, while the more problematic clients would receive a tailor-made service from outside contractors.

By now the range of concepts I had ingested over the previous month were beginning to revolve in every waking, and probably sleeping, hour. I went on reading the material from my crate over the Christmas break, between family obligations, but I needed a clear period to put my thoughts on paper. As New Year approached my wife was struck down by a vicious bout of food poisoning – so all our social engagements were cancelled. I settled down at my computer to draft.

In the next three days, over the New Year period, I hammered out a basic text of some 7,000 words, assembling the key concepts. I wrote that the Government's aspiration for an 80 percent employment rate could be achieved, and that it would be economically beneficial for both the UK and for the Exchequer. However, it implied new and innovative policies. The Government would also need to recast the way it assessed its spending framework in this area. There should be more spending on getting the people with most difficulty back to work. The programme to achieve this should be outsourced and payment should be based on successful outcomes, which would allow it to be self-funding, and would encourage a more individualised approach.

Much of the focus would have to concentrate on those on Incapacity Benefit and lone parents, not least because these two categories comprised the bulk of inactive individuals. The official statistics divided the working age population three ways. Active individuals were either in work or were unemployed but looking for work. Individuals were defined as "inactive" if they were not looking for work and many of them were supported by state benefits which did not have a work requirement. On the disabled I wrote: "On average these individuals spend more than five years on benefit (and typically do not leave it for employment). The financial value of such individuals moving into the labour force is substantial."

On Lone Parents I recommended that from 2010, when universal nursery provision was planned, they should work or train from when the youngest child was five.

I drafted the section on funding carefully, fully aware of the Treasury rule which kept a rigid distinction between two types of expenditure. There was the DEL – the Departmental Expenditure Limit – which covered the Department's annual running costs, including the costs of running the Jobcentres and the New Deals. Then there was AME – the

Annually Managed Expenditure – which provided the cash that was paid out in benefits. The latter dwarfed the former. But, as I pointed out in my report, "Clearly, given the active market policies now pursued in the UK, there is a close link between the two. Cuts in spending in DEL could lose the Exchequer much more in AME than its DEL savings."

So I recommended an exercise to link the two spending types more closely. This was really cover for the specific recommendation to allow large-scale funding for my proposed programme. "Contractors should be paid on the basis that individuals are placed in jobs, stay in them, earn promotion and move out of the benefit system over a period of, say, three years. This should encourage contractors to provide the long-term support and skill provision to allow such returns to be earned. The back-loaded nature of the payments to contractors should also allow the system to finance itself post facto out of AME savings. The length of the relationship with individual clients requires that the contracts are let for a period of seven years or so."

Finally, I turned to the most difficult issue of all: the shape of the benefit system itself. There was no point in ramping up spending to support people into the labour market if the benefit system itself provided a fundamental disincentive to take part. I concluded: "The benefits of moving to a single system of benefits for all people of working age lie principally in the simplicity and clarity of the incentives it would allow. Accordingly this report recommends that a new benefit replaces Jobseekers Allowance (JSA – the standard benefit for the unemployed), Income Support (IS – available in the main for lone parents) and Incapacity Benefit (IB – for the disabled and soon to become the Employment and Support Allowance or ESA)." Even as I wrote I was dubious about whether I would have the time or resources to lock down a recommendation as fundamental as this.

The draft was littered with figures in square brackets and titles in bold for non-existent tables and graphs. Nevertheless, when I brought it into the Department in the New Year there was palpable shock. Later Phill Wells joked: "We thought you'd come bumbling into the Department asking things like: 'What does JSA stand for?'"

Now they had something to get their teeth into. The Ministerial team had moved from Richmond House at the turn of the year into Caxton

House, just behind Westminster's Methodist Central Hall. They brought most of the officials with them and it was here that Isobel and Tony started chopping the text up into the various chapters. Alongside them, Phill got to work assembling the mountain of analysis that I had demanded. I worked on fleshing out the key sections, going into detail on the contracting model, the funding and the issues surrounding a single benefit. Each draft would circulate round the Department, with officials throwing in corrections and improvements – as well as removing anything they found too contentious.

Isobel said: "You should be ready to see outsiders soon, David. Once we've cleaned up your filthy capital markets' language. You cannot say things like 'the wretched of the earth'."

"It was a joke," I protested. "It's the title of a book by Frantz Fanon."

"You cannot say it, even if it's a joke and even if it's the title of a famous book which no-one's heard of. The correct expressions are 'furthest from the labour market', 'the most vulnerable' and 'the hard to help'."

From mid-January I started meeting a series of external experts and interested parties, or 'stakeholders' in the Whitehall jargon.

Roy Sainsbury, a professor at York University's Social Policy Research Unit, brought a paper with him on benefit reform. "We need a single working age benefit," he told me forcefully. "Just do it. It should support welfare-to-work strategies for all claimants and it needs to break down the barriers stopping disabled people working. That includes all the uncertainty of moving between Incapacity Benefit and JSA, the incentive to stay 'sick' because of the higher rate of incapacity payment, and the contradiction people face between being on an out of work benefit and expectations to move to work."

It was one thing to declare the need for a single benefit; another thing to design one. By the end of January, I was recommending a common basic allowance with one additional premium for work-related activity and another for disability. But I was deeply uncertain about the costs and the impacts of such a change and all the fundamental questions it raised. Should the payment go to households or to individuals? How angry would the Chancellor be if we incorporated the tax credit system? Should housing benefit be included?

I told Leigh Lewis of my concern. "I simply don't have the time to look at the benefit structure properly," I confessed. "It's a big modelling job." Our relationship had improved immeasurably since I had drawn the distinction between the JCP volume related business and the contractors' more individual provision.

"Look, David, in these papers it's often best to concentrate on a particular area. You can't expect to cover absolutely everything. Best keep that section pretty vague."

In the final version I explored some of the design options, concluding: "There is a strong case for moving towards a single system of working age benefits, ideally a single benefit." My proposal for a Commission to examine this was watered down to: "Debate on further reform should be informed by detailed modelling on the impacts on work incentives, costs and benefits (for individuals, the Exchequer and society) and take into account the interactions between all out-of-work and in-work support. This should call on existing expertise in academia, think-tanks and the private and public sectors." This was the one part of my report which Government barely acknowledged. Unknown to me, however, my challenge was taken up. It was to bear fruit two-and-a-half years later.

Other meetings were less problematic. Ian Charlesworth, the Chief Executive of the Shaw Trust, biggest of the voluntary groups working in welfare, provided a powerful illustration of why an outcome-based payment would work. "Let's take the case of someone who needs five interventions to get into work. If the state specifies four of those interventions, we can do them and get paid – but that person still won't get a job. If you pay me to get him a job, I'll make damn sure that I do all five of them."

I got a valuable endorsement of my proposed division between the JCP volume business and the more individualised approach required from the contractors from one of the largest companies looking to enter the market, Serco. This was a company I had advised some years earlier when I was an investment banker.

"We'd like to take the whole caseload, David, like they do in Australia," Chris Hyman, the Chief Executive told me.

"I'm proposing two very different business models," I explained. "JCP will continue to do the standard volume business while contractors will only be paid if they get someone into a job and keep them there for a quite extended period. That's what the State wants; not short-term job entries but attachment to the world of work. I think you would find it quite hard to combine those two business models."

Grudgingly, Chris Hyman agreed. His obvious interest in the detailed proposals, as well as that of some of his top managers, gave me confidence that the business structure I was developing would appeal to the corporate world. Given the amount of capital the contractors would need to fund the upfront investment, I believed that it was inevitable that corporates would undertake the bulk of the work.

In all I was to hold more than 20 meetings with interested groups as drafting proceeded. Despite Isobel's discipline, I sometimes couldn't resist incorporating the odd joke. At one meeting I cut loose with my views on the benefit bill in the Annually Managed Expenditure, or AME, category of the Government's accounts. "It's like the Holy Roman Empire, which Voltaire dismissed as neither Holy, Roman nor an Empire. Expenditure on benefits is not 'Annual'; it's an open-ended obligation. It's not 'Managed'; it's paid out on demand. I wouldn't even categorise it as 'Expenditure'; it's waste. That's why I'm exploring using the savings from reducing the benefit bill to fund programmes to get people into work. Those programmes are in the Departmental Expenditure Limit (DEL) category, and the Treasury split the two categories in 1998 and resists mixing them."

By now Phill Wells was locking down the key figures behind the payment by results structure. The value of moving someone off disability benefits into work was worth £9,000 a year to the Exchequer. "Wow," I said. "That's quite a lot more than I thought." The savings for the unemployed and lone parents were somewhat lower, but still appreciable.

Phill and I took Gareth Davies through the numbers in late January.

"These figures mean that savings to the State could run at up to £9 billion a year, once the programmes have got into gear." I told him. "We can therefore justify creating a big programme to get these benefits – in the region of £3 billion to £4 billion a year. That's a multiple of our current spend of roughly £1 billion."

"And have you now got a figure for what all this could be worth to the country; the scale of the prize?" asked Gareth.

"Phill's been working on the GDP (Gross Domestic Product) impact that you asked for. If we get to the 80 percent employment target, we would increase the country's output by 2.5 percent, or £30 billion, per year by 2030."

"That would give Tony the big prize that he's looking for," concluded Gareth.

By the end of the month we were ready to see Tony Blair. At mid-morning on 30 January Gareth led us into No. 10 and down a short passage-way to the Prime Minister's cosy ground-floor study, where we sat on the couches which took up one half of the room. Disconcertingly Tony Blair's face was caked in heavy make-up. (He was due to make a public appearance with the French Presidential aspirant Nicolas Sarkozy immediately afterwards.)

My presentation was 125 words on a single sheet of paper, describing my structure in 12 steps and checking off the six issues that were raised by it.

"Absolutely central to this proposal is the link between DEL and AME. Without it, this big programme cannot be funded, "I explained. "I am proposing a substantial widening of what JCP does, making it the front end for all benefits – for the disabled, for their partners, for single parents. This is a big step forward from the New Deal structure, and there will be sensitivities about that. (I didn't need to spell out that it would be Gordon Brown who would be sensitive). I want Lone Parents to start looking for work when their youngest is five, not 16. I am arguing that we should aim to get people off Incapacity Benefit, even if they have been on it for years and, finally, I am recommending a single benefit even though I will not have been able to work out the proposition in any detail."

Blair focused thoroughly on the proposals. He concluded: "This is very good; just what we want. What are the arrangements for launching it?"

"The Treasury are talking about it being for internal use only and not for publication," warned Gareth.

Blair laughed. Diaries quickly came out and a date less than five weeks away was pinpointed for public launch. And then we left him to his Sarkozy visit. I would have been still more impressed by his composure if I had known that his previous meeting was with a Scotland Yard detective investigating the extent of his personal involvement in the Cash for Honours scandal that was then raging.

I was intensely worried about whether my DEL-AME link would get through. Without it I had no funding and all my proposals would collapse.

An avuncular Leigh Lewis said: "David, you're not the first person to see the absurdity of keeping DEL and AME so separate. It's like a castle defended by Treasury officials. People have stormed it and been thrown off the battlements again and again to lie battered in the ditch. The key difference in this model is that you've transferred the risk to the private sector. So this time there's a chance that you may succeed in taking the castle."

CHAPTER 2

Blunting the Salami-slicer

Any optimism that the passage of my paper would be smooth evaporated in February. Out of the blue Shriti Vadera called me. "David, I hear you've written a powerful paper on welfare." I knew Shriti well. We had been colleagues at S.G. Warburg/UBS before she left to work for Gordon Brown at the Treasury in 1999. Indeed, she had worked for me on a couple of deals at the bank. She had been intensely hard-working and driven then; now her tone exuded far greater authority. In the eight years working for Brown she had developed a formidable reputation for driving through, with some force, his initiatives on the private sector and international finance. I discovered later that she had enthusiastically endorsed my appointment and accordingly would take internal flak if my performance was unsatisfactory. She came quickly to the point of the call. "Your problem is that your paper will be lost with regime change," she advised. "You might think of arranging for it to be delayed for a couple of months so that Gordon can announce the main elements in the Budget. Then it will become Gordon's initiative."

"Shriti, how on earth am I going to be able to delay it? The whole No. 10 machine is in full swing. If it needs delaying, I'm sure there are resources in the Treasury that can arrange it." There was a grunt at the other end of the phone. "Let me go back and see what we can do."

At least this implied endorsement was a definite step up from the earlier Treasury attitude. Through January they had been telling Departmental officials that the report should remain private and not be published.

But on this occasion the Treasury machine ran up against a determined Prime Minister. On the last weekend in February Tony Blair told Gordon Brown that the report would definitely be launched on Monday, 5 March. Gareth Davies told me later that week that Blair had been blunt: "If you aren't there it will look as if you are against radical reform in an important part of the Government's agenda." In this period of intense manoeuvre to take over as leader, Brown decided that he needed to be at the launch.

It did not mean that he needed to accept the contents of my report, however. On Monday evening I got a call from Shriti: "I've got more information. Gordon is in fact prepared to support the review. However, it needs large sections removed. We're not talking about redrafting. We're talking about cutting it to a third of its length." I didn't answer.

She was back on the phone early the next morning. "Come round and see Gordon at 6:30 this evening." That sparked a series of meetings in the Department. At mid-morning I went to see Leigh Lewis. The Permanent Secretary seemed mildly amused at my predicament. "When Adair Turner was doing his pensions report Gordon ended up throwing the PowerPoint slides at him." Having braced me for the likely tone of the meeting, he ended with the Mandarin-style advice: "You may wish to hold firm." Later I was called in for a meeting with an anxious John Hutton: "Gordon is concerned about the statement that we are not going to meet the child poverty target. He doesn't like the financial model for the transfer of risk. He doesn't like the seven-year contracts or the cost benefit analysis."

As dusk fell, I walked over to the handsome Treasury building on Horse Guards road. I was expected at the reception desk and taken straight upstairs to the Ministerial Corridor. Briefly I waited in the Chancellor's private office – a large room still bustling with civil servants despite the hour. Then I was ushered into Gordon Brown's study, where he was waiting for me with Shriti. It was a surprisingly small, even cosy, room. At the far end was Gordon Brown's desk and there was just room for a couch on the side wall, alongside two armchairs. The Chancellor stood up from the far armchair to welcome me, as I made my way to the one facing him. Shriti was on the couch.

"You know Shriti?" His tone was unexpectedly friendly.

"I'm one of the few people who have both had Shriti working for them and worked for her."

"We all work for Shriti. I should tell you what happened at the Vatican a couple of weeks ago over our vaccine project. Their security systems are not too efficient. The Queen of Jordan was visiting at the same time and they mixed them up. So Shriti was being ushered through, while the Queen was penned up in a room with the secretaries and they wouldn't let her out."

"Shriti would make a good Queen of Jordan."

"She would indeed." Then, "You'll be interested in doing some more on this in the months to come?"

This was an unexpected overture, a probe into what he could offer me in return for co-operation. "Oh, I'm not sure," I demurred. "I've got to get back to my Palestinians. I've been badly neglecting them in the last few weeks."

"Absolutely, absolutely; we need you to do that, don't we Shriti." Abruptly the atmosphere of bonhomie disappeared and the conversation switched to the topic in hand. He opened my report at the fourth chapter, dealing with contracting out. "This table is all wrong." His forefinger, nail bitten to the quick, stabbed at it angrily.

The table was at the heart of the cost/benefit estimates to demonstrate the savings when people were taken off welfare and found work. Phill Wells had laboured long and hard on the model. "I think it's pretty reliable."

"No. It doesn't show the costs to use when a Lone Parent goes to work."

"Yes it does. Look, £2,200."

"It's much more than that. It's £3,400. Besides, there are a lot of costs in moving someone from benefit to work."

We were getting bogged down. Inspiration struck as a route out of the impasse. "This is the gross effect," I said. "I could change the title to make it clear it's gross."

He seized on the meaningless distinction. "Yes, you should change the language. But really the whole table is unacceptable laid out like this. It simply gives ammunition to the Tories."

"They're just my estimates. I'll make clear in the text that they're my estimates and I could write a foreword making it clear."

"If it's in tabular form in a report like this people will use them against us."

"All right. I'll take out the table and use the actual figures in narrative form." This first concession was at least purely presentational. The next was more substantial, although hardly central.

"It's also unacceptable that you say the child poverty target won't be met."

"I can take that out for you."

"Good. Now why don't you talk to my officials about sorting out the rest of it?"

"I really don't want to. They've already had a meeting with my team this afternoon."

"How do you know all this will work anyway?" He was referring to my proposal that contractors should develop a three-year relationship with claimants to help them get into work and stay there for three years.

"I'm saying we should pilot it."

"Where does it say that? It doesn't say that."

"It does." I riffled through the pages in a failed attempt to locate the paragraph (which had been moved to the last section of the draft). "It does," I repeated. "And I can absolutely re-emphasise that in the text."

Shriti interrupted: "Your next meeting is waiting." He stood up. "I will champion this and it will happen. But you must understand that you can't tie the Government to spending and specific timetables. I'll leave you to sort it out with the team." Having softened me up to his satisfaction, he hurried out of the room, presumably unaware that bullying by chief executives and finance directors was the daily fare of investment bankers.

Shriti took me to a small office next door and left me to the tender mercies of two Treasury officials and another trusted Special Adviser, Spencer Livermore. Despite his youth – he was in his early thirties – Spencer Livermore had spent the last eight years as a Treasury Special Adviser and was immensely experienced. Thin and composed, he maintained a cold and ascetic façade as we settled into the negotiation.

It was a gruelling two-hour session. They started working through the draft, paragraph by paragraph.

"You can't have the child poverty discussion in the second chapter."

"I'm happy to move it to the fifth chapter."

"Take out the 80 percent target rate for employment."

"It's a current aspiration for the Government. I'm happy to leave it as an aspiration."

"All of Chapter 4 has to go."

"I will not budge on Chapter 4."

"Take out this section on skills."

I started to laugh. "That's a direct summary of what was published in the Leitch paper, which you commissioned." (Sandy Leitch had published the final report of his 'Review of Skills' less than three months earlier.) [10]

Spencer Livermore tried to justify the demand: "There was some very contested drafting that went into Leitch, so it has to be exact."

It was a turning point. Patronisingly I proposed: "Why don't you send me an exact draft tomorrow and then we'll change it."

"I'll have someone look at it."

After that I stiffened my opposition to each of their proposals. By 9.15 pm they were ready to give up and I walked out of the Treasury building onto Horse Guards Road pleased not to have given anything away.

The ambush was, of course, just the start of the process. Next day Isobel was under attack from a Treasury team who were emailing amendments through on an industrial scale. "There seem to be about 12 of them pushing this stuff through," she said in despair. "They are taking the report to bits."

I took a look at some of the amendments that had come through. "Actually, some of these are quite helpful. Accidentally. They haven't had time to co-ordinate their approaches. We'll just go through them and you can email back 'David accepts this amendment' to the ones we like and 'David does not accept this amendment' to the ones we don't." It was a long day but Isobel and the team soon got into the swing of telling the Treasury what to do with their drafting proposals.

Shriti, now thoroughly regretting her initial sponsorship of my appointment, felt responsible for getting me back under control, even though welfare was far from her own brief. She was back on the phone early in the evening as I was walking down Whitehall, from Caxton House to the Adelphi. "Right, I'll get straight to what they tell me we really must have. "This isn't 'Nice to Have' from officials. These are political red lines which we must have. You've got to take out the £9,000, the 2.5 percent, the £3-4bn and . . . are you there? . . . "

"I'm listening."

". . . and the table on Lone Parents."

"Well Shriti, what I'm proposing is to write Gordon a letter laying out what I've been able to adjust and where I can't move."

Her tone took on an alarmed urgency. "Do not write a letter. You must not write a letter. We know exactly what changes you have made. You've no idea. It would leak all over the media. I'm warning you as a friend: do not write a letter." The phone went dead. Ignorant as I was of the armaments of political infighting, I had stumbled on a potent weapon.

I was under the arches at Charing Cross when Shriti phoned back. I pre-empted her: "Shriti, I'm not prepared to move on any of these matters. And on the 2.5 percent GDP boost, I've had pressure the opposite way from someone who's next door. They want to have a prize to announce." We talked on through the evening playing with different formulations.

But the position had hardened again by the following morning, the Thursday just five days before the launch. "You must take out the £3-4bn and the 2.5 percent boost to GDP. Gordon has talked to Tony and he's agreed to take out the 2.5 percent. So just do it."

"I don't care," I replied, hurrying round to Caxton House to get to the bottom of the conversation between Chancellor and Prime Minister. Soon I was being bombarded with texts from Shriti: "We asked the PM who said he was more than happy to remove the 2.5 percent. Are you now telling me it was never No. 10?"

I slipped into John Hutton's empty office and phoned Shriti in a rage, which was partly genuine and partly tactical. "I'm not changing a word. Not a word. Do you hear me? I don't care what anyone says, I'm not changing a word."

I had not managed to close the door all the way so the private office team outside were all trying to disguise their smirks at my tirade. One of them hurried across to ask me whether I'd like a tea or coffee – an immediate reward for standing up to one of the Civil Service's bête noires. Gareth phoned in to clarify the facts surrounding the 2.5 percent discussion. Luckily my disbelief had been well-founded. "The Prime Minister didn't agree to anything. Gordon caught him unprepared and said the numbers were all wrong. Tony just said he'd look into it."

Later that day, Shriti and I made up, agreeing that we wouldn't allow what had happened to undermine our long personal relationship. The implication, however, was that I had lost my go-between with the Chancellor and would have to find another route to agree any final compromises.

On Friday Gordon Brown signalled his support for the launch in an article in the *Financial Times* which read as if it had been dictated by him word for word. "In the first real indication of how he intends to overhaul the public sector if he takes over from Tony Blair later this year, the Chancellor will join forces on Monday with John Hutton,

Work and Pensions Secretary, to unveil a far-reaching review of welfare-to-work policy by David Freud, a former investment banker."[11] It went on to re-assure John Hutton of his position: "Mr Hutton, meanwhile, is clearly being wooed by the Brown camp as someone who will remain in Cabinet."

Gareth congratulated: "Well, you've won. Gordon's effectively committed to supporting this. So you can decide what to do. Gordon has gone to Tony to complain about the 2.5 percent and the £3-4 billion scale of the programme. But it's up to you."

My central concern through the whole process had been to protect the DEL-AME switch, without which the whole paper would fall. After Gareth left, I said to John Hutton, "Look I'm prepared to agree a package deal in principle. I'm not going through drafting anymore. They'll go on salami-slicing me. The deal is: they get rid of the 2.5 percent and I switch from £3-4bn to multibillion, which equals more or less the same figure. I keep the £9,000 and I keep all my drafting on Chapter 4 in particular. That consolidates the DEL-AME switch. You'll have to find a way of delivering the proposition. I've blown up my negotiation route."

In the end the route was through the Civil Service, with John Oliver, the Principal Private Secretary dealing with his direct counterpart in the Chancellor's office. My compromise was accepted.

With the Monday launch looming, now it was John Hutton's turn to become nervous.

"David, I'd be really grateful if you'd remove the specific age of five for lone parents. Could you say 12, with further reductions to follow, without specifying them?"

I had no interest in annoying my main sponsor. "Of course," I replied.

Bright and early on the first Monday of March I made my way to No. 10 and climbed the stairway, lined with the pictures of previous Prime Ministers. Technicians were busy transforming the two elegant reception rooms on the first floor into a stage set, headed by a table on the platform alongside a screen for the slides. Television lights were being set up on their stands. "It's the first time the Prime Minister and Chancellor have been together in public since the autumn," Gareth told me. Soon the room was filled with journalists and broadcasters. My report, titled by my team member Tony Wilson *Reducing dependency, increasing opportunity; options for the future of welfare to work*, was about to go public.

John Hutton kicked off proceedings, saying: "When I commissioned David Freud late last year to review our welfare-to-work strategy, I wanted someone to look afresh at the challenges facing our country's welfare system and outline the changes we would need to make to ensure that our historic ambition of creating the right to work could become a modern-day reality for all our people."

Tony Blair was next and put on a presentational master-class; on top of the material, relaxed, convincing. He made sure to emphasise the role of the voluntary sector in the contracting system: "On the basis of the expansion of the private and voluntary and charitable sectors in delivering work programmes for people as well as the usual public sector programmes, then they will be able to play a far greater role in assisting us with this process, getting people off benefit into work, finding the right skills and, most important of all, making sure that people stay in work." He concluded: "We need to make sure . . . that you get a virtuous circle where more people are coming off benefit and into work, where there's greater support for families with children and where, at the same time, we're able to raise the numbers of people in work to pay for the welfare state of the future."

Then it was my turn. I started with the figures, saying that low unemployment allowed us to tackle the most disadvantaged. "There are 7.8 million people who are economically inactive, of which 4.4 million are on the main benefits. 3.1 million of them have been on those benefits for a year and sometimes for much longer than a year. So, the goal in this report is to tackle the real social disadvantage that this 3.1 million figure represents. I support the Government aspiration to move to 80 percent employment as soon as possible and that implies reducing the number on long-term benefit by 1.3 million people."

I described how the contracting system would work. Then I moved on to disability claimants, whom I argued should become part of the system. I stuck to the agreed line on Lone Parents: "I'm looking to bring down the age at which the youngest child is, from 16 to 12 to bring them into the regime," adding, "it should move younger still in years to come, subject to adequate support and provision."

I closed with the analysis I had salvaged from Gordon Brown, who would be following me at the lectern. The 'harder to help' would be switched to programmes contracted to the private and voluntary sectors.

"I envisage this will be a multibillion-pound market." I went through the figures retained in Chapter 4: "It costs the State £9,000 to keep someone on Incapacity Benefit for a year, and once someone has been on Incapacity Benefit for a year they are on average going to stay on it for eight years. That represents a net present cost to the State of £62,000. So turning around two-fifths of those people back into work will have a major impact on the level of GDP in the country and on the public finances long-term, if we can achieve it." I might have lost the 2.5 percent of GDP figure, but I was not going to lose the importance of the direction of travel.

If Tony Blair had given a master-class in presentational skills, Gordon Brown gave one on how to position oneself to become the next Prime Minister. First, he took control of the next stages: "I want to say how the Budget and Spending Review will build on the excellent work that has been announced today." Then he told the journalists how successful his New Deal had been: "The New Deal has made it possible for more people to be in work in Britain, 29 million people, than ever before."

He had a carefully chosen form of words for my report. "This starts a new time of employment and welfare reform which I will champion." Clearly, I thought, that did not suggest any intention to champion the reforms I was recommending. As for my contracting out system, he shied away from dependence on commercial companies: "I particularly favour extending the role of voluntary organisations in offering one-to-one personal advice and coaching." Despite myself I was impressed at how he had managed to rise to Tony Blair's challenge of joining the platform for radical welfare reform, without supporting it.

Gary Gibbon, political editor for *Channel 4 News*, was the first with a question: "You talked about the wraparound childcare perhaps eventually allowing you to bring down the age even further of children when lone parents come off benefit. What's the target there?"

Too precipitately I answered: "Every country in the world is jealous of the Scandinavian countries which have a norm of getting parents, lone parents as well as other parents, back to work incredibly fast. There the norms are down to three years and clearly they have put a lot of resource and investment into making that happen . . . It would be very nice to be in a country where there was that kind of support . . . "I realised I had now strayed far into dangerous territory and tried, ineffectually, to get back onto safe ground . . . "But that's outside my scope."

Tony Blair did his best to rescue me: "I think the important thing to emphasise about this is that as you provide more help and support so you can bring the age down where you're expecting lone parents to come off benefit and into work."

Unintentionally I had provided the headlines for much of the next day's popular press. The *Daily Mail, The Sun, The Daily Telegraph, The Independent* and *The Daily Express* all led on lone parents being "forced" into work when their youngest child turned three. It was an early lesson in how the political press would turn a hint or implication into a full-blown proposition. Indeed, as a new entrant into the world of politics, this was the first time I fully realised how politicians, and others on their stage, could not afford a stray word or phrase that could be distorted into a caricature of their position. Luckily, on this occasion, no damage was done.

The day was not over for John Hutton. Back at the Department I was told: "There's an Urgent Question scheduled for 3:30 this afternoon."

"What does that mean?" I asked. Isobel explained: "The Lib Dems are complaining that your report should have been announced in Parliament first and are demanding that the Secretary of State makes a Statement about it. They don't seem to be attacking your report; quite the opposite, they're saying it's of great importance. You should go along to see what they all say about it."

So I queued up to go into the public gallery, protected from the Commons Chamber by its glass shield, and sat on the benches to watch my first ministerial grilling. It was a peculiarly pleasurable experience, with all three parties endorsing my report. John Hutton concluded his opening statement: "The recommendations represent the opportunity for a step change in the nature of our welfare system in the United Kingdom."

David Laws for the Liberal Democrats demanded: "Does the Secretary of State agree that David Freud has done an excellent job in nine weeks in reviewing some of the challenges in the benefits system? Will he accept our support for a large part of the Freud proposals?"

From the Conservative benches, Philip Hammond, the Shadow welfare spokesman, said: "The focus on transferring risk to the private and voluntary sector and incentivising longer-term support reflects much of the Opposition's thinking . . . We therefore welcome the thrust of the proposals."

Remarkably, there was not a single voice of dissent among the 14 MPs who spoke. Somehow, I had hit the political sweet spot. From the perspective of the Left I was proposing a substantial increase in the level of support to get people back to work while from the Right I was increasing the level of expectation on them to find a job.

The one institution I had confronted head-on was the Treasury – by funding the programme through what became widely known as the DEL-AME switch. I had decided that its rule of keeping a rigid distinction between the two forms of expenditure was the softest target. Almost by definition an Independent Reviewer for the Government is going to meet substantial opposition. If a solution is acceptable to all sides and Departments it would already have been adopted. So the role of the Reviewer is to explore whose door to kick down. And then stand firm when the injured party fights back. Many of the Reviews commissioned by the last Labour Government – and there were more than 30 – were savagely watered down in their closing stages in this way. Most were quickly forgotten as a result.

With the support of Tony Blair, I was able to stand firm against his Chancellor and kept the shape and scope of my recommendations. As a result I represented radical welfare reform in the public arena. In the words of the Institute for Government, I "had come to symbolise who owned the policy area." [12]

That position was to open up a new career.

PART II

MANOEUVRES

March 2007 – February 2009

CHAPTER 3

Change of Regime

"Has there been much reaction from the Lone Parent groups?" John Hutton asked when we gathered in his office the next day.

"Remarkably little," said one of the officials. "A bit of grumbling about the need for better childcare but they're remarkably calm about moving the age."

The Secretary of State was far too polite to mention my gaffe in alluding to the age of three - as indeed was everyone else in the team gathered round his large beech table to discuss next steps.

"Well, on that basis, we'll go straight to 12 next year and seven as soon as possible after that." It was my first direct experience of policy creation. The muted public reaction to my accidental creation of headlines about mothers being "forced" to work when their youngest was three had given the Government carte blanche to move ahead on my original proposal, despite earlier nervousness.

"And let's move aggressively on the rest of David's recommendations. I want the Green Paper out pretty swiftly. We need to keep the pressure up on this. What else can we do?"

"We've got the conference coming up in three weeks."

"Ah yes, Jim Murphy's conference; we need to really get behind it." Jim was the second Minister in the Department, responsible for Employment and Welfare Reform. He had been running a series of seminars and conferences about the future of welfare in the months I had been in the Department. I had not bothered myself much with his activity, seeing it as a communication rather than design exercise.

The conference on 26 March 2007, however, was on a much grander scale than anything he had organised up till then. Some 300 delegates gathered in the Baroque Methodist Central Hall in Westminster. Many of them were international. There was a heavyweight US delegation, including Ron Haskins, whom I had visited in December on my trip to Washington. There were speakers from many of the countries with leading programmes in the welfare field – Australia, the Netherlands, Denmark, New Zealand and Germany. In his keynote speech John Hutton called for those interested to comment on "the proposed radical extension of support from the private and voluntary sectors; the need for greater benefit simplification; and the renewal of the contract of rights and responsibilities in our welfare system." After him, I made much the same speech as at the launch of my report. The conference generated a palpable sense of movement and change – just as it was designed to do.

Meanwhile the drafting of the Green Paper responding to my report was proceeding apace. I was given a lesson in policy creation by Isobel. "First you have an Independent Report, like yours," she explained. "Then you can have a Consultation Document. In that the Government puts out various options and asks for views from the public. Next step is a Green Paper, which is a little bit more specific about what the Government wants to do, but is still asking for views. The final step is a White Paper which outlines the proposals and leads to legislation."

"So you're not planning a consultation document here?"

"We don't necessarily go through all the steps each time. Here we're planning to go straight to a Green Paper."

"And it looks pretty good doesn't it? It's basically endorsing all the proposals in my report."

"Well don't get your hopes up too high. There's a story doing the rounds that the Treasury are drafting an alternative Green Paper. And you can imagine how emasculated your stuff would be in that."

Her warning was all too prescient. By now 'Regime Change', as Shriti had put it, was imminent. On 10 May Tony Blair announced that he would be resigning as Prime Minister in late June. No other politician could be found willing, or able, to stand against his heir apparent, Gordon Brown. So within a week the Chancellor found himself unopposed in his long campaign to become Prime Minister.

Nevertheless, John Hutton remained adamant that the reform programme would stay on track. A week before the hand-over he gave a speech saying: "I know there are some who hope the coming political transition will mean the Government goes cool on the prospect of further radical welfare reform to benefit the hardest to help. They will be disappointed." [13]

Mysteriously, during the interregnum, the Green Paper failed to appear. And when Brown took over formally on 27 June, John Hutton was swiftly transferred from the Department to become the Secretary of State of the newly-formed Department of Business, Enterprise and Regulatory Reform. In his place at DWP was the veteran politician Peter Hain. He had spent his early childhood in southern Africa and launched his public career in the late 1960s with direct action movements against apartheid, before moving into politics proper. As a Labour Minister he had at one time or another covered Trade and Industry, Wales, Northern Ireland and the Foreign Office.

Now he got his marching orders from Gordon Brown. A participant in the meeting to agree his appointment told me (some time later) that Peter Hain asked: "Have you any particular guidance on how you want me to run the Department?"

"Yes," Gordon apparently growled. "Don't be like Hutton."

I had no expectations that I would continue my relationship with the Department after Gordon Brown took over, which proved a realistic supposition. Nor was I particularly concerned, given the amount of work to catch up on at my main job, the Portland Trust. I became an outside observer of events, called on by the media to comment occasionally. Peter Hain made no effort to contact me.

However, my recommendations now found renewed impetus in the shape of Nick Timmins, the leading journalist on public policy, who wrote for the *Financial Times*. He had made his name writing the definitive account of the Welfare State, from Beveridge onward, titled *The Five Giants*.[14] He was assiduous in chasing down the implications of a support system that could channel substantial funds towards helping the most disadvantaged. His coverage when my report came out was extensive and accurate. It focused on the business implications of my structure, in which companies with capital – so-called prime contractors – would establish consortia to handle the challenge: "A dozen large private sector 'prime contractors' will take over responsibility for getting the long-term unemployed off benefits and into work in what could become a 'multibillion-pound' welfare industry,"[15] he wrote. At the time I was pleased to see that my compromise "multibillion" phrase had maintained the concept of substantial scale.

The Green Paper, when it arrived in mid-July, was far from the drafts

I had seen six weeks earlier.[16] The only clear-cut recommendation concerned Lone Parents, who would be transferred to Jobseekers Allowance when their youngest child was 12 from October 2008 and seven from October 2010.

Otherwise it was very significantly watered down. There was a nod to working with the private sector but no detail as to how this would be achieved. In the *Financial Times*, Nick Timmins focused on the backsliding in a piece headlined: 'Business 'uncertain' about jobs plan role'.[17] He wrote: "Rather than settle on the contracting model, the Green Paper says the Department will undertake 'a detailed exercise' to work out the role of prime contractors."

Shortly afterwards Nick came into the Department to interview Peter Hain. It was a foolish move by the new Secretary of State. One of the consequences of the rapid turn-over of Ministers was that they tended to understand their briefs far less well than informed outsiders; and there was no-one more expert on the welfare state than Nick Timmins.

This failed attempt at damage control became the splash in the *Financial Times*.[18] Peter Hain told Nick that the prime contractor route was "not my preferred option", although there remained big potential for the private and voluntary sector. He still was keen on a "crusade" for jobs, despite the near-15 percent cut in the Department's budget planned for the subsequent three years.

Nick asked: "Isn't this a long way short of proposals that Freud described as developing over time into an annual multibillion market?"

Peter was reduced to: "Yes, but Freud is not the Secretary of State."

Nick went on pushing. Without the capital that only the private sector could provide there would be no 'DEL-AME' switch and no large programmes. "How can upfront investment be found to sustain the Government's ambition?"

Haplessly Peter Hain insisted: "By just working more efficiently." This was self-evidently ludicrous.

Nick's summary of the interview put the challenge straight to the Prime Minister. "Private companies' hopes of getting huge new welfare-to-work contracts suffered a severe setback yesterday in what many will see as the first clear sign of the Brown Government retreating from Tony Blair's commitment to a much bigger private role in public services."

On the next day, the beginning of August 2007, Nick described the hostile reception to his exclusive story, with quotes from the CBI warning of "real concern about the mixed messages from Ministers on the future of public service reform." [19]

Nick kept up the pressure. A week later he was giving inside details about how John Hutton had signed off proposals to award 20 to 25 big welfare-to-work contracts to private companies. He wrote: "A final draft of the welfare reform Green Paper had been completed, insiders say, and sent to the Treasury and No. 10 just days before the transition from Tony Blair to Gordon Brown." [20]

Much later I heard from officials that the telephone lines between No. 10 and Peter Hain sizzled after each of these stories, galvanised by Nick's accusations of Prime Ministerial back-sliding.

It was only now that I was summoned to see Peter Hain. We sat awkwardly in the blue couches in the corner of his room, accompanied by a couple of officials.

There wasn't much small talk. "Describe how your system would work," he probed.

Slightly puzzled, I launched into a description of the contracting system. There was nothing much to add to my report – which he could presumably read, if he hadn't already. I kept it brief. He didn't seem focused on what I was saying anyway.

When I paused, he said: "I see." Then added: "We wouldn't want a private monopoly replacing a public monopoly."

"Of course not," I replied. "And there's no reason to see a monopoly develop if the contracting is done effectively."

"We're in the same place," he concluded.

It was a short meeting and it was only a few days later that I realised what he was seeking to achieve. In mid-September he swallowed his preferences in a speech to the Institute for Public Policy Research: "No one has gone cool on reform. The reality is we will work with large-scale providers. They can bring scale and integration."

As ever, the score was kept by the *Financial Times* in a piece entitled "Hain changes welfare-to-work tone." [21] And now I discovered the reason for my meeting. "Mr Hain said he had spoken to Mr Freud, who was 'in the same place' and shared his concerns about big contracts replacing a public monopoly with a private monopoly." It was a volte-face due entirely to the perseverance of Nick Timmins – a volte-face designed to maintain the Prime Minister's public commitment to welfare reform, regardless of the embarrassment created for one of his Secretaries of State. My meeting with Peter Hain was aimed at identifying me with the Government position, getting me to respond positively - or at least not disagree - when he said we were 'in the same place'.

I might have been new to the political process, but I knew enough to maintain my independence - particularly from a Government dominated by Gordon Brown. Right from the outset I had made sure that I had open lines to the other parties, briefing them on my report before it was launched. I was rather too open with Philip Hammond, the Conservative welfare spokesman, when I described the tortuous process of drafting. "I kept the essentials in the report, but Gordon Brown was pretty hostile through the process. He dragged me into the Treasury and demanded a lot of cuts."

Hammond endorsed the report on its launch and by early June he was asking questions in the Commons about the drafting process. Did "Ministers and officials in his Department and in other Departments" suggest amendments? Less than a week later *The Daily Telegraph* carried a story about me being "hauled into the Treasury" to present my findings. "He said hello, got a 45-minute rant from Gordon ... Then he was marched into a room full of advisers who shredded him." [22]

Meanwhile David Ruffley, one of the Conservative Shadow welfare team called me up: "We want you to do a speech at a conference about your report. Will you be able to do it?"

"Of course," I answered. The conference, on 7 June during the Blair-Brown interregnum, was hosted by the leading City lawyers Clifford Chance and was titled 'Welfare Reform: What the Government's Freud Review means for the Private and Voluntary Sector'. It was the first time for me to meet George Osborne, the Shadow Chancellor, who dashed in to deliver the keynote speech. However, it was Philip Hammond who made the political point. "There is an opportunity here to fulfil social and economic imperatives without exposure of the public purse. It is less clear that Gordon Brown is committed to this approach."

Apart from Philip Hammond and George Osborne it was the standard round of speakers and issues. The significance lay in the fact that the Conservatives were now exploring how they could claim ownership in welfare, an area that had long belonged to Labour. David Ruffley was bubbling with excitement at the end of the morning. "This has really worked to get the leadership's attention; just the fact that George came. It's the first time that he has shown any interest in welfare at all."

Shortly after Peter Hain took over from John Hutton, the Conservatives had their own reshuffle, with Chris Grayling taking over from Philip Hammond at the beginning of July. My first encounter was at a breakfast meeting in late autumn 2007 to discuss welfare. Both Chris Grayling and George Osborne were in attendance.

"We're doing a lot of work in this area and we'd like to feel we could call on you every now and then," said Chris. "That is if you don't feel you're tied into the Labour Government."

"Absolutely not," I assured him. "I wrote the Government of the day an Independent Report which is available to anyone across the political spectrum seeking policy ideas. I might add that I am not, and never have been, a Labour supporter. In fact, I've voted Conservative as long as I can remember."

"Did John Hutton know that?" asked George.

"No. He never asked. I've always kept my political views to myself – until today, I suppose. As a banker you learn to work for whoever hires you."

George was clearly searching me out. He had been Shadow Chancellor for just over two years and, at 37, retained his boyish looks. He proved less interested in the economics of welfare and instead, applying his considerable charm, set about finding out about my background. He was particularly interested in my experience in privatisation and rail. He wanted to know how we had managed to float Eurotunnel and rescue the Channel Tunnel Rail Link. "They know how to do rail properly in Japan," he told me. "When I visited last year they took me for a ride on the Maglev test track."

"What a coincidence. My wife and I were there a few weeks ago and were taken on it; unbelievable – 500kph and hardly a tremor."

"Mind you they had to start braking as soon as they reached top speed or they would have run off the test-track." We spent the rest of the breakfast swopping stories about developments in Maglev, or magnetic levitation, which used powerful magnets to raise high-speed trains above the track to reduce wheel-to-rail friction. Temporarily the problems of welfare were forgotten.

But Chris Grayling was absolutely focused on the topic. By December

I was sharing a platform with him, and the Conservatives were moving to adopt my proposals. He declared: "In Australia, many parts of the United States, the Netherlands and elsewhere a combination of tougher conditionality and well-focused support programmes to get people back into work have delivered real reductions to welfare rolls.

"Gordon Brown spotted that years ago, but his solution has always been top-down state programmes that simply haven't delivered what he promised.

"It's a particular pleasure to be speaking alongside David Freud today ... In David Freud's work and the experience of other countries, we believe there is a solution to be found. And the next Conservative Government will find it."[23] One could not fail to be struck by his imposing height – 6ft 5in – which enhanced the impact of his assured delivery. His background in the media industry, where he had worked for the *BBC* and *Channel 4*, had clearly enhanced his presentational flair.

Early in the New Year he was on the phone. "David, we're putting out our Shadow Green Paper next Tuesday. I'll send you a copy. We'd like you on the platform at the launch, so let me know whether you can agree with it."

I went through the sections.[24] The language was toughened up, but most of them were in line with – indeed, based on – my recommendations. In particular the Shadow Green Paper explicitly endorsed the DEL-AME switch. One of the proposals was novel. It called for a complete reassessment of all those claiming Incapacity Benefit and the use of this assessment as the basis on which the disabled would be allocated to the contractors. This had always been a loose element in my own design. It would be highly risky if contractors were responsible for selecting the individuals they thought were capable of going back to work. There would inevitably be cases in which inappropriate choices would be made – of severely ill people – which would throw the whole scheme into disrepute. This risk would be mitigated if selection was through a formal route.

I joined the launch conference in Brixton, where David Cameron described the key elements: "First of all, we will give everyone a proper assessment, whether they are on Incapacity Benefit or on jobseeker's allowance. We will give everyone the help they need, the training they need to get back to work. And we will use the most modern methods to make sure this happens. And the absolute keystone is ensuring that the agencies responsible for returning people to work are paid on results."

When I followed, I emphasised that I was talking from a position of complete political independence. "Of central importance is that Mr Cameron has announced a clear commitment this morning to overturn and modernise the artificial accounting distinction between programme costs and welfare payments." [25]

Meanwhile welfare policy was in stasis as Peter Hain faced political melt-down. He could not account for the funding of his campaign during the previous year to become Deputy Leader of the Labour Party, which put him in breach of electoral law. Despite his public volte-face in September, I placed little hope in the Government endorsing my proposals. That cynicism was reinforced when I went to see Tony Blair on the first floor of his grand office in Grosvenor Square in the autumn of 2007. The meeting was about Palestine, where he was now the lead international diplomat, but at the end he asked me how my welfare proposals were proceeding.

"Still in play," I hazarded, cautiously.

He shook his head in mild disgust. "With Gordon there, good luck with that."

Peter Hain tried the defence of incompetence, or chaos, in the administration of his campaign. But he was unable to sustain it. On 24 January 2008, the Electoral Commission referred the failure to report donations to the police and his position became untenable. Abruptly, he resigned as Secretary of State. I doubted whether his departure would make much difference to the Government's suspicion of me and my proposals.

CHAPTER 4

Inside the Department

The morning after Peter Hain's departure, in late January 2008, my phone rang as I was on my way to our house in East Kent. I stopped in Morrison's car-park, outside Gravesend, to take the call. It was James Purnell, the new and youthful Secretary of State at the Department.

"David, I would like to ask you to become my adviser on how to implement your reforms."

Put like that, I could hardly refuse. "I would be delighted." I told him. The invitation followed his initial meeting with officials and advisers the previous day, when he came into the Department. "I want to return to John Hutton's reform agenda. How do I get the message out that I intend to make radical welfare changes?" he asked.

"You could get David Freud in as your adviser. That would send the message," suggested Gareth Davies, still the No. 10 adviser on welfare.

My new role was announced three days later. Monday's *Financial Times* carried the story that: "The appointment is a clear signal that the private sector will be given a significantly enhanced role . . ." [26] It was a position apparently endorsed by Gordon Brown, who joined his new Secretary of State on a conference platform that morning.

The Daily Telegraph was quick to follow up with a request for an interview, which I granted without much thought. A couple of days later two journalists, in the shape of Rachel Sylvester and Alice Thomson arrived at my second-floor office at the Portland Trust in Portland Place. If I had been more aware of their reputation - they were dubbed 'the dangerous sisters' - I would have been less relaxed.

They probed the numbers of disabled people and lone parents that could be helped back to work. Carefully I stuck to the numbers in my report: "There are about 3.1 million people not working. I think we can get 1.4 million back to work." As they stood up to leave, Rachel asked as an apparent afterthought: "What do you think the real figure for incapacity should be?"

Too casually I murmured: "I suspect it's a lot closer to the 700,000 we had when the rot started in the 1980s than the one we have now." I was to discover that this was a dangerously imprecise way to refer to the figures for reducing incapacity claimants in my report – a 1 million reduction from 2.7 million.

I spent a couple of days in the Department getting my marching orders and sorting out the mechanics of my appointment. James Purnell had joined the Cabinet – its youngest member at 37 – as Secretary of State for Culture Media and Sport seven months earlier. He had been close to Tony Blair, working on research for him in Opposition. Now he was in charge of the biggest Department in Government. He had an immense youthful charm: "David, I need you to put all this together: the life chances agenda, contract structures, incentives to personalise the service." He had clearly absorbed his brief very quickly.

I popped in to see Leigh Lewis, the Permanent Secretary, to agree my appointment letter. "You need to clear any interviews with us."

I replied: "I'm happy with that, except that I've just given one to *The Daily Telegraph*."

"Well, that should be all right."

He could not have been more wrong.

Saturday's *Telegraph* splash was a ruthless distortion of my remarks. Headlined, '1.9 million on benefit "should get back to work"', the opening paragraph stated: "Up to two thirds of people claiming incapacity benefit are not entitled to the state's handout, the Government's new welfare adviser warns today." [27]

Infuriatingly, the inside story carried the numbers I had used in my report. It even recorded my exact expression "a lot closer" – rather than the entire increase in the disability roll since the 1980s implied by the splash. [28] But the exact quotation inside the paper was irrelevant given the inflammatory front page.

My phone started to ring as every paper sought to follow up the story. I had a brutal choice. Disavowing the story would undermine the active approach I was encouraging towards the long-term inactive and unemployed. I quickly realised that, however distorted, I had to stand by the story.

The day was full of interviews, from a radio truck parked outside my London house to a visit to *Channel 4 News* at Grays Inn Road in the evening. James Purnell was waiting for me at the turnstiles as I came out at 8pm. "That's enough now, David. We need to put this to bed."

Later he told me that he had been on the receiving end of considerable abuse from Gordon Brown. James had agreed my appointment without clearing it. Now the Prime Minister was furious: "I told you that bastard would dump us in it."

In fact, the pressure slackened off remarkably quickly. James told me (again later): "When the polls came in they showed that your story did rather well for us. It put us ahead of the Conservatives on welfare for the first time. So Gordon backed off."

Despite this inauspicious start, or maybe because of it, I was settled in the Labour Markets team in the second main Departmental office in London, off the Strand in the Adelphi building. This was a 10-minute walk from the main office in Caxton House, where the Ministerial team was based. Adam Sharples, in charge, proposed: "I always think it's good to have an end date with these roles. Should we say a year?" Clearly, from the Department's perspective, my main symbolic purpose had been fulfilled.

In mid-February I had my first meeting with Alan Cave. He had joined the Department from the private sector shortly after I wrote my report. Confident and effective, he had not been idle. He took me through the plans to launch the Flexible New Deal. I was genuinely impressed. He was proposing a new structure of incentives for the contractors working to help people into work, which ramped up the reward for performance. This would pay half the total return once someone was in work for three months and a further 30 percent if that job lasted for six months. It didn't go as far as my payment by results model but it would be a most useful stepping stone in building up an industry which could take the risks involved in it.

"Did Peter Hain know you were cooking all this up?" I asked.

"More or less," he replied carefully. I took him to mean less.

He wanted my help in persuading James Purnell to roll it out in phases, rather than all at once. I thought the arguments made sense and I tested them carefully at a meeting with companies interested in becoming contractors which took place later in the month.

When we next met, I advised: "James, you're trying to create an industry which can take quite substantial risk here. It makes sense to do it in two bites. It means you can keep the competitive pressure up and incorporate improvements in round two." James grimaced as he agreed. The unspoken concern was that round two would inevitably fall after the next election, which Labour was projected to lose.

At the end of February 2008, companies interested in becoming back-to-work operators attended the launch of the Department's Commissioning Strategy at KPMG's London headquarters in Salisbury Square. James Purnell laid out a structure of larger, longer contracts rewarding job outcomes rather than process. The contractors would be encouraged to run consortia which included so-called third sector – voluntary and charitable – organisations. He told them: "We will judge the success of our providers on the outcome that they deliver. We are committed to developing a mature market, where competition will drive innovation, improve value for money and enhance the effectiveness of all participants."

I was given a five-minute slot to endorse the strategy – which I was happy to do. The process of applying the principles would start with the Flexible New Deal and the first tranche of contracts – covering some 60 percent of the country – would be operating from October 2009.

With James' aggressively pushing the agenda, spring of 2008 was busy. By May I was meeting with Treasury officials to discuss how to implement the DEL-AME switch. The central issue was how to estimate and deal with 'deadweight' – the jargon term for an outcome that would have happened anyway. A proportion of people flow off benefits naturally and the Government would only want to pay contractors for success above this level.

I was becoming more knowledgeable about the Department as each month passed and I met more of the officials and front-line operatives within it. My immediate contacts were the policy officials, of whom there were around 1,000, many of them based in London to be available to Ministers. But the wider operation was focused on delivery, with more than 100,000 employees in the Department as a whole. The biggest group – about 70,000 – operated out of JCP, which ran some 800 outlets in town centres. JCP was the public face of the Department, where unemployed claimants would be required to attend fortnightly to 'sign on' as a condition of receiving benefit. One of the officials described the approach to me: "Basically it's a great big nagging service. And it works. People move off benefit more quickly when we require them to sign on than when we don't."

This approach was all very well when the service concentrated on those capable of working. It was likely to be far less effective when people had deep-seated problems which needed to be tackled before they could take their place in the labour market – whether it was illiteracy, chronic back pain or drug abuse. And there would need to be a transformation in the front-line service to tackle such problems.

I was taken aback at one meeting I had with a group from the Job-centres responsible for operations, who were complaining about how ineffective some of the policies were. Innocently I asked: "What has been the response to these issues?"

"We don't talk about them." The operations team were wary of raising issues with the policy officers based at headquarters, let alone with ministers. It was a culture that was genuinely back-to-front. In all effective operations I had come across in the private sector, feedback from the front-line was central to decision-making.

Benefit delivery was scattered across about 80 back-office centres, many of them situated to satisfy the political imperative of job creation in depressed parts of the country. They were responsible for delivering an extremely complex skein of benefits – each with different entitlement, withdrawal and tapering rates. One official illustrated the problems this created with the shocking fact: "If you are a benefit claimant with reasonably complicated circumstances, your papers will be lost around 40 percent of the time."

It reminded me of the need to modernise the welfare system, preferably with a single benefit. At my next meeting I raised the issue with James.

"The best way of getting a single benefit structure would be to set up a Commission to investigate the issue," I argued.

He wasn't keen. "The trouble is that a Commission would run away with the issue and come up with completely unaffordable proposals. It would go outside our control."

I only discovered much later that James had broached the option of introducing a single benefit with Gordon Brown, who turned it down because of the likely political backlash from incorporating child benefit into the structure. The Government continued to pay lip service to the idea, but there would not be a concrete agenda towards achieving the goal.

Politics was definitely on the agenda, however. Just before the summer recess James moved to match Chris Graylings' hard line on incapacity benefits. The Consultation Paper put out in July 2008 stated: "Between 2009 and 2013 all incapacity benefits claimants will be reassessed using a medical assessment called the Work Capability Assessment (WCA)". It also stated that the replacement for Incapacity Benefit, called the Employment and Support Allowance, would comprise two divisions. The Support Group would not be expected to work while "those in the Work-Related Activity Group will be expected to engage with a personalised programme of back-to-work support." [29]

The disability lobbies seemed to accept Waddell and Burton's conclusion that work would be good for the disabled. I spoke at a large gathering organised by the disability network Radar, held at the Oval conference centre in London, where an informal vote showed overwhelming approval of the concept that, with adequate and appropriate protections, "the majority of disabled people can and should work". The most moving moment, for me, was when a young disabled woman with learning difficulties demanded loudly: "Will someone give me a job? I want a job."

Greater concern was expressed in mid-September, after the summer recess, when we gathered to promote the Consultation Paper at a conference held at the Park Plaza hotel in London's Victoria. There was some mild disruption from a group of four disabled people, protesting that we had broken the mantra of the disability lobby; "Nothing about us, without us." Two got into the auditorium and interrupted proceedings briefly.

But the context in which we were operating was about to be wrenched into dramatically new territory. As we waited to go on the platform (before the interruption) I confided to Steve Timms, Jim Murphy's successor as Minister for Employment and Welfare Reform: "We're in for a dreadful crisis. And we're going to be hit in ways that we can't yet fathom. It is going to drive all our activity from now on."

It was 15 September 2008, the Monday of the collapse of Lehman Brothers, one of the major New York-based investment banks. The rescue talks in New York over the weekend had failed and the news that the company had declared bankruptcy was just emerging. The financial sector was about to go into anaphylactic shock, in the words of Ben Bernanke, Chairman of America's Central Bank, the Federal Reserve.

The impact in the real world was dramatic. Already the unemployment figures announced in mid-October showed the biggest jump since the previous recession – 17 years previously – with an increase of 164,000. Those were the figures for the three months to August, before the collapse of Lehman. The figures were about to get much worse and the strain was reflected in JCP activity. From September my right hand was Caroline Haynes, who had worked at the National Employment Panel (an organisation funded by the Department) for the previous five years, and kept me informed as to what was happening on the ground.

"They've got security stopping people coming into the Jobcentres – they're so many. Some of the Jobcentres are being overwhelmed," she told me as the redundancies began to mount through the autumn.

Inevitably the centre of attention was shifting elsewhere, particularly given the imperative to rescue the banking system after the precipitate collapse of Lehman.

I kept on working. The follow up to the Consultation Paper was a White Paper, launched on 10 December, which incorporated most of the agenda in my Report. The main item was the wholesale move of people from Incapacity Benefit to the new Employment and Support Allowance. It announced five DEL-AME pathfinders – to develop the best way of operating the approach – and there was even a nod towards the single benefit. "We will explore whether, over the longer-term, a single working age benefit is the right approach."

I was also involved in a taskforce which explored how to help the charitable sector compete for contracts for welfare to work. Under the energetic chairmanship of Tony Hawkhead, Chief Executive of the charity Groundwork UK, it concluded that the sector needed more financial provision, an expanded skills-base and a greater appetite for risk.

But all this was happening in a grim political context. The polls for Labour had turned sour after Gordon Brown's honeymoon in the late summer of 2007. His 'bottling' – as the Conservatives dubbed it – of a snap autumn election undermined his image and by year end he was trailing. By the autumn of 2008 he was thoroughly behind and a modest recovery during his successful handling of the bank bailout did not last beyond the end of the year. Stories about his over-bearing behaviour were rife and there was deep discontent among Labour MPs.

I was not involved in the immediate response to the prospect of a surge in unemployment. Later in the year there were internal rumours about youth unemployment schemes that bore a remarkable resemblance to the New Deals. The leadership for these initiatives was coming from No. 10 and Gordon Brown's instincts proved even more statist in a crisis than in stable times. The Future Jobs Fund, when it was announced at the following Budget, in April 2009, proved remarkably similar to his traditional programmes.

I was feeling increasingly marginalised and irrelevant. However 'radical' my sponsor – James Purnell – might have wished to be, it was becoming clear that in the crisis, decision-making had reverted to No. 10.

CHAPTER 5

The Conservatives Pounce

Unbeknown to me, another door was opening. My contacts with the Conservative leadership had not dried up with my appointment by James Purnell. Soon after the collapse of Lehman, towards the end of September 2008, I got a call out of the blue from George Osborne.

"David, we are planning to propose going ahead with a high-speed rail line from London to Manchester at Conference next week. I want to announce that you are our adviser on it. We're going to put some serious resource into it. I've got a half-million budget for you to build a team to do it."

I was strongly tempted. Big rail projects had a way of working their way into people's imagination once they had experienced them; in my case I had already notched up Eurotunnel and the Channel Tunnel Railway Link. "But George," I replied regretfully, "I'm advising James Purnell on how to implement my welfare reforms."

"That's all right," said George breezily. "You can advise Labour on welfare and the Conservatives on transport."

"That seems a bit far-fetched to me," I confessed. "But if you think it could work, I'm happy to give James a call to see if he could live with it too."

"No, you better not do that. James is a good guy but he's bound to warn the centre what we're planning. And I can't afford to have the announcement disrupted."

"Sadly, we'll have to leave it then," I closed. "Maybe when I've finished this stint with the Government?"

The next call came at the beginning of 2009. Could I come to see him in his office in Parliament? I went through the rigmarole of security at Portcullis House and was led through to the next-door building, originally used by New Scotland Yard, the Norman Shaw South Building. Here, on the second floor, George Osborne shared an office suite with David

Cameron, with space for their support team. Outside his room sat two formidable advisers in the shape of Matt Hancock and Rupert Harrison, who combined youth and joviality in equal measure. They joined us round the small table in George's office.

This was not about rail. "David, we're creating an Economic Recovery Committee to help us develop policies to run the economy. There are some big names on it from the private sector and we'd like you to join it."

I told him: "I'd like to take part in principle. My appointment with the Government is coming to an end this month, so I'll be clear to be a member. I should probably leave a 'cordon sanitaire' of a month or two between resigning and taking this on."

By now David Cameron had come into the room. "We'd very much like you to do it," he said. "But we need to announce this quite soon and we'll add your name to the team later when you can join in."

So we reached agreement in principle. As I left, I unburdened to David Cameron: "Of course, the real problem in welfare has been the astonishing turnover of Ministers and Secretaries of State in the Department. I think the average length of stay by Secretaries of State has been something like nine months. You can't work out where the toilets are in that time, let alone conduct a thorough-going reform. People should stay in post for years to get on top of the issues."

Subsequent events suggest that David Cameron took these remarks as a proposition.

It was some weeks later that we met again. I had gone skiing with my son in late January and was pre-occupied with launching the Third Sector Taskforce report on my return. [30] So it wasn't till a week into February that I was able to come back to sort out the details of my putative membership of the new Committee. In fact, David Cameron had announced the Committee and its membership on the previous day and I was able to study the details in the press as I travelled in.

As soon as I had settled down in George's office – this time in one of the small armchairs – David Cameron joined us.

"Right," he said. "We want you to join the Economic Recovery Committee. In addition, Gordon Brown has written to say that we can appoint two Peers to balance his three appointments in October – Peter Mandelson, Paul Myners and Stephen Carter. We would like to make you one of them. You would become our spokesman on welfare reform in the House of

Lords. If we win the next election and form the Government you will become a Minister of State in the Department for Work and Pensions."

I was caught totally by surprise and couldn't think of anything to say. I had retired from the Portland Trust at the turn of the year and my agreed time with the Department for Work and Pensions was coming to an end. I was looking forward to a period of relaxation; this highly stressful challenge was the last thing that I had expected. David Cameron probably interpreted my silence as playing hard to get.

"This opportunity is unlikely to come up again. I doubt we'll be invited to put forward any more Peers before the next election. That's just how it is. So we need to take a decision pretty soon."

Having delivered the offer, he left me with George. There followed the most absurd negotiation of my life. Despite my initial surprise, my instinctive reaction was to accept. I thought that the Conservatives would win and here was a chance to take direct responsibility for my reform programme, rather than advising at one remove. However, I was fully conscious of the scale of the obligation this would represent and was cautious about taking the step without further consideration, particularly given the inevitable imposition on my family.

"Can I have a week to think about it?" I asked George.

"There's quite a lot of time pressure on us. Can't you do it quicker than that? Two days?" After haggling, we settled on three days.

I didn't need the three days. I talked it through with my wife Cilla, whose initial hostile reaction reflected her social despair at the prospect of a peerage. "You really want to take this on, don't you?"

"Yes."

"Well go for it then."

I was travelling to Birmingham on a visit with Caroline Haynes the next morning. When we arrived, I excused myself as we walked across Victoria Square. I stood on the steps facing Thomason's classical Council House as I made the call to George.

"George, I didn't need the three days. I would like to accept your proposal."

The next day, Thursday 12 February, I was back in George's office to make the final arrangements. They planned to announce the appointment on the weekend. "You need to be a member of the Conservative Party when it goes out," insisted David Cameron.

"I'll do it in Dover," I suggested. "I've got a home in the constituency."

"They'll need you more down there than in London," said George. "And Charlie Elphicke is the candidate. He's a good guy. He'll be able to sort out your membership."

"It's all on-line," I told them, to their surprise. "I can become a member in the next five minutes." Which I did.

"Have you got any issues with the tax man?" David checked. "Usually it takes a few months to clear these appointments and it's not public beforehand. In your case there's no way to keep it quiet through that process. Once we put in your name the other side will leak it pretty viciously, so we'll have to pre-empt with our own announcement. You've got to be suitable to become a peer. In particular your tax affairs must be in order."

"My taxes are up to date."

"OK," concluded David, "We're good to go. This was a good idea of yours, George."

David Cameron was right about the risk. The other peerage was offered to Sir Richard Dannat, retiring army Chief of the General Staff. In the event it was put on hold as concerns were voiced about the propriety of taking on a political role so quickly and it was not till the end of 2010 that Sir Richard finally joined the Lords.

The story started to leak on Saturday morning. I was on the tennis court when my phone rang. It was John Williams, Special Adviser to John Hutton, with whom I had worked so closely on my Report. "David, there's a story doing the rounds that you're switching to the Conservatives."

"It's true."

"A lot of people will be very upset. They gave you a platform. It's not too late to change your mind."

"John. I know and I'm grateful. But I am now committed to doing this. I want to carry out the work in office and this is the opportunity to do that."

"You're burning your boats," he pointed out. "You're relying on the outcome of the next election."

It was the most painful of the calls I was to take that morning. Evidently someone in No. 10 was orchestrating the campaign. Shriti Vadera put in a call 15 minutes later. "This will be used politically. You do understand?" Later she texted: "Meant to say congratulations."

James Purnell did not call, though he told me later that he got "a complete earful" from Gordon Brown.

John Hutton's call was the most relaxed. "Good luck and I wish you well with your reform efforts." He could report back that he had made the call with a clear conscience.

As a game of tennis, it left a lot to be desired.

The headlines the next morning were, unsurprisingly, highly politicised. The story led *The Sunday Times*, a position it earned because George Osborne's team had sold it as a key defection. 'Tories steal welfare guru David Freud from Gordon Brown,' read the headline. "The resignation of such a senior figure is a significant blow for the Prime Minister who faces growing criticism as unemployment nudges 2 million." [31] In *The Sunday Telegraph* the second headline summarised: 'David Cameron has recruited one of Labour's most influential advisers on welfare reform to help him deal with 'mass unemployment'.' [32]

It may have labelled me as a turncoat but as a political attack on the Prime Minister, the Conservatives had delivered a heavy blow. Within days Rachel Sylvester, one of 'the dangerous sisters' now moved to *The Times*, was writing off Gordon Brown in a piece whose sub-heading summarised: 'The defection of the Government's welfare guru is the latest sign that Gordon Brown is heading inexorably to defeat.' [33]

Some time later I complained, mildly, to Rupert Harrison at the ruthless way they had used my appointment to undermine the Brown Government.

"I know," he replied unrepentantly. "Wonderful, wasn't it."

The story I enjoyed most ascribed a Machiavellian competence to my move. Anne McElvoy wrote in the *Evening Standard*: "Sir David has behaved like a City dealmaker (his old job). He has held out for the best possible offer from the Tories since last September." [34] Putting aside the knighthood I had mysteriously been awarded by part of the media, I wish my career-planning had been somewhere close to this fantasy.

My resignation letter to James Purnell emphasised how well we had got on. "I would like to stress how much I have enjoyed and appreciated working for you to improve the shape of welfare provision in this country."

In the event James would not outstay me for long. He could not bear working for Gordon Brown. Later he told me: "Brown meetings are awful. He has this way of saying that what you're suggesting is based on some theoretical model and 'it's like some other approach' when it's got nothing to do with them; a way of sounding informed and brow-beating you at the same time."

Sensationally, James walked out of the Cabinet in early June 2009, calling on Gordon Brown "to stand aside to give our party a fighting chance of winning" the next election.

By then I was deeply involved in my new role. And the omens were mixed. George had told me: "You'll be working with Theresa May." She had replaced Chris Grayling as Shadow Work and Pensions Secretary a matter of weeks before my move. George made no secret of his contempt for her. "The journalists have been asking me what on earth we were thinking of, putting someone so uninspired in the role. I've been telling them to watch this space and that we've got a surprise for them – that's you."

It was a useful premonition of the tensions I would have to face.

PART III
OPPOSITION

February 2009 – May 2010

CHAPTER 6

Get Britain Working

"They really gave me the third degree," Caroline Haynes, my aide at the Department, told me when we met up at a coffee shop. It was early February 2009, a couple of days after my dramatic exit from the Department. "I told them I didn't have any advance knowledge about your controlled explosion but they didn't seem to believe me. I've been stuck in a small room ever since like a prisoner in isolation."

"I'm sorry. I didn't tell you for your own protection; doesn't seem to have worked, though. Anyway, I've set a meeting for you with George Osborne's chief of staff, Matt Hancock. I've got to work up a Conservative unemployment plan in time for the autumn Conference and George is prepared to fund a team."

The interview was a formality. Caroline was found a desk working for George Osborne before the end of the month. Our combined knowledge put us in a position to build a strategy which reflected the reality of current Government programmes and infrastructure. This meant we overcame the key obstacle for external policy-makers: an inability to track the complexity of what's going on within a Department of State. Indeed, it is because of this lack of detailed insider knowledge that Opposition parties rarely have coherent, fully-worked through plans ready for implementation on achieving office. By the beginning of May the team was rounded out with the recruitment of a young and effective analyst in the shape of Antony Hawkins, on secondment from the Shaftesbury Partnership, an organisation fostering social reform.

Theresa May's office was in the main Parliament building, up an obscure staircase and down a narrow corridor. It was quite a cosy suite of panelled rooms, furnished with the standard, slightly aging Commons' green sofas and armchairs.

"Margaret Thatcher had these rooms when she was in Opposition," she told me. She pushed out her feet as she sat on her armchair, forcing me to notice. "My kitten heels," she said. She had intrigued the Press with her choice of footwear at the Conservative Conference in 2002, and I imagine a discussion about shoes had become a standard introductory topic. This was the limit of the small talk in what was an oddly formal meeting.

She had pursued a career in one of the more obscure branches of the financial services industry, in clearing payments, before becoming an MP in 1997. Here she rose rapidly to become the most senior of the female Conservative Shadow Ministers. She was not an empathetic politician.

She chose her words with great caution as we made arrangements for me to work on the unemployment plan. "Make sure I see all the drafts," she told me. "I need to clear everything before it goes to the Policy Board." It was inevitably going to be uncomfortable. I was tasked with assembling policy proposals for approval by the leadership of the party – the Policy Board. Moreover, Caroline and Antony worked for me out of George Osborne's office. Clearly, she regarded me with deep, and undisguised, suspicion. To a politician with her acute antennae, it was not difficult to see me as an instrument designed by Osborne and Cameron to remove her authority for her Departmental brief. If George Osborne had not bothered to disguise from me his contempt for her, she could hardly have remained oblivious to it.

Through the spring and early summer, I began to assemble a package for tackling the unemployment crisis. There were strict limits on its contents. George told me: "David, you've got to stay within the Labour spending plans. I don't care how you adjust the spending within the overall budget, but we've got to be able to say that the plans are fully-costed and fully-funded."

"That won't be easy," I pointed out. "Labour has already made a series of unfunded commitments."

When I discussed the issue with Theresa, she was quick to add her own constraint: "You've got to stick with all the public commitments we've made in the past. Otherwise we'll be accused of U-turns. And don't talk about changing the Flexible New Deal. We shouldn't look as if we are going to tear up Government contracts." I bit my tongue. I could hardly create a new set of policies without making some changes.

Theresa was at her best when defending established policy. She seemed much less comfortable at the prospect of transforming it.

With these constraints in place, I focused our efforts on building a set of programmes that would tackle the immediate unemployment crisis caused by the developing recession, particularly as it affected the young. These were to form the base of my first presentation to the Policy Board in late July. As we were writing it, the numbers out of work were swelling rapidly; in the spring quarter (to May) more than a quarter of a million joined the ranks of the unemployed. Ominously, the rate of increase was faster than in the previous three deep recessions.

By far the biggest area of spend we worked on was to expand the number of apprenticeships. Here the policy detail was built up by David Willetts and his team. David (dubbed "two-brains" for his formidable analytic capability) was the Shadow Innovation, Universities and Skills Minister – a Conservative stalwart from the Thatcher Government. He found the funding for the increase by switching more than £2 billion from a more generalised Labour programme for training people in work (Train to Gain).

Other initiatives for building up the skills of the young unemployed included work placements; mentoring with sole traders such as plumbers; a combined training/work placement scheme in the service industry; more money for further education. We also rebooted the Enterprise Allowance Scheme, one of the key Conservative programmes of the 1980s to encourage entrepreneurs. All of this was incorporated under the brand of Renewal UK, and there were to be up to 1,000 community-based Renewal Centres to provide mutual help and support from voluntary organisations.

Ahead of the Policy Board meeting I held meetings with key individuals. First was Nick Boles, who had been charged by David Cameron to make sure that civil servants would be able to implement Conservative policies. He was to become an MP the following year. "It's great," he said. "They'll be gagging for it."

Less successful was my meeting with Steve Hilton. Steve was David Cameron's Director of Strategy. He had a mythical reputation among the staff of the leadership suite. "If you want something done, go to Steve", one of them told me. He was responsible for Cameron's rebranding of the party to make it greener and more progressive. He was dressed in tee-shirt and baggy shorts, a combative sartorial style for which he was already well-known.

He seemed to know little about the complexities of the welfare system. "I don't like this," he declared airily. "It's much too bureaucratic. You shouldn't involve the state at all. What we need is a call to social responsibility." I would have understood his vehemence better if I had known he was constructing one of Cameron's central concepts for the election revolving round the Big Society. This ideology aimed to devolve power to local communities, in which people would be encouraged to take an active part.

"But," I argued, "The welfare system is a massive engine of the State. You can't replace it with volunteers in the middle of a crisis. You've got to use the tools to hand."

The Policy Board review was a rushed affair, with only 45 minutes to go through the paper. All the players were round the table: David Cameron and George Osborne; Theresa May and David Willetts; Steve Hilton; and finally Philip Hammond, then Shadow Chief Secretary to the Treasury and responsible for spending decisions.

"We cannot let today's newly unemployed become tomorrow's structurally unemployed," I opened as I introduced the paper. "Not least as there is strong evidence that an extended period out of work is seriously damaging to health and leads to depression. So this is a two-year emergency programme which will be overseen by a Cabinet Committee reporting to the Prime Minister."

David Cameron responded: "I don't want to hear about people being depressed. It may be true but I don't want to hear it."

It was not a great start. Given the time constraint, I ran quickly through the programmes. They were clearly dissatisfied with the low level of ambition in the programme.

David Cameron instructed: "It needs to be crunchier." Inwardly, I cheered. I could take this as a mandate to overturn Theresa's restrictions on the core welfare programmes. However, I had exulted too soon.

Just as the meeting was about to break up, Steve Hilton interjected: "I don't agree with the approach here."

David Cameron was visibly annoyed. "It's no good you coming up with that right at the end of the session." But his annoyance did not mean that the intervention was dismissed. Instead, Steve Hilton was commissioned to come up with an alternative plan.

While he was flailing, I settled down to create the 'crunchier' plan that David Cameron called for. In early August, Caroline Haynes and I retired to my home in East Kent and started composing.

"Let's just assemble the whole package we wanted under Labour, but couldn't get," I proposed.

"It needs a punchy name. What shall we call it?"

After lunch I walked round the garden, trying out various constructs. "I know," I decided. "The Work Programme; does what it says on the tin."

We wrote: "An incoming Conservative Government will introduce a comprehensive strategy to tackle unemployment and welfare in the emergency period following the next election.

"The flagship will be The Work Programme – a set of outcome-based measures in which providers in the private and third sectors will support both the newly unemployed as well as those traditionally excluded from the workforce.

"The Work Programme will replace Flexible New Deal Phase 2, due to be contracted next summer, while we will seek to renegotiate FND1 into the wider scope of The Work Programme."

The next day Bee Roycroft, chief of staff to Theresa, and her researcher, Joanna Penn, came down by train to join us. We spent the day building up and refining the paper.

In the following week we were in a position to see Steve Hilton, who remained resolutely opposed to the bureaucracy involved in what he called top-down programmes. I explained: "The unfortunate reality is that an element of compulsion is required in welfare to work programmes. At that point voluntary processes and community support break down. So you inevitably need some form of bureaucracy."

Without the counter-paper he had committed too, his position was weak. "Most of these people are illiterate," he told us. "We should make them do a compulsory course. The only people who know how to teach literacy are the army. They do a brilliant course in Harrogate."

Smiling sweetly, Bee Roycroft skewered him with some elegance: "Isn't that a top-down programme?" The conclusion from the meeting was that we would turn the paper into a policy proposal.

There was still niggling from Theresa, phoning from her holiday in the Alps. "I don't like the name. See if you can find something better. Build up the National Enterprise scheme and drop all this stuff about restructuring the benefit system. That's all too risky." Otherwise, with her own staff now genuinely committed, our approach was cleared.

No-one came up with a better name.

In parallel with the policy work, I was building a network of businesses and people who would endorse and support our programmes. Clearly it was vital that the welfare to work industry did not disparage The Work Programme when it was announced, requiring some careful preliminary briefing here. Elsewhere, the inspiration for work-based mentoring by sole traders came from a social enterprise called Working Rite; the training/work experience module was developed with the services industry, in the shape of Skillsmart Retail and People1st (who represented the hospitality industry); The Bright Ideas Trust endorsed our training strategy for young entrepreneurs; and the Conservative Kent County Council provided a useful model for vocational training.

My most enjoyable piece of relationship-building was with the Conservative Mayor of London, Boris Johnson. I already knew his policy director, Anthony Browne, who got in touch the day after my appointment as Shadow welfare spokesman. London had a series of employment programmes, on which he wanted me to help. To do so, I formally became an adviser to the Mayor. He had been setting up the 'Boris bike' rental scheme on the day of our meeting and hurried into his office late, cycling rucksack over his shoulder and blond hair more than usually dishevelled.

"Look at this," he said: "My key for unlocking the bikes." He threw it over to me. "You can keep it if you like." As I examined it he realised: "Actually, I'd better have it back. It's got my bank card details on it."

I had been cycling to work in London since 1976. "What we really need is segregated cycle lanes. You could create cycle-ways by joining up secondary roads. All you'd need to do is knock-out the ground floors of the key houses in between those roads."

"Can you draw me up a map of that?" he asked.

"I would if I had the time; but I don't," I replied regretfully. "I'd better do some work for you on welfare."

Despite the rambling nature of this encounter, I reached agreement with the London Mayoral team for them to launch some of our programmes in the capital immediately after they were announced at the autumn Conference. It may have been symbolic, but it would give the whole approach momentum as we headed towards the election.

Through August and early September we worked to complete the policy document, now named *Get Britain Working*. The Renewal concept was junked and most of the modules were renamed with work in their title in line with The Work Programme. We had Work Clubs, Work for Yourself, Work Together, Work Pairing. For the Policy Board on 10 September 2009 we prepared a summary paper alongside the full document. After the last experience I was apprehensive.

We gathered in the Shadow Cabinet Room in the original Parliament buildings, in a group that had expanded considerably. We were getting close to Conference now and this would be a key component. I went through the main points and waited for someone to come in with a damaging broadside.

To my relief the first substantive intervention came from Ken Clarke and it was positive: "I've read the whole document through. It's different from the summary paper. And it's very good. It summarises the whole situation and makes some excellent proposals. I think it will probably cost rather more than David has told us but I think that's fine. We should be prepared to help the unemployed in a recession." Ken was one of the most experienced Ministers of modern times, with a reputation among many as the best Chancellor we have had. His endorsement effectively wrapped up unanimous support for the paper.

I spent the run up to Conference arguing with Theresa on the detailed contents of the document.

"We can't have anything commercial in the document," she insisted.

"Fine; but there's got to be enough to make sure that people know what the structure is." I worked out that this concern translated into her wanting to make a grand flourish in her speech. She planned to say that we would not sign the second stage of Labour's Flexible New Deal Contracts after the election and this was why she didn't want it mentioned in the document.

"You can't give any detail about when people will move onto The Work Programme. Our Green paper said everyone at six months."

I disagreed: "It's unaffordable; people older than 25 will have to move at the one-year point."

The battling concluded with a pointless and debilitating row on who was to compose the summary. I refused to back down and the end result was a document that laid out the programme in a comprehensive way.

By now Steve Hilton, who was planning the contents of the Conference, had become quite an enthusiast. His email to Caroline and me suggested: "I think we can put together a really amazing session which will be quite unlike anything we usually do, and would involve a number of Shadow Cabinet members as well as David (Freud) and Theresa. I was thinking Willetts, Gove, Ken Clarke – and also Sayeeda Warsi . . .

"Doing it like this would be a perfect kick-start for Conference, a serious substantive plan involving a team approach right across the Departments, focused on the big issue we will need to deal with."

He did not accept my suggestion to have Boris Johnson join the launch, however. It meant all our work to build the perception that London would be carrying out the programme ahead of the election was wasted.

This was only the second Conservative Conference I had attended and the Manchester centre was buzzing at the prospect of a win at the next election. There were TV cameras all over and one had to be careful not be ambushed by strategically positioned interviewers. More importantly, one had to avoid the 'waiter' outside the conference hall pressing a glass of champagne into one's hand. Indeed, the Party Chairman had banned the drink to stop the slew of pictures of senior Conservative politicians holding a flute at a time the party was emphasising the importance of national austerity.

We presented *Get Britain Working* in the main conference hall in the Monday afternoon slot. Steve Hilton's plan was implemented, with one addition; James Dyson, inventor of the bagless vacuum cleaner, launched the session talking about the need for better support for scientists and engineers. Then we introduced the document, which had been thoroughly trailed in the press over the weekend. It seemed to go down well.

I was amused two days later when we had another session on stage. Theresa announced, as she had planned, that she would not sign the second stage of the Flexible New Deal contracts. Nobody bothered to report her dramatic statement.

The following week, when I saw George Osborne to plan the follow-up, I could not refrain from expressing my frustration with Theresa.

"She made producing this document an extremely difficult process. I didn't complain to you directly because you can't run to Mamma every time there's a problem, but I want you to know what I and the team have been through."

"Yes, I was kept up to date on what a pain all this was proving."

"She's very reluctant to think structurally and yet she can be extraordinarily obstinate on points of detail. On top of that she's got very poor judgement. So on issue after issue – no welfare, no growth measures, no change in existing policy – she would stop me working.

"It was only after the Policy Board – where David [Cameron] made it clear he wanted these things – that I could go ahead. She is very insecure, so was very manipulative about her position. The effect was to create two teams battling with each other. In Government that would be suicide. The civil servants would play us off before we'd sat down to lunch."

"None of this comes as any surprise to me," George sympathised. "Will you be able to work with her for the next six months?"

"Of course; I'm just saying that if you want a revolution in welfare you won't get it pairing us together in the Department."

CHAPTER 7

Lords and Legislation

By now I was a fully-fledged member of the House of Lords. It had been quite a process. The Lords Appointments Commission had vetted my peerage 'for propriety' in just over two months. The papers were then sent by No. 10 to the Queen and it was early June 2009 by the time I received formal notification from the clerk to the Crown. Before I could be 'introduced' to the Lords, however, I was taken down one of the more obscure byways of the UK constitution to select a new name.

The College of Arms is a red-brick building tucked into Queen Victoria Street in the City of London, up the hill from Blackfriars. Somehow it had survived, much of it, since the seventeenth century. In a book-lined study covered with papers I met Peter Gwynne-Jones, grandly titled the Garter Principal King of Arms. We got through the business of the day speedily.

"You're only a Baron, so you can't have a City in your title. I had a terrible time with Digby Jones, who insisted on being Baron Jones of Birmingham. I told him he couldn't have a City but he was quite emphatic."

"I was thinking of Eastry, the village where I have my home in Kent."

"Oh, a village is fine."

"Should I clear it with the parish council, do you think, as a courtesy?"

"No. I wouldn't do that; sets a bad precedent. I don't suppose you'll want to change your present surname? You can change it to whatever you want."

"I'll stick with Freud."

"So it'll be Lord Freud of Eastry. Now what coat of arms do you want?" We had come to the main point of the meeting – the commercial opportunity to sell me a coat of arms for £5,000. It was not an item whose deficiency had previously occurred to me. Peter Gwynne-Jones quickly made me aware of what I had been missing. He was in his late 60s, red-faced with a donnish, idiosyncratic enthusiasm. Since his appointment in 1995 he had re-invigorated the College by encouraging a large number of applications from individuals for new coats of arms, many of which he had designed himself.

"Well Freude means happy in German and bats are the heraldic symbol for happiness. So your shield should have a bat supporting it on each side." Clearly, resistance was useless.

At our next meeting, to finalise the shield he had designed, he asked: "Did you decide on a motto?"

"How about *Frangar non Flectar*?," I suggested. "It's based on something in Livy and I haven't seen it used by anyone else." It meant 'broken but not deflected' and I had a feeling that the motto was likely to reflect the reality of the job I had taken on. In the event I was grateful to have succumbed to Peter Gwynne-Jones' sales pitch. The heraldic master-designer retired in the spring of the following year and died shortly afterwards.

The House of Lords is a complex, subtle institution, whose ways would take a life-time to learn. It is centred on an exquisite legislative Chamber, presided over by an elaborately carved throne within a gilded canopy. Around the Chamber is a labyrinth of offices and meeting rooms, showing distinct signs of deterioration after 150-plus years of heavy use. With four offset working levels it is easy to get lost.

New members enjoy an initial welcome of the utmost warmth. My introduction took place at the end of June. Accompanied by two Lords, Jeffrey Sterling and Tristan Garel-Jones, I was arrayed in a splendid red robe and slowly paced through the main doorway of the Chamber to the large table in the centre. Here I swore to be faithful to the Queen and then paced out between the supporting Lords, shaking hands with the Lord Speaker to the standard cheer from Peers.

Before I could begin to take on my role as welfare spokesman in the Lords, there was one more hurdle. This was a maiden speech, traditionally not politically contentious and welcomed, regardless of worth, by fellow-Peers as a piece of oratory on a par with Churchill's. My first opportunity came up on 10 July, when I spoke in a Bill on autism.

After a few words on autism, I turned to the debt I owed to the country. It was a way to explain my motivation for the work I had undertaken: "My family arrived here 71 years ago at a very difficult time for this country and the world. . . I place on record in this place and at this very difficult time my gratitude to this great country for all that it has done to nurture the Freud family and other families who have come here for freedom and to achieve their potential."

The House broke up less than a fortnight later and would not reassemble until well into October, after the conference season. When it did reconvene, I would be ready to start learning my new trade: how to function on the Front Bench of the House of Lords. It would be a vital part of my education. The Lords were to become central to achieving the welfare reform I had embarked on.

I was just in time to take part in the last three weeks of the Welfare Reform Bill that James Purnell had launched at the beginning of 2009. Since it was based on the December White Paper, I was familiar with the contents. The process of legislation is quite drawn out. Each mainstream Bill goes through four similar stages in both the Commons and the Lords, usually starting in the Commons. Discussion is organised by amendments proposed by the non-Government parties, which are then either accepted or rejected. Rejection is easier for a Government in the Commons where it has a majority. In practice it is only vulnerable when there is a rebellion of its own backbenchers. So debate can often be cursory and few concessions are made. In the Lords the Government does not have an inbuilt majority, with a group of non-aligned Crossbenchers holding the balance of power. As a result, there is much more give and take and an elaborate, careful courtesy as all participants strive to avoid giving unnecessary offence.

Each Bill is introduced to each of the Houses at First Reading, when its name is read out. This is followed by Second Reading, which in the Lords is often a full-day affair at which interested Peers make speeches on the positions they are planning to adopt. The subsequent Committee Stage is usually a discovery process. Here participants test out the strength of each other's arguments. In the Commons external witnesses can be invited to give evidence during this stage. While there is voting in the Commons, many Bills in the Lords are dealt with outside the main Chamber in Grand Committee, where there is no voting.

Battle is joined at Report Stage and this was the point in the progress of the Welfare Reform Bill at which I took over as Conservative spokesman. On Day One I put up a single amendment, which I had inherited from previous stages of the Bill. It covered a familiar topic, the issue that I had inadvertently blundered over at the launch of my report, about when lone parents should be required to take part in activity. Government policy had moved with great speed here, and the Bill was looking to require lone parents to take part in 'work-related activity' when their youngest was three and four, compared with the inactivity permitted to the sixteenth year when I wrote. In this case, paradoxically, I was looking to soften the penalties imposed for non-compliance for a parent whose child was under five. I had cleared the position with David Cameron, through Theresa, and the amendment simply stated that such parents would not face a financial penalty. [35]

The House of Lords is made up of a varied group of people. There is a large contingent of former politicians. Alongside them are experts and leaders in key areas – ranging from the law to farming. Welfare had its own devotees and this Bill served as my introduction to a group of Peers who followed every twist and turn of the legislation.

Patricia Hollis had spent eight years as Lords Minister in the Department under Labour and had developed a deep knowledge of the welfare system. Elegant and authoritative, with flaming red hair and a flair for building complex arguments out of abstruse elements in the system, she now demanded: "Although the noble Lord, Lord Freud, said that there could be sanctions other than financial ones, he did not give us a single instance. I would like to know what they look like."

I replied: "Clearly taking people's time is effective … Making the way money is collected rather more inconvenient is effective. Controls on how money is spent and in what form are another."

The Labour Minister taking the Bill through the House was Bill McKenzie. His background as an accountant was reflected in a forensic questioning style. "The noble Lord said that one of the sanctions that might be introduced would be to restrict how people spent their money. Will he elaborate on that for us?"

I ducked: "I was giving the noble Lord some thoughts and I think I have given enough."

In this case I had reached an agreement with the Liberal Democrats to support the amendment. So I was in a strong position. I used the formula to call for a vote: "I would like to test the opinion of the House."

After an equally formulaic call from the Lord Speaker: "As many as are of that opinion say 'Content'," and the equivalent call for the 'Not-Contents', she called out "Division".

The bells rang in the corridors and Peers emerged from their offices, where many had been watching the debate on their monitors. The Conservative and Liberal Democrat Peers, together with the majority of Crossbenchers, filed over to the door to the left of the throne and entered the narrow corridor running alongside the Chamber – the Lobby. In two files they passed the Parliamentary Clerks who crossed through their names one by one, registering they were 'content' with the amendment. At the far end of the Chamber the Labour Peers and a handful of Crossbenchers filed through the 'not content' Lobby.

Back in the Chamber we waited for the Tellers from the two lobbies to come in with the score, which was jotted down by the Clerk at the central desk. The senior Teller from the winning side was then given the figures to bring to the Lord Speaker, who sat at the head of the Chamber on a red couch known from medieval times as the Woolsack. There was a rumble of jubilation when the slip was handed to the Conservative chief whip, Joyce Anelay. It was close.

"The contents 103; Not-Contents 97," called the Lord Speaker.

In truth, when the Conservatives moved a rare ameliorating amendment, they could expect support from the tender-hearted Lords on the Crossbenches and the Liberal Democrats, so the victory was hardly unexpected. Nevertheless, it was a heady moment. "Well done," congratulated one experienced Conservative Peer afterwards. "Your first vote and you won it. Many Opposition spokesmen go for years before they have a victory."

The triumph was short-lived. The Bill progressed through the final formal stage of Third Reading, which tidied it up. It was then sent back to the Commons in a process named ping pong. In this, the amendments inserted by the Lords were voted on by the Commons. Traditionally, the differences go back and forth between the two Houses until they are resolved. In the Commons, the Government overturned my amendment, with only a handful of rebels.

"The Liberal Democrats tell me they will support us if we change it back," I told the Conservative Shadow Leader of the House, Tom Strathclyde. He was one of the 92 Peers who had survived the dismissal of most hereditary Lords in 2000. He was both jovial and had a doctor's soothing avuncular way about him.

"David, I'm sure you could win but the convention is that we only send it back once. You need to withdraw gracefully now."

My next – and final – Bill in Opposition was on Labour legislation to eradicate child poverty by 2020.

"This is bonkers," I confided to Theresa. "These income transfers simply don't tackle the real problems. Shouldn't we just oppose it?"

"It's a political trap ahead of the election," Theresa explained sourly.

"We can't afford to oppose it and allow Labour to say that we don't care about child poverty."

Restricted thus, my attack on the Bill concentrated on its inadequacies. As an unexpected bonus, the research required to tackle the issues helped me to hone my own views on how to tackle poverty. In contrast to Government Ministers, who can rely on large Departmental teams writing their speeches, Opposition spokesmen are obliged to prepare the bulk of their material themselves. The preparation work was much greater but the process required a more intensive application of brain to subject matter.

In my Second Reading speech I pointed out that on some measures child poverty had hardly changed over the previous decade, despite income transfers nearly doubling. I suggested: "Perhaps it is not the case that child poverty has risen despite money being transferred to the poorest sections of the community, but maybe the financial transfers themselves have masked poverty and created poverty traps." [36]

I concluded with our own agenda: "We have the lowest child well-being in a comparison of 21 rich countries. The Government's child poverty targeting regime has failed ... For that reason, our policy in this area will concentrate on the causes of poverty and inadequate child welfare, with particular focus on the four main drivers: family breakdown, addiction, inadequate education and skills, and work."

The half-year in Opposition was invaluable in allowing me to learn how to operate. It was becoming second nature to address a fellow peer in debate as the 'Noble Lord' or 'Noble Lady' and never to use the word 'You'. If a peer stood up, I would know this to be an intervention and that the calls of 'order' were made to alert me to the need to 'give way', or sit down, to allow the point to be made. All the little conventions needed to become second nature: bowing to the throne; sitting when the Lord Speaker stood; not passing between the Woolsack and the Despatch Box. Mastery of those conventions would allow me to focus on the things that really mattered; the content of the work; the emotional tone of my address; the appropriate way to respond to difficult questions.

I would need that experience all the more as our ambition in welfare reform took wing. Out of the blue, my proposal to reform the benefit system itself – shunted into the long grass by the Labour Government – had been revived.

CHAPTER 8

Enter Iain Duncan Smith

I first met Iain Duncan Smith in early June 2009 with Theresa May. The meeting was in her room and he was keeping us up to date with developments at the Centre for Social Justice (CSJ), which he had set up in 2004. Iain's establishment of this foundation was the stuff of legend. In 2003 he had been brutally rejected as Leader of the Conservative Party by Conservative MPs, unpersuaded by his adoption of the label of the "Quiet Man". But the year before, in 2002, he had made a public commitment to a powerful social agenda. This followed his visit to the depressed Easterhouse estate in Glasgow. Amid the drug strewn debris, he seems to have had a genuine epiphany. He told the Conservative Conference in Harrogate that his ambition was for the party to be one "that doesn't just drive past Easterhouse on the motorway." Despite his ousting, he had held to the vision with the founding of the CSJ, which had rapidly come to represent the voice of right-wing thinking in social policy.

He was anything but quiet at our meeting. "We'll be publishing the findings of *Breakthrough Britain* next month," he told us. This was a piece of work commissioned by David Cameron 18 months earlier to make policy recommendations in the social sphere for the Conservative Party. [37]

"It's going to find that the single most important thing we can do to tackle poverty is to support stable family life.

"The next thing we're going to publish is our report on how to transform the benefit system. We've got a team on it now, led by the London leader of the Oliver Wyman management consulting firm, called Stephen Brien. He really is committed to the project and is doing an extraordinary job. We'd like to brief you on it when it's ready in the autumn."

The promised briefing on *Dynamic Benefits* took place a week before it was formally launched on 16 September 2009. [38] It was held in one of the modern rooms of Portcullis House, which had projection facilities, and we were joined by its principal author, Stephen Brien.

Iain opened: "We've been seeing all the media ahead of the launch." He then drew out some of the themes for us. "The key issue is that it remains financially pointless for people on benefits to take a job, due to the loss of those benefits. Stephen has developed a structure that gets rid of that problem."

Stephen Brien put up some charts. "The central problem is the very high withdrawal rates of the different benefits," he explained. "Nearly 2 million working people currently suffer marginal rates of withdrawal of more than 60 percent. Some are even more than 90 percent."

"We've built our own model which includes the effects of the changes we're making, so it's dynamic. We've designed a two-component system: a Universal Work Credit and a Universal Life Credit. We're proposing a standard 55 percent withdrawal rate." Sometimes he spoke so fast in his enthusiasm that his words fell over themselves. "We've also boosted the amount of money people can earn before benefits are withdrawn, to encourage people into work.

"The overall effect would be self-financing in the medium-term once you take the tax gains and the reduced administration costs into account." The reason the report was called *Dynamic Benefits* was because it took into account the positive – dynamic – behavioural change that the system would encourage, reducing the number of people who relied on state benefits and the cost of the system.

I started to delve into the detail with him. I was impressed by the way he had modelled a common structure which could be tuned to the needs of each individual.

"So you are taking the elements of the current system of benefits for each individual, adding them all up and then withdrawing the total pot as they start to earn money?" I checked.

"Exactly," he agreed. "And we'll include all the main benefits – we counted 51 in total – council tax benefit, child benefit, disability benefits."

"So everything will be means-tested."

Crucially the new system would incorporate the tax credits which Gordon Brown had introduced in 2003. These consisted of a child tax credit for those on low income, whether or not they were in work, and a working tax credit to supplement low wages. They had been kept entirely separate from out of work benefits and had been given to the tax authorities in the shape of Her Majesty's Revenue and Customs (HMRC), rather than DWP, to run. They had grown rapidly to more than £20 billion a year. By integrating the two systems, Stephen's structure effectively used the tax credit funds to provide a smooth reduction in benefits as people's earnings increased.

At the far end of the table Iain could sense Theresa's cool hesitancy as well as her irritation at my obvious interest. Knowing her reluctance to engage in new ideas with an outside audience, let alone a structure as complicated as this, I was unsurprised by her being in 'listening mode'. Iain insisted: "If we're serious about tackling poverty and getting people into work we have to do this. There is simply no other way."

"We'll have to look at it in detail," she replied crisply.

We next assembled at an evening fringe meeting on the Monday of the Conference in October. It was hosted by CSJ in the shape of its formidable executive director Philippa Stroud. Both Theresa and I spoke, but the event was designed as a platform for Stephen to explain *Dynamic Benefits*.

Afterwards Theresa complained to me: "If they're trying to simplify the system, why are they introducing two new benefits?" It was a fair point.

While Theresa was lukewarm about *Dynamic Benefits*, the message had clearly got home to David Cameron. In his closing speech to the Conference two days later he focused on the high rates at which benefits were withdrawn.

"In Gordon Brown's Britain if you're a single mother with two kids earning £150 a week, the withdrawal of benefits and the additional taxes mean that for every extra pound you earn, you keep just 4p.

"What kind of incentive is that? Thirty years ago this party won an election fighting against 98 percent tax rates on the richest. Today I want us to show even more anger about 96 percent tax rates on the poorest."[39]

He then threw in another surprise. "And in that fight, there's one person this party can rely on. He's the man who has dedicated himself to the cause of social justice and shown great courage in standing up for those least able to stand up for themselves: Iain Duncan Smith. And I am proud to announce today that if we win the election he will be responsible in Government for bringing together all our work to help mend the broken society." With this announcement David Cameron brought Iain Duncan Smith back into the fold, with a public commitment that he would run a

Cabinet sub-committee on Social Justice. There was no talk of him running specific Departments, but the ambiguity of his role further undermined Theresa's responsibility for the welfare agenda.

At our wash-up meeting after Conference, George Osborne told me: "I want to have a meeting with you and Iain and Theresa to discuss what to do about *Dynamic Benefits*. We have to be careful to make sure that this does not go public before an election.

"In my view we must do enough analysis to make sure we understand the direction of travel and that we're happy to go along it. I'd be most interested to explore it in real detail."

By the time the email went out the next day the invitees had expanded to include Steve Hilton and the Conservative fixer, Oliver Letwin. There was also a full cast list from the various support teams. However, it was not to be.

Theresa reasserted her authority with an email. "As I have already allocated work on this issue within my team and have asked Andrew Selous and Mark Harper to take on this issue rather than David Freud it would make more sense for them to be at the meeting instead of David." She concluded glibly: "I suspect no-one was aware of the work that had already been set in motion."

Iain was on the phone to me the next day: "I know Theresa pretty well. This is not her ball game. It's too complex. She feels people are raiding her territory and she wants to establish that she's in charge; but it's not her ball game."

He continued: "We've got an implementation group embedded in each of the Departments now at mid-ranking level. So all we need to do is keep going with the implementation. The idea would be just to get you involved unofficially in that process and that's what we will arrange."

George's meeting was cancelled and it didn't take long for Iain to clear my involvement. At our kick-off meeting in his Parliamentary office in early December, he told me: "I want you to turn it into practical politics, David."

This initiated a series of weekly meetings between Stephen and me, typically at the Costa coffee shop under his office in Baker Street. He was in his early forties and one of the cleverest people I had ever met. He was born into an academic family in Dublin and inherited a strong sense of public mission from, in particular, his maternal grandfather. He had an education to match – with no fewer than four degrees: three in computation, including a doctorate from Oxford, as well as an MA in Law for good measure. He had been working for Oliver Wyman since 1997 and headed their London office. He had always planned to branch into public policy work and the opportunity to tackle the ills of the welfare state for the Centre for Social Justice had been too attractive to turn down. It allowed him to develop the concept of the taper which had been inspired in 1995 by Samuel Britain's *Capitalism with a Human Face.* [40]

"How on earth did you do all this modelling?" I asked. My inability to model the welfare system in the time-scale had been the key factor in preventing an outright recommendation in my report to move to a single benefit.

"Well I got a young modeller – Daniel Khoo – and just built it up. I don't think he knew enough at the outset to realise what an enormous task he was embarked on."

"And what got you going in the first place?"

"Well, we saw the recommendation in your report to run detailed modelling for a single benefit system. No one was taking up the challenge, so we thought we'd have a go."

"If we're going for simplicity," I said, "shouldn't we plump for a single benefit rather than the two you've got here? Theresa made the point and it's a fair one. Would that be a problem?"

"No, not really; it's not essential."

"Then probably the most important challenge is to call it something snappy. I leave that in your hands."

When we next met he had the answer: "How about 'Universal Credit'?"

I approved. It was somewhere between the 'Tax Credits' Gordon Brown had created for low-income earners and the 'universal benefit' catch-all to describe those payments that went to all in the appropriate category, like child benefit.

"You won't like this, Stephen," I warned, "I don't think we can risk putting all the benefits into the new system. We should probably exclude child benefit. That goes to all mothers, including the middle-class ones, and there would be uproar if that was means-tested and removed from them. The other payment we should leave outside is the Disability Living Allowance. That's not means-tested now and we would be taking on the disability lobby if we included it. If those two groups became our opponents, Universal Credit would be still-born."

I had dumped a lot of remodelling on him and I had one more request. "We'll have to be careful with double counting. The Treasury will be all over us on the savings from the DEL-AME switch as we get people back to work. We can't claim savings from the same people going back to work because of the better incentives under Universal Credit."

Each week we went through the theoretical issues. At the beginning of 2010 we moved onto the practical ones around how we could implement the system and the time-scale for doing it. In an early draft of my 2007 report I had estimated that it would take at least eight years to introduce – an estimate that had been carefully excised during the vetting process. A lot of that timetable was consumed by the legislative process. I had undoubtedly under-estimated how long it would take to adjust the Pay-As-You-Earn (PAYE) system run by the taxman to provide a feed of what people were earning. That information would be essential to allow us to pay working people their Universal Credit top-up automatically.

Now Stephen went off to meet the consultancy team at the accountants Price Waterhouse Coopers, who were closest to the Government IT systems involved.

"Well they think it's a brilliant idea," he reported. "They think it is eminently doable and that it should have been done years ago."

"That's very encouraging," I prompted.

"But they think it will take eight years to do. Updating the PAYE system will be a major challenge."

I looked at him in dismay. "That's no good. I can just imagine wandering in to see David Cameron and telling him we've got this wizard wheeze and it'll be ready halfway through the Parliament after next if you're lucky. Basically, I think we're dead in the water." We finished our cappuccini in gloomy silence.

It looked as if we would have to give up.

CHAPTER 9

Moment of Serendipity

In February 2010 we seemed to have hit a complete road-block on devising any practical way to reform the structure of the benefit system. Stephen and I started to consider how to break the bad news to Iain.

At this point of despair, I experienced a moment of complete serendipity. In mid-February I met a representative from Vocalink in the House of Lords bar for morning coffee. The meeting had been put in my diary by Philip Hammond, the Shadow Chief Secretary to the Treasury, with whom I had been working closely on the costings for *Get Britain Working*.

We settled ourselves beside the window overlooking the Thames. Initially I was puzzled as Peter Seymour introduced himself to me. "What is Vocalink, when it's at home?" I asked.

"I'm sorry, we've just changed our name. We're BACS; we're the electronic system for making payments from one bank account to another. We've been working on a real-time PAYE project with the tax people and Philip thought you'd be interested."

The penny dropped. Peter Seymour, head of Government and Public Service at the company, explained how they had been involved in a project over the last four years to update the creaking PAYE system – in which employers only reported what they paid their staff at the end of the year.

"It's a prototype system on a desktop computer," he explained. "But it works perfectly well and should be straight-forward to scale up. We've been calling it PAYE2. We can provide the Government the payments information in each period, monthly say, so that it can work out the proper tax."

"And presumably the amount of benefit to which each person is entitled?"

It was a breakthrough. We only heard about the pilot because the tax authorities had decided it was not worth pursuing and had abandoned it. Peter Seymour was vigorously circling Opposition politicians to see if, somehow, he could bring the project back to life. I immediately saw this as the solution to our problem. It would allow the state to pay the right amount of benefit on an immediate and automatic basis while saving the Universal Credit project the four years of development time which had already been invested.

Within a month Vocalink had sent me a short paper fleshing out the proposition. "Our proposals would seek to use the existing BACS infrastructure to create a centralised PAYE2 system that would calculate an individual's tax, deductions and benefits in real-time from gross employer submissions." [41]

The costs of creating this centralised system were estimated at £200 million and a Government that got to work on day one could have a central tax calculation 'go live' in 2012. With changes to the benefit system undertaken in parallel, roll-out of welfare reform could proceed thereafter. Their paper showed the roll-out of the reform from 2013 onwards, although it was ambiguous about its pace.

Iain was visibly excited when Stephen and I took him through the paper. Given its authoritative source he now had real ammunition to justify his ambition to transform the system.

"We need to take George through this," he told us. He set up a meeting, although with George increasingly tied up preparing for the election, it wasn't until a fortnight later that it took place.

Meanwhile I was fighting fires on a different front. We were following up the *Get Britain Working* document with a planned announcement about the launch of one of its components, the Service Academy. This would offer a short training course combined with work experience for unemployed youngsters. Critically the launch would be supported by 20 companies in the hospitality, leisure and tourism sector.

Suddenly, the companies that had indicated their support were dropping out. Theresa was furious. "How has this happened?" she demanded. "Whose fault is it?" Quickly her wrath became focused on my team member Caroline Haynes, who had sent out the emails to the 20 companies seeking final confirmation.

It was hardly Caroline's fault, as she explained in a careful email. "I have spoken to a number of people this morning and the sudden reservations of some companies is down to perceived tighter polling." The big

Conservative leads of 2009 had evaporated in February and the polling organisation YouGov in the *Sun* was now showing the party ahead by only 4 or 5 points. Companies naturally did not want to endorse publicly a party that might not win.

There was no time to be wasted – certainly not in allocating blame. While Theresa fumed, Caroline and I hit the phones and begged chief executives to reaffirm their commitment. We didn't get all 20, but there were some very big names in the group of 11 that elected to stay on board, including Gala Coral, Pizza Express, Travelodge and Starbucks. It was enough to go ahead with the launch, at which I particularly enjoyed Theresa's gracious thanks to the industry: "We welcome the support being given by businesses in the hospitality industry and their commitment to helping to tackle unemployment." [42]

It was late afternoon on the first day of April that we finally went to see George. He was based in a small corner office of the floor in the Millbank Tower which had become the hub of the Conservative election machine. We passed rows of desks with volunteers busy phoning electors. Iain led the way, with Philippa Stroud and me close behind.

It was an uncomfortable, cramped meeting. We explained the break-through; how we could use information from the tax system as a base for a single unified benefit in the shape of Universal Credit. George was unenthusiastic. The polls had continued to be obstinately discouraging and he must have been feeling the pressure.

"You cannot be serious if you think you can introduce a complete reform of both the tax system and the benefit system just five weeks ahead of an election. Not a word of this must get out. If it does, I will leak against you." By then I had learned that the threat of being 'leaked against' was the most potent weapon in the modern politician's armoury. It implied a full-scale media attack on the victim's plans, motivation and, no doubt, sanity.

He softened somewhat when he addressed me. "David, why don't you work with David Gauke in the Shadow Treasury team to see how this real-time PAYE might work? I'll let him know you'll be calling."

We left the meeting considerably deflated. When I phoned David Gauke the next day, he already seemed well-informed about the PAYE2 trial. Vocalink had come calling on him as well.

"David," he told me at our meeting the following week, "I want to introduce this new system if at all possible. The PAYE system is completely decrepit and badly needs updating, so it makes sense to modernise it. If we can help you with welfare reform at the same time, that's a bonus."

"Let's just move ahead in parallel then." I suggested. "I'll get on with preparing an action paper for DWP and I'll leave you to handle HMRC. We can get the two Departments together immediately after a new Government is formed – assuming it's us. Let's stay in touch in case either of us runs into difficulties."

David knew that he had a challenge on his hands, based on the scepticism of the senior leadership team at HMRC. Later he told me: "When I raised the prospect of PAYE reform before the election with Lesley Strathie, the HMRC Chief Executive, she jokingly formed a cross with her fingers in terror at the prospect." He explained: "The view of the HMRC leadership was that the reform was too ambitious and that the organisation was in too fragile a condition." The merger between its two component parts – the Inland Revenue and Customs and Excise – had only been completed in 2005, while the introduction of tax credits had expanded its responsibilities still further. Finally, the previous Chief Executive had been forced to resign in late 2007 when discs containing the details of child benefit claimants were lost.

David and I talked regularly in the following weeks. Both of us stuck with our commitments in completing the work required. The relationship I formed with David Gauke in that period was to be a key factor in achieving the changes we were seeking.

Given George Osborne's reaction, it came as no surprise that the Conservative Manifesto made no mention of any of this. While it promised to tackle welfare dependency and the causes of poverty, the solution proffered was Steve Hilton's Big Society, with its unspecific remedies. The Manifesto did incorporate, however, all the elements of the *Get Britain Working* document: The Work Programme, Service Academies, Work Pairing and apprenticeships. [43]

While I worked through the election period in getting our ducks in a row, we were careful not to breathe a word about Universal Credit in public. In the event it was Theresa May who was leaked against. The authoritative political commentator Fraser Nelson wrote in *The Daily Telegraph*: "With a nine-year track record of achieving precisely nothing in Opposition, May is spectacularly ill-suited to what should be the toughest task in government. It is not enough for her to have David Freud, a banker turned welfare adviser, in the wings. There is only one man appropriate for this job.

"Duncan Smith wanted to stay on the back benches, to be a Wilberforce-style campaigner rather than be part of a cabinet. But now there is a compelling case for him to head a new Department of Social Justice."[44]

In the run-up to the 2010 election on 6 May, the Conservative lead became far shakier than I had expected. At the same time my enthusiasm for taking on the arduous task of reforming the welfare system had severely diminished. I had already warned George Osborne that I could not envisage achieving anything with Theresa May as my Secretary of State. Now I determined that I would turn down outright any job in the Department if she was to be my boss.

PART IV

PERSUASION

May 2010 – November 2010

CHAPTER 10

Minister for Wefare Reform

The election, held on 6 May 2010, was dominated by the television debates. The fresh-faced Liberal Democrat leader, Nick Clegg, adopted a highly effective technique of looking straight at the camera as he made his pitch to the TV audience. He undoubtedly saved his party from the squeeze on its vote that it looked likely to suffer as a by-product of Conservative recovery. At the same time Labour, with Gordon Brown at the helm, did much better than I anticipated – an expectation probably biased by my own experience of him. So, the outright Conservative lead melted away and, at 306 seats, the party was 20 short of an outright majority.

I was a bystander, watching the TV screens with the rest of the country as the coalition talks with the Liberal Democrats, with their 57 seats, stretched over the next five days. The details were kept tight until Tuesday evening, when agreement was reached and David Cameron went to Buckingham Palace to be invited to form a Government by the Queen. Just before he set off, invitations went out to Conservative MPs and Peers to a meeting at 10 pm in the largest Committee Room in the Palace of Westminster, the wood-panelled Number 14 presided over by the large, sombre painting of Gladstone's 1868 Cabinet.

It was crowded and raucous, with many standing at the back. David Cameron entered to a standing ovation of clapping, cheering and desk thumping. He could hardly get out half a sentence without being interrupted by a renewed outburst. "I would only be Prime Minister now..." (cheers) and "I would only have taken a call from Barrack Obama..." (more cheers). Clearly, he had far less need to justify the agreement than he had expected. He emphasised that the Welfare Reform agenda was one of the main areas in which the Conservative strategy had been fully incorporated. He then handed over to William Hague, leader of the negotiating team, who quickly ran through the main features of the

Coalition Agreement, aiming to show that these were all elements that the party could live with.

The next day the Cabinet appointments began to come through. Early on came the surprise news that Theresa May was appointed Home Secretary. Hypocritically I texted: "Theresa, many congrats; though you will be missed on the DWP front." She replied: "I'm pleased but also sorry not to be able to put our plans in practice."

Now I settled down at my desk at home to wonder whether I would be appointed or not. Clearly all the Conservative plans for Government were up in the air. With five Cabinet posts going to the Liberal Democrats, plus another 18 junior minister jobs, there would be a terrible squeeze on Conservative appointments. To give a major portfolio to a non-MP, when there were so many MPs to satisfy, might well be a step too far.

Coming back from holiday in Florence, Iain Duncan Smith was caught by surprise when Ed Llewellyn, Downing Street head of staff, phoned to offer him the job of Secretary of State for DWP. "I asked for an hour to discuss it with Betsy," he told me later. Betsy – his wife – told him he would regret it if he turned away from the chance to put all the work into practice.

Iain went on: "Originally they told me the Employment slot would go to Greg Clark. Later it turned out to be Chris Grayling. They warned that there was a lot of social damage I would have to control. Chris had obviously turned down a lot of other options." Chris Grayling had been the Shadow Home Secretary, so the role of Minister of State for Employment was a significant downward step.

The first I knew of these developments was by text from the astonishingly well-informed Tim Stone, the former colleague who had proposed I should write the Welfare to Work review. In the early evening of Wednesday he wrote: "Am assuming you're still in there with IDS and Grayling?" Chris Grayling's appointment was my first solid indication that I was not, after all, going to get the Minister of State job Osborne and Cameron had promised.

Shortly afterwards Philippa Stroud rang up: "Can you join a meeting with Iain and officials tomorrow morning."

"I haven't been appointed yet. And I might well not be. It would look quite wrong to come in beforehand."

"Oh, I didn't realise. Iain is very keen for you to come in. We're arranging to get tax credits away from HMRC."

"Don't do that," I cautioned. "I've heard from Vocalink that HMRC are digging their heels in about losing tax credits. It would be a complete waste of time to have a turf war when we need their co-operation to get a real-time PAYE system off the ground."

"Too late, I'm afraid," Philippa confessed. "We've already started the process."

Philippa was now Iain's Special Adviser. She was driven by her concern for the disadvantaged. In her early twenties she turned her back on the career in international banking that beckoned in order to help the poor and homeless. Her initiation was working with addicts in the slum area of Hong Kong's Walled City. In her late thirties she was lured from the social project she was running in Birmingham to join the team setting up Iain's Centre for Social Justice in London. Within a matter of weeks, she became the Chief Executive of the organisation and was instrumental in developing the *Breakthrough Britain* studies commissioned by David Cameron.

After six years with the CSJ, she had thrown her hat in the ring to become an MP, fighting the Liberal Democrat constituency of Sutton and Cheam. However, Nick Clegg's stunning performance in the TV debates held off the Conservative challenge in their key seats, and it was retained – narrowly – by Paul Burstow. She was in limbo for only a few days; Iain's first act as a Secretary of State was to appoint her his Special Adviser.

She was deeply, and privately, religious. She fought the political battles that we were to face with an intensity driven by her concern for the poorest in society. At times her emotions could break through. "I know the damage that certain behaviours cause," she told me later. "It makes me angry when people in positions of power do not use that power to help the most vulnerable."

The next day was strange and jittery. Would I be called up? If I was, what would the job be? Would I want it? When would the call come? Hours stretched by as I waited at home with my phone to hand. I was sharing the emotional roller-coaster of all the Conservative and Liberal Democrat contenders as the appointment process reached the junior ministerial ranks. Theresa was no longer an obstacle, but with Chris Grayling's appointment as a second-rank Minister of State I was going down the pecking order. By the afternoon I had reached the decision that I would accept a job only if it entailed running the welfare reform agenda. I had seen the role of a typical Lord's Minister in a Department;

the core function was to push through legislation created by one of the Common's Ministers. I really did not fancy the idea of being a 'legislative jockey' where I would not be adding value significantly beyond that of any other Lord.

So I was in a fractious mood when, at 6.35 pm, the call finally came through from Tom Strathclyde, Leader of the Conservatives in the Lords. "Lord Freud, I'm sorry we've kept you waiting. It has been extremely hard to get everything sorted out. The reason it's me calling is that we decided that we've simply got to let everyone know where they stand, so David is calling the MPs and I'm calling the Lords. I can't emphasise how hard it's been to get people jobs and we've been badly squeezed. So your job is to go into the DWP as the Parliamentary Under-Secretary. David emphasises that you are driving the welfare reform process."

A Parliamentary Under-Secretary was the third ministerial rank after Secretary of State and Minister of State. Tom Strathclyde might have proposed that I would be driving the welfare reform process but as a third-rank Minister I would be in danger of not having adequate authority. In that event the job might well morph into the jockey role I didn't want. "Tom, I don't want to do it. It's not what I came in to do."

"Right, I'll get David onto you straight away. Stay near the phone. The next call you get will be from the Prime Minister's office."

There followed the conversation which opens this book. When David Cameron came through, I congratulated him on his strategic touch in creating the Coalition.

"Well, that's very kind. We've got ourselves into a position where we can have stable Government for the very difficult times we are facing. I'm sorry this is on the phone until you can come in here next week."

I went straight to the issue at hand. "I don't want to do the job Tom offered because it's not what I came in to do. I came in to do welfare reform."

"That's exactly what we want you to do."

"I spent last summer sorting out a Conservative welfare reform strategy and that is what I wanted to make sure was put into effect. I don't particularly want to be a legislative jockey in the Lords."

"That's exactly what IDS wants you to do. The job description is much more important than anything else. He is going to be a chairman figure so you will be in charge."

"Can I be called Minister for Welfare Reform?"

"Yes, and you can have access to me. Ed have you got that." Ed Llew-ellyn was the new Prime Minister's chief of staff and was listening in.

"I'll take you up on that. In particular I may need to talk to you about a project to integrate benefits, tax credits and tax, which will need your support."

"Well, the Treasury will also have something to say on that."

"Yes, of course. They'll be part of this process." I had a final try for the senior rank I had been promised. "Can I be a Minister of State?"

"The trouble is I haven't any more Ministers of State to give away."

"I see. Well on the basis of the title of Minister for Welfare Reform and access I'm pleased to accept the offer."

"Done."

Chris Grayling was among the callers that evening. I commiserated with him over his disappointment. "I'm slightly shocked at the way you didn't get the Home Secretary job, but I'm delighted to be working with you again."

"There are not many reasons to be pleased in the last two days," he con-fessed, "but being part of a team with IDS and you is one of them." Then he got to the point of the call: "I see you driving the Reform agenda, while I get on with the Welfare-to-Work stuff that we've developed."

He was transparently staking out his turf. In practice I was happy to acquiesce. The principles of The Work Programme had already been developed in considerable detail, while the creation of Universal Credit was a far greater challenge and would require all my efforts. "I'll be most pleased to help you with the Welfare-to-Work stuff, if you think it would be helpful, particularly on the contract commissioning," I told him.

Next morning, the Friday of a tumultuous week, I cycled into the Lords to change into my suit, as was my traditional practice. While I was in my Lords' office, I was called up by the Department wanting to know where I was. I walked the short distance to Caxton House in Tothill Street. Waiting for me at the entrance was Leigh Lewis, the Permanent Secret-ary, with whom I had developed a good relationship in my time at the Department. With him was someone I did not know, but who was to become my key support in the years ahead, my designated Private Secret-ary, Jessica Yuille.

They took me into the downstairs reception, where I was impressed to see that my photograph was already on display alongside those of the other new Ministers. Then we took the lift to the Ministerial floor, the fourth, to a large office which would be mine. Outside, the rest of my team was gathered. This was my 'private office', a team of four led by Jessica, whose job was to make sure I was briefed for every encounter, my diary ran smoothly and that all decisions were followed up. That team soon expanded to six as my portfolio took shape.

I barely had time to talk to each of them before it was time to walk down the corridor to Iain's office to join the other Ministers and senior officials. This was a meeting to discuss the Emergency Budget that was planned for late June, just over five weeks away. There was little time for niceties or introductions. Big reductions in spending were required for the next five years, on top of those already announced by the Labour Government in March. Most immediately we had to cut the direct spending of the Department by £285 million in the current year. But the Treasury wanted substantial reductions in the benefits paid out over the period. Iain told us: "I'd like Ministers to work with their officials on what is feasible for those cuts. Clearly we don't have much time."

Iain was pushing ahead with the plan to take over tax credits. "We should aim to take over the tax credits policy team as soon as possible. Then we need a short Bill so that we can take over the whole system." I felt deeply embarrassed as he went through the plans with an enthusiastic Departmental team. I was probably more responsible than anyone else for setting this particular hare running. It flowed from the formal pre-election meeting between Leigh Lewis and Theresa May and her team in the previous autumn. At that meeting I had explained that if we were going to integrate the benefits system it made sense to start by bringing the administration of the two arms together. The tax credit system of supplemental payments to the low-paid – launched by Gordon Brown seven years earlier – had been separately administered by the tax authorities to avoid the stigma attached to the receipt of benefits. The Department had always deeply resented the structural snub, and the endorsement of this meeting had set off a whole tranche of work within the Department as to how the take-over would be effected. However, in the last few days I had been warned by Vocalink, the company that had developed the real-time PAYE system, that HMRC was reluctant to lose tax credits. I warned Iain privately that the last thing we needed was to dissipate our energies in a battle over administration.

By Monday Iain was sounding less confident. He came into my office to tell me: "George has been spooked by officials. They've told him it will cost £300 million. It's all nonsense of course. The real cost is £30 million or so."

I consoled him: "The real goal is to get integration of benefits, tax credits and tax so it may not matter if we don't get immediate control as long as we get the integration."

I was to find working with Iain a straight-forward proposition. He proved able to build a core group who were intensely loyal – both to him and to the vision for reforming welfare. That group included senior civil servants, advisers and more junior politicians. He never positioned himself as a strictly analytical practitioner but, despite slurs on his intelligence (not least those attributed to George Osborne), he could conduct a master-class in simplifying complex issues.

He found it less easy to build a broad coalition among his senior political colleagues. In meetings he could talk too much, as if plentiful explanation was sufficient to bring people aboard. This weakened his ability to recognise where others were coming from. He was focused on ensuring that his message was consistent, internally and externally. He was demanding of his civil servants and could be dogmatic with them, since he was anxious not to allow leeway for wavering. However, they were able to deliver bad news when necessary and they soon learned that they could come down the corridor to me and work through any problematic issue afterwards (an arrangement of which he was well aware).

His greatest weakness was to prove a pathological difficulty in persuading and winning over his seniors. Perhaps this stemmed from his experience in the hierarchical command structures of the British Army, where direction flowed downwards. Whatever the reason, he could find himself bereft of coherent expression in meetings with David Cameron and George Osborne.

The next 11 weeks, till the end of the Parliamentary session on 30 July, were to be extraordinarily intense. The priority was to get Universal Credit off the ground. This had to be achieved in the context of Treasury demands to make substantial cuts to expenditure, which required going through virtually all the Department's programmes to identify savings which would inflict the least damage. At the same time, we were committed to introducing The Work Programme. I was the only member of the Conservative Shadow welfare team to have made the transition into

Government. This entailed a series of meetings explaining to officials and other Ministers what our policy was on various issues, and digging out the background papers.

It was a tight Ministerial team, down from six under Labour to five – responsible for £160 billion of expenditure a year. Chris Grayling was the Minister of State for Employment, overseeing JCP as well as the employment programmes. Alongside was another Conservative, Maria Miller, the Parliamentary Under-Secretary with responsibility for the sensitive disability portfolio. Steve Webb was the Liberal Democrat member of the team, the Minister of State for Pensions, who was ambitious to achieve significant reform in this area. My own portfolio – Welfare Reform – was inevitably the most complex. As well as Universal Credit, I was responsible for many of the elements it would incorporate, such as Housing Benefit and the efforts to control fraud and error in the system. My portfolio also included the team within DWP which helped people with health issues join, and remain in, the workforce.

The adage 'be careful what you wish for' frequently came to mind in those early weeks. I may have insisted on the reform portfolio – indeed it was the only reason to take on the job – but the price was a daunting workload. I had to represent the whole Department and carry through its legislation in the House of Lords on my own, covering the ground for which four Ministers in the Commons were responsible.

And now I learned that being a Minister was very different from working as an advisor to the Department. Sitting on my desk when I arrived was a large white file entitled: 'Welcome', which had been assembled by Jessica Yuille, my Private Secretary. With more than 150 pages of text and tables it laid out the key facts and figures about the Department, the options for reform that the Conservatives had committed themselves to, and my obligations in the role. Developing policy with the civil servants was only a first step. I would have to build up relationships with the various outside bodies that were influential, the so-called stakeholders. That meant regular one-on-one meetings with groups like Citizen's Advice and the National Housing Federation. There would also be speeches to deliver, whenever we needed to announce or explain a policy step.

Media handling was a full-time activity for the Department, with Press releases to be prepared and cleared more or less daily. Where policy needed to be defended or announcements made, Ministers would undertake interviews on radio and television, usually at short notice, disrupting the diary for the day.

The Lords would be time-consuming. The Department needed to pass numerous pieces of what was called secondary legislation a year (70 over 2010, for example). These contained the real detail of the regulations behind the main legislation. Each needed to be passed, often after debate, by both Houses. Oral Questions would also soak up preparation time. In the Lords, each day began with a session of questions to Ministers. The opening question to each Minister was known, and indeed printed in the Order of Business for the day. The follow-ups lasted for seven minutes or so and came spontaneously from Peers round the House – so would cover a wide ambit. My very first oral question two weeks later was, bizarrely, on the risks posed by synthetic biology – an obligation flowing from the Department's responsibility for Health and Safety. My main struggle on that occasion was to remember how to distinguish and pronounce mycoplasma mycoides and mycoplasma capricolum, the two bacteria involved in the question.

Sitting in the in-tray was a pile of letters which required Ministerial signature. This was an industry in itself. In Jessica's welcome she wrote: "We received over 3,500 Commons and 180 Lords Written Parliamentary Questions in 2008/9 and over 1,000 pieces of correspondence a month from MPs, Peers and key stakeholders which are signed by Ministers." I would be responsible for all those covering my parts of the portfolio. Half the ground floor of the Department was made up of teams of officials producing this mound of paperwork. In the early months, needing to change the New Labour language and justifications we had inherited, each draft letter from officials needed extensive revision and rebalancing. Later, as the templates were recreated and I could recognise the standard paragraphs at a glance, I became able to scan each letter for signature much more rapidly.

Finally, there was the importance of building relationships through an organisation of more than 100,000 people, most of them involved in delivering the Department's services. I would need to visit and talk to the various teams round the country for which I was ultimately responsible. My Welcome pack suggested that it would send a really positive signal if I were to go to one of DWP's offices – probably a Jobcentre – in my first week.

"Let's make an early start," I suggested to Jessica, "and go round each floor of this building to say hello to the various teams." We kicked off the process with a visit to the employment policy team for half an hour in the first week. However, that was as far as we got, as the volume of work and number of priority meetings became overwhelming.

The private office run by Jessica represented one of the marvels of the British Civil Service. It was to underpin my ability to handle all the activity necessary to reform the welfare system. The team was responsible for making sure that I was fully informed for all my meetings and Parliamentary encounters. They would set up my engagements, arrange my briefings for them, record the outcomes and then follow up to make sure that agreed actions were undertaken. Inside the lead-lined Red Box which I took home every weekend they carefully assembled all the material I needed to prepare for the week ahead – a task that usually took at least a day-and-a-half. As the challenge of the job peaked later in the year, my diary secretary told me, with some pride: "I've got you up to 16 meetings a day this week." The team's loyal and hard-working support was the bedrock which allowed me to concentrate my energy on taking the myriad decisions necessary.

CHAPTER 11

What's the Catch?

Top of the priority list was to get Universal Credit under way. I had spent the election period preparing a policy paper on introducing the new benefit structure, leaning on the work done by Vocalink and helped by Stephen Brien. By Tuesday 18 May 2010 – 12 days after the election – the officials were ready for the kick-off meeting with me to go through it.

The paper started: "Our aim is to integrate PAYE, benefits and tax credits into a single system within two years on a real-time basis. Benefits payments will be withdrawn at a steady rate to incentivise an additional 410,000 households back into the work-force and a net 530,000 households to increase their participation. A broadly self-financing structure directs additional funds to poor people (reducing child poverty by 175,000) at modest cost to those higher up the scale."

It went on: "This opportunity arises through using a Single Account System developed by Vocalink (BACS), which already makes 96 percent of salary payments and 98 percent of state benefits. It has recently developed Faster Payments infrastructures which can handle the requirements. It has also built (working with Treasury over the last four years) a working prototype of a centralised PAYE2 system that would calculate an individual's tax, deductions and credits and benefits entitlements in real time from gross employer submissions."

I then summarised the savings that would accrue to the Treasury, pointing to an annual reduction in fraud and error of £2 billion and similar operational savings from system simplification. It also envisaged a straight-forward transition. "Existing benefits will be unchanged. Each household's benefits will be packaged within a single "wrapper" and withdrawn at a constant 55 percent of post-tax earnings." This was shorthand for recipients retaining 45p of each extra pound they earned.

On timing I leaned heavily on the Vocalink estimates. "Rollout of PAYE2 collection could commence early 2011 in parallel with the commencement of the single account design phase. This would ensure that central tax calculation could 'go live' in 2012 enabling the roll out of welfare reform based on single tax and benefit account information." The table I adopted from Vocalink showed this roll-out proceeding thereafter.

The paper set the agenda for the next few weeks. Using the formal acronym for Her Majesty's Treasury (HMT), I wrote: "A joint HMT/HMRC/DWP working party should be established immediately under HMT/DWP ministerial chairmanship to report within 50 days on a robust project plan to achieve these objectives. In particular it will need to establish that a real-time system can be launched within the proposed time-table. Updated costs and savings should be established." I had already talked to David Gauke on the weekend to clear this procedural approach. He had been installed as Exchequer Secretary to the Treasury, responsible for HMRC. He told me he was working to establish a team that could work with ours.

The key DWP officials gathered round the large beech table in my office. They included Sue Owen, overall head of the policy advisory group; Neil Couling, responsible for benefits policy; Malcolm Whitehouse, No. 2 in the IT Department; and Trevor Huddleston, the Strategy Director responsible for pulling together individual policy areas.

Trevor, earnest and boyish-looking, pointed out: "We've already got an initiative to get to a single working age benefit, based on the recommendation in your 2007 report."

"Well this is how to achieve it," I replied. "We can build on the work that Vocalink has done to get up-to-date information on what we should be paying people who are doing some work."

They warmed to the idea rapidly. Malcom Whitehouse from the IT Department, sitting halfway down the table, was the most positive. "This could really work," he said. "I've already sounded out our contractors and they don't think it should be too complicated to do."

We had two sessions going over the proposition on that first day. I asked: "Can we just lift the people from their existing benefits and drop them into Universal Credit electronically? After all, they'll be getting the same benefits. It's effectively a new wrapper."

Neil Couling had grown up in the Department and had immense knowledge about the various benefit structures. He was a formidable decision-maker in his own right. He shook his head. "Our legacy systems wouldn't allow us to do the transfer. Besides, there would be far too many mistakes and anomalies between the various benefits for us to sort out. It would be far more efficient to start from scratch and get everyone to apply afresh."

The most interesting comment came from Sue Owen, head welfare strategy, just after the meeting. Sue had enjoyed a stellar civil service career between No. 10, the Treasury and Foreign Office. She was perky and approachable. Now, still sitting at my table, she revealed: "I'm absolutely furious. We've been meeting the tax credits team for weeks and they never mentioned it. This could have saved us all the work of assembling the information about pay in our system design." In reality it was more than likely that the tax credits people themselves didn't know about this particular project because it had been conducted in an entirely separate part of HMRC, the PAYE personal tax team. Nevertheless, this was a remarkable example of outsiders bringing in more information about what Government was doing than Government itself knew.

Sue chuckled: "The general idea, David, is for us to come up with policy proposals, not for the Ministers. We want to do this. We all recognise that it's the one chance we'll have to get rid of the creaking, broken system we're locked into operating now." Her remark reminded me of the frightening estimate one official had given me while I was researching my Report: "If your benefit claim is relatively complicated, we will manage to lose your papers about 40 percent of the time and you'll have to start all over again."

On Thursday Iain came into my office to say: "It looks like we won't be getting Tax Credits, which may not disappoint you too much. But I'm insisting we push ahead with the integration of the system. If we can't do that, there's no point me doing this job."

I was relieved that this false start had been abandoned. "It may be for the best," I consoled him. "If our structure works, we'll effectively be eliminating the Tax Credits operation and it'll be pretty unpleasant to be the Department responsible for closing it down."

His conversations at Cabinet level had been more encouraging. "The Lib Dems are really up for this," he told me. "We'll need to be in a position to give a presentation to Clegg in the next couple of weeks – and Cameron for that matter, too."

On the following Wednesday, just two weeks into the new Government, we held the first joint meeting of the benefit reform group in David Gauke's elegant office in the Treasury. It may have been introductory but it got the process under way. I was both encouraged and relieved by the positive responses from Steve Lamey, Director General of the tax credits operation. I had been worried that he had been concerned about transferring tax credits to DWP. Now, ironically, it looked as if he would prove a real ally in the creation of Universal Credit.

Treasury officials wanted to see a series of alternative approaches to our reform structure. At the second meeting, a week later, they went through some of the options they had worked up. These represented in the main a series of cost-cutting measures, although they did produce an idea for an over-riding single taper, which would fit on top of the existing benefit structure. It looked ferociously complicated, both to understand and administer. I told Matt Oakley, the senior Treasury official: "I think you'll be surprised at how long it takes to make some of these one-off changes by comparison with redoing the entire architecture."

By the next week we were ready to see the Prime Minister. We met in the small office on the ground floor of 10 Downing Street in which I had seen Tony Blair, sitting on the same sofa and armchairs. Alongside the Prime Minister was George Osborne, with his chief of staff Rupert Harrison on a hardback chair behind. Jeremy Heywood, newly installed as Permanent Secretary to Downing Street and the Prime Minister's 'fixer', was also present. Our team comprised Iain, Leigh Lewis and Philippa Stroud.

David Cameron started: "How's it all going?"

I replied: "We're really pleased with the energy and enthusiasm the DWP are showing in getting behind our programme." I then launched into the presentation. This was the key chance to sell the concept to the Prime Minister and Chancellor and I was not going to underplay it.

"This is about the challenge you set at the Conference in October, to get rid of the very high rate at which benefits are withdrawn from people with modest earnings" At this point I was pleased to see the Prime Minister nodding in recognition of the issue.

"We are spending the welfare money, but we are locking people into dependency. There are two issues. There is no or limited financial incentive for many to work and there is also a real fear factor in leaving dependency. The risk/reward ratio is wrong.

"Piecemeal reform is not enough. In recent months we have been working to develop the concepts in *Dynamic Benefits*. We developed a simple combined system, where recipients always know where they are. They always keep 45p in the pound. That's how the maths work.

"We had a breakthrough in March. We were working on the system architecture along the lines of the *Dynamic Benefits* analysis, but the IT development would be five years plus – smack into the worst point of the electoral timetable. Then we learned of the work to create a real-time system for tax and tax credits. That was transformational. It means we can use information on people's multiple salary payments and benefit entitlements to produce real time benefits and tax credit payments. We can erase error, drive down fraud and eliminate tax disregards. That is some billions of pounds of AME savings. By simplifying payment systems we can also obtain further billions of DEL savings eventually."

"What about Disability Living Allowance and child benefit?" asked George Osborne. I had excluded these two deliberately, fearing hostile public reaction. I replied: "We haven't included them in the architectural model. We will have the choice of doing that."

David Cameron said: "I understand the option. We will be able to take that as a distinct political decision." Then he asked: "How risky will this be?"

I interpreted the question to refer to the risk to benefit recipients. "We should be able to cut across to the new system, so it should be less risky than many structures."

George, in the middle of a major exercise in reducing the Government's costs, wanted concrete assurances on the assumptions around the numbers moving into work. He pushed for the economic gains from introducing the new system. "What about the dynamic effects? How much have you taken into account?"

Given the major modelling exercise we were now embarking on, I was reluctant to over-commit to him: "We're not quite there yet."

"Come on, Lord Freud," George gave an ironic emphasis to a title which he had, after all, been instrumental in bestowing.

"About £2 billion, we think."

Iain was less worried about the subtleties: "£2 billion is the figure," he confirmed.

David Cameron was clearly taken with the concept: "This seems incredibly simple. What's the catch?"

"None," I assured him. "It really should be doable, subject to the intensive due diligence we have under way now."

The Prime Minister closed with a positive endorsement: "Let's aim to have this in a robust state for the Spending Review in the autumn. And we can also reference it in the Budget statement."

Afterwards Leigh said quietly to me: "I think you did that really well."

A week later we went to see Nick Clegg in his grand office in Whitehall. The presentation ran along similar lines. The Deputy Prime Minister was clearly impressed by the proposition. "I'm a devotee," he declared at the end. The steadfast support of the Liberal Democrats in the months and years to come was to prove critical to the programme.

While Universal Credit had not been mentioned in the Conservative Manifesto, an accelerated set of new employment programmes had been a centrepiece. Now, the Department was working full-tilt to introduce – on an expedited basis – the programmes laid out in *Get Britain Working*, including The Work Programme.

Alan Cave, the head of employment programme commissioning, with whom I had worked closely when I was James Purnell's adviser, came to see me in my office. "David, I think we shouldn't bother with introducing The Work Programme in half the country and waiting for the Flexible New Deal to run its course before going ahead in the other half. We should just rip up the Flexible New Deal contracts and cover the whole country with The Work Programme straight-away." As adviser to James Purnell, I had persuaded him to introduce the Flexible New Deal in two waves, with the second one due after the election.

"Won't the contractors sue us if we do that?"

"We'll have to pay a bit of compensation but I don't think they'll sue. They won't want to attack a Government at the height of its popularity on one of its keynote Manifesto programmes."

WHAT'S THE CATCH? · 105

"Ok. Let's go for it," I agreed, both surprised and pleased to see the programme get off to such an aggressive start.

Chris Grayling, never a man to settle for half-measures, was equally keen. By the third week of the Government, Chris and I were making speeches to the contractors describing the plans to introduce The Work Programme. We felt confident enough to leave some heavy hints that we were planning to close the Flexible New Deal early, although Chris would only make the formal announcement four months later in October.

CHAPTER 12

Reform for Cuts

Alongside Universal Credit, the Department was working full tilt on the cuts demanded by the Chancellor for his looming Budget. Here the housing benefit bill was a central target, where expenditure was both substantial and rising – up 50 percent in real terms over the previous decade. This was part of my portfolio and at the beginning of June 2010 I assembled the housing policy team in my office for an evening session to go through our options. I had spent the previous weekend reading through the mound of background materials they had supplied.

"It strikes me that setting rents at the halfway point for comparable properties is a charter for private landlords to set the level there, whether the property is worth it or not," I observed. Some 40 percent of housing expenditure went to benefit recipients who rented from private landlords.

"Well, there's an incentive for the tenant to negotiate a lower figure," the team pointed out, tongue in cheek.

"So you send these people, who are perhaps not the most trained negotiators in the world, out to landlords with a price target on their heads? Whoever thought that would work? Let's just cut the level to the 30th percentile of the market rate. That way we should get private landlords to take some of the pain."

It would raise some money, but not enough to satisfy the Chancellor. "We could cap the maximum amount paid in rent," the team suggested. This would be a worthwhile amount.

Finally I prompted: "These are measures that hit the private sector. Is there anything we can do to reduce costs in the public sector?" The majority of housing benefit recipients were in social housing, where the landlords provided homes at lower rents – often because the capital costs had been subsidised. Many of the homes had been built by local councils.

"Is there a way we could encourage housing benefit tenants with homes larger than they need to switch?" I asked. "I'm thinking of people whose children have moved out. Perhaps they could be offered an alternative. If they refuse three times, say, we could reduce their benefit."

By Thursday the team had put together a letter with the proposals that we discussed for me to send to Iain. He accepted them and they became a significant part of the negotiations with the Treasury for the Emergency Budget.

The bulk of the face-to-face negotiations were handled by officials from the two Departments, with the positions laid out in letters. Direct meetings between the politicians were rare, usually set up to resolve the final elements. A lot of gamesmanship was involved in establishing the nature of a 'cut' in the benefit expenditure, or AME, budget. This was because the language of cuts in Government was not quite what it seemed. It referred to cuts in projections, not cuts in spending from one year to the next. The Chancellor needed to announce the biggest possible cuts in his Budget – to impress the audiences to which he was appealing, not least the lenders of the international capital markets. However, the actual reduction would be considerably less and five-year forward projections involved imaginative construction of the theoretical base from which these reductions were made.

Given the speed with which the Treasury was working, the negotiations were anyway truncated. A week later we were presented with the first cut of the Treasury proposals. The private sector housing cuts were adopted in their entirety. When it came to social housing, the proposal had been brutally simplified. The Treasury proposition simply imposed a reduction in benefit on anyone who had surplus bedrooms. It would be introduced in one step, in April 2013. There would be no process of offering alternative accommodation before the reduction was applied: instead there would be a discretionary pot of money to deal with cases of hardship.

At the Departmental Ministerial meeting I expressed my shock at the structure of the programme. "How can they think it's a good idea to impose this in one go? It will be really ugly."

Iain sighed, "David, I don't think it will be any use fighting over this. They are determined to introduce it." Later he told me: "Given the speed with which they turned this idea round I think they had already developed the structure under Labour and were just waiting to push it out."

A complicated battle between George's desire for cuts to the welfare budget and our determination to introduce Universal Credit was focused on the numbers in the Treasury spreadsheet over the last week. Treasury officials were prone to take savings on a one-off basis which we argued could only be delivered through our reforms. Iain complained: "They're grabbing all the gains from introducing Universal Credit. At this rate there'll be no business case to justify it."

By Friday the two Departments were at logger-heads over the level of expected savings to use to justify the introduction of Universal Credit. We wanted to use the figure of £1.5 billion to £2 billion.

I managed to get through to David Gauke on Saturday morning. I told him I was concerned that there were no numbers attached to the proposal. "If I was George and I saw a massive transformation without numbers attached, I wouldn't feel very compelled."

He reassured me: "Yes, but Justine and I will tell him this looks really worth doing. We just don't want numbers floating about that the Treasury team have not checked out." He warned: "I'm worried that if Justine and I don't get something into the Chancellor's box shortly there won't be anything for the Budget." Justine Greening was the Economic Secretary in the Treasury alongside him.

David's goodwill was too important to push the issue any further.

Iain was in his constituency surgery when I phoned him. I told him: "I've agreed to drop the numbers. I don't think it matters that much. We need a solid reference in the Budget itself to kick-start the process."

Iain answered: "Well in that case you better get hold of Philippa fast, because I've just sent her in to battle the Treasury. We've been fighting them all yesterday evening to hold out the changes to the Employment and Support Allowance till we have a reform process and we've just won."

Philippa was still feeling bruised by her encounter with the Treasury team. "I don't care about the numbers," she told me. "These guys have no idea about the social impact of this stuff and they don't care."

Three days later, on 22 June, George Osborne stood up to deliver his first – Emergency – Budget. He outlined £17 billion of annual cuts by 2014–15 on top of the £44 billion already committed to, albeit not identified, in the Labour Budget three months earlier. The biggest target was the welfare system, representing two-thirds of the extra reduction. The respected Institute for Fiscal Studies concluded that the country faced the "longest, deepest period of cuts to public services spending at least since World War II." [45]

For benefit recipients, real pain was involved. On top of the housing cuts, which would mount to some £2 billion per annum, the inflation index for welfare and other payments was changed from the Retail Price Index (RPI) to the more slowly growing Consumer Price Index (CPI). There were a series of reductions to tax credits, for which the Treasury had direct responsibility, and the introduction of a medical assessment for Disability Living Allowance.

From my perspective the most important element, on the day, was that Osborne delivered on the agreement to refer to our reform programme, albeit in the weakest form possible. "My Right Honourable Friend the Secretary of State for Work and Pensions will bring forward proposals to further reform the benefits system as a tool to support work and encourage aspiration in time for the Autumn Spending Review," he announced.

If we thought that these cuts were the end of the story we were in for a rude awakening. Within a month we discovered that further welfare savings would need to be investigated as part of the Spending Review process. We would be required to develop a comprehensive range of targeted savings measures alongside our work on the Universal Credit model.

Relations between the two Departments rapidly broke down in the face of the Treasury scepticism over our reforms, which officials made no effort to disguise. Iain could see his agenda withering away as the pressure for further cuts built up. At Ministerial meetings we worked through spreadsheets of savings looking for the billions that the Treasury was pressing for. At one meeting with DWP officials Iain urged extreme caution in the provision of data to the Treasury. "They just take our savings measures and factor them in without any allowance for the reforms needed to produce them."

He focused his rage on one of the officials at the Treasury who was blunt in their opposition to the reform agenda. I was not present at the ensuing row between Iain and the Chancellor. The details became public within weeks, with *The Mail on Sunday* recording – from an un-named source – that Iain had told the Chancellor: "I am not prepared to tolerate the appalling way you treat my Department. Your officials must show more respect to my staff. They do not deserve to be treated in such an arrogant and rude way." [46]

The Prime Minister was clearly unsettled – presumably by his Chancellor – when we went to see him again in mid-July. Jeremy Heywood received us in the lobby of No. 10, after we handed over our mobile phones and started to walk across the chequerboard tiled floor. He had become a key figure in the Government, David Cameron's fixer across a huge range of issues. His face was open and guileless behind his rimless glasses; his delivery succinct in his slight northern accent. Now he warned Iain about how to handle the Prime Minister as we walked down the corridor: "He's nervous. Keep it tight." He added: "I've staked my reputation on this, so you better deliver."

This time I was a bystander in the discussion, with the Prime Minister wanting to test the confidence of the civil servants to undertake the reform. (In fact, I was waiting for a summons to a vote in the Lords, which duly came, so that I had to leave No. 10 partway through the meeting.)

The formal paper under discussion covered the Prime Minister's main concerns, around those people who would lose from the changeover, reductions in the cost of welfare overall and the scale of the IT challenge. It priced and discussed some of the cuts we could make to child benefit and the Employment and Support Allowance. On the IT challenge the paper concluded: "This would be an IT development of moderate scale, which DWP and its suppliers are confident of handling within budget and timescale."

Leigh Lewis, the Department's Permanent Secretary, duly gave his administrative assurance: "I'm in agreement with the document."

David Cameron said: "Clearly there's been a lot of work put into this and I'm persuaded of the case."

He then turned to the publicity plan and complained that Iain had not laid the groundwork for a story of such massive scale.

Iain defended himself: "We've been out there with the media regularly telling them about the need for reform. We've been laying the groundwork before we came into Government with *Dynamic Benefits*. There is now a general expectation in the media that we will undertake reform."

Grudgingly the Prime Minister agreed. "All right, you can do a speech and a document. But make it theoretical, like an English Literature essay."

Before the 'essay' – in practice a Green Paper entitled *21st Century Welfare* – could go out as agreed at the end of July, the Department and Treasury needed to come to terms. Oliver Letwin, the Minister of State for Policy who was proving increasingly indispensable in resolving internal Government rows, was set to broker the peace. With a week to go before publication, Philippa drove up to Chequers, the Prime Minister's grace and favour country residence, to meet him and Rupert Harrison, the Chancellor's main aide.

There they agreed a process of co-operation on both reform and Spending Review negotiations. Most importantly, Oliver proposed that the Spending Review announcement would be closely followed by a Welfare Reform White Paper in November. This would allow the Government "to announce the Spending Review cuts in the context of a positive welfare reform narrative," according to the carefully-drafted read-out from the meeting.

Philippa told me: "We also agreed that everyone who is transferred to Universal Credit will have their existing level of benefit protected. That means that we won't have losers." This was an expensive commitment, although the cost would be reduced by designing the protection to fall away when people's circumstances changed substantially.

The following Monday at the internal review meeting, Iain was jubilant: "We have all our stuff. We have a commitment to the White Paper, which we didn't have before. And we can expect Treasury co-operation in the next few months."

The Green Paper focused on the failures of the current welfare system to generate the right behavioural responses, pointing to poor work incentives and complexity. It contained five options for reform but it was clear that Universal Credit was by far and away the front-runner. The Treasury alternative of 'A Single Unified Taper' got some space in the document but each of the other three ('A Single Working Age Benefit'; the so-called 'Mirrlees model'; 'Negative Income Tax') were effectively dismissed in half a page each. [47] The launch took place two days after the Parliamentary session ended at the innovative Bromley by Bow health centre in East London. As Iain had promised the Prime Minister, it went by largely unremarked because it had been generally expected.

The Department had assembled a 50-strong team to build the detail behind the reform of the welfare system. Stephen Brien was now seconded to the Department, on a temporary basis, and he joined me in addressing the team at the kick-off meeting in late June. We spelled out our ambitions to this group, who were experts in all the individual parts of the current welfare system. Later one of them confided to me that, despite the apparent enthusiasm, many of them did not believe we would be able to pull off the transformation.

The analysts got to work replicating the model built by Stephen in *Dynamic Benefits*, using the detailed figures that the Department possessed. The first outputs were deeply discouraging – coming nowhere near the savings that Stephen had projected.

"You better find out what's gone wrong," I told him, "and work with them to get something halfway acceptable."

The Department's analysts were working with data that was far more comprehensive than any outsider could access, so it was not surprising that they were turning up deficiencies in the *Dynamic Benefits* model. It emerged that some of them were material. Nevertheless, it should be possible to mitigate the damage by adjusting some of the assumptions.

Stephen got to work. "I've been fine-tuning it, but the Treasury team won't let us incorporate the gains from moving more people into work. Plus, there does seem to be a genuine problem with the people who get mortgage relief. I got them to model an assumption that people would not be eligible for it if they did any work at all. Finally, Oliver's deal to offer everyone transitional relief is pretty expensive."

"Where have you got it to?"

"We still take a lot of people out of poverty; we still improve work incentives but the taper rate has gone up to 65 percent." Stephen had modelled 55 percent in *Dynamics Benefits*, which meant people kept 45 pence in every extra pound they earned. Now they would keep only 35 pence. As the Treasury battle to achieve further cuts in the Autumn Spending Review intensified, all the assumptions in Universal Credit were coming under scrutiny. The approach in *Dynamic Benefits* – to put some of the gains from more people going to work into a more generous taper – was an early casualty.

"I have a nasty feeling that there's a tipping point somewhere, at which people decide it's worth working," I brooded. "The trouble is that we don't know where it is. Retaining 35 pence in the pound seems a lot further from the tipping point than 45 pence."

I consoled myself: "Mind you, there will be significant gains from simplicity alone. We'll be cutting the risk from trying out a job; people won't have to switch back and forth from benefits to tax credits; and it'll be much easier to understand how much money they'll keep if they work more hours. We won't be able to model that, but we should surely talk about it."

Nor was it straightforward in HMRC. Steve Lamey had become a surprise convert to updating the PAYE system. At an early meeting he declared: "This is something that has a positive business case for the individual bits, but may not be absolutely compelling. When you put them together it becomes really compelling." Later he confided that his deputy had warned him that he would be reprimanded for cutting across decisions that were reserved for the Treasury. He cheered himself up: "Still I haven't been reprimanded yet, so let's wait and see."

Despite his enthusiasm (for which, in the event, no reprimand was forthcoming), HMRC was not prepared to rely on the full Vocalink version, which involved monitoring the actual payments going through the banking system. Steve Lamey explained at our regular joint meeting: "The tax people are concerned about the time to adopt this safely. They've developed an interim step, which we've called PAYEGLET or piglet for short, which will give us near real-time figures."

David Gauke said: "The issue we have to worry about is that the trans- formation doesn't stop at piglet but that we go on to PAYE2. I'm sure we'll find a way to lock that in. By the way, we better stop calling it piglet right now, or we'll end up referring to it that way in public."

The Vocalink PAYE2 proposal had been to track wage payments as they went through the banking system, producing an automated real- time data feed to HMRC. The interim system (never again referred to as piglet) had a very different approach. It relied on employers forward- ing the information about wage payments to HMRC, as soon as they were made. HMRC would then make that information available to DWP. In practice it meant an exercise to get the providers to add an extra button to their payroll software which employers could use to transmit the information about payments immediately after the bank transfer instructions had been sent. It also meant abandoning Vocalink as a supplier, despite their pivotal role in developing the conceptual base for Universal Credit. My efforts in the following years to move to their real-time approach took me down several byways of the banking system but I was unable to resuscitate PAYE2.

The concordat with the Treasury held through the Parliamentary recess as the steps between the Green and White Paper were being negotiated. A series of costed options for benefit cuts was provided to the Treasury by the Department. At the same time the Treasury demanded reductions in the underlying running costs of the Department in excess of 25 percent over the term of the Parliament. This was hardly consistent with their quest for major initiatives to rein in benefit spending. As far as Universal Credit was concerned, the key elements were rapidly being assembled under the control of Neil Couling, an old hand at the Department who very much understood the way the figures worked.

One looming problem emerged over council tax benefit, one of the means-tested elements we were modelling as part of Universal Credit. The Treasury wanted a £500 million reduction in this subsidy. At the same time Eric Pickles, the Secretary of State for the Department of Communities and Local Government, had announced that Local Authorities would take control of their budgets and set their own priorities. This left an awkward ambiguity as to whether the Department or individual Local Authorities would run the council tax benefit scheme and be responsible for the cut.

"We'll just have to write a careful section leaving it open," Neil told me. "We won't have time to rebuild the model excluding it, anyway."

"We should do all we can to keep it," I argued. "The last thing we want is another fiddly means-tested benefit with different rules, taper rates and cut-off points for each Local Authority. We're trying to sweep all that away with Universal Credit. Simplicity is the key."

The two big ticket items in the negotiation were Child Benefit and Disability payments. Child benefit was paid out to all parents, regardless of their income, and cut across the Universal Credit approach of directing welfare payments to the poorest. I had excluded it due to its political sensitivity; under pressure we now suggested its inclusion for annual savings mounting to £6 billion.

The disability cut we were working on put a time limit on the period the less severely disabled could as of right receive Employment and Support Allowance – a so-called contributory benefit paid without a means test to those who had made sufficient national insurance contributions. This would be cut from an indefinite period to a year, although the time period would remain unrestricted for the severely disabled. At the same time, we were already committed to retesting disability recipients, which needed costing. There were a large number of smaller items which went back and forth. We sent over reductions in some of the universal payments to pensioners, such as winter fuel and free TV licences. These were quickly ruled out by the Prime Minister, who was to fiercely defend pensioner benefits throughout his time in office, reflecting the commitments he made during the election campaign.

The IT department remained confident that the project was achievable. I double-checked with Joe Harley, the overall head of IT, who told me: "We've a strong record on IT. We brought in both the Employment and Support Allowance system and the modernised payments platform successfully. Those programmes are both bigger than the new systems we'll need for Universal Credit." Joe was highly respected and enlarged his job to become overall head of IT for the Government at the turn of the year. So I took considerable comfort from his informal re-assurance.

In the light of the implementation problems that subsequently emerged, this assurance proved way off the mark. Universal Credit proved to be much bigger than anything the Department – and possibly Government as a whole – had ever attempted. Even in retrospect it is difficult to explain the over-optimism. In part it was based on ignorance. Government had never attempted an interactive system on this scale, with such obvious security ramifications. Government outsourcing strategy meant the Department commissioned most development work, leaving it bereft of hands-on development expertise. Yet outside contractors had imperfect knowledge of the scale and complexity of a benefits system which would dispense the best part of £100 billion a year. It was a classic case of 'you don't know what you don't know'. At that stage I certainly did not have the expertise to challenge the assurance, nor an understanding of the weakness of the IT function which led to it.

The final element in the agreement between Treasury and the Department was the *Get Britain Working* agenda, particularly The Work Programme. This was to be funded by the benefits saved from getting people into work, through the DEL-AME switch which the Treasury still hated but, as a specific Coalition concordat commitment, could not reject. Through the summer Chris Grayling and I visited the various companies whom we expected to bid. My former investment banking colleagues at UBS looked through the assumptions and concluded that we could offer them an adequate reward, although already the negotiations with Treasury officials about the returns we could offer to the companies was turning testy. The only programme in the *Get Britain Working* package that failed to get through was 'Work Pairing', where sole traders mentored a disadvantaged apprentice. Year after year I tried to start up this programme, which I thought particularly promising, and year after year there was never the funding.

By the week before Conference, in late September 2010, the main elements of the agreement had fallen into place. Universal Credit and The Work Programme would go ahead. Although the Chancellor and Prime Minister shied away from incorporating child benefit in Universal Credit, the Chancellor had decided to remove it from higher rate tax-payers. The contributory disability payment was limited to one year.

Inadvertently, I nearly managed to upset the whole delicate balance. I met up with Rosie Bennett, *The Times* social affairs correspondent, with whom I thought I could build a useful long-term relationship – feeding her a stream of stories about the development of welfare reform. It was a model common from my days as a journalist in the 1970s and early-1980s (when I worked at the *Financial Times*). The stories would break news although hopefully be biased in favour of the source.

Carefully I suggested what she might write ahead of our planned Conference announcements. "You could say that 'Universal Credit has emerged from the Green Paper consultation as the favoured reform option and is likely to be announced shortly.' Please keep it till the weekend."

Journalism had moved on since my time. My strictures on waiting till the weekend were ignored as Rosie led Friday's newspaper with the headline that Iain had defeated the Chancellor to get Universal Credit. 'Duncan Smith wins reform battle with Treasury' declared the sub-heading on the front page. [48]

Next morning Philippa told me: "They're hopping mad in the Treasury. They were threatening to cancel the whole deal. I've had to spend the morning soothing them and explaining it was a cock-up not a planned leak." After that, despite a long letter from Rosie who seemed to have real-ised only in retrospect that she had burned a source good for hundreds of stories, I gave up any thought of symbiotic relationships with journalists.

The Conference was held that year in Birmingham. We duly trooped up for the round of fringe meetings and our appearance on the platform on Tuesday. I was outside the main hall watching the screens when George spoke the day before.

It was with mounting dismay that I heard him say: "So I can announce today that for the first time we will introduce a limit on the total amount of benefits any one family can receive.

"And the limit will be set according to this very simple principle: Unless they have disabilities to cope with, no family should get more from living on benefits than the average family gets from going out to work.

"No more open-ended cheque-book. A maximum limit on benefits for those out of work; set at the level that the average working family earns."[49]

It was the story of the day. From my perspective it was a parallel welfare policy which cut across both the simplicity and fairness we were trying to create in Universal Credit. A Benefit Cap made little sense in a system designed to provide each family what it needed.

"We'll have to own it," Iain told me, preparing to announce Universal Credit to Conference the next day. "At least it sends out a signal about the limits to welfare. By the way, I want you to implement it."

Much later Rupert Harrison told me: "I know it didn't make much in the way of savings but when we tested the policy it polled off the charts. We've never had such a popular policy."

The agreement was confirmed in a series of announcements over the next six weeks. In the week after Conference, I repeated Iain's oral statement in the Lords. This spelled out that we would shortly launch a White Paper and legislation introducing Universal Credit; that we would fulfill the commitment to test those applying for disability and that we would start the bidding process for The Work Programme in December.

When quizzed on the Benefit Cap, I stuck carefully to our official line: "The noble Lord asked whether the £500 Benefit Cap is fair. Many hardworking families do not achieve a rate of £35,000 gross. It puts things into context for them when people on benefits can get more than that. Therefore, our aim is to cap what people can get. This will come in towards the end of this Parliament and we have a lot of measures, including the cap on housing, to work the process through. So, yes, it is fair."[50]

The following week featured the Spending Review, on 20 October, when George took a further substantial bite out of public spending. Welfare measures accounted for a significant proportion, mounting to £7 billion a year by the end of the Parliament. This was on top of the £11 billion taken out in the Emergency Budget.

It was almost an anti-climax when we finally launched the White

Paper on 11 November: *Universal Credit: welfare that works*.[51] Nick Clegg joined Iain on the platform in Arlington House, a hostel for the homeless in London's Camden Town. His presence reflected the strong support from the junior partner in the Coalition for these reforms. Indeed, Nick Clegg claimed direct parentage in his speech: "That is what today's announcements are about; returning welfare in this country back to its original purpose. Nearly 70 years ago, its architect, the great Liberal William Beveridge imagined a system that gave people protection from cradle to grave but not one that would act as a crutch every day in between."

In the formal oral statement by Iain in the Commons, and repeated by me in the Lords, we laid out the results of all the modelling: "Our guarantee is crystal clear: if you take a job, you will receive more income. Some 2.5 million households will get higher entitlements as a result of the move to Universal Credit.

"The new transparency in the system will also produce a substantial increase in the take-up of benefits and tax credits. Taken together, we estimate that these effects will help lift as many as 350,000 children and 500,000 adults out of poverty. That is our analysis of just the static effects of reform.

"Analysing the dynamic effects is not easy, but we estimate that the reforms could reduce the number of workless households by about 300,000. Let me also provide assurance about the transition. We will financially protect those who move across to the Universal Credit system. There will be no losers."[52]

Labour found it hard to complain. Bill McKenzie, my opposite number in the Lords, echoed the qualified support of Douglas Alexander in the Commons: "Let me be clear that we support the strategic direction of the proposals, but what counts is the decency with which they are implemented. We will work constructively with the Government to seek to ensure that that is the case."[53]

We were through. We had taken a mauling in the process, with some painful dilution of the original vision. In particular, we had a much less generous taper and had lost council tax benefit. Jobless households were estimated to fall by only 300,000, compared with 410,000 in my paper in May. A number of distortions of the original vision of simplicity had been introduced, of which the most notable were the Benefit Cap and the charge for excess bedrooms in social housing. Funds would be available to ameliorate the worst impact of these, although they would be handed out on a discretionary basis. Nor did we have much flexibility to fund further wrinkles in the system as we uncovered greater detail. However, the Government had embarked on the most substantial reform of the welfare system since its inception. Now the challenge was to undertake the detailed design and implementation of the project, to which I turned my attention.

In retrospect, we had slipped through the narrowest of windows. In the early days of the Coalition the Departments were allowed considerable autonomy, an autonomy which eroded steadily over the next five years. At the same time few of the other Departments had developed their own agenda with which we could come into conflict – the main exception being Eric Pickle's localism drive, which was partly responsible for the loss of council tax benefit from Universal Credit.

The nervous support of David Cameron and the more solid enthusiasm of Nick Clegg were enough, just, to counter the mounting opposition of George Osborne. In the first three months he seemed to move from mildly helpful observer (putting me together with David Gauke, for instance) into a position of some hostility. That change in attitude was, I am convinced, fed by sceptical Treasury officials. While no-one could accuse Iain of being a skilled negotiator, I doubt there was any alternative to the belligerence that he displayed, alongside his obduracy and determination, if the agenda was to be pushed through against this kind of opposition.

David Gauke, from within the Treasury, was in one of the best positions to assess the roots of hostility we faced in introducing Universal Credit. Much later he summed up for me: "Quite apart from the institutional suspicion the Treasury felt for DWP, the Treasury simply did not believe that fancy welfare structures were needed to bring down costs. They believed that ramping up conditionality was the key to bringing down the number of unemployed.

"As for George, he just wondered what on earth you guys were doing – launching a massive reform, which would never work anyway given the history of welfare reform. It was a major distraction from his central goal of driving down the deficit in his austerity programme. Besides, he didn't trust Iain to carry it off successfully."

I was, and remain, firmly of the view that real reductions in the cost of welfare can only flow from carefully constructed reform, with the savings emerging over a number of years. This is because welfare recipients are perfectly capable of adjusting their behaviour to take advantage of any new rules in the system. The six-monthly cuts process we had just endured – twice – was antithetical to this. The Treasury process arms its team with a spreadsheet and encourages a process of tweaking existing pro-grammes to score gains. This seems to me conceptually wrong-headed, since it takes little account of the behavioural changes that these adjust-ments are likely to generate.

There was no post-war precedent in the UK for the introduction of absolute cuts in welfare on the scale of 2010. And we were under no illus-ion about the difficulty we would have delivering them. However distaste-ful, I never considered resigning in this period – given my determination to create a welfare system with an effective architecture. The cuts were an inevitable part of the deal.

I ended the first six months profoundly disillusioned with the Treasury. My perception was that the average age of the Department was 29 and many were as arrogant as only 29-year-olds out of their depth can be. The staff turnover rate was running at 25 percent. They didn't own the policies they had forced on us. They had done their job once the spreadsheet was cleared by the Office for Budget Responsibility and many would be off to fresh pastures shortly there-after.

PART V

PRIVILEGE

November 2010 – March 2012

CHAPTER 13

Holding the Line

"Does he realise that this conjures up a picture of Tory and Liberal hard-faced men sitting around a table in Westminster plotting to deprive the poorest people of some financial aid?" demanded Tommy McAvoy, a pugnacious Glaswegian Lord and former Labour MP. "Is he proud of that?" [54] The Coalition Government had made its cuts, and now it had both to legislate for them – and defend them. On this occasion I was on the receiving end of an Oral Question in the Lords in the spring of 2011, some three months after the Spending Review. Tommy McAvoy was protesting two of the Government's most discomfiting 2010 cuts – to the maternity grant and the health in pregnancy grant.

I had a fraction of a second to decide my response. It was at the end of the allotted seven minutes, so I could close my session with it. With the major legislation coming up it was vital to staunch attacks on our presumed malevolence.

"My Lords," I exclaimed. "I am not proud of a previous Government who threw bits and pieces of money around like an out-of-control farm-yard muck spreader." I brought my hand down emphatically. To my surprise it hit the raised wooden despatch box with a thump (one of the disadvantages of being quite short). "We are making coherent provision for the most disadvantaged in a way that you could not." I thumped the box again, deliberately this time, as the microphone amplified the effect.

Hansard recorded the reaction of the Chamber: "Oh!"

Afterwards the senior official of the House, David Leakey or Black Rod (whose ceremonial duty at State Opening was to strike the Commons' door with his staff), came up to me: "Could you be a bit careful with the Despatch Box? It's quite fragile."

The next day, as I was tackling another question entirely, the Labour Peer and former European Commissioner Stanley Clinton-Davis intervened. "Would the Minister apologise for yesterday's tantrum? I am very concerned about his mental health." [55]

I didn't rise to the poorly expressed insult, which earned a frisson of disapproval round the Chamber. "My Lords, the expert in thumping Palace woodwork, who is Black Rod of course, suggested that I did not make a habit of maltreating the furniture. I am happy to take that advice to heart."

The cuts and fundamental reform we had announced meant we were now committed to a major legislative programme. Some of the cuts could be made through secondary legislation, which was relatively rapid to introduce. Most of it would require primary legislation, which was much more time consuming. A typical Bill would take about a year to receive Royal Assent, during which time it would pass through both the Commons and the Lords in matching stages. Inevitably most of the focus would concentrate on the Lords' stages. Without the Commons' inbuilt majority, it was essential to persuade enough of the independent Crossbenchers to support the Government if it was to carry the legislation. The opportunity was not lost on stakeholders and other interested parties. Often it was during the Lords' stages that they would mount campaigns to change those parts of the legislation they didn't like.

This meant I would have to rely on coherent argument and the effective marshalling of fact if I was to get the legislation through. I would also have to be prepared to compromise and negotiate where differences were intractable and where the Crossbenchers were united against the Government.

The first challenge came over the reductions in private sector housing benefit, announced in the July 2010 Emergency Budget and which we were introducing rapidly through secondary legislation. The Commons Work and Pensions Select Committee was quick to look at the issue and I was summoned to appear for an extended session in early November 2010 where MPs, particularly Labour MPs, argued that we would create homelessness on a substantial scale. [56]

I took friendly fire from the Liberal Democrat MP, Stephen Lloyd, who pointed out: "'*The Observer* a couple of weekends ago ran a long story that 82,000 people in London will be made homeless on the basis of the changes you are bringing in."

I told them the figures were exaggerated. "In many, many markets, when you are a 40 percent purchaser and you are changing the terms of trade, there is nowhere else for many landlords to go. Now, I know that is not the case in every market and there are different sub-markets, but as an average and as a whole, that is what we would expect to happen".

I pointed out that a gap had opened up between the rents paid by non-benefit low income families and benefit recipients. "Just take a Lewisham resident, for instance, in a one-bedroom property. The housing benefit tenant would be paying £185; the low-income working household would be paying £172. That is an example. Let's take – what is a nice place to go? Brighton and Hove; that's lovely – on a two-bedroom property there, a housing benefit tenant is paying £190 and the low-income working household pays £178."

The Labour MP Glenda Jackson, former star of films such as *Women in Love* and *A Touch of Class*, used her histrionic skills in a way that clearly undermined the patience of the rest of the Committee. She told me: "We are talking about people who do not take work because they are afraid that if they take low-paid work, they will lose their home. I am asking you what figures you have on the number of such claimants at the moment who will inevitably lose their homes."

"I am completely baffled by your question."

"Well, I must be honest: I am completely baffled by your answers."

Fortunately, her tone was not reflected in the Committee's final report, published at the end of the year, which concluded: "We support the Government's objective of managing the costs of housing benefit." Anne Begg, the Chairman of the Committee, admitted: "It is hard to say exactly what the impact of these changes will be." The Committee's main fire was directed at the provision to reduce the housing benefit of the long-term unemployed – another cut which had infuriated me when it was imposed by the Treasury. Our own statutory adviser, the Social Security Advisory Committee, had been considerably more brutal: "These measures must impact disproportionately on those low-income households with the least financial resilience and the fewest options for managing their lives and their finances". In the event, we managed to reverse this particular measure.

The formal challenge to the housing cuts took place in January 2011, over the regulations which we had submitted to Parliament. For quite different reasons it was a period of exceptional turbulence for Lords' business – over the Government's plan to reduce the number of MPs in the Parliamentary Voting System and Constituencies Bill. To get it through the Committee Stage, we would have to sit overnight on the 17 January and old hands warned that the danger points for this elderly group would be 1am and 4am in the morning. This was when people were most likely to die. Doctors were available right through the night, just in case.

In the event nobody died. Luckily, I had my office to myself, so after the vote at midnight I pulled the cushions off the sofas onto the floor and got into my sleeping bag. I had just got to sleep when the bells for the next vote rang, at about 3 am, so I got dressed to go down. There was not much conversation in the Lobby.

"I'm not sleeping with you again," complained one elderly Baroness to an equally elderly Lord. "You snore."

The housing regulations were now looming and the Labour Opposition were proposing to overturn them in their entirety – in the shape of a Fatal Motion. My whip was John Taylor, who was proving to be a skilled operator. Indeed, he proved his capability on one occasion when I was felled by a motor-bike while hurrying over Abingdon Street to answer a complex pensions question in the Chamber. As an ambulance carried me off to St Thomas', he took hold of the file and successfully extemporised his way through the responses. None in the Chamber realised his total lack of preparation. A former Chairman of the National Conservative Convention, he warned me: "The House looks likely to support the 'Fatal' on this unless we make some kind of concession."

It was rare for Fatal Motions to be laid down and rarer still for there to be a vote on them – particularly a successful vote. However, emotions were clearly running high on this issue.

"You need to do a deal with Lord Best. He's the acknowledged leader in housing. Basically, if Richard Best is on your side, the rest of the Crossbenchers will follow his lead."

Still groggy from lack of sleep overnight Monday, I met Richard on Wednesday evening. He set out his position: "I want to see a proper review of the impact of these measures next year and annually thereafter. That'll give you the ammunition to fight the Treasury for some in-flight adjustments if the results are as bad as we think."

"I think I can manage that," I told him. I had cleared the concession with Iain earlier in the week. "I'll need to look at the timing carefully.

Also, none of us will want this independent body assessing the changes in perpetuity. In practice they will be overtaken by all the other changes we are planning." Later I emailed him the relevant section of my speech to be sure that it met with his approval.

It was my first Lords' deal as a Minister. Labour called in all their Peers to vote on their Fatal Motion, but lost their nerve as news of the concession Richard Best had obtained percolated out. [57] Opening for the Opposition was Jim Knight, who vigorously condemned the measures and quoted an official report from 2006: "It is consistent both with the Lords' role in Parliament as a revising Chamber, and with Parliament's role in relation to delegated legislation, for the Lords to threaten to defeat a Statutory Instrument."

The drama faded out of the evening, however, when he closed: "In keeping with the constructive nature of this Opposition, our respect for convention and our desire to be helpful to the House, I intend to withdraw my Motion at the end of the debate."

Equally Richard Best declared himself satisfied with the commitment I had made for an interim report in 2012 and a full report in 2013. He added: "I think that there must be an implied commitment, in setting up this review, to the Government's changing course if that is necessary – perhaps in quite a radical way." He was to be disappointed.

Our two mainstream Bills were launched in February. The Welfare Reform Bill, incorporating Universal Credit, entered the Commons process first. It required a major effort over December and January to get ready. The other Bill, aimed mainly at accelerating the timetable for raising the state pension age, was much shorter and came to me in the Lords first. It pulled forward the equalisation of women's pensions from 2020 to 2018 and the completion of the subsequent increase to 66 in the retirement age of both genders down from 2024 to 2020. It had been a key element of the Spending Review in the previous October and saved the public finances £30 billion.

The speeches at Second Reading left me in no doubt that there would be serious opposition to the acceleration. The pension expert Jeannie Drake made the initial Labour speech with her measured, almost pedantic, delivery. "In the face of increasing life expectancy, I accept that raising the state pension age is part of the solution to maintaining a sustainable state pension system that supports private pension saving.

"As a principle, however, the manner and timing of any increase in the state pension must give people fair and proper notice and sufficient time to adjust, and ensure that the impact is not unfair and disproportionate for particular groups. The acceleration of the timetable to achieve the equalisation of pension age for women and men, from April 2020 to November 2018, does not meet that principle and breaks the promise made in the Coalition agreement not to start increasing the state pension age to 66 for women before 2020." [58]

Steve Webb, the Pensions Minister, and I joined Iain and the officials to discuss our options. I told them: "We've got a group of women hard hit by this and I'm worried about losing with a lot of Coalition Peers going against. There are three options as I see it. Draw the line at 18 months, which costs £1 billion; Steve's scheme to stop at a year and claw back later by putting both men and women up to 66 and a bit; or some mitigation through pension credit for the very poorest, though the Department says that is fraught with legal difficulty."

Iain sent the officials out of his office. "If there is an amendment at 66-plus that's an amendment which the Treasury can think about during the Commons' stages. You never know, it might stick. I don't want to hear any more about it."

Afterwards I sat in Steve's office discussing how we might send an indication to the Commons about what might be acceptable to the Lords further along in the process. He proposed: "We could have an amendment from a backbencher like Archy Kirkwood".

I had learned from the housing Fatal. I suggested: "Better from a Crossbencher; how about Sally Greengross?" Sally occupied the same influential role in pensions as Richard Best in housing.

"That's a very good idea. Although it will be extremely difficult for her to draft an amendment that actually works," said Steve.

I wrote Sally an unsigned note about which groups to try to protect and directed her to the Clerks in the Lords to help her with the drafting of the amendment.

In the event the Opposition strategy at the all-important Report stage backfired. [59] Bill McKenzie separated his blockbuster amendment from Sally Greengross' more modest proposal. I pointed out that his proposal to delay the move to 66 for both men and women by two years would cost the State £10 billion. "We simply cannot go on ignoring the increases in life expectancy," I argued. Bill pressed ahead with calling the vote – which he lost by a margin of 12 on a big turnout (214-226).

We started the debate all over again, albeit on the Greengross amendment. This limited the extra period any women would have to work to one year at the much cheaper cost of £2 billion. Her formulation failed to work, however, since it backtracked on the legal commitment to equalise the state pension age.

"As structured, it risks breaching the European directive and being unlawful. Therefore, I am not in a position to support the amendment," I concluded regretfully. With my eye on the future stages, and anticipating a loss, I added: "This House has expressed strong feeling on this matter and the message has undoubtedly gone out loud and clear."

To my surprise I won the Division on this amendment as well, again by a margin of 12 (203-215). There was one final vote – keeping a more generous time-table for making the means-tested pension credit available, but Bill McKenzie's tactics now began to have an impact as Peers drifted away to 7pm dinner appointments. With attendance down 71, the final vote was won by a handsome 41 (153-194).

Iain was ecstatic. Next morning he was on the phone: "I just wanted to ring you to congratulate you on getting the Bill through. This is really significant. It means that we have real credibility with the Treasury in driving through the new Single Tier state pension." This was a major simplification that Steve Webb had embarked on, replacing the basic state pension and the earnings-related state pension with a single flat rate structure.

The denouement took place half-a-year later, after Steve had fought for an amelioration worth £1 billion, which capped the delay any woman would experience at 18 months. When the Bill came back from the Commons with this measure in it, there was one final attempt by Bill McKenzie to revert to his original proposal.

I was careful to pay tribute to Sally Greengross. "Our amendment takes her amendment as the starting point and provides the same notice for the first women affected by a one-year rise." [60]

When Bill McKenzie called his vote, the Crossbenchers split in half with Sally leading 32 into the Government Lobby. This was enough to produce a significant victory and the passage of the Bill. It would also open the door to years of ferocious pressure from the group of women affected, under the WASPI campaign – Women against State Pension Inequality.

At the turn of the year, all this was far in the future. The work-load seemed to increase every time I looked round. Quite apart from Universal Credit, a series of issues forced their way into my diary. Once I started reforming one element of the welfare system, I found myself unable to resist being dragged into investigating the knock-on issues in contiguous areas. Many of these issues concerned health – unsurprisingly, as poor health and disability – at about £50 billion – absorbed a considerable proportion of the Department's working age budget.

Mental health was the most intractable problem, still an affliction with real stigma attached. People with mild to moderate mental health issues accounted for about 40 percent of those moving onto long-term disability benefits. If we wanted to get the numbers down, we would need to develop a better mental health strategy. One of the officials from Nice (the National Institute for Health and Care Excellence) advised me: "You should look into the work of Aaron Antonovski, who analysed the health outcomes of concentration camp survivors. He discovered that while survivors faced similar pressures, some were more resilient than others. That resilience comes from a sense of 'coherence'. You should talk to Harry Burns, the Chief Medical Officer in Scotland, who is the leading advocate of the approach in this country."

It was a transformational theory, awkwardly named Salutogenesis, which I read up in detail (as well as visiting Harry Burns). Indeed, it provided an over-arching rationale for our efforts to transform the welfare system. In a speech at the time I explained: "By disempowering people – as the legacy welfare system does – we effectively remove people's ability to develop a coherent world view. That undermines their resilience, which makes them sick. It's no accident that the number of disability claimants recording mental health issues soars the longer they are on the benefit." I set in train work to develop programmes to help people with mental health issues.

Carol Black had put out her Report recommending the switch from 'sick note' to 'fit note' in March 2008, a year after my Report on welfare to work.[61] In September 2010 we travelled to Leicester and Birmingham to see two of the resulting pilots. She told me: "The trouble is the GPs still won't focus on how best to get their patients back to work. Too many just sign them off."

"We need to intervene much earlier," I said. "We need to get help to people in the period when they are on sickness absence from their place of work and well before they end up on benefits, by which time it's too late. Would you do another review on it? You can be as radical as you like."

I was also worried about the adults with severe learning difficulties, such as Down's Syndrome and cerebral palsy. Employers had become increasingly reluctant to offer them paid work after the strict laws on the minimum wage were introduced in 1999. The plea of the young lady at the Radar disability conference in 2008 continued to haunt me: "Will someone give me a job? I want a job."

I crossed the corridor to my colleague Maria Miller's room. "Maria, I've just been researching an Australian model for what they call Social Firms. If a company takes on at least 25 percent of workers who are profoundly disadvantaged, they are forgiven all pay-roll taxes in compensation. These are workers who will always need close supervision. Quite a few supermarkets in Australia have become Social Firms. Do you think it will fly with the disability lobby here?"

Maria was enthusiastic about the concept but considerably deflated when we met again: "I've talked to the lobby," she told me. "They won't have it. They believe disabled people should be treated exactly the same as fully able-bodied people – as a matter of principle."

"It's a principle that has denied more than 90 percent of people with severe learning difficulties the fulfilment of having a job," I replied glumly. "They spend their days sitting in common rooms watching day-time television." It was an issue that would nearly destroy my political career.

I inherited another pressing health issue from my predecessor in the job, Bill McKenzie. He had commissioned a formal report into the scandal of mesothelioma which was waiting for me when I arrived in office. This terrible form of cancer developed many years after exposure to asbestos, possibly 40 years or more. It was one of the most painful ways to die, as I could attest, since it had carried off my own father. All workers should have been covered by standard employer liability insurance. However, with the passage of years the insurance industry had lost the records in a significant minority of cases, leaving the victims and their families uncompensated. I embarked on what was to prove an extended negotiation with the insurers to find a solution.

Outside health, I found we had a problem with the Credit Union movement. Under the previous Government, the Department had ploughed up to £70 million a year into the sector, which provided loans and financial services to poorer communities on a non-profit basis. I asked one of my former colleagues from the financial markets to take a quick look at the sustainability of the sector before we took a decision to continue the subsidy. Paul Ruddle's analysis was damning. "They don't have a viable business model. It costs £100 to make their average loan of £400, on which they earn £27," he told me. "Virtually all the growth in the sector in recent years seems to have come from the DWP money." We needed a strategy to make the sector viable.

The Work Programme, promoted vigorously by Chris Grayling, was moving ahead rapidly. The Invitation to Tender was published in December and there was a session on the structure for the likely bidders on the third floor of Caxton House. We needed to ascertain the response of the sector.

Chris concluded his description of the package by saying: "You can make shed-loads of money by performing."

I reinforced his salesmanship: "For the first time we have an uncapped reward structure – based on the DEL-AME switch. Price differentiation means that you will be rewarded for helping the most difficult."

One of the leaders of the industry, Richard Johnson of Serco, got up from his corner seat and addressed the room. Serco was one of the major contracting companies I had talked to four years earlier when formulating my original report. Its interest had reinforced my confidence in the design. Now Richard put the pressure on: "You have just said this structure is designed to incentivise us to perform but I have to tell you that this does not provide adequate returns. If one was coming fresh to this one would not bid. I have to warn you that on these terms there will be market failure." It was a blatant attempt to get us to reduce our demands or, alternatively, drive down the value of the other bids. Such gamesmanship had been effective when the Flexible New Deal was being marketed, persuading James Purnell to soften the terms.

Chris took it head on. "We have looked at this very carefully, using some top advisers and investment banks. It is perfectly possible to make very good returns and the cash flow break-even has been carefully structured so that the capital requirements are not too difficult."

Only one other bidder rose to put pressure on us. Otherwise the audience resolutely refused to join the attack. Later, when we met to assess the reaction, we decided to adjust the terms very little, given what seemed broad acceptance.

My main focus over the period, however, was to get Universal Credit in good enough shape to go through the legislative mill. Through December and into January 2011 we tackled a series of issues and it became more and more apparent how complex the detail of rebuilding the entire welfare system actually was.

Philippa, Stephen and I gathered some 20 officials in one of the large downstairs meeting rooms to decide on the frequency of payment.

"Will people be able to budget for monthly payments?" Philippa asked. Neil Couling replied: "When we moved from weekly to fortnightly payments everyone forecast it would be the end of the world but people handled it just fine. They'll manage a move to monthly payments just as well."

"I never realised time was so complicated," I confessed. "Weeks simply don't cut across to months at any level."

"We'll have to use daily rates for some elements, like sanctions," one of the officials explained.

"In practice I don't think we have any other choice than monthly," I concluded. "We're bringing together the tax credit assessment, which is an annual process, with the fortnightly benefit structure. Most employers pay monthly and we want people on the employment cycle. We'll need to be able to pay people more frequently when they're in real difficulty, though."

The most intractable issues were dubbed the 'frightful eight', and required a series of papers and meetings to lock down. Stephen developed a clever way of providing the promised transitional protection. "We'll establish any cash loss at the point of transfer and add an element to Universal Credit. That will erode as Universal Credit rates move up," he explained to me.

On Carers, Neil Couling said: "Either include them in Universal Credit, or exclude them. All the intermediate options are too complicated."

I thought aloud: "The simplest solution is to put them into Universal Credit and not support rich Carers. But that will provoke real anger."

At the second meeting of the day on the issue Iain concluded: "I sense that they could be really difficult. Everyone loves a Carer. Hey, what's not to like? We must get Universal Credit through and not risk it by trying to include them."

Shortly afterwards Neil relented and brought me an intermediate structure. Carers Allowance would continue as an independent payment but there would be an element in Universal Credit as well. "That's quite elegant," I congratulated him.

He was insistent on getting rid of the various rates and premiums for disability. "These are not consistently applied at all. They don't work. We need just the two main disability rates, which can be higher to compensate."

We were going back and forth with Council Tax Benefit. I was still hopeful that we could retain it in Universal Credit, even if it had notionally been 'localised'. Eric Pickles at the Department for Communities and Local Government (DCLG) was not particularly keen to take ownership; but then, neither was DWP. Ownership implied finding the £500 million a year of savings announced by the Chancellor.

When questioned on whether it would be retained in Universal Credit at a conference in March I replied, incautiously but luckily quite cryptically: "I can assure you that we are not going to let a ha'porth of tar around council tax benefit undermine Universal Credit."

As the pressure from the Treasury ramped up for Eric to take responsibility, I ran into Danny Alexander, the Liberal Democrat Chief Secretary to the Treasury. "You realise you're undermining Universal Credit with what you're doing, don't you?" I reproached him.

"Find me the £500 million," was his crisp retort.

It wasn't the only problem we had with Eric's Department. It was deeply concerned about our plans to stop paying social landlords directly and instead give tenants the responsibility to make their rental payments. The social landlords argued that the impact in terms of arrears would create serious damage to their finances. I set up a series of meetings with the Housing Minister, Grant Shapps, to iron out the differences.

The DWP housing team, accustomed to handling DCLG, developed the idea of piloting how tenants would react in practice. Grant reacted with genuine concern at our plan to launch these 'direct payment demonstration projects'.

"Don't get me wrong, I'm a real enthusiast for the UC," he told us. "But we're announcing the Affordable Rent project in July and we can't afford the industry to get a whiff of these demonstrator projects."

I replied: "I'm sure we can agree on the timing of announcements.

But I need the wholehearted and speedy support of your team to make sure we produce projects that work both for Universal Credit and the financing of social housing."

Philippa was most concerned about the Budget cut to childcare subsidy in working tax credit (rolling over into Universal Credit), down from 80 percent to 70 percent. The provisions around self-employment needed considerable work as did the question of how Universal Credit would deal with all the benefits which were linked to the welfare system. This was a major complexity. Other Government Departments piggy-backed on people's rights to DWP benefits to provide additional support – a process known as passporting. So a JSA recipient, for example, would be passported to free medical prescriptions by the Department of Health and legal aid by the Ministry of Justice. The children of a lone parent on Income Support were among several categories to receive free school meals from the Department of Education. This Department would build still further on the system to make a payment to schools known as the pupil premium – reflecting the greater challenge of educating poorer pupils – based on the number taking such meals. Chris Grayling suggested: "Why don't we see if the Social Security Advisory Committee can help us out?"

Not surprisingly, the detail round some of these measures was sketchy as the Bill entered the Commons in February 2011. Government was expected to put considerable information alongside primary legislation to allow Parliament to scrutinise it properly. Often this would include full drafts of the secondary legislation which would subsequently be issued – or at least full explanations of what that legislation would be. With a measure such as Universal Credit, which would eventually require no fewer than 300 pages of secondary legislation, this was a daunting requirement.

Liam Byrne led for the Opposition. He had learned the hard way about the danger of making jokes in politics. His tongue-in-cheek note for his successor at the Treasury less than a year earlier – 'I'm afraid there is no money' – backfired badly. The Conservatives delighted in using it to lambast Labour's financial record. Now he showed no flicker of humour as he condemned the Bill because "the proposal of the Universal Credit as it stands creates uncertainty for thousands of people in the United Kingdom." [62] He cited lack of clarity over childcare, housing benefit, free school meals and council tax benefit alongside a list of other shortcomings.

When the Bill entered the Committee Stage at the end of March 2011, Chris Grayling tried to pre-empt the attacks on the lack of detail. He introduced the first two clauses on Universal Credit as creating "the framework for the new benefit".

"For want of a better way of explaining it, they will create a bookcase on which we can lodge the books of the detail of the future benefit system.

"The Bill and the debate are about building that bookcase. We will do our best to explain our initial intentions about what should be put on the shelves but . . . the debate is not about the detailed content of every single book." [63]

With Maria Miller he led no fewer than 26 separate Committee sessions on the Bill over the next two months. It was a grueling process although the number of votes called was relatively modest at 16. They broke along party lines for the Government (normally 14-10) each time they were called.

"I'm planning to make no concessions at all during the Commons stages," Chris assured me. "I'm leaving all the concessions for the Lords, where you'll need them." In practice he made one small change in the status of secondary legislation.

The Commons scrutiny process concluded at a gallop in mid-June, with only two days put aside for the final two stages – Report and Third Reading. Iain was contemptuous of Opposition objections that the process had been truncated. "They have complained that we did not allow enough time for consideration of issues on Report and then, on the day before yesterday, they proceeded to talk for more than an hour on amendments that they did not even push to a vote." [64]

Reflecting the solid support for the Bill on the Coalition side, it passed its final stage with a majority of 50 (288-238). It would be a very different story when the Bill came to the Lords.

CHAPTER 14

The Lords' Den

The Welfare Reform Bill was scheduled to receive its Second Reading in the House of Lords on 13 September 2011. It would take an intensive six months before we could hope to see it pass. I made ready with some trepidation. Three Ministers had taken it through the Commons, where an inbuilt majority at every stage meant they were in total control of the process. I was on my own in the Lords and, rather than turning to cordial political abuse when hard-pressed, my arguments had to be focused on persuading Crossbenchers as to the soundness of the Government's position.

I had prepared carefully for the Second Reading. This was the set-piece at which interested Peers laid out their concerns and foreshadowed the key issues on which they would look for changes and concessions. I had organised an elaborate programme of briefings for the various groups, meeting with Labour Peers, Conservatives, Liberal Democrats and Cross-benchers separately.

The process had begun with a meeting with my opposite number Bill McKenzie where I promised: "I'll get you all the information I can through this process. I want to make sure that debate is well-informed. There's no point Peers grabbing the wrong end of the stick and waggling it vigorously, so I'll make the officials available for seminars ahead of our consideration of the various parts."

"It's a bit of a two-edged sword for you," Bill said sympathetically. "The better we understand it, the better focused our criticism."

I replied: "I don't see this as a desperately political process."

"We may have the odd political flurry."

"Yes, we can have a bit of fun, but I'd like to keep it restrained. I'd also like to use the Committee as a discovery stage and leave the voting for Report."

This was reasonably standard procedure but it was good to get it confirmed. "Yes, that should be broadly OK," he agreed.

At Second Reading, in the early afternoon, I laid out my stall: "These measures lay the groundwork for the main purpose of this Bill, the creation of Universal Credit, the most radical reform of the welfare system since its invention.

"With the creation of Universal Credit this Bill does not just allow for the development of a new benefit, it creates the conditions for attitudinal and behavioural change. It bridges the gulf that has opened up between unemployment and work, and delivers a benefits system that is about people not process, one that is flexible and responsive."

I settled into my seat to listen to the reaction of 50 Peers, a process that would take seven-and-a-half hours and close with my response to the issues they raised. [65] Some of the speakers were among the most expert in the welfare system in the country and they could call on intensive analysis of the issues by the various lobby groups. In my corner was the 'Box', a group of four or five officials segregated into what looked like an enclosed Elizabethan church pew at the rear alongside the Government benches. They would produce briefings for my responses, which would be brought over by one of the House of Lords doormen – in plenty of time for a set-piece like Second Reading but invariably too late when in the middle of the cut and thrust of debate.

Early on it was clear that Peers were happy with Universal Credit. Patricia Hollis, a previous (Labour) incumbent in my Ministerial role and acknowledged doyenne of welfare, declared: "Most benefits and credits have different income thresholds, different taper rates, different backdating rules, different eligibility criteria, different linking rules, different passporting arrangements, different savings caps and different payment patterns.

"Not surprisingly, therefore, we have error, fraud, underclaiming and overlapping built into the system, to say nothing of complexity, confusion and high administrative cost. The result is that it is a full-time job being poor. We need a robust, easily understood structure that reduces the risk while increasing the reward of working as the most effective route out of poverty. I am hoping that the Universal Credit will deliver this."

In common with several other Peers, she then went on to warn: "The architecture is being undermined by the cuts agenda and we risk Universal Credit failing." She reserved her main ire for the Eric Pickles'

Department of Communities and Local Government: "It is a complete idiocy for it to localise and cut council tax benefit, undermining Universal Credit rules. It sends an Exocet through UC. With friends like the DCLG, who needs an Opposition?" I began to wonder whether my office had been bugged.

Archy Kirkwood, eight years the Chairman of the Commons Work and Pensions Select Committee, made the same attack. "I agree that the structure and the architecture of the Bill are perfectly defensible . . . but it is at risk of being prejudiced because of the degree to which these cuts have come on the back of it."

As a Liberal Democrat, he was now a Coalition Government backbencher so I paid particular attention to this influential figure when he rejected the Chancellor's Benefit Cap.

"We have a system of entitlements in our social security system and, if you have the entitlements, you get the benefit. Here is an arbitrary system coming in and overlaying that by saying, 'Well, you may well be entitled to it but we think it's too much'.

"I give the Minister fair warning that I cannot support the Benefit Cap as it is currently cast." So here was one potential rebellion in the Government's ranks. Clearly, I would be having more problems with the other parts of this portmanteau bill than with its centrepiece, Universal Credit.

More ominous still was the speech from James Mackay, former Lord Chancellor under the Thatcher and Major Governments. He took aim at the reform of the child maintenance system and the charging structure we were introducing for parents who wished to use state support. This was a part of the Bill that had received almost no interest in the Commons process. Now James Mackay said: "I am entirely in favour of parents who have encountered difficulty in their relationships, for whatever reason, trying really hard to resolve the maintenance of their children amicably.

"Sadly, there is a hard core of parents who will do everything that they can to avoid their liability. It is for those who are left with the care of the children that this service is essential, as the Department's research itself shows. Where the absent parent is traced, I am all in favour of his having to pay for the consequences of his attempt to evade his responsibility but I cannot see any fairness whatever in charging the parent who has been left in the lurch for that service." Given the extraordinary regard with which Mackay was held on the Conservative benches, this was a warning about a potential rebellion from the heart of the majority ruling party.

I was not surprised by the wide range of attacks on the various disability provisions. What I had not quite expected, however, was the vehemence with which they were delivered; not least, by people who were themselves disabled. Crossbencher Colin Low, who was blind, was both extraordinarily articulate and utterly brutal: "Research by the think tank Demos has shown that, far from being protected from the worst of the cuts, disabled families face losses of £2,000 to £3,000 over the course of this Parliament. Overall, it estimates that disabled people will lose £9 billion in welfare support." He took particular aim at the removal of some of the extra disability payments from Universal Credit.

The diminutive and doughty Crossbencher Jane Campbell, suffering spinal muscular atrophy with undimmed energy, was desperately concerned at the replacement of Disability Living Allowance (DLA) with the Personal Independence Payment (PIP). DLA was regarded as outdated by the Government because in too many cases it was based on self-assessment, without regular review. It was being replaced by the entirely new PIP structure, in which inability to perform a range of specific tasks were scored and totalled. Jane finished with an emotional twist of the knife: "From my mailbag, it is obvious that many disabled people expect to lose their independence."

Closely linked to disability was concern about our treatment of cancer sufferers. Crossbencher Narendra Patel, former President of the Royal College of Obstetricians and Gynaecologists, declared: "The Government's proposals to time-limit contributory-based Employment and Support Allowance (ESA) to 12 months are unfair and wrong. In my experience, 12 months is simply not long enough for many cancer patients to be well enough to return to work."

Bill McKenzie could appeal to plenty of Crossbench allies as he spelled out the areas in which the official Opposition would probe and seek changes. The measures to reduce rents for people with spare bedrooms "are illogical, wretched provisions that must be exposed and opposed," he declared. He took aim at the Benefit Cap; he would want the time limit on contributory ESA moved out to two years; he would aim to protect the disability premia in the switchover to Universal Credit.

When I stood up to respond it was already past 10pm. I opened in conventional Lords' style by congratulating the speakers, with the slightest of twists.

"I am extremely pleased that the debate has been both informed and committed. I may not have enjoyed some of the things I heard but it has certainly been extraordinarily well considered."

I responded to several of the issues but, given the complexity of the changes, I was careful to emphasise the process of communication during the next stage of the Bill.

"Over the next few weeks I shall publish a great deal of detailed information which was previously provided in Committee in another place. It will include notes on every regulation-making power in the Bill, full policy briefing notes and, where possible, illustrative draft regulations which will go into considerably more detail than has previously been published.

"In addition, as we approach each section of debate in Committee, I will ensure that officials from the Department for Work and Pensions are available to host briefing meetings for noble Lords. These sessions will be a further opportunity to go over the detail of each clause before it is debated in Committee. I hope that both these sessions and the additional information that will be published will be of use to the House and will go a reasonable way to answering many of the questions and specific points raised today."

There was no opposition to giving the Bill a second Reading, paving the way to the intensive process of the Committee Stage. This stage is strikingly different in the Lords by comparison with the Commons. The Commons Committee is hand-picked by each side, with a number reflecting the balance between the parties in the Chamber. So the Government is always in a majority unless rebellious backbenchers have been selected.

In the Lords any interested peer can turn up to the Grand Committee and take part, although there is no voting. A second room, the Moses Room, is reserved for Grand Committee proceedings. However, on this occasion it was deemed too small, so the plan was to use the much larger Committee Room 4 for the duration. This room was in the Committee Corridor of the Palace of Westminster on the first floor.

Time pressure meant Parliament restarted while the Conservative Conference was underway in early October. I hurried back for the first session of Grand Committee on Tuesday, straight into a row on the suitability of Room 4 for the process. The combative George Foulkes (like Tommy McAvoy a former Scottish Labour MP) complained vehemently: "I think it is very difficult to have started the Welfare Reform Bill Grand Committee in this totally inadequate room, dealing with something that is so important when it should have been dealt with much more appropriately on the Floor of the House, and it is going to create tremendous difficulties not only for people with mobility problems but for all of us with regard to 10-minute Divisions and a number of other things." [66]

I kept quiet during this opening manoeuvre. In fact, Room 4 was big and convenient, with the desks for Peers set up in a large square and rows of seats for observers. Across the square I was facing a line of interested Labour Peers. Behind me were five or six rotating officials from the Department, marshalled by the Bill captain, Phill Wells, (previously the analyst whose figures had stood up to Gordon Brown's assault). I would need their quick-fire support, passing forward notes, given the tactic of the Labour group. They would let the prepared responses to each amendment through and then grill me intensively as each issue drew to a close.

There were 17 four-hour sessions through October and November, of which the first 10 concentrated on Universal Credit.

The best single speech came from Patricia Hollis, when she eviscerated the decision to remove Council Tax Benefit from Universal Credit. [67]

"As for the consultation . . . only one page, page 10, offers five principles – well, at any rate, five claims – for localising CTB. The other 39 pages are spent trying to overcome the difficulties that will result.

"Of its five claims – I cannot really call them principles – on one page of a 40-page document, the first is absurd, the second is fallacious, the third is false, the fourth is sophistry and the fifth is cruel. That is before we get to the 39 pages of problems that the DCLG itself identifies."

I found it difficult to keep a grin off my face. Tony Newton, a former Conservative Secretary of State for Social Security under Mrs Thatcher, observed: "Maybe the Minister has some wonderful answers that I cannot predict; I am just glad that I am not in his position. I think that we have had a devastating critique of this proposal, and I will take some persuading that it makes any sense."

I resisted the temptation to agree wholeheartedly and stuck to an anodyne party line.

Richard Best attacked the direct payment of housing costs to tenants rather than landlords. "The Tenants and Residents Organisations of England (TAROE) strongly support giving tenants the right to choose.

"Organisations representing landlords – the Residential Landlords Association, the National Housing Federation, the housing federations in Scotland and Wales, the British Property Federation, the National Federation of ALMOs and others – are worried that rent arrears will escalate as tenants prioritise other debts." [68]

I had done a lot of work on this. In September I had travelled up to Birmingham to the National Housing Federation and delivered a speech announcing the demonstration projects to find out how social tenants would handle taking responsibility for paying their own rent.

I replied firmly: "One of the key principles of our welfare reforms is to make the whole experience of claiming benefits as close as possible to the experience of receiving a wage or salary. The choices available to working households do not include opting for their employer to pay the landlord directly.

"I am not convinced by the argument that so-called tenant choice is genuine choice. Effective choice exists only when the balance of power is equal between tenants and landlords. When power is in the hands of land-lords, tenant choice becomes landlord choice, and that, of course, leads to the situation we have at the moment where 95 percent of claimants reputedly choose to have their housing benefit paid direct to the landlord."

I fended off several of the pressure points with carefully timed an-nouncements or commitments. We announced another £300 million for childcare, which Philippa had worked hard to win. An issue that caught me unawares was how Carers would be passported onto their benefit (and UC element) once the Personal Independence Payment was introduced. Patricia Hollis did not disguise her concern: "Too much depends on how you align the two rates of disability allowance; the passporting of Carer's Allowance will depend on it; and, in turn whole issues such as couple conditionality, in-work payments and the like will depend on that. We cannot deal with earlier sections of the Bill if we do not know what the implications of this are." [69]

They threatened to delay further stages of the Bill until the inform-ation was available. This was a potent threat given the imperative to finish the Bill before the next financial year, when some of the first savings were planned. I promised to have the decision by the Report stage of the Bill and later, privately, told them I hoped to relieve their concerns by passporting Carers from all levels of PIP.

The simplification of the disability elements in Universal Credit – and the alignment of the child and adult rates – was roundly attacked. I had to admit that there would be some losers from the changeover and my defence that the differences were not very large did little to appease Peers. This would clearly go to a vote at the next stage.

In area after area I was given food for thought, much of it highly valuable, particularly from Labour Peers. Rita Donaghy warned that we were under-estimating the difficulties we would face in the area of self-employment. Jeannie Drake protested that we were being too mean with pension saving. Ruth Lister, a life-long poverty campaigner, probed our arrangements for the most vulnerable. In each case I was to go back and pursue the issues they raised. Perhaps the most significant issue – reflecting Ruth Lister's concerns – was how best to look after the people who simply would not be able to manage an arm's length relationship with the welfare system. I started to look at how to provide individual support for these vulnerable groups. The Peers had responded to my open policy on information by focusing carefully on the key issues. We may have been debating across the political divide, but I was genuinely impressed.

Disability came up early in the process. Bill McKenzie complained about the Prime Minister's language. He quoted the Conference speech of the previous day in which David Cameron had announced: "For years you've been conned by Governments. To keep the unemployment figures down, they've parked as many people as possible on the sick; two and a half million, to be exact. Not officially unemployed, but claiming welfare, no questions asked."

McKenzie said: "Nobody who has any knowledge of the benefits system could reasonably accept that as a fair representation of the situation in recent years." He added: "The impact of this is to stigmatise people on benefits, and we should be deeply worried about that." [70]

In the Prime Minister's defence, I explained: "Let me just make it absolutely clear what the Prime Minister was saying in the slightly more technical language that we understand in this Committee. The Prime Minister was making the point that we had created a series of inactive benefits onto which people were put and then left without any route back into the workplace."

Drily Bill McKenzie replied: "If that is what the Prime Minister was intending to say, his usual high command of the English language eluded him."

This set up five fraught sessions on the disability provisions in the Bill, outside Universal Credit. The line of desks to my right was now filled with Peers, usually from the Crossbenches, who were themselves disabled.

The measure to limit to one year the amount of time people could stay on the lower tier of contributory ESA was heavily criticised. (The clumsy formal title for the lower tier was the Work-Related Activity Group or WRAG). Delyth Morgan, Chief Executive of the Breast Cancer campaign, warned: "This measure will affect people with a degenerative condition who qualify for the Work-Related Activity Group but whose benefit expires before their condition deteriorates, to the extent that they would be eligible for the Support Group." (The Support Group represented the upper tier of ESA.)

Peers also focused on the problems for cancer patients. Narendra Patel said: "People who have a terminal diagnosis but who are expected to live for longer than six months currently can still be placed in the WRAG and will therefore be subject to time-limiting. This means someone who has a prognosis of two years and is placed in the WRAG could lose their support after one year, even though they may have only one year left to live."

Bill McKenzie summed up: "The overall tenor of our very powerful debate this afternoon is clearly to the effect that people are extremely unhappy with these provisions." [71]

I could see that I would need significant concessions in this area.

Unsurprisingly Peers were suspicious of the replacement of Disability Allowance (DLA), by the Personal Independence Payment (PIP), suspicion that extended to the new name. I deployed a series of concessions and indications here to fend off attack. I would look again, or 'take back', the measure to extend the waiting period from three months to six; I would concede a major evaluation of the impact of the new benefit. Finally, I was able to indicate that we would drop a hated measure in the October Spending Review, which removed mobility funds from those in residential care. The result was that the introduction of PIP went through unscathed.

The penultimate session concentrated on the Benefit Cap, another area where I was in sympathy with my attackers. Given the aggressive way that this bit on people, Philippa and I had spent several sessions going through what a sensible set of concessions might be. We both rather liked the idea of increasing its level by excluding child benefit from the mix. I found myself goading the Grand Committee in this direction.

Ruth Lister demanded: "There has been talk about a level playing field. Will he explain to the Committee how the Government justify the fact that child benefit is being taken into account on one side of the equation and not on the other when we know that all those families on median earnings are getting child benefit?"[72]

Insouciantly I replied: "I acknowledge that we are not comparing like with like. We are looking at a sensible level at which to put the maximum benefit payment. The level that we are looking at is the equivalent of a household earning £35,000. I think that one can over-elaborate the logic, which I will not attempt to do here." This was a Lordly way of admitting there was no logic to my position.

Grand Committee closed with James Mackay reiterating that he was not happy with charging mothers for the new child support services. "Unless some change of heart occurs, I may raise it again," he warned my new whip, Rupert de Mauley, who had taken over from John Taylor. [73]

Before we could begin the next stage of the Bill – Report – I needed to assemble a range of concessions from the Government machinery. The most pressing was the passporting arrangement for Carers from PIP, which I had promised Patricia Hollis. Philippa warned me: "The Treasury and No. 10 are playing games."

This was exasperating: "I can't afford to renege on my word here. I promised this for before Report and if I don't deliver my word will be worth nothing for all the other things we need. Tell them I'm preparing a letter to Patricia on Carers which will essentially have them passported from all of PIP."

Two days later, on Friday afternoon, just three days before Report, Philippa rang to interrupt a game of tennis.

"No. 10 and the Treasury want to review our proposal to passport Carers from all PIP," she told me. "The Department didn't think it needed clearance to shape the arrangement but No. 10 thinks they do."

She put on Hugh Harris from the No. 10 Policy Unit. He told me: "It's a £300 million decision and I think it's only right that the Quad at least has the option of not doing it, even if they probably won't use it. The Quad meets Thursday so it's only a delay of a few days." The Quad was a regular meeting to resolve pressing issues between the Conservative Prime Minister and Chancellor with the Liberal Democrat Deputy Prime Minister and Chief Secretary to the Treasury.

I replied: "Well, it's high risk. In practice the numbers being passported will depend on where we set the thresholds. I have promised the statement before the Report stage starts and without it there is a real possibility that the Report stage is aborted till after Xmas. Then we could lose the start-up to ESA time-limiting. I have also informed Hollis that she will be receiving a letter from me with this information. It's an expensive way to obtain an option we'll be highly unlikely to want to exercise."

Under pressure No. 10 folded and with some relief I sent the letter on Monday – albeit on the same day as we plunged into Report. This stage of the Bill was moved to the main Chamber, where there would be six sessions of about six hours each, with the emphasis on voting.

Day One concentrated on Universal Credit, where I won a series of tight votes over: monthly payments; the simplification of the child disability payments (to my surprise); and on removing council tax benefit from the structure (a victory I found it hard to exult over).

After that victories became much scarcer, although the number of votes was reasonably modest and many amendments were withdrawn.

Richard Best withdrew his amendment on direct payments of rent. Instead, he concentrated his fire on the spare bedroom measure, dubbing it the 'so-called bedroom tax' for the first time in public. It was a phrase that Labour took up with alacrity and was to haunt the Government (and me) for years. My announcement that there would be a further £30 million a year put in the discretionary housing pot to support disabled people who had made adaptations to their homes, as well as foster carers, cut little ice and I lost significantly, with rebels from both Coalition parties.

I won a vote on PIP but fared much worse on the measure to limit the time the less severely disabled (or WRAG) could stay on the more generous Employment and Support Allowance. Here I went down three times, quite badly.

It was late January 2012 by the penultimate day on Report. This was a set-piece round the Benefit Cap, where the Bishop of Ripon and Leeds had picked up my gauntlet and put in an amendment excluding child benefit. The Bishops had been roundly excoriated in the Press for their pains. One of them told me, wonderingly: "I've had pictures of my Palace all over the *Daily Mail*." They won, but only by 15 on a big turn-out (252-237).

The final day of Report was a fiasco, with James Mackay making good his threat to rebel on charging mothers for child support services. Labour could just sit back and watch with joy as a series of Conservatives stood up to support him in his stand.

Only Elizabeth Berridge, on the Conservative benches, was brave enough to point out: "Although much has been said on behalf of mothers, who are in the majority in this situation, of course it is not as simple to say that just because the mother has the care of the children she is not some-times at fault for the fact that maintenance is not paid." [74]

The 'not content' Lobby seemed almost empty as I passed through, to see the biggest defeat on a Bill of the whole Coalition Government period, 270-128. A major exercise would be needed to turn this round.

The Lords would not finish with the Bill till a week later, when the final stage of Third Reading took place on the last day of January. This stage is designed to tidy up anomalies without returning to matters which had already been dealt with. However, the Crossbencher Molly Meacher decided to rerun the vote on the simplified disability elements for children in Universal Credit. Seven weeks earlier I had narrowly won the original vote; this time – on a much bigger turn-out – I lost a remarkably similar amendment by 15 (246-230). It was the only loss I took on Universal Credit.

Iain was in a rage with James Mackay. "I saw him before the vote in private and I thought we had an agreement. Then he goes straight off to *The Guardian* and tells them we're working on concessions. The trouble is that he was never a real Conservative, even under Thatcher."

Our strategy for getting the Bill through was to invoke Financial Priv-ilege. This was a device, rarely used, through which the Commons imposed its will on the Lords, turning down their amendments because they cost too much. At our meeting to discuss Bill handling, Iain decided: "We need to be tough and push it through with Financial Privilege. We need to tell MPs that this is the cuts agenda and we can't afford as a Coalition to lose these sums."

I pointed out: "Some of these amendments don't actually cost us anything."

Iain was adamant. "That doesn't matter. We'll just do it as a package."

"I think I'll still have to give concessions." I had been looking at the detail of how Financial Privilege worked and it didn't seem quite the constitutional silver bullet advertised. "They can still send back other amendments in response."

We worked up a series of concessions in preparation for the negotiations. Most urgent was the child support issue. Here we decided to cut the upfront charge for the parents with care (usually mothers) from £100 to £20. I held a one-to-one meeting with one of James Mackay's Conservative supporters, Tim Boswell.

Maria Miller, who was responsible for the policy, told me: "You've got to win this in the Lords, David, because I'm not sure I can hold our side if it comes back again to the Commons." She was insistent that we could not give anything away on the level of the regular fee the resident parent would have to pay to use the service.

With Boswell I rehearsed my main argument: "We didn't explain properly that we are giving £5 billion plus to lone parents that we don't take back if they get maintenance. That's money on top; an extra £1 billion. So, if the running fee is £100 million a year, that represents about 2 percent of the total that the state provides or arranges."

He was clearly wobbling. "Well, we can look at the rates again in regulations. I can withdraw and leave the gloves on the table."

Later I met with Tony Newton and Norman Fowler (another former Conservative Secretary of State responsible for Social Security). Iain joined us. Norman Fowler explained: "There's great concern over the use of Financial Privilege and that it forms some kind of precedent. It's got caught up, unfortunately, with the concerns people have about the moves to abolish the Lords."

Iain replied: "The truth is that we applied Privilege because this is an absolutely key Bill at a pretty extraordinary time. It doesn't set a precedent for other Bills or for future Social Security Bills."

Norman Fowler concluded: "Well, if David could make that clear that would be extremely useful."

The Bishops were clearly very uncomfortable at their central role in attacking the Benefit Cap. I felt somewhat guilty for encouraging them through my responses in Committee, particularly as the concessions that the Treasury eventually accepted were quite different; a grace period of nine months and more discretionary payments for Local Authorities to dispense. I explained: "You've got between the Coalition and Labour on what will be a major battle ground for the next election."

James Bell, the Bishop of Ripon and Leeds, divulged: "We've had thousands of emails abusing us".

"Can I give you some advice?" I suggested. "Why don't you just declare victory? The concessions we've given add up to £110 million in the first year, compared with your £120 million proposal, and our approach will help people right across the piece, while the child benefit proposal just lifts a third out of the impact."

James Bell responded: "We're very concerned about the language all this is being conducted in, with all this abuse of scroungers."

I assured him: "I'm happy to say what I really think when we get to the Chamber, which is that the State sets expectation in the way that it establishes and runs a benefit system and we've given out the message to too many that dependency is acceptable."

Bill McKenzie suggested that we write the Bill in a way that would allow regulations to extend the one-year time limit on receiving the WRAG. "I can see that you will want to impose a one-year limit on the WRAG, but couldn't the Bill be phrased to allow it to be longer if the regulations are changed."

I replied: "We'll look at it". This was a concession that the Treasury accepted with alacrity.

The Department had done a deal on cancer sufferers. I told Narendra Patel: "We've reached agreement with Macmillan on the three issues of how cancer sufferers get into the Support Group, how they switch into it from the WRAG if they deteriorate and how they can stay in it if they have problems and I'm prepared to spell all that out."

He replied: "On that basis I'll be happy to withdraw my amendment."

Molly Meacher was equally helpful over her late Third Reading amendment to our simplification of disability rates in Universal Credit. I promised: "I'll have a close look at the definitions of child DLA in a reasonable period, probably three years to allow the option of us looking at it in the context of the introduction of a child PIP."

I did less well with Richard Best over the spare bedrooms. I told him:

"The best thing I can offer is to do really comprehensive research on what's happening in social housing. That way we'll know what the problems are and will be in a position to work with the Treasury on how to solve a specific problem."

Richard Best replied: "Well that's one idea, but I am under terrific pressure to come up with an amendment which protects people." Two days later he emailed that he was not going to accept the research approach.

So I was reasonably confident that we would dispose of most of the issues in the first round of ping pong. This was the process (which I had first experienced – and described – from the Opposition perspective in October 2009) by which the Commons and Lords settled on the same version of the Bill. The Commons would accept or reject Lords amendments and Ping the Bill back to the Lords who would consider those that had been rejected and either accept the Commons position; propose an alternative amendment to pong back; or insist on – and therefore also pong back – the original amendment. The use of Financial Privilege effectively cut off the last of the three options – as Tom Strathclyde, Leader of the House, explained to the Chamber. [75]

"The only effect of the Privilege reason is to send the signal that it is unprofitable for the Lords to persist with amendments in lieu on the same lines as the original," he explained. I was grateful that he took on the task of explaining our use of Financial Privilege ahead of the main business of the day.

Tom summarised: "On the Welfare Reform Bill, the Commons authorities found that Privilege was engaged in 46 of the 110 Lords amendments. The Government asked the Commons to agree to 35 of those 46 amendments and to reject the remaining 11.

"In agreeing to those 35 Lords amendments, each a concession to this House, the Commons waived its Financial Privilege for more than £300 million of public expenditure. Therefore, we are really talking only about the remaining 11 Lords amendments, which, on policy grounds, the Government could not accept and which they asked the House of Commons to reject. When the Commons voted to reject each of those amendments, the only reason it could cite was Privilege."

Tom closed by referring to the issue of reforming the House of Lords. "This House should be reformed only if it can be more assertive, stronger and better able to hold the Government to account and if it can challenge the views of the House of Commons. Otherwise, why on earth would we bother with all of this?"

I picked up the point when I took over from Tom.

"I want to pick up on the comment made by my Noble Friend: why would we bother with all this? I am considering all the work that has been done on this Bill, and as I look around noble Lords I can see that the most astonishing amount of energy has been put into this Bill through its Committee and Report stages.

"I have seen a lot of changes in this Bill as a direct result of that work. I shall name a few of those changes because it is easy to forget what we have done with this Bill.

"On ESA time-limiting, we accepted the need to make amendments to protect those with degenerative conditions. On the Benefit Cap, we have put in a nine-month grace period and exempted those in the Support Group of ESA, again in response to debates in this House.

"On PIP, we have made a number of changes to the required-period condition and have restored the mobility component for those in residential homes. Within Universal Credit, we have put in £300 million a year to afford additional childcare. That all added up in this Spending Review period to £638 million. Looked at as an ongoing cost when Universal Credit is introduced, it amounts to an extra £518 million per annum in a steady state.

"Each of those concessions was made as a direct result of the debates that we had in this House. I think, bluntly, there was a point at which the Government decided they could not afford any more. The cost of the amendments that we sent through would have been £2.1 billion in this Spending Review period."

The concession strategy held. Molly Meacher accepted the review on children; Ruth Lister withdrew without concession on her measure to protect youngsters flowing onto contributory ESA; Narendra Patel also withdrew following our agreement on cancer sufferers. On the time limit for ESA, I accepted Bill McKenzie's amendments.

His response was characteristically double-edged: "I am very grateful to the Minister for his acceptance of those amendments. He helped to draft them so he should accept them."

There was a wobble over the Benefit Cap. James Bell, the Bishop of Ripon and Leeds, declared victory, as agreed: "I am very grateful for the substantial government response to the earlier amendment, not least for that promise of an evaluation of the cap after a year of its operation."

On this issue, Bill McKenzie was less easy to please. He presented a complicated proposal to regionalise the cap, a strictly political move to preserve the idea that Labour was for the popular Benefit Cap, albeit not this version of it.

The Lords saw through this pretty fast, with Tony Newton pointing out: "Housing costs do not vary on a regional basis or even on a district or city or borough basis; they vary on a street-by-street basis. Is that what the noble Lord has in mind? If so, it would become a complete administrative nightmare. He needs to think very carefully before pressing this particular line, whatever its intellectual attractions."

Bill McKenzie lost the vote handsomely (134–223).

Luckily, when it came to child support, James Mackay was on holiday and his position was taken by the more emollient Tim Boswell. I proposed pushing the issue of charging forward into the regulations. I also committed to hold public consultations and involve Peers fully in the process, as well as publishing a review within 30 months of the measure's introduction.

It was enough. Tim Boswell concluded: "We can now have a constructive discussion which will lead to a satisfactory outcome."

Richard Best was still holding out on the spare rooms, however. He put in an alternative amendment protecting tenants who were not expected to work – such as the disabled, carers and mothers with young children – where there was no alternative accommodation. He won the vote he called, but rather narrowly (236–226). It went back to the Commons.

Here there was no sign of wavering among the Coalition backbenchers and the measure was overturned in line with the Government's majority (316–263). This left nowhere for Richard to go and we reverted to the offer I made to him originally of thorough research on the impact of the measure. In the Chamber I committed: "We will carry out research on this measure, once it has been introduced, to understand the effects of the changes, but I do not see the need to put that in the Bill."

The Bill was through. We had got Universal Credit across the line, while the Chancellor had got his cuts. It was rather too much of a burden for one person to carry, however.

On the day the Bill received Royal assent, 8 March 2012, I could feel the acid building in my stomach. By mid-morning on Monday, four days later, my oesophagus was clenching and I had to go home, where I spent the rest of the week, till the drugs began to work. I had, almost literally, bitten off more than I could comfortably chew.

My ill-health had not been triggered solely by the stress of taking the legislation through the public arena of the Lords. At the same time, behind the scenes, the problems of building the new benefit system were mounting. We now turn back 15 months to follow this story from the outset.

PART VI

AGILE

November 2010 – December 2012

CHAPTER 15

Digital by Default

"I can't get money out of my account," I explained over the phone to the banking official.

"I'm afraid it's frozen. You'll have to go into your branch to unfreeze it."

"Why?"

"I'm not at liberty to say," he replied curtly.

It was an inconvenience I ceased resenting when my bank manager explained that a fraudster had captured my unused telephone identity and the bank had intervened to block his attempt to transfer funds from my account. It reinforced for me the importance of building security into Universal Credit. We would be creating Universal Credit on a digital platform, which meant the systems for preventing fraud would need to be at least as effective as those of my bank.

The 'digital' decision emerged over the first half-year. The Green Paper in July 2010 described customers making a single application. "The claims process would be as simple as possible and would build on existing plans within the Department for Work and Pensions to develop full online services." [76] It seemed an obvious approach and I welcomed it without needing specific briefing.

By the November White Paper, the approach was explicit. The Department would "make extensive use of online technology to allow people to better manage their claim and understand the benefits of entering paid work." [77]

The White Paper explained: "The introduction of Universal Credit provides the opportunity to transform the delivery of in and out-of-work benefits into a service fit for the 21st century. The Government's principles of increasing access to online services and maximising service efficiency lie at the heart of our delivery proposals for Universal Credit."

In this, the Department was echoing Government policy. Less than a fortnight after the White Paper was published, Martha Lane Fox, the UK 'Digital Champion', put out her Report stating: "Shifting to digital-only services has huge cost-saving potential. Directgov should be the default platform for information and transactional services, enabling all Government transactions to be carried out via digital channels by 2015." [78] Francis Maude, the Minister for the Cabinet Office, responded in a press release whose title included the evocative – and prescriptive – phrase 'digital by default'. He announced: "We will use digital technology to drive better services and lower costs." [79]

Work on building the system began as soon as the White Paper was published. Four months later, in early March 2011, I assembled the team to discuss my security concerns. I described my banking fraud problem to them. "I'm sure this happens to thousands of people and the bank has systems to catch it. When I look at Universal Credit it has all the same security issues as a bank. It's fine for people to make their initial applications online; but if we allow people to go in again to change their details – or find out what they're going to be paid – it's just like online banking. Fraudsters from all over the world will try to get in to divert the funds.

"So the question I've got is: what are we doing about cyber-fraud and online security?"

There was an uncomfortable silence. Malcolm Whitehouse, the director of IT for the project, confessed: "We've not had to do this before and we need to make better arrangements. We'll come back to you on how we're going to tackle it." It took months for answers to start to emerge. Meanwhile I was mollified to see that cyber-fraud now became registered as one of the major risks for the programme.

Malcolm had moved with great speed to get the IT part of the programme under way. This meant that implementation began in parallel with the legislative process described in the previous chapter. Indeed, we held the first formal meeting on implementation a week before the White Paper was published in November 2010. He told me: "We're going to develop the IT on an Agile basis."

"What does that mean?" I asked.

"It's what they've been doing in the private sector for the last ten years or so. It means that we develop the IT in bite-sized chunks and test it out as we go. That means it's much more flexible than the waterfall approach, which we traditionally use. With the waterfall you take the full specification, from which you build the whole thing in one go, which can take years. Then you test the complete system and hope it works."

"It sounds pretty attractive," I told him. "We don't know the way users will react to a lot of this, so if we can test as we go we'll really reduce our risk. We're a long way off building a full specification in any case. Who's going to do the work?"

"We'll be using our traditional suppliers: IBM, HP and Accenture. We've got long-standing contracts with them."

"Do they know how to do it in an Agile way?"

"They're up for it. They know that Agile is the future for IT development."

It was with some relief that I heard this plan. The White Paper had laid out a time-table to introduce Universal Credit from October 2013, with completion of the transfer over the subsequent four years. In 2010 that seemed an eternity away but I was all too aware that much of the time would be eaten up by legislation. A full specification could only be produced on completion of the regulations – which would lay out the detailed design of the structure – and the earliest they could be ready would be sometime in 2012 (in the event the timetable slipped to the end of that year). Either way, that left precious little time to build a traditional waterfall project.

I had anyway been pleased that the Department had come up with a time-table that mirrored the one produced for me by Vocalink. Now I could see that the planned adoption of Agile methodology must have been a key factor underpinning that time-table, since it meant we would be able to start building sooner than I had envisaged. Any concerns I might have had were dispelled by the avuncular confidence of Joe Harley, overall head of IT for the Department, who was also being appointed the Government's Chief Information Officer.

In an interview in the trade press a few months later he described how the welfare reform agenda would help the public sector "achieve more participation and engagement with the public by relying on a more agile delivery of ICT (Information and Communications Technology) with the increased adoption and provision of more online transactional services." [80]

Later, when a slipping time-table came under retrospective scrutiny, the question came up as to whether Iain or I had put the Department under pressure at the outset to launch in 2013. I was not conscious of any such pressure, although the officials would have been all too aware of the timing of the next election. The paper I wrote with Vocalink support was also explicit in anticipating a 2013 launch. In retrospect it seems to me that a politically convenient time-table was accepted too easily by officials who did not adequately understand the challenge that was being set. Once the time-table became public, Iain became adamant that we should stick to it.

The Department saw change at the top over the year end. Leigh Lewis, the Permanent Secretary, retired and Iain selected as his replacement Robert Devereux, who had been running the Department of Transport. He had spent six years of his career at the Department, so was hardly coming in cold. Iain told me: "They didn't expect me to pick him. He's very bright and a bit different. You'll like him." Iain was right. I found Robert to be lively, clever and effective in marshalling a team round him.

The other major change was the appointment of Terry Moran as the Senior Responsible Owner (or SRO) of Universal Credit. Over the previous decade the Civil Service had developed a dual control structure for managing projects. The SRO function had been introduced to take responsibility for ensuring that projects met their overall objectives. Alongside was the Programme Director, with day by day responsibility for running the project, a role taken in the early months by Chris Hayes from within the Department. The way that these two leaders interacted was clearly central to the outcome of projects and there was no clear delineation of the two roles. The SRO could be anything from the full-time executive leader of a project to a part-time chairman figure monitoring the performance of the Programme Director.

Terry's appointment was clearly conceived in the former – more involved – mode. He had joined the Department as a school leaver, steadily working his way up. Now he was Chief Executive of the Pensions, Disability and Carers Service, responsible for more than half the benefits paid out by the Department. It was one of Leigh Lewis' last personnel decisions before his departure. "David, I know Universal Credit is the biggest challenge this Department faces and in Terry I've given you the best of the best."

My first formal meeting with Terry took place at the end of November 2010, a day before he formally switched into his new role. He took me through his plans in some detail.

"Your UC Programme Board is too big," I told him. "You've got 23 people on it. That's a talking shop, not a decision-making body. I think when you see Iain you should be suggesting a plan to get it down to say nine."

"Thanks for the indication," he replied carefully. He struck me as earnest and hard-working, clearly focused on the fine detail of the challenge ahead.

We also needed to make sure that Stephen Brien was fully involved. He had been seconded from management consultants Oliver Wyman over the period of the Green and White Papers. Now that Universal Credit had got the go-ahead, he would be invaluable in the process of detailed development over the next couple of years.

"I'm feeling pretty guilty about taking two years leave of absence when Oliver Wyman thought they were investing in a position in Universal Credit," Stephen told me.

"I completely understand that," I told him. "You took a calculated risk that it would work out and in practice it has come to this outcome. We should make a direct request of Oliver Wyman. Tell them Universal Credit is too important for us not to use the resource you represent."

In the event, my attempts to reach an amicable agreement with the consultancy got nowhere and Stephen cut his links with Oliver Wyman to become an Expert Adviser to the Department. He was to become my eyes and ears as to how the programme was being implemented, albeit at the cost of some suspicion from the civil service establishment.

Terry commissioned the consultants McKinsey to help work out who should deliver Universal Credit. This was a live question since major elements were currently managed by three different organisations. DWP ran the out-of-work benefits, HMRC the in-work tax credits and 380 Local Authorities delivered housing benefit.

"We've concluded that if we're going to hit the time-table the only realistic option is for delivery by DWP, with face-to-face service continuing to take place in Jobcentres," Terry told me. "After 2017 we can look at other models, like using external providers."

With the Report stage of the Pensions Bill safely navigated, in April 2011 Malcolm Whitehouse took me up to the Agile hothouse just outside the northern town of Warrington, at the Birchwood business park.

"It's conveniently placed to get staff together from all over the country," he explained as we entered a large modern office block and went up in the lift. His ebullient deputy, Steve Dover, Director for Major Programmes, took us through progress when we got upstairs.

"As you know, we're doing this on an Agile basis, so we build it up in stages, which we call Leaps. Each of the Leaps are made up with short intensive Sprints of a fortnight or so. We reckon we'll need five Leaps in total before we launch in October 2013, and we'll need more afterwards. We started Leap One in February and we plan to finish it in a couple of months, so you're here as we get stuck into the detail of its content. The Leaps will speed up as we get going.

"The way we're doing it is through individual stories for people going through the Universal Credit system. We start with the simpler stories, individuals with standard requirements, for example. Then we'll build up the stories to include couples with more and more complex situations."

Malcolm added: "We've got about 190 stories to do over the Leaps."

Steve Dover said: "Let's go and see them elaborating the first story."

He led us through the large open-plan area, with walls lined with white-boards and post-it notes, into one of the large conference rooms. Here the team was assembled in a rectangle of desks facing a large screen. The team was made up of around 20 people from the various contractors and DWP operations staff. We sat to one side as they worked through the 'story'. (No doubt it was as much a demonstration for the visitors as a genuine exercise.)

Up on the screen 'Tom' was working through his application for Univ-ersal Credit. "Now 'Tom' doesn't need support for his housing, but we'll still need his address so we can identify him," explained the session leader. " 'Tom' also needs to tell us what his last job was and when it stopped."

One of the team interjected: "Won't we know that from the real-time feed?"

"Not while he's making the initial application."

For the rest of the hour, the team picked the process apart from various perspectives. It became quite clear to me that the precision involved in building the software was critical in translating Universal Credit's broad-brush policy objectives into reality. I determined to visit as often as possible.

A month later I was back in the conference room to see the team elaborating the application process for a couple. We watched as 'Liam' and 'Yasmin' negotiated the process of making a joint claim.

"One of them starts the process and fills in their details, then the other takes over and completes their part of the application process."

"What happens if 'Liam' refuses to complete his part? Let's say he won't agree to all the conditionality."

"We can either stop the application entirely or let 'Yasmin' continue as a single applicant." The session leader looked over to me. "I guess that's going to be a policy decision."

"What does it mean to 'be a couple'?" I asked.

"We put information tags next to anything that people might want more information on, so they can just check."

"Yes, but this one is pretty vague – about living together like a couple."

"That's because it's not a phrase defined in law. It's based on hundreds of pages of case law which are impossible to summarise."

Later in the morning one of the contractors took me through a mock-up of a possible add-on to the system.

"On this page we're summarising your level of earnings and how much Universal Credit you're entitled to. The two together show the total amount you've got to live on this month. Then we add this option so you can look at what would happen if you earned some more. You put in the extra hours in this space and the programme tells you how much the total you've got to live on goes up."

"I like that," I responded. "We should try to include it, if we can."

Back in London I told Stephen Brien. "Make sure you spend as much time as you can in Warrington. The officials here can theorise about policy as much as they want. They are building the system up there, making the detailed decisions on how it actually operates."

He went up with Iain to visit in mid-June and came back convinced. "I got my moment of epiphany when you told me that the system was actually being built in Warrington. When I got there last week, I found out they were doing exactly that."

By now the team had begun to focus on the issues of security. They employed a consultant from Detica, one of the leading firms in the field, to advise on how best to set up the defences for Universal Credit.

When we met, Richard Dykes explained the critical elements to secure the system against fraud. "In particular you will need to make sure that Universal Credit is able to cross-check what applicants say against all the other systems with information about them. You need to create data links with all kinds of systems – private and public – credit reference agencies, the land registry, motor vehicle licensing and so on."

"Do we have powers to do that?" I asked. It was a murky area. The short answer seemed to be that while we had considerable powers, each connection would need to be justified on an individual basis.

Stephen Brien and I were beginning to worry about the organisation of the project, which seemed to lack drive and focus. We couldn't pinpoint who was specifically responsible for delivering various components of the plan.

"They still haven't got a structure that really makes sure that people are forced to deliver," Stephen observed to me. "They need someone in charge of marketing, or what the product is; someone for delivering the IT like Malcolm Whitehouse, but he's spread too thin; and someone to manage the organisation and the transition."

I replied: "I'd like to see those people in an organogram with smiling faces and job descriptions on my wall. And the other thing I want to see is a top expert responsible for cyber-security. Not seconded in, but with his whole career depending on it."

I talked over our concerns with Robert Devereux, the Permanent Secretary. It was a prickly conversation.

"Have you been talking to Stephen? Have you told Terry this?"

"Yes, I have talked to Stephen and no, I haven't been able to talk to Terry yet. Anyway, I thought it was only right that I should talk to you first." After he calmed down, he agreed that our proposals were in line with how he was reshaping the Department.

Terry Moran was now firmly in the saddle and in June 2011 he set about re-organising the operation. Malcom Whitehouse was promoted to Programme Director, taking over from Chris Hayes. The Programme Board was re-organised and shrunk, albeit only modestly. At least more senior people were now on it. In effect the IT Department strengthened its position, with Joe Harley (overall head of IT) joining Malcolm Whitehouse on the Board. However, the other two positions in which Stephen and I wanted strong characters remained less well focused. In particular, the job of shaping the product, Service Design, was reserved for a senior official who would not be able to start work for another eight months.

Terry asked me to join the new Board. At the first meeting, in late June, he presented me: "David is here as one of the Board, and has been proposed because of what he has got to add."

"I know this is somewhat unusual," I told them. "I need to make it clear that I am not sitting formally as a Minister, but on even terms with other Board members." Traditionally Ministers do not sit on implementation Boards, given the convention that the politicians deliver instructions which the Board delivers. In a re-organisation as all-encompassing as the introduction of Universal Credit, however, it was already clear that the conventional three-way separation between political demand, policy design and operational implementation had broken down. If the political demands were to be deliverable in this instance, they needed to reflect the day-by-day reality of processes on the ground. My presence would not work if everything I said was taken as an instruction.

The re-organisation took a toll on Stephen's relationship with the civil service. He joked: "They tell me I've got 'psychological problems'," meaning that the team resented his access to Iain and me.

"Well don't fix them. It's vital you keep the information flowing to us."

With the Lords stages of the Welfare Bill looming, I was becoming increasingly concerned at the way that Universal Credit policy was being developed. I told both Robert Devereux and Terry Moran that we needed to change our approach.

"When we had lots of separate benefits it might have made sense to have a number of separate teams working on them, each in its own silo. That way the team could concentrate its expertise and when people moved on it was relatively straight-forward for a newcomer to pick up the brief – especially if there was good documentation.

"That's not going to work with Universal Credit. The team needs to be able to understand the full width of the benefit system and that means that silos won't work. You need a unit of officials – pretty senior ones, too – to cover the whole of Universal Credit. I call it a 'mash' unit."

Robert responded by promoting one of his smartest officials to take on the challenge. Paul McComb took up the role of Deputy Director, Welfare Policy, in June. He proved to have acute antennae as to how the wind was blowing – among politicians as well as civil servants. He was soon setting up a series of meetings with me and his team – each of them focused on an area of Universal Credit, but working closely together. Through June I joined a series of workshops on some of the most problematic areas: how would conditionality work; how should we treat various forms of income; what should be our policy on the self-employed?

It allowed us to write the policy notes for the Lords, but I could see that much greater detail would be needed for the detailed regulations.

Iain was broadly content to let me get on with moulding the shape of the benefit. Occasionally he would develop a bee in his bonnet.

"Everyone needs to pay their own rent," he declared at a meeting he called to discuss the support we provided for housing. "If you're in a job you pay your own rent and Universal Credit should be no different – whether you're in social housing or private housing."

"Absolutely," I proceeded to disagree. "That will be the default. We just need to make sure there's an effective fall-back if people are simply not able to." The previous Labour Government had moved to 'direct payments' for private sector tenants, but around 24 percent of the more vulnerable still relied on 'managed payments' directly from Local Authorities to landlords. Since the social sector tenants were by and large more vulnerable than private sector tenants, I reckoned that the fall-back would be needed by about a third of tenants. Iain repeated his point a couple of times, but in the end did not respond to my counter-proposal. I had learned this was his favoured way of indicating that he would not oppose my strategy.

Sometimes Government processes proved absolutely immovable, even if they were ludicrous.

"Why," I asked the financial control team, "does the total cost of the Universal Credit business case include both our capital expenditure as well as all the depreciation? That's simply double counting."

"That's how the Treasury want us to prepare it. It's based on international accounting standards."

When I saw the Treasury team, they told me that they were bound by the accounting standard, even if it represented double counting.

"All we're doing is building in a bias against capital in public projects, which cannot make sense," I told them. Despite my exasperation, I did not have time to take the issue any further.

As in the previous year, we were too busy to take much holiday through the 2011 summer recess period and were in and out of the Department through August. In early September we gathered in Iain's room in the Commons to take stock of Universal Credit's progress through the summer. In particular we wanted to know how well planning was progressing for the Leaps – the stages in the system build.

A full cast of officials were present. As well as Terry Moran (the SRO), Malcom Whitehouse (Programme Director) and Neil Couling (head of benefits policy) were facing us across the wide beech table in Iain's office. Terry told us: "We've reduced Leap 2 from 28 percent of the total build to 21 percent." There was silence. This represented a cut of a quarter in the planned activity for the period.

He hurried on: "I am absolutely comfortable that this is the right thing to do and that we are still on track."

Iain reacted with cold fury: "I've got No. 10 and the Treasury on my back worried that we can do this to time and if we come up with a shortfall like this there'll be no holding them. Our lives will be absolute misery and that means your lives. You have got to get a way of getting most of it back."

Afterwards, when the officials had left, he held me back: "They're taking holidays at this critical period and as a result we're now late. It's the civil service mentality. If this was the private sector all holidays would be stopped when you're doing a key project at a critical time. I want you to work closely with Stephen to get the figures sorted on this."

Later that afternoon, when I met Malcolm, I told him: "Boost Leap 2 to 25 percent somehow and then leave a final shortfall of 3 percent due to policy delays, which Iain will be able to justify."

The timing was all the more dangerous since the programme was facing its second external review by the Major Projects Authority. The first had been a cursory 'Starting Gate' review six months earlier, which found that the programme had made an 'impressively strong start". [81] The second was likely to be far less complimentary given the delay. I discovered that the figures showing the full 7 percent shortfall had already been circulated to the Board, which meant they would be available to the MPA, so our attempts to recoup the shortfall were redundant.

In mid-October I hosted a group of journalists on a trip to Warrington. After going through the Agile approach and 'Tom' story-line, they quizzed me on the concerns that No. 10 and the Treasury had about the programme.

"The plans are on time and on budget," I assured them. "It's right that Downing Street is following this key reform closely. This is the most radical redesign of the welfare system since its creation and we are taking an equally radical approach to the design and build of technology to deliver it."

The report by the Major Projects Authority team was delivered to Terry in November 2011. It scored the project Amber/Red and expressed serious concerns about the strength of the management team.

The Major Projects Authority - or MPA - had been formally established by Francis Maude eight months earlier, as a joint undertaking of the Treasury and Cabinet Office. It was designed to beef up the review of Government projects, based on the recommendations of David Pitchford, an Australian who had been the Chief Operating Officer of the Melbourne Commonwealth Games in 2006 and was brought over to become the first Chief Executive of the MPA. Its teeth derived from the mandatory nature of its involvement and the way Treasury funding was tied to compliance with its recommendations. In this early period it was building its operational approach and personnel.

It used a traffic light rating system for projects. At least it had not scored Universal Credit as Red - which meant that successful delivery was unachievable. Amber/Red meant that successful delivery of Universal Credit was in doubt, "with major risks or issues apparent in a number of key areas."

Philippa told me: "I heard that Jeremy Heywood's view at No. 10 is that the rating for Universal Credit is going to remain as red as Lenin's underpants till the day it starts operating. That's because it's such a complex project."

From his role as Minister for the Cabinet Office, Francis Maude was to have a major impact on the Universal Credit project, both in its set-up phase and later, when it ran into difficulties. He had become a junior minister in the Thatcher Government in his early thirties, although there had been a hiatus to his political career when he lost his Parliamentary seat in 1992. I first ran into him a couple of years later, when he was working for the American investment bank, Morgan Stanley. Then, we were engaged in a complicated dance over the mandate to float Railtrack (which I describe in my book on the City). [82]

Back in Parliament in 2005, Francis became Chairman of the Conservative Party and was closely associated with the successful leadership takeover by David Cameron. Improving the efficiency of Government now became his central purpose and, in Government again, he pursued the goal with real intensity. In meetings he could prove ferocious in driving towards a particular objective and he was deeply suspicious of the motivations of particular groups of civil servants. He could be single-minded and very focused when pushing through one of his projects, some-times failing to see a wider picture. With a domed forehead enhanced by his swept-back hairstyle, I found him approachable and good company when we didn't have a particular issue between us.

The establishment of the Major Projects Authority was only one of the ways the Cabinet Office, under his direction, was assembling the struc-tures to control Departmental projects. All significant IT expenditure had to be cleared by the Cabinet Office. A year earlier Francis was already telling the Conservative Conference: "We've reviewed over 300 Govern-ment projects worth nearly £3 billion, and we've stopped over £1 billion." [83]

He had also served notice on the IT industry that the big contracts to which they were accustomed were on the way out. At the end of 2010 he told an audience of key Government suppliers, including BT, Hewlett Packard, IBM and CapGemini: "The days of the mega IT contracts are over, we will need you to rethink the way you approach projects, making them smaller, off the shelf and open source where possible." [84]

The Department had, so far, stayed on the right side of this particular pronouncement. Francis visited Warrington shortly after my trip with the journalists to see the way we were building the new system. In a doc-ument published by the Cabinet Office a few months later, in the spring of 2012, Universal Credit was still being held up as an exemplar, despite the MPA review. "Universal Credit, currently the largest ICT programme in Government, continues to innovate on the application of Agile prin-ciples at the level of a major programme." [85]

There was one other area in which the Cabinet Office were keen to see progress. Malcolm Whitehouse explained it to me at one of our regular meetings. "They want to set up a market in identity assurance."

"How would that work?"

"Instead of each individual having to establish their identity with each internet service they want to use, they would establish their identity with an independent service provider, who would then be able to verify them and transfer them onto Universal Credit, or any other internet service which adopted the system. Individuals could choose which service provider to use."

"Sounds clever; it would cut out all these damn passwords I have to remember. Does it add to our risks?"

"Given our time-table we'll need to be the first to adopt it, so we'll have to get on with organising it pretty rapidly. Our back-up is to provide our own gateway, which will be more expensive."

Malcom responded to the MPA review by arranging to put in a deputy to take control of end-to-end programme planning. But while the management team was being strengthened at this level, it had just been weakened elsewhere. A month earlier Robert Devereux had told me: "I've decided to appoint Terry as the Chief Operations Officer for the Department. Don't worry; he'll still be the SRO for Universal Credit."

"Won't that be too much for one person?"

Robert explained his rationale: "Universal Credit will transform the way that this Department works, so it makes sense for the same person to be responsible for operations and UC. That way we will make sure that the system we develop will translate smoothly into operational mode." However much this might have made sense, it was inevitable that Terry would move from the executive leader model of SRO to that of part-time chairman. Indeed, my impression in the following months was that he didn't have time to do much more for Universal Credit than chair the regular Programme Boards.

The second blow was the loss of Paul McComb from his job of running the Universal Credit policy team – my 'mash' unit. Here I was outgunned by Iain, whose Principal Private Secretary, John-Paul Marks, had been transferred by Robert into Operations. Iain selected Paul to replace him and all I could do was moan: "Just as you've got on top of the policy issues, you're sugaring off and I'll have to start all over again."

"Don't worry, David, I'll be just down the corridor to help out," Paul replied cheerfully. Paul was to play a major role in the future battles to make Universal Credit a reality. However, it was to be another three years before I again felt comfortable that we had a coherent overview of Universal Credit policy coming from the Department.

Slowly Universal Credit was assembling a capability in securing the system against cyber and other forms of fraud. Bob Lovett was appointed head of security and was building a team around him. He told me he was working on two main initiatives. The Integrated Risk and Intelligence Service – IRIS for short – was designed to counter fraud by individuals by cross checking with other data sources. As for the second initiative, Bob told me: "To counter cyber-fraud I'm looking at putting in a powerful new system. We don't just have to stop the hackers breaching the perimeter; we have to have levels of defence inside the system itself. It's the equivalent of the Tower of London with its outer and inner walls. We're calling that system Cerberus." Cerberus was the three-headed dog guarding the entrance to the underworld in Greek mythology. It seemed an apt enough analogy.

I had been invited to a Government-wide meeting on cyber strategy in July 2011, chaired by the Foreign Secretary, William Hague, in the Cabinet Office's Cobra meeting room. I rather disrupted the cosy consensus around the proposition that the Government needed to work on an integrated strategy to face the threats. Feeling like an interloper among the experts in cyber warfare I told them: "The strategy is too slow for us. We have a hard stop in October 2013 and we need the Government to introduce particular initiatives on the distributed hub and identity assurance which will cost £63 million. Otherwise we'll have to adopt a less effective defence for ourselves."

William Hague elegantly disguised his surprise, saying: "It looks as if there should be a sub-committee on this."

Francis Maude responded: "Absolutely and I'm happy to run with it."

When I saw the incoming Permanent Secretary of the Cabinet Office, Ian Watmore, in December at a meeting of Universal Credit's Senior Sponsorship Group, I returned to the issue.

"I'm particularly concerned that the general Government progress on cyber fraud is on our time-table, particularly since we have now had to take the decision to act as pathfinder in this area," I complained.

Ian Watmore deflected me elegantly: "That's not quite how I recall the history."

"Well, let's not go over history," I responded. "Are you satisfied that the arrangements now in place are adequate for us to have an integrated Government cyber fraud strategy?"

"Yes, we are recruiting strongly and have people wandering around in flip-flops like a proper Google office."

In the interstices of time left while I was buried in the Bill, I made good my resolution to see the top 20 or so members of the Universal Credit team on a face to face basis before the end of the 2011. Malcolm Whitehouse joined me at the meetings. "I want to see an organogram of their faces pinned up on my wall, with their responsibilities laid out," I told him. We went through each of their roles and what they were responsible for, individual by individual. It was clearly a useful process – for him as well as for me. I never did get my organogram, though. The culture of ownership in the Civil Service was heavily diluted by the rapid turnover of personnel.

Stephen was following my instruction to spend time in Warrington. In November he told me: "I'm going up to Warrington to go through each of the stories in Leap 2, to see if they hang together."

"Hasn't anybody done that?"

"Doesn't look like it."

I lamented the loss of Paul McComb: "That's what we need a 'mash unit' for: to understand the system as a whole. I'm still worried that I haven't had any policy issues coming back up to me for reconsideration because they don't work in practice."

Stephen offered some back-handed reassurance: "Don't worry; we're getting something for you on contributory benefits not working as part of Universal Credit."

"Ouch, I won't like that."

Many more things that I wouldn't like were about to emerge.

CHAPTER 16

Timetable under Pressure

On my behalf, Stephen Brien was watching closely what was happening with the development of Universal Credit. His input was all the more valuable in the period in which I was effectively buried steering the Welfare Reform Bill through the Lords. He came in to see me in December 2011 to report: "We're coming under real pressure from the contractors to delay the launch by six months."

It was my first confirmation that some of the set-up problems were going to necessitate adjusting our ambitions. I told him: "We need to work through the detail of the programme to establish what is realistic. That's the key job for Malcolm's new deputy."

My attitude to the time-table was that it should be kept tight to maintain pressure on the team to deliver. It could be carefully relaxed when absolutely required. I was to discover that my private sector approach on this was deeply flawed. In the political arena a time-table change was a gift to any Opposition politician needing to claim Government incompetence.

Apart from my concern over the lack of feedback from Warrington, I was genuinely surprised that autumn to discover that the team there was not actually building the system. "Once we've elaborated it," Malcolm explained, "we send it over to India where they do the actual coding."

"That doesn't sound particularly Agile," I told him.

"With a big project like this it's the most efficient way of doing it," he assured me.

Martha Lane Fox had come to visit in mid-November. I knew her from my City days, when she was preparing lastminute.com (of which she was joint owner) for a stock market listing. She was still limping heavily from a car accident seven years earlier in which she had been badly injured.

She was keen for me to get close to Mike Bracken, who was setting up the Government Digital Service. "He's a good guy," she told me. "Could you please see him as soon as possible? You'll like him."

I saw Mike within a month when he dropped by my office for a courtesy visit. Francis Maude had appointed him the Executive Director of Digital in the summer and now he was busy building the scale and capability of the Government Digital Service. He assured me that he was available to help me and the team implement Universal Credit successfully.

The next time I saw him was less relaxed. Francis Maude asked me to come into the Cabinet Office immediately after the New Year recess in January 2012. It was an early morning meeting which I attended with Steve Dover. Francis was sitting on an armchair with his two recent IT appointments, Mike Bracken and Liam Maxwell, lined up on the couch. (Liam was in charge of IT 'Futures' in the Cabinet Office.) It smelled like the ambush that it was.

Coldly Francis stated: "We agreed a common timetable on the introduction of a Government-wide identity service and the next thing we see is an advertisement for Identity Assurance services from DWP, which we had to stop. What on earth is going on?"

It took me a bit of time to work out that the Universal Credit team had fouled up. I needed to avoid diverting blame to Steve Dover, so I had to capitulate pretty completely.

"Well, as you know I am driving the team pretty hard to keep to a really demanding schedule and it looks as if someone may have been over-zealous." After a little toing and froing, I was able to agree that we would put out a joint advertisement.

"We now have an agreed 8-week timetable to get a cross-Government position and I am most happy to abide by that."

"Wow," breathed Steve Dover afterwards. "We were lucky to get out with our skins."

The advertisement did go out in early March 2012 but the incident left a difficult legacy between the DWP and Cabinet Office.

In February the Department organised a trip for the senior Universal Credit team, including Iain, to GCHQ – the Government Communications Headquarters – in Cheltenham. We were taken round the facilities and given a vivid picture of the extensive, international nature of the cyber-fraud business. At the mid-morning wrap-up session, the GCHQ team warned us that Universal Credit would be under sustained attack and that we would be the first of the Government's digital systems to face the challenge.

Iain asked whether GCHQ could take over responsibility for our security. The GCHQ Director, Iain Lobban, replied: "That's not within our central scope, nor do we have a budget for it."

I suggested: "I think we need to make sure we have the appropriate Government-wide governance for this, which should include DWP, HMRC, Cabinet Office and GCHQ. Then we can develop the right operating arms under it."

Iain Duncan Smith joked: "We wouldn't have started Universal Credit if we knew all this was coming at us." Nobody laughed.

Shortly afterwards Liam Maxwell came to my office, ostensibly to discuss real-time information but actually to express his concerns about the Integrated Risk and Intelligence Service – IRIS. This was one of the two systems that Bob Lovett was developing, designed to cross-check benefit claims against other data sources. It proposed using BT's network to transmit the information round the system. The meeting was our first face-to-face encounter and the first time I had seen him since Francis Maude's ambush at the beginning of the year. He told me: "I think there are some off-the-shelf components we could use for IRIS which would save money. I should be able to find some Cabinet Office resource to help you get it right."

Given the helpful tone of the discussion, it came as a shock when the Cabinet Office slashed back the budget for IRIS from the £17 million requested to an interim £4 million. They argued that there was confusion as to the scope of the project and there was no technical, operational or technical leadership in place.

We found it hard to counter their concern, however much it was resented. Robert Devereux pointed out that a lot of the disquiet was based on the scale of the BT contract – an approach the Cabinet Office had already approved. He added, "However, I do think that we need to look at how the whole programme is managed."

"We need to get the right person running this," I told him.

The worst of the pressure was mitigated through enlisting Joe Harley's help in our response. However, this was the last time we were able to use Joe – the Chief Information Officer for the Government as a whole – as a shield from the demands of the Cabinet Office. Joe was to retire little more than a week later at the end of March 2012.

I put IRIS on 'credit watch', an expression borrowed from the credit rating agencies operating in the financial markets and which I applied to any programme that needed intense senior involvement. I would have weekly meetings with the whole team until the project was back on track.

A month after the letter arrived, one of the senior DWP civil servants, Sue Moore, had taken charge of IRIS. I met her on her third day on the project.

"What do you make of it?" I asked.

"Scary," she told me. But already she seemed to have a grip.

Robert Devereux had also grasped the challenge set by the Cabinet Office on using an outside service. "The issue is whether we should let an outsider have our information, which I'm dead against.

"Just inform Francis that you are satisfied that we have dealt with this issue and that we are proceeding in the way we decide. We can't afford to let Cabinet Office delay us any further."

By early May much of the steam had been taken out of the row and Liam backed down in the face of our concerns about the security of sensitive data if we were to use a service. I was able to write to Iain telling him: "This programme is now back on the critical path for Universal Credit delivery."

A little later Liam took me up to see MoD Corsham in Wiltshire, where the defence establishment headquartered its security control operation. There were valuable lessons for Universal Credit, for which we were already designing a Joint Security Operations Centre – or JSOC. When I wrote to Iain afterwards, I told him: "It's clearly important that the security operations staff understand both the technicalities of cyber security as well as day-to-day business operations in order to maintain the service for legitimate users.

"Whoever is on duty needs to be able to take the decisions about what to 'turn off' and to understand the operational impact."

On the way back I told Liam: "I don't mind you shaking the tree if you're concerned about things the Department is doing. But please don't undermine the time-table."

While I was dealing with the closing stages of the Welfare Bill in early 2012, Malcolm Whitehouse's new deputy was getting on top of the roll-out strategy. He had appointed Karolin Nakonz into the job, seconded from IBM, and she proved a formidable operator.

At the end of February 2012 we held a meeting in Iain's room in which Karolin took us through the exercise to pin down what would be delivered and when it would be delivered. Alongside this time-table was, crucially, what would be automated and when. It was perfectly possible to undertake a reasonable volume of activity on a more manual basis, which is what the Department was already doing with existing benefits. The issue was the extent of such activity.

She was able to present a coherent plan to which there wasn't a lot to add. "We need to take the number put on UC down from about 750,000 in the first six months to 400-500,000 in order to de-risk it," she concluded. "It will take us to the end of March to work out a specific migration plan."

I told Iain: "On that basis I'm happy with the shape of this."

Even before the Bill was wrapped up in February, we embarked on the exercise of creating the 300 pages of detailed regulations that would have to be approved by Parliament before Universal Credit could be launched. The process took an intensive five months. Two and three times a week, Departmental officials would gather in my room to face a grilling from me, Philippa and Stephen Brien. We went through more than 60 submissions. Many addressed complex issues and we found a considerable number of contradictory approaches to similar questions which needed to be made consistent.

As Stephen had warned, contributory benefits – which were not means tested and which recipients received as of right – were an early casualty, proving impossible to integrate with Universal Credit. The myriad of other issues we dealt with included: a determination that both 'Yasmin' and 'Liam' needed to sign a claimant commitment to make a valid claim; continuation of the support for disabled students that existed in the legacy system; grace periods for the self-employed before they were assumed to earn a minimum income.

I was particularly worried about the five-week period before people received their first monthly payment of Universal Credit. I told the team: "The one thing we can't afford is a rolling crisis of people coming onto UC and having a cash flow crunch. What has happened to the fortnight's cash flow we save?"

"They get it as they go off UC," the official tasked with this issue responded.

Philippa emphasised my point: "The one thing that the Secretary of State won't accept is throwing all these people into debt at the start of their UC experience. It's political dynamite."

The cost of providing an upfront grant to cover the shortfall would be £3 billion over the period during which UC was introduced and there was no way the Treasury would wear this figure. I countered by pointing out that the shortfall was effectively being seized by the Treasury and sent the team back to try again. "I'm not convinced where the cash flow has disappeared to."

This was an issue that we worried at for month after month. Eventually I was forced to create an advances, or loans, process to soften the impact.

I decided that we should send the draft regulations in their entirety to the Government's statutory advisory body, SSAC or the Social Security Advisory Committee, with plenty of time for consideration. This was not strictly necessary, since regulations based on new primary legislation were not included in SSAC's remit. However, with a new Chairman in place – Paul Gray – the Committee did an extraordinarily thorough job. It raised a series of problem areas, where I was happy to make the recommended changes, and ironed out a large number of technical glitches in the drafting. The exercise reset what had historically proved an over-adversarial relationship between the Department and the Committee.

One area of the project which was proving surprisingly free of problems was the real-time information system for PAYE for which HMRC was responsible. The tax authorities had experienced a series of public blow-ups in developing IT, and their cautious approach reflected the lessons learned. They were building the system on the old-fashioned safety-first waterfall basis and steadily expanding the user groups as they scaled it up.

In my regular formal meeting with David Gauke in January 2012 his team was able to report that the RTI pilot would start as planned in April. The initial 10 employers would build up to 300 over the first three months; with another 1,300 coming on stream in July and 200,000 in November. Integration testing with Universal Credit would start in August.

This was all based on the 'interim' solution which we had adopted early in the process. There would inevitably be discrepancies between the reports from employers and what some employees actually received in their bank accounts – which we dubbed LMI, or 'Late, Missing and Incorrect'. Only a move to using the actual transfers through the banking system – our original Vocalink-inspired 'strategic' solution – would eliminate this.

Peter Seymour of Vocalink – my inspiration for the Universal Credit structure – made no secret of his dismay at the approach that we had taken. It was pretty evident that he had been lobbying MPs and others over the shortfalls of the 'interim' solution. In February he told David

Gauke and me: "We're being cut out of the process and are really worried that you are not going to do the strategic solution."

I assured him: "We have just launched a process to move towards the solution. However, I have to point out that your lobbying is now really endangering the process. People are using the issue to raise doubt about the timing and prospects of getting Universal Credit developed and that undermines our ability to get all our stakeholders to work with us. David and I are your best friends in this whole process and you are not helping us."

The lobbying stopped. For David and me the encounter sparked an extended process of engagement with the banks' payment industry. Our efforts to make sure that the payments through the banking system carried enough information for us to arrive at a reliable Universal Credit disbursement were to take us on a long and complicated journey.

The debates at Committee stage in mid-December 2011 about how the most vulnerable would cope with Universal Credit pointed up a genuine problem. While the majority would be able to handle monthly payments and digital access, Peers warned that a minority would find it too challenging.

Archy Kirkwood cautioned: "I do not believe that the 15 percent of the family households at the bottom end of the income distribution will be anywhere near using these things comfortably." [86]

I reassured them: "We have begun working with Local Authorities, housing associations and the relevant third sector organisations to develop guidance around who might qualify for more frequent payments or the direct payment of a proportion of an award to a third party, such as a landlord."

But I didn't think this would be enough for the most vulnerable groups. So it was good timing that the next morning Merrick Cockell came to my office. He was Leader of the Conservative Kensington and Chelsea council but was meeting me in his capacity as Chairman of the Local Government Association.

"We want to help you with Universal Credit but we're not sure how," he told me. "Maybe we should set up some pilots to test it out." We set up a small meeting of Local Authority leaders at the end of January. It was to prove a valuable exercise.

I explained: "We are building a volume operation with Universal Credit, but in practice we are now as a Government looking to the Local Authorities to look after the most vulnerable, whether it's Discretionary Housing Payments, managed rental payments direct to landlords, the social fund or the duty to house the homeless. So we have to make sure the two systems butt up to each other smoothly."

Paul Martin, the Chief Executive of Wandsworth Council and a member of the UC Programme Board, replied: "If that's the message, you need to get it out to Local Authorities because it's not what they think the plan is." We agreed the rough outline of a series of pilots to test how Local Authorities could support people in difficulties with Universal Credit.

I did not think the team was gripping this problem. In late May 2012, I set up a meeting with Katherine Courtney, responsible for the Universal Credit service proposition, to focus our efforts.

"I'm very concerned about the interconnection of a group of issues which have real urgency. How we treat vulnerable people; what our payment exception service is; how does that play into banking support and who do we ask to help us? If, as I think, it'll be the LAs we need to tell them what we want by late autumn at the latest. That's why I'm putting this issue on 'credit watch'."

On a visit to Warrington at the end of March 2012, Steve Dover was more subdued than usual. I quizzed him on the progress of the stories. "We've had to change our approach. It was too disruptive to break into the same code and expand it incrementally with each story. So we're doing larger chunks."

Yet again, it didn't sound very Agile.

Stephen told me a little later. "They're pushing ahead with the Leaps, but they keep stripping out the really difficult bits. It's like a snowplough charging up the centre of the road, leaving all the knotty problems heaped up on the kerbs behind it."

Neil Couling, Director of Working Age Benefits, was equally frustrated. "I'm available to help them but they simply won't utilise me." In the late summer he was to move on to the challenging job of running the Jobcentres.

Nevertheless, with Karolin's delivery plan taking shape, we decided on setting up a pathfinder in April 2013, six months ahead of the formal launch. Malcolm told me: "We've been talking to Greater Manchester and they're pretty keen. We would aim to set it up in four different authorities there."

I described the approach to Iain in my weekly letter to him: "It will be a rolling pathfinder, starting in April 2013 but continuing beyond

Universal Credit go-live in October, allowing us to test different systems, products and behavioural outcomes before they are rolled out nationally. We will set up a 'war room' to monitor the pathfinder and to bring together people from different parts of the programme to tackle problems as soon as they emerge."

We reached agreement with four Local Authorities in the North West – Tameside, Oldham, Wigan and Warrington – and were able to announce the plan in May 2012.

I was still deeply nervous about how well the system would be functioning in the early period. One area I thought might prove problematic was our planned introduction of a civil penalty of £50 for people who provided the wrong information to the Department. In May I recommended that we delayed its introduction in Universal Credit for the first year.

To my surprise, Iain dug in his heels. "We can't slow down on this. It's vital to send a message to people that they can't give us the wrong information."

"My concern is to get a smooth introduction of Universal Credit and not to have stories around about fines because our system is unfair. It may be that we have blue throbbing screens that drive people to make mistakes."

"Are you saying that you don't believe the system will have all this ironed out?" he demanded.

"A lot will have been ironed out, but there may well be clusters of errors, perhaps caused by cultural differences we don't understand well enough. At least let us have some wriggle room, and keep it under review."

"You can have the review. But the system must function and we are testing it thoroughly to make sure it does." Iain had a way of asserting what he wished to be the case.

"Well, I don't think we have a meeting of minds on this."

He concluded: "We'll have to touch heads like Vulcans to sort it out."

It was the first time I could remember him rejecting one of my recommendations.

He was less certain than he made out and had been calling for a Red Team review of the team's progress. His military background attracted him to this approach, popularised by the US defence establishment, in which an independent group challenges an existing operation to improve its effectiveness.

Malcolm had been resisting the exercise but now he believed that enough material had been developed for a challenge exercise to be valuable. He asked the technology consulting firm Capgemini to organise the process.

Meanwhile Karolin Nakonz was promoted within IBM and came to the end of her secondment as Malcolm's deputy. I was deeply sorry to see her move on. Even though she was an outsider, the loss of a key person at a critical time would inevitably damage the project and reflected the casual attitude to turnover that was endemic to the Civil Service.

Her replacement had worked his way up the civil service. He told me: "I am absolutely not a one-for-one replacement of Karolin. I will take a lot of the back office off Malcolm, but won't be solving the immediate crises like Karolin did."

It was an expert in finding solutions for IT crises that I wanted. When I caught up with Philippa later, I unloaded my disappointment on her: "That's the big difference with the Civil Service and the private sector. They simply don't value people properly. They think that any Grade 6 is interchangeable with any other."

The new deputy presented his plan to 'Go to Amber' to the Programme Board with commendable rapidity. It was a line-by-line response to the shortcomings set out by the Major Projects Authority in its May report, which again showed an Amber/Red score, repeating many of the previous concerns about the security of the system and the capability of the team.

It seemed to me too mechanistic a response, conceived almost as an independent exercise, rather than as a way of addressing the structural issues surrounding the design and security of the system. In the semi-public forum of the Programme Board I gently observed: "Well, that's a pretty ambitious target."

Security issues were proving increasingly difficult. The expansion of Bob Lovett's security team, and their placement in the Warrington IT factory, seemed to have made matters worse rather than better.

Stephen Brien told me: "The security team is refusing to allow claimants to see their claim."

"Well that's simply unacceptable. You can see where you are with the banks and Amazon, so there must be a solution here."

"That's what I've told them. There must be a level of risk that the Accounting Officer – Robert Devereux – and the Minister are prepared to tolerate. The trouble is that relatively junior guys with the security brief are taking very critical decisions and there's not enough pushback." Stephen spent the next three days buried in detail, going up to Warrington to sort through key screens.

A couple of days later I received the conclusions of another Red Team exercise – on the risks of online fraud – commissioned after our trip to Cheltenham. With GCHQ and HMRC involved, alongside staff from DWP, it was a litany of flaws and made for grim reading.

The links between app design, security and the IRIS teams were ineffective; invalid assumptions were being made by the technical teams on what was acceptable to the business; there was a lack of corporate balance between usability and security; poor understanding of dependencies between Universal Credit components and little consideration was being given to the technical implications of business design activities.

A fortnight later Stephen Brien came back to report: "It's really bad. I've been spending the last two days in Warrington and the security problem is simply not sorted and we're not going to sort it in time. We're going to have to savagely descope the pathfinder and October launch. There simply isn't time."

I told him: "We need a crisis programme on security."

"Yes, I've been setting up a team. The trouble is that the security people have come in late and they are being provided pre-cooked solutions which are not acceptable. I sympathise with them."

I tried to console him: "I'm not so worried about the pathfinder. We can man-mark the initial people for fraud." I left the implications for the October launch unstated.

Stephen and I were able to brief Iain after the weekend.

Stephen summed up: "They're running seriously behind on integrating security and the claimant journey."

"Why aren't they on top of it?" Iain demanded. "I'm very concerned about the progress on the next releases. I don't think the senior team knows what's happening."

Bob Lovett had assembled a big hitting team to defend Universal Credit from cyber-attack. His plan was to provide layers of security in Cerberus with a consortium made up of IBM, HP and BT.

"It'll cost £55 million to put in place," he told me, after a meeting with the three companies. "We're putting the application into the Cabinet Office at the last minute and we may need a bit of support from you to get it through."

In the event spending approval from the Cabinet Office was not forth-coming, despite my recent trip to Corsham with Liam Maxwell. It was a rerun of the IRIS encounter, with the Cabinet Office arguing that the pro-position was both over-specified and over-priced. Liam was now Deputy Government Chief Information Officer and with Joe Harley's retirement we had little protection.

Robert Devereux told me: "Liam usually has a point. I've been looking at this in great detail. I think we are sorting out the over-specification that we've got. When it comes to Cabinet Office clearance, Liam's point is that we haven't put this out to competition and we'll end up at the mercy of the suppliers for years to come, whether there are break clauses or not. In the end I think I am persuaded that the costs of a six months delay to the whole programme outweigh the extra costs we may be get-ting into here."

The Cabinet Office refused to budge on Cerberus and we had to aban-don the scheme. The final decision, to switch to a radically downsized £2 million interim solution, took place in a very different context. At the end of July 2012, the Red Team Review that Iain had demanded on the whole programme became available.

It was a somewhat unconventional Red Team in terms of its inde-pendence, because four of the five members of the review team were client directors from the IT contractors. So they were marking their own homework and the conclusions were delicately stated.

It found that the Pathfinder should be deliverable; that material change was required to achieve the Launch in October 2013, where it should be possible to retain much of the 'original ambition'; however, a detailed re-plan of the IT and non-IT strands beyond the launch was required. The security issue remained problematic.

The Review was much less guarded when it came to the operation of the programme. Here it found a 'fortress-like' approach, unwilling to look outside itself for support. There was an 'authoritarian' or 'brutal' leader-ship style, according to many of the people they interviewed. Plans for the various programme strands were not well-connected.

At the conference call with the senior management team in early August to address the issues we agreed a four-stage process. First, we needed to sort out security, then organise the pathfinder, plan the October launch and then a pathway beyond. We left the cultural issues aside for the time being. Iain summed up: "We're creating a new benefit system here, and using technology as a tool to help us. We can perform some of the elements manually where it's efficient."

He was trying out the statement for size before going public with the line.

There was politics to deal with before the implications of the Red Team review. I was on a visit to Leeds on the day of the Cabinet reshuffle in early September. The newspapers were full of reports that Iain had been offered a switch to the Ministry of Justice. When he turned it down it had gone to Chris Grayling. Maria Miller had also been promoted to the Cabinet, taking on the Department of Culture, Olympics, Media and Sport. My new Ministerial colleagues were Mark Hoban and Mike Penning.

When I saw Iain the next day I told him: "I'm extremely relieved that you're still here. It was nice for you to be given a choice about going to Justice?"

"There was no alternative. If I'd walked, the whole reshuffle would have blown up before it happened."

"Why the offer of Justice?"

"The Treasury want me out."

"Who in the Treasury?"

"The whole lot; the senior officials and George. They can't bear that this Department is meeting them on level terms. It always used to be under their thumb. They want to carve up Universal Credit and I'm blocking them."

Iain spent the next fortnight fighting the battle to cement his position. By mid-September he was cock-a-hoop when he popped into my office.

"The Heywood opposition was flushed out by Fraser Nelson in *The Spectator* last week. Make sure you read the piece. I've just seen the Chancellor and he says he'll support Universal Credit, but was concerned about his cuts. I told him we sent over a paper with a freeze and various other options in the summer, but he doesn't read his briefings. He looked blank when I asked him whether he'd read it. Heywood has asked to see me this evening and now that he's been uncovered he's going to have to over-compensate about how much he's supporting us."

Fraser had written a lead article in the magazine headlined 'The Universal Credit crunch'. In it he wrote: "Sir Jeremy Heywood, the civil servant effectively running Britain, is letting it be known that he is 'sceptical' about Duncan Smith's mission. This, in Whitehall is the equivalent of a go-slow order." He concluded: "The Prime Minister should throw his weight behind Duncan Smith rather than seeking to remove him. He ought to remind Sir Jeremy that, as head of the civil service, he is paid not to be 'sceptical' about Government policy but to implement it." [87]

One of Iain's first acts on being re-installed in office was to endorse Robert Devereux's proposal for a regular weekly meeting of the senior executives of the Department. This would review the progress of the various programmes we had in hand. Robert had made the proposal to regularise Iain's habit of demanding meetings at short notice on any day of the week. I joined him as the other Minister on this Ministerial Change and Delivery Group or MCDG. Among the Departmental Executives attending were Robert Devereux; the newly-promoted Finance Director Mike Driver and the equally new head of IT, Philip Langsdale, whom I was looking forward to getting to know.

The first meeting, in late September 2012, looked at progress in Universal Credit. Terry Moran looked quite shaken as he admitted: "We are not in a position to provide a firm update of our plans. We seem to be on course to begin the pathfinder but there is less certainty round the October launch.

"I've spent the last day and a half going through the plans and I am not happy with the progress we're making. Some of the team seem to be on top of their objectives, but from others the responses suggest they don't have a grasp of what's needed."

Iain replied: "Well, I've made a very clear commitment to all my colleagues, including the Prime Minister and the Chancellor, that we are able to deliver this – so the Department needs to push hard and make all the changes required."

A little after the meeting Philippa told me: "Iain has just asked Stephen to become the No 2 in the structure between Terry and Malcolm."

Later in the day, when I saw Stephen, I asked him: "What is Terry planning?"

"Quite a lot of changes".

"I'm concerned that Terry will go at the team with a meat axe. We can't afford to lose the knowledge and experience the current team have. The changes should be carefully judged, with people's roles concentrated where they are over-stretched and their weaknesses balanced up with other colleague's strengths."

First thing on the following Monday Stephen came into my office.

"Got some news," he told me. "Terry is not coming in. The team spent Friday going over the plans at Philip Langsdale's house. On Sunday Terry rang Robert to say he wasn't coming in today."

Later, Robert Devereux told me that the Friday meeting had been quite fruitful, with new plans being developed to restructure the project. However, when he had a follow-up conversation with Terry on Sunday, Robert realised he would not be able to come back for some considerable time.

On Monday evening I had a meeting with Philip Langsdale and Stephen. By then, it was clear that Terry was seriously ill and Robert Devereux had appointed Philip to take over as acting Senior Responsible Owner for Universal Credit. Terry had become overwhelmed by the scale of the demands on him.

Three years later, in a piece for *The Guardian's* 'Time to Talk' column, he wrote: "I took on more and more until the weight of my responsibilities and my ability to discharge them just grew too much for me.

"While I occasionally hinted to others that I had too much on, I couldn't find the courage to say it outright until it was too late, and by then I was ill with depression." [88]

Philip was a big company IT professional with a string of achievements under his belt. At the BBC he had led the introduction of Freeview; at Asda he had created a store-driven ordering system; while over his previous four years at the British Airports Authority he had transformed Heathrow's real-time systems. He had an infectious charm and a personal style that inspired confidence.

He had been appointed in May to take over from Joe Harley but it wasn't till the beginning of September that he had taken up the post. Soon afterwards he was in a motorised wheelchair, as his illness – Motor Neurone Disease – advanced. He never referred to his fatal condition and it took only a few minutes in his company to disregard it entirely.

That first evening with Stephen was spent going through the individuals in the programme and discussing the damaging culture in the Universal Credit project team that the Red Team had identified.

I warned: "I am concerned that we don't make overhasty decisions on exiting particular individuals. On balance I think they're pretty good and highly motivated – but need adjustments to their roles."

The next morning Robert slipped into my office to say: "We've had all these proposals to move people around, but I'm not sure whether the real issue isn't Malcolm. He should be all over this re-planning and he isn't. I've asked Philip to find out if there's a world-class project manager we can grab and he's looking into it."

A few days later Philip told me: "I've taken your advice about not focusing on particular individuals. I've decided that we need a new leader. They can take decisions on who they want in the team.

"I told my wife that UC is a bit like a bus travelling round the country getting stuck in dead-ends and mud all the time. And everyone rushes up to change the wheels and shock absorbers rather than working out why it's getting stuck in the first place."

Philip got an immediate grip on the programme. He decided that more resource was needed on delivering the pathfinder and then the launch in the following October. His search for a new Programme Director came up with an internal candidate in the shape of Hilary Reynolds, a level-headed official just back from a spell in New Zealand, who was in post by the beginning of November. Alongside, he appointed two senior DWP officials to run the pathfinder (now called Phase 1) and launch (Phase 2) in the shape of Janice Hartley and Sue Moore (who had worked on the IRIS programme).

We set up a regular Monday meeting for Hilary, Philip, Stephen and me to review progress. On Hilary's first day in post, 5 November 2012, we went through some of the IT design problems. I observed: "I can't understand why they haven't built the system using the smallest possible elements and adding them together."

Philip agreed: "It is inherently bad design to start with a household, when you should use the unit components. I'm concerned we're simply building another legacy system."

Hopefully I suggested: "It might be quite straight-forward to fix, mightn't it?"

Philip sighed: "No, it will probably be desperately hard to fix. We're taking a deep dive into design to see what other areas may be wrong. Is there anything else you want the system to do?"

I went through my wish list: "I want to make sure that we can run randomised control experiments at minimal cost on all the key parameters, by putting a flag on people we are monitoring."

I continued: "I'm also most concerned that we haven't ever built a 'Mash Unit', so that there is a place within the organisation which understands how the system is meant to fit together."

When we reviewed governance, I recommended: "My only advice is to get the numbers down. A Programme Board of five or six, if you possibly can."

Philip replied: "I suspect the main decisions will be made in a kitchen cabinet of the people in this room." In sharp contrast to Terry's response to the identical advice, Philip brought the number on the Programme Board down to six by the next day.

Later Hilary went through some of the people she would be moving out of the programme. "There just hasn't been enough grip," she said.

The next day at the Ministerial Change and Delivery Group (MCDG), Philip told us: "We have now got 450 consultants from Accenture working on this, which is way overkill. We need to build more cleverly than we are."

In his overview of the week Philip told us that he had instituted a review of the underlying system architecture to explore the concerns about the design flexibility. He also set up a Major Projects Authority review for January.

There were clear signs of re-invigoration and progress. An intense week was required to sort out the claimant-facing user screens, which had been incoherent when I reviewed them a month earlier. They were dramatically improved. The process for managing changes in benefit claimants' circumstances was next for the same intensive treatment.

Beyond the immediate IT build, the operational components began to come together. The claimant commitment was integrated into the system; the 'knowledge hub', for Jobcentre staff to check procedures was moving ahead; I was even given a reasonable first draft of an integrated exceptions process for the most vulnerable. This linked into the Local Authority pilots I had agreed to at the beginning of the year.

The public fall-out from the loss of Terry and Malcolm was relatively limited. For the Opposition, Liam Byrne told *The Independent on Sunday*: "Universal Credit is in danger of descending into total chaos." [89] However, there was little follow-up to the story warning that the project was already a year behind schedule because of computer glitches.

It was a period of intensive effort. By the end of the November I told Hilary: "I'm very concerned about the number of people who are becoming exhausted doing Universal Credit. You have to take some of them aside and give them a few days off. Both Philip and Stephen are two of those I'm most worried about."

"I'm going through the team and making sure they have job specifications they can manage and proper support where needed," she assured me.

One of the outcomes from the refocused activity was a greater realism in the team about what was achievable. The MCDG meeting in early December 2012 proved particularly uncomfortable. Iain was full of flu and Philip was at home, ill with a chest infection.

Sue Moore went through the design for the Phase 2 launch in October 2013. "We will have to use the structure we've built for Phase 1."

I asked for confirmation: "So users will only be able to apply on the system at the time of October launch and will not be able to go back into the system to change their circumstances."

She confirmed: "Yes."

Given the undeveloped state of our security design it was hardly a surprise. Before there was real consternation I observed: "Well that might just work, but it depends critically on when the next drop happens. If it's not till April 2014 it will look really bad."

Iain concluded: "This is simply not satisfactory, but I suppose you have clearance to explore the implications." Philippa was clearly furious.

Later in the week she told me: "I'm so angry about Tuesday's meeting. We had no warning about the conclusion. Sue's got to understand the political consequences of not having proper IT at the time of launch."

I told her: "I think Sue tells it like it is. If she says we can't have it, then we probably can't."

Later with Stephen I said: "If we don't have a proper system in time for October, we're going to have to think about fall-backs. Maybe in June after a few months of pathfinder we should announce a problem which pushes us back a few months and that October will effectively be an expanded pathfinder."

Even though Philip stayed at home through December, finding it difficult to shake off his chest infection, Hilary ploughed on with ensuring Phase 1 would be ready for the spring and that the scope for Phase 2 would be completed by year end. I went home for the Christmas recess feeling mildly confident. Somehow, we would struggle through.

That mood evaporated within a few days. At midday on Christmas Eve Stephen rang me to say: "David, awful news. Philip Langsdale has died."

I was stunned. I phoned Iain: "Yes, it happened two days ago. The Department owes him an awful lot. He got the UC process back on track."

PART VII

WRITE-OFF

January 2013 – January 2014

CHAPTER 17

Poacher Turns Gamekeeper

The immediate shock of Philip Langsdale's death had eased by the time I caught up with Robert Devereux after the recess. Robert consoled me: "He made an incredible impact in just four months and got us pointed in the right direction. He was enjoying himself hugely in the job and remember - with Motor Neurone Disease - it was always going to happen. It just happened sooner than we expected."

He told me he had been working right through the Christmas break to sort out the repercussions of Philip's death. He was following Philip's recommendation for a new CIO in the shape of Andy Nelson. The second vacant role was that of SRO for Universal Credit. "Now I've just got to see if I can get David Pitchford out of the Cabinet Office."

In the meantime one of the senior Departmental hands, Mark Fisher, took on the job of SRO, while Hilary Reynolds stayed put as the Pro-gramme Director. So the Universal Credit programme, after only two years, was now being run by the third incarnation of each of the two principal officers.

The immediate issue through the rest of January proved to be pass-ported benefits. These were payments and concessions on offer from various Government bodies and Local Authorities based on people's entitlement to the Department's main welfare payments. I had asked the Social Services Advisory Committee to look at this problem and in the previous spring Professor Janet Walker, SSAC's deputy chair, had written a report into how passported benefits might work within the Universal Credit system. [90] The report detailed the extensive number of free and discounted services - primarily in health, education, utilities and access to justice - which could be accessed by recipients of Jobseekers Allow-ance and other benefits. Clearly, the traditional direct entitlement would no longer work in an integrated system in which people with higher levels of earnings were eligible for Universal Credit. I had worked with Janet Walker to develop a strategic solution in which some of the largest passported benefits – particularly free school meals – could effectively be incorporated in the Universal Credit structure itself. That would take some years to establish.

Meanwhile we were working with the other Departments to develop an interim solution as to how they might continue to piggy-back on the DWP's welfare system. We needed to agree what level of earnings would give people eligibility for the main passported benefits so that we could design these thresholds into the system. In mid-January I joined a meeting with Ministers from the three most interested Departments, chaired by the Government's fixer-in-chief, Oliver Letwin. Oliver's habitual, and somewhat patrician, air of light-hearted amusement belied his intense analytical capability and his sheer appetite for hard work.

At the beginning Oliver Letwin complained: "No-one will get any free school meals if their total income needs to be below £6,000."

I pointed out: "That's not total income, that's their earnings thresholds."

"Oh, that's better then." He added, with typical self-deprecation: "I told you I didn't understand this stuff."

I described the longer-term strategic solution of incorporating some of the major passported benefits like free school meals into Universal Credit. "We could develop a way for people to claim their school meal costs upfront in Universal Credit and then it would be tapered away as they earned more money. That would be a much fairer and more graduated way of supporting people."

Oliver liked the structure: "I see that, and it's very good."

David Laws was the Liberal Democrat Minister of State for Schools in the Department for Education presided over by the Conservative Michael Gove. He interrupted: "We're here to reach a deal on the interim period not the longer term."

Oliver Letwin replied: "But it's very important that we know where we're going."

That was as far as the supportive noises went. Oliver was poring over an A3 document I'd never seen. He concluded: "There are 100s-of-thousands of losers here and that's a sure-fire election loser. We can't go ahead with UC on this basis. I know Iain will be very disappointed."

'Disappointed' would be a relaxed way of describing Iain's reaction, I thought to myself. Oliver hazarded that protecting recipients could cost £100s of millions.

David Laws asked: "When do we need to agree this deal?"

"The 14 February," I told him.

Oliver concluded: "On that basis we'd better have a Quad on Monday."

In the event, when the Department's analysts had a chance to look at the figures more closely, the number of losers melted away. So the idea of referring the issue to the regular Quad meeting of David Cameron and George Osborne with Nick Clegg and Danny Alexander was quietly dropped.

Iain was at his most adamant as we prepared for my next meeting the following week.

He demanded: "How did their paper get tabled? This is what happens all the time. They have a paper with nonsense figures on it and then we get pulled all over the place. They've got to withdraw this paper and use our paper or we should refuse to go to the meeting. These people (he meant the Cabinet Office) are outrageous."

Then he turned to the number of thresholds – the various levels of earnings at which entitlements to particular passported benefits would cut in and out. "I'm terrified about this. We should have a maximum of three, otherwise it gets too complicated and we'll have delays."

I kept my mouth shut for most of the meeting, adhering to a firm instruction from my Private Secretary, Jessica Yuille. At the end I said: "We're pretty close to a deal. The real number of losers is pretty low and we can handle up to six thresholds. So our focus tomorrow should be to get a deal which allows us enough time to build the system. I've given them a decision deadline of 14 February."

The meeting the next day opened with a somewhat uncomfortable-looking David Laws stating: "Michael is determined that there will be no losers of any kind from this." His Secretary of State, Michael Gove, had clearly given him some strict requirements.

Oliver came riding to the defence. "Looking at these numbers I don't think we've got a problem. We'll be able to say there'll be no cash losers. If Michael wants to defend opportunity losers as well that is not a problem for Universal Credit; Education will have to work out who they are and pay for them out of its own budget."

I drew the discussion on the number of thresholds to a close by stating:

"Departments only need four thresholds so can we agree on that. We need to have agreement in order to build the system."

David Laws wasn't satisfied: "We'd like to have one in the middle at say £10,000, just in case."

I conceded: "Ok, four and a spare." With six in hand, I was happy to settle at five.

While this was enough to continue building the system, in the event Michael Gove refused to reach a final agreement on the threshold levels. But within a matter of days this peripheral threat to Universal Credit was forgotten as a far more deadly assault loomed.

The Major Projects Authority review agreed by Philip began in late January and was led by Dr Norma Wood, a seasoned operator for the MPA.

Within days concerns about the findings were beginning to circulate. As we carried our coffees along Tothill Street, Iain anticipated: "They are going to complain about lack of clarity about roles and have a go at Stephen Brien. The Cabinet Office will use it to try to take control. It's a blatant power grab."

The next day Paul McComb, Iain's Principal Private Secretary, briefed me on the implications of what the report was likely to contain. "They don't think the security is in any fit state.

"They think that we're opening up our core systems to the outside world and that security needs to have been designed at the heart of the system rather than as an add-on. We may be faced with difficult decisions about going ahead for longer without being online. After all, there's only a relatively small financial benefit from the online element. Most of the £29 billion economic upside is due to the nature of the benefit itself."

Robert Devereux took me through the issue of our IT architecture. "Mike Bracken and Liam Maxwell, as well as Ian Levy from GCHQ, all think we should just dump our existing system and go with a modern cloud based one. I'm not convinced that's right, given that we've got all these legacy systems they've got to interrelate with."

He was baffled as to how to handle the Cabinet Office: "We've got £8 million to spend on IT for this month, but the drip feed of clearances is really damaging progress, especially as it is effectively resisting steps that it is too late to do anything about. The trouble is that the people in the Cabinet Office all represent different fiefdoms which don't relate or even necessarily like each other. So it's impossible to control."

The draft report from the MPA, which arrived on my desk late on Wednesday, 6 February, was damning. The entire delivery approach needed to be rethought to safeguard the successful delivery of the policy intent. The rating was Red, meaning 'successful delivery of the project appears to be unachievable'.

The next morning I told Philippa: "It's fair, but the language is bad."

Philippa said: "We're trying to make them change it. If it leaks, which it will, it's going to be pretty terminal."

"Will they change the language?"

"I don't think so. They want us to wake up and smell the coffee."

When I talked to Iain later, he told me: "I had Norma in and told her that I had ordered the Red Team process. That we were onto the issues and that her review didn't reflect it."

But the Cabinet Office now held all the cards, and Iain was realistic enough to recognise it. He briefed me on the developments across the weekend on the following Tuesday.

"The Cabinet Office set up the MPA review to bring it all to a head. As soon as I saw the draft on Wednesday night I knew that it was awful and that I only had one chance to turn it round. I phoned Francis on Thursday night and said that if it went through like that I would have to write my resignation letter and apologise that I had let everyone down.

"Francis assured me that he absolutely didn't want UC to fail. We spent Friday sorting out some of the language, but the fundamental criticism was that we didn't have a blueprint.

"I went in to see Francis yesterday. In the private meeting before I asked for David Pitchford to take over as SRO. He told me that he was too busy on the Major Projects Authority. So when the others came in - Mike Bracken, Stephen Kelly and so on - I just addressed them. I said straight to him: there's only one man that can sort this out and that's you David. You know the programme and can go in and put it on the right lines.

"Afterwards Bracken and Kelly and the others gathered round Francis and insisted that David should do it. It's interesting that later they were following me out saying: 'We can sort this out for you. It can be done'.

"David's conditions were that he would come for three months and report directly to me - that's you and me, on the political side - and not to the Permanent Secretary. They don't trust Robert and that's a serious problem. I told David that if he had any disagreement with Robert, I would side with him. In fact Robert did say yes to all the requirements, more or less. That means David can start tomorrow."

Effectively, the agreement meant that Iain had secured one of the Cabinet Office's main poaching assets to be a gamekeeper for the project

"Congratulations," I told him. "You've seized triumph from the jaws of disaster." My overblown reaction reflected relief that Universal Credit was still on the road, at least for the time being.

The next day, on 13 February, I focused on pushing through all the secondary legislation to turn the Welfare Reform Act into reality. I had prepared thoroughly for this, with a dedicated team working over the previous half-year to ensure that our communications with the key stakeholders were effective. A large amount of information had been provided to Peers, along with access to officials in various sessions. The measures would be taken in sequence in one long session on the floor of the House.

If I thought this would be successful as a tactic to exhaust the Opposition, I was to be disappointed. In practice I was the person exhausted as we ploughed through seven separate sets of regulations – rebuilding the welfare system in great detail – without a break from four in the afternoon till 11 at night. Luckily, I managed to sneak in a chocolate bar for sustenance, despite the strict convention against eating in the Chamber. There was only one vote – of regret that Universal Credit would not achieve its aims – which I won comfortably (169–239). At last we had a clear legislative base defining what Universal Credit was.

The team building the pathfinder, under Janice Hartley, continued to push ahead. By late-February she reported that the Universal Credit code for the launch had been completed and was now being intensively tested. She told me: "Sixty-two days to go. We are regaining the test days we lost. It'll be tight." The plan was to launch on 29 April. I arranged to spend our next meeting going through our contingency plans to deal with any problems.

David Pitchford's first priority as the new Chief Executive of Universal Credit was to resolve the central criticism of the Major Projects Authority review – that there was no Blueprint or over-arching business architecture for the new system in steady state. He brought back Dr Norma Wood, the leader of the Review, to build the Blueprint. She was a blunt no-nonsense executive, with many years of experience and a low toleration of ambiguity. She immediately set about marshalling the Universal Credit team in the Department to assemble the document, called the Universal Credit Steady State Blueprint.

The new arrangements included reporting to a Ministerial Oversight Group, or MOG, made up of Ministers and officials from the Treasury and Cabinet Office, as well as Iain and myself from the Department. Its first meeting was held in Iain's office at the end of February.

Iain opened the meeting: "It's the Pitchford show."

David Pitchford had cut his teeth in the Office of the Tasmanian Governor – in his home town of Hobart – before moving on to manage major development projects, such as Palm Jumeirah City in Dubai. He was a big man in his fifties, with an open face and straight-forward manner.

To my relief, he began his report by confirming: "I've decided we're going ahead with the pathfinder." This meant we would establish a presence on the ground for the new system. He went on to warn: "We still need to explore the nature of expansion in October."

Oliver Letwin asked: "When are you planning to get a permanent Chief Executive?"

Robert replied: "I've seen three first class people who are all available. We're not going through the formal process to get them so they should be at work comfortably within the three months."

"That's wonderful news," said Oliver. "With a Chief Executive and a pathfinder we may have a successful programme yet."

Danny Alexander, the Liberal Democrat Chief Secretary to the Treasury asked: "Will you be testing the behavioural change sparked by the introduction?"

Iain replied: "Absolutely."

I cautioned: "But the main elements we are establishing with the pathfinder are our own business processes. There are something like 426 to test through."

At the end of the meeting David Pitchford warned Iain and me privately: "Most of the team are accepting their new roles, but Hilary is wobbly."

I asked to see Hilary as soon as I heard the warning but she resigned before I could talk to her. When we met the next day, she told me: "There wasn't room for a Programme Director and a Chief Executive. I've told Robert I can't go on. I had my first proper night's sleep for a long time last night."

I told her: "Well you have been looking terrible, which just shows the pressure of this programme. Thank you for all you have done. You have put together a first-class team."

Stephen Kelly was one of Francis Maude's recent appointments, a former private sector Chief Executive in Information Technology, brought in six months earlier as the Government's first Chief Operating Officer as well as running the Cabinet Office's Efficiency and Reform Group. He was elegant, articulate and unfailingly positive. He also had real experience in the area. He started his career at ICL in the 1980s building the 'Opstrat' back-office system for DWP's precursor, the Department of Social Security. "I think it cost close to £2 billion and was the largest live operational system in the world in terms of user-numbers." He told me. He was "revisiting memory lane 30 years later" because Opstrat was still operating as part of the Department's legacy systems. Luckily, he joined Iain and David Pitchford on a trip to two of the pathfinder Jobcentre offices, and the Bolton service centre, at the end of February.

At our next Ministerial Oversight meeting he showed all the enthusiasm of a recent convert. He told us: "What really matters is the people on the ground. They are going to make this work. The trouble is that people here don't get out of Whitehall enough to see what's really happening on the ground. We're going to get this through and at below the budgeted cost."

Later that day Stephen Brien explained to me for the first time the real problem with the IT. "The Oracle system is a black box. It does the analysis of what people are entitled to, but it's outside the control of the system - so we don't know what happens in it and we can't control what people do there."

I was genuinely taken aback: "Dear God. And I thought the Oracle programme was the best thing since sliced bread." It was one of the first IT demonstrations Malcom Whitehouse had taken me to, in October 2010. The programme - Oracle Policy Modelling, or OPA - translated documents into executable business rules, which meant it could work out people's entitlement to Universal Credit from our policy documents and legislation. I had tested some basic propositions and the programme's ability to respond accurately had left me deeply impressed.

Stephen's role as deputy SRO did not survive regime change. "I've been thrown off the UC team," he told me.

"Why? I told Pitch that you and I were the only people left with an overview of where we are."

I suspected that there was a reluctance to have people aboard raising some of the problems the new approach would generate.

David Pitchford (whom we now mostly referred to as 'Pitch') told us that, for the time being, the contractors had agreed to keep working on the pathfinder mostly for free. At our next weekly Oversight Meeting he said: "They will continue to work, but they want guarantees of continued involvement."

Francis Maude reacted: "We're not guaranteeing anything for those dinosaurs. We want a modern approach to this and those guys are simply unable to provide it." Already the Cabinet Office was looking to blame the contractors for the problems in the build.

In the second week of April Norma Wood took me through the draft of the Universal Credit Steady State Blueprint. Much of the document was a basic recapitulation of the aims of Universal Credit, with timelines for establishing better governance, financial reporting systems and renegotiated supplier contracts. The transformative proposition was that the architecture for security would be brought into the heart of the system and integrated with the business and system architectures. This would require the building of an entirely new version of Universal Credit. The designer of this approach was Tom Loosemore, Mike Bracken's deputy in the Government Digital Service, who had been seconded over to us to establish what it would take to create a safe online service. I found him genuinely impressive.

When the Ministerial team went through the Blueprint a week later Tom Loosemore demonstrated how the user interface might look with a mocked-up computer screen.

Francis Maude was delighted at this apparent proof of the efficacy and speed of his digital team. "That's excellent," he enthused. "When will that be ready to go?"

Tom Loosemore looked embarrassed. "I can't emphasise enough that there's nothing behind this. It's all smoke and mirrors."

As we left the meeting, Stephen Kelly comforted me that a minimum viable product could be ready in a matter of months. "Don't worry, David. We'll get this done for you." (He was assuming, he told me later, that the current build would be terminated.)

The timetable was looking difficult if we wanted to go ahead with any kind of expansion in October, the date to which we were publicly committed for the formal launch. I asked David Pitchford: "When are the plans going to be ready?"

"We're looking for final approval on 22 June."

"Well on that timetable we need to get something going beforehand in order to have any options for October."

I communicated with Iain through Paul McComb. I told him: "The only solution is to go national with the pathfinder in October."

Paul said: "Iain is on that page too. The only trouble is that we won't know if it's robust enough to scale up for another two weeks. If that Blueprint satisfies them, that's fine with us. The only thing we have to make sure of is that we get a commitment to October before Pitch leaves on 9 May."

The Cabinet Office were now focusing their ire on the contractors and we spent considerable time in the Ministerial Oversight Group being briefed on various plans to take them to court for the way they had performed in this contract. In the end however, the Cabinet Office decided there were no grounds for action. Nevertheless, David Pitchford wanted to squeeze them further before allowing the pathfinder to proceed. "We need to pull down the cost of ongoing support from the original £32 million to the current £27 million down to nearer £22 million."

He got close enough to allow the pathfinder to proceed and five days before the late-April launch my team brought in the formal Statutory Instrument for me to sign. The title was almost as long as the text and deeply obscure: *The Welfare Reform Act 2012 (Commencement No. 9 and Transitional and Transitory Provisions and Commencement No. 8 and Savings and Transitional Provisions (Amendment)) Order 2013.*

It was an historic moment. It meant, finally, that the Government was committed to pushing ahead with Universal Credit. Neil Couling, now Work Services Director, had come back to act as SRO for the pathfinder launch decision and judged that while the IT build was quite limited, the risks were manageable. Only 7,000 people would be taken onto the system and they would be a narrow group of straight-forward claimants. At the same time, we had scaled back the initial launch to a single Job-centre – Ashton under Lyne – with Wigan, Warrington and Oldham to follow in July.

The launch was deliberately low-key but it kept a sense of momentum around the project at a time of high vulnerability. I certainly found it useful in the months ahead. When one journalist asserted that Universal Credit was in chaos and running late, I took some pleasure in replying robustly: "We started six months before schedule; I'd hardly call that running late."

Even before the pathfinder launch, Robert had succeeded in landing a big name to take over from David Pitchford as Chief Executive. Howard Shiplee was the Construction Director at the Olympic Delivery Authority which had successfully delivered the Olympic Park the year before. Like me, he was in his sixties. Robert told me: "I know he's a construction man and knows nothing about welfare, but he knows how to drive a programme forward. He sees this as his last big challenge before retirement." Howard's experience spanned the world, from Hong Kong to the Middle East. He was cheerful and enthusiastic and clearly had a deep understanding of management structures. The added complexity of dealing with incoherent Government approval processes, however, were to drive him to barely suppressed fury.

He was appointed in time to attend the set-piece meeting on 9 May, at which David Pitchford delivered his recommendations. I was taken through them by David Pitchford and Norma Wood ahead of the main meeting. The central recommendation was to build a new digital system, which could be done with great rapidity. Rather than starting with simple cases and ramping up the complexity, as at Warrington, they would take the full range of complicated cases at the outset. They would be ready to trial that system on 100 people in a year's time – in the spring of 2014. In the summer there would be a trial for 1,000 people and the third stage would test the system with 10,000 people in the final quarter of the year. That would allow full operation of the system from the beginning of 2015. A separate team would be needed to build this digital system, which would operate in a truly Agile way.

I was relieved to see that Norma Wood had incorporated some expansion of the existing system in October. It was, however, extremely modest.

I told her: "I'm concerned at the slow build up before the switch-over to the digital system. Surely we can do more than 17,500 on the pathfinder basis?"

Norma Wood was unrelenting: "The organisation can't handle the volumes."

Ahead of the main meeting Paul McComb told me: "Iain's strategy is to smile and wave. He's told Howard Shiplee he wants to start in October and close down JSA and tax credits at the beginning of 2015, so the introduction of UC is irreversible."

Iain opened the main meeting by saying: "I accept these recommendations in their entirety."

Francis Maude asked a series of leading questions on how much of the existing system would need to be written off. Clearly a big write-off would make the position of the Accounting Officer – Robert Devereux – untenable.

"How much of the system can be re-used?" he asked. "If most of the spend has been nugatory then we need to be honest about that."

David Pitchford replied: "CIS and the payment system can be re-used but the balance will need to be defined and built."

Francis Maude stated: "That assessment needs to be done in a very clear way."

Later in the meeting he changed the angle of attack: "The Chief Executive of UC should report directly to the Secretary of State."

Howard Shiplee demurred: "I'll need to work within DWP. That means I need a relationship with the Permanent Secretary."

After the formal meeting there was a row with Mike Bracken, who told Howard Shiplee that he would not leave Tom Loosemore in the Universal Credit team to develop the architecture of the proposed new system. They went into a side-room to negotiate. Robert told me: "We can't spend three months training up a key guy in UC just to have him leave again."

We had successfully responded to the MPA review and established the first stage of the process that we were later to dub 'the reset'. However, the Cabinet Office was far from finished with the Department.

Political tension had grown through spring 2013, as the Treasury cuts became imminent. Most public fury was directed at the reduction in housing benefit for those with spare bedrooms, which took effect at the beginning of the financial year in April. Labour had enthusiastically adopted the label of 'Bedroom Tax' introduced in the Lords by Richard Best and was vigorously attacking the Government over it, ably supported by the *Daily Mirror* and *The People* newspapers.

David Orr, Chief Executive of the National Housing Federation, warned me: "The bedroom tax is a disaster and we will be campaigning against it vigorously."

I corrected him: "Well, of course, it's not a tax."

"But that's what we're going to go on calling it."

I had changed the name from the original and incomprehensible 'social sector size criteria' to the 'under-occupation charge'. Within a few weeks this new name was overtaken. In early March Iain pronounced: "We've been caught out on the labelling here. We need to call it the Removal of the Spare Room Subsidy from today. Steve (Webb) used it in the debate last week and it went down very well." We explored what concessions we could make and agreed to hold fire till May, when we could see how the introduction went. "Meanwhile," he concluded, "we absolutely have to hold the line."

Nobody told the Prime Minister. As I was travelling to St Andrews to be lambasted by councillors and officials from the Convention of Scottish Local Authorities, David Cameron was facing the leader of the Opposition, Ed Miliband, at Prime Minister's Questions. While we had been holding firm for months, he folded when Ed Miliband pressed him: "Will he admit that the vast majority of disabled people will get no help from the hardship fund and will be hit by his bedroom tax?"

"Anyone with severely disabled children is exempt," he declared – inaccurately. Afterwards one of the officials told me: "It was a cock up in No. 10, but they've just come back and said 'make it so'."

A month later the UK Uncut protest group held demonstrations at Iain's home in Buckinghamshire and my semi-detached in North London. The sign outside my house, staunchly defended in my absence by a row of yellow-jacketed police, declared: 'Who Wants to Evict a Millionaire?' Iain's protest was staged in his front garden and had several disabled participants. When we compared notes he told me: "They got into my garden and I found later they had broken into my garage. I think they were hoping to find a fancy car, but there was only an old tractor in there."

One of my other responsibilities, George Osborne's Benefit Cap, was also due to be introduced in April. I had been warned by the officials in the previous autumn that the IT wouldn't be ready in time. "We'll have to go manually till July. That means we can only do 2,000 a month for the first three months, not the main stock of 40,000."

With the problems looming in Universal Credit, as well as a three-month delay in another programme, the Child Maintenance Service, I found it difficult to muster much surprise.

"We had better make a virtue of incrementalism, then," I told them. "Develop a strategy to build up the programme slowly so that we test the processes ahead of the volumes." The team came back with a plan to introduce the cap initially in four Local Authorities and I made time to talk to the officials in each of the chosen councils during the spring.

This stealthy 'go slow' strategy triggered a furious rebuke from No. 10, warning that the Implementation Unit in the Cabinet Office needed to be kept fully informed about the development of programmes.

The most uncomfortable task that spring, however, was Parliamentary. The Appeal Court had ruled that sanctions had been improperly imposed on people who failed to attend mandatory back to work programmes. It found that the information about the programmes, and the letters sent to claimants, were too sketchy. This would lose the Exchequer £130 million and we introduced an Emergency Bill, with retrospective effect, to maintain the sanctions. The Opposition in the Commons let the Bill through in a day but in the Lords there were a series of votes against the measure (which I won). Nevertheless, I found our justification almost as threadbare as the most effective lawyer in the House, David Pannick, who argued: "The Bill breaches the fundamental constitutional principle that penalties should not be imposed on persons by reason of conduct that was lawful at the time of their action." He was unmoved by the prospect of saving £130 million. "The rule of law is simply priceless. One cannot put a price on complying with the rule of law and basic constitutional requirements."

These issues – complex and demanding as they were – were overshadowed by the problems of Universal Credit, where hostilities with the Cabinet Office were about to resume.

CHAPTER 18

The Twin Track

The tussle between the Department and the Cabinet Office was exacerbated by Francis Maude's growing suspicion of Robert Devereux. The origins lay with Francis' drive to improve the efficiency of Government and in particular his strategy of functional leadership. He explained this in a later Speaker's Lecture; "The Civil Service needs strong functional leadership at the centre of government." He continued: "Every Department claims that what it does is completely unique and distinctive, and of course much is genuinely unique. But most of their requirements for property, IT and digital procurement, HR, finance and project management are common to the whole of government. And even when they are not, you still need one place where there's a critical mass of technical expertise." [91]

As the biggest spending Department, DWP was clearly a key component in achieving this centralising agenda. However, again and again Francis found it slow and reluctant, whether on his project to share services or to stop the process of automatic payment of union dues by staff. He felt that the DWP was not giving him the right information and laid the blame at Robert's door.

By mid-May 2013, Howard Shiplee was firmly in the Universal Credit driving seat and our period of tutelage under David Pitchford was over. The Cabinet Office no longer had direct control over the direction of travel. Once again, they resorted to using their weapons of influence to exert pressure from the outside. Most ominously, they put in place yet another review of the project by the Major Projects Authority, less than six months after the previous body-blow. I presumed this was designed to give them the ability to dictate our next steps.

I was still trying to absorb the implications of the Pitchford initiative. In particular I felt deeply uncertain about the best way to proceed with the IT. The Blueprint summary, produced under great time pressure by

David Pitchford and Norma Wood, seemed to me to be a fairly cursory document. The hundreds of pages behind it, which I went through carefully, looked as if they had been thrown together in great haste – as they were. On the other hand, I gravely doubted whether the security issues of the initial build could ever be resolved. I thought Mike Bracken's team was undoubtedly right in arguing for a design which integrated the security with the architecture of the system.

In mid-May I went to see Mike in his headquarters in Holborn. I could already see what Ian Watmore, the Cabinet Office Permanent Secretary, meant when he said that it looked like a proper Google office. Teams in T-shirts were hard at work at their computer stations across the Government Digital Service floor in Aviation House.

When we sat down in one of the meeting rooms Mike Bracken spelled out how the world of computing had moved on over the last 15 years.

"The Department simply hasn't got many of the key skills required to run a project like this. Essentially, over the last 15 years it has become a function for commissioning work from the dinosaur providers. That's what they know how to do. The trouble is that they are about 15 years behind the times and their skills have atrophied. There are lots of good medium-sized companies that have given up trying to get Government business. There are simply too many barriers that we put up and they can't be bothered anymore."

He now seemed to be genuinely keen to help. "I've put a team together and I've assembled space over at Victoria Street (alongside the Joint Security Operations Centre) for them to build the system. It will start at 20 to 40 people and then can grow to 80 or so." I was relieved to hear him confirm that Tom Loosemore was a key figure of the team.

I was concerned at the separation from the mainstream systems. I explained: "The trouble is that Universal Credit will become the platform for the whole Department and when the project is built it will have to be docked into the other systems. So our challenge will be to get this docking to happen." I arranged to meet him on a regular basis, along with Howard.

Francis Maude resumed probing the value of our investment at the Ministerial Oversight Group meeting in early June.

"Why is only £34 million written off?" he demanded. "The bulk of the expenditure is nugatory."

Mike Driver, the Department's Finance Director explained: "This is the figure for the work redone in the previous financial year. The remaining

£260 million will be on our books as an asset until we decide what to do. So we may write it down at some stage, depending on how long we use the software."

Robert told us: "The £34 million is the figure that the NAO is agreeing we should write off." His confidence was based on feedback from the National Audit Office team working on the Department's draft accounts for the previous year. In the event, that response from the NAO hardened and the Department faced a long battle to arrive at a figure. It was the issue that determined the Cabinet Office on killing the pathfinder, since Francis wanted to force a big write-off.

Howard now raised the issue of expanding the pathfinder in October. Before the meeting he had asked me to support him on releasing the funds for this next step.

I declared: "If we are going to follow the Blueprint, we will need to approve funding shortly to do some further work to hit the October target." There was no response.

It took Iain to state: "I should just confirm that this group has accepted the Blueprint?" Silence was assumed to be consent. But the silence was ominous.

Two days later I had a bleak meeting with Philippa, where we discussed how to expand the pathfinder. I asked her: "Does the Cabinet Office understand the political implications of not having anything to do in October?"

Philippa replied: "All they care about is that they can have a big write-off on what we have done so that they can blame the civil service. They want Robert's head."

The Cabinet Office was preparing to unleash another highly hostile report from The Major Projects Authority.

The issue came to a head that June weekend. On Monday morning Paul McComb rushed in to tell me what had been happening.

"No. 10 went nuclear when they heard what's been happening. The new MPA review has chunks put in the summary which have nothing inside. It's saying that some of the Blueprint recommendations - like establishing the team - haven't been carried out, when Howard only got the Blueprint while the review was happening. We asked the Treasury whether they were behind this and they ran for the hills. So the report is going to be dumped.

"Francis told Iain that there was no problem. We should just say that we've wasted all the money and the civil service has let us down.

"I don't know what Howard makes of all this. He told Iain that if the review by the MPA went ahead he was off."

The next day Howard joined me for my new series of regular meetings with Mike Bracken. We went through the four critical roles in the new build being established in Victoria Street: IT Architect, Security Architect, Business Architect and someone who understood the Business Processes. Mike agreed to set up a Memorandum of Understanding for the terms on which he would make GDS services available to us. He pointed out, however: "We're just trying to help you set up the capability to do it yourselves. We're not doing it for you."

At the end of the meeting Howard told him that he was planning to go ahead with the 17,500 expansion in October. "I will have to use the existing suppliers to do so."

Mike warned: "That will be very difficult for us."

Despite his concerns, the build up at Victoria Street, with Tom Loosemore in charge, proceeded smoothly. I walked the 100 yards to the new office at the end of June to see how it was going. Tom told me: "We're going to start with a partnered couple to set ourselves a challenge." They were beginning to look at some of the tougher problems – on how to incorporate contributory benefits and manage the occasions, such as at Christmas and Easter, when two monthly payments might be made in a single month. I told him: "I want to make sure that we don't lose the knowledge that has already been built up in the original build and that you come to me with the tough issues straight away. I commit to a rapid turn-round on them."

This commitment reflected an earlier, gloomy, conversation with Stephen Brien. "The trouble is that nobody knows anything," he told me. "They are risking making all the same mistakes again."

I met weekly with the new 'Policy Solutions Group' through July to resolve the issues holding up progress in Victoria Street. Although we had already dealt with many of these during the original design, we needed to go over them again to make sure our hard-won knowledge was not lost and that decisions were still appropriate in a digital context. We decided on keeping contributory benefits outside Universal Credit (again), worked through the issues of couple claiming, determined that digital signatures were adequate, explored how to adjust for intermittent earnings and developed a policy for taking over tax credit debt.

Meanwhile, Robert was engaged with the National Audit Office on the issue of writing down Universal Credit expenditure. In early July he came into my office to show me the letter from the NAO, which rejected our defence that we didn't know whether or not the current expenditure was nugatory – or wasted – at this stage.

"I'm not prepared to publish the accounts if we haven't worked this out. I'm asking a top auditor from PWC to act as mediator between us," he told me.

The battle on the report and accounts went back and forth, delaying their publication for month after month. But while the Department could delay issuing the annual report, albeit with some embarrassment, there was little it could do to slow the National Audit Office's separate report on Universal Credit for the Public Accounts Committee (PAC). This was due for publication in early September. Meanwhile we were due to provide evidence to the Work and Pensions Select Committee in July.

When we met to plan strategy our head of communications, John Shield, pointed out: "We've got a shit-storm in store when the NAO and PAC go for us in the autumn."

I told him: "My instinct is that we could announce bad news but we need to announce the plan of what we're going to do at the same time. Otherwise we look rudderless."

On the day of the Work and Pensions Select Committee hearing, 10 July, we put out an announcement that another six Jobcentres – in each of the regions – would begin to take new claims to the benefit as we rolled out the programme from October. The expansion would start at the Hammersmith Jobcentre, with Rugby, Inverness, Harrogate, Bath and Shotton to follow in subsequent months. The minimalist launch was seen by the Press as another sign that we were falling behind schedule, although on a busy news day coverage was limited.

In front of the Select Committee, however, we argued strongly that the strategy was based on the need to roll out the programme safely. Anne Begg, the thoughtful Chair of the Committee observed: "As a Committee, we have said that we would rather you get it right than rush it. However, there is rushing it and there is a snail's pace." [92]

Iain was adamant that whatever the initial process "we are bound to the time-scales set. Between October 2013 and 2017, all those who fall within the ambit of Universal Credit will be on Universal Credit."

Howard Shiplee concurred: "I see no reason why this programme cannot be delivered within the due dates that have been established and within the budgets that have been allocated to us."

Our performance bought us another two months. We still needed to develop a strategy to take the project forward and a hostile report from the NAO would ratchet up the pressure.

In the event, the report was just about as harsh as it could be. [93] The best thing about it was the ambiguous title – *Early Progress* – since it found precious little. It laid out a detailed time-line of the project, revealing for the first time the 'reset' process under David Pitchford. It concluded: "At this early stage of the Universal Credit programme the Department has not achieved value for money.

"The Department has delayed rolling out Universal Credit to claimants, has had weak control of the programme, and has been unable to assess the value of the systems it spent over £300 million to develop. These problems represent a significant setback to Universal Credit and raise wider concerns about the Department's ability to deal with weak programme management, over-optimistic timescales, and a lack of openness about progress."

There were clear signs of briefing from the Cabinet Office: "The Cabinet Office does not consider that the Department has at any point prior to the reset appropriately adopted an Agile approach to managing the Universal Credit programme." This blithely ignored the Cabinet Office's own public endorsement of the Department's Agile strategy just 18 months earlier.

The NAO cast severe doubt on whether we would be able to maintain our time-table: "To keep to the 2017 completion date, the Department would have to migrate a large volume of claimants within a short time frame."

It did include – as some small mitigation – the observation: "Universal Credit is a key programme for the Department, and it is still entirely feasible that it goes on to achieve considerable benefits for society." The observation had been a hard-won concession to the Department.

As the publication date of 5 September 2013 loomed, Iain called me into his office. "I think it makes sense for you to handle the media," he said blandly. "While it's a report on civil service failings, all the journalists will be interested in is the political angle." He added: "You've got to stay absolutely rock solid on the timetable. Otherwise they'll use it as an excuse to kill Universal Credit. It doesn't have any friends out there." He was trying to downplay the importance of the report by putting up a junior minister against it. I suspected that this request would probably be terminal for my continuing in the role. "I'm happy to do it," I told him. If it meant that the project would survive, I was quite prepared to be sacrificed.

In fact I was not put to the test. When Craig Oliver, the head of communications at No. 10, heard the plan he insisted that Iain front the major media on the day. (I ended up doing the regional round in the afternoon.)

Robert was extremely anxious. He came into my rehearsal to make detailed points: "We knew there were problems and we put Philip in position to sort them – which he was doing. Then he died."

I replied: "There's no way I can go into this kind of detail."

He confided: "I like this job and I want to keep it."

He would have taken little comfort from the way Iain laid the blame squarely on Departmental officials. On the morning the NAO report was issued he told the BBC: "I lost faith in the ability of the civil servants to be able to manage this programme so we brought in people from outside – we brought in the Cabinet Office working with my colleagues – to ensure that this programme could be delivered within the scope of how it was planned." [94]

Even though the report was prepared for the Public Accounts Committee, the Speaker of the Commons was happy to allow Liam Byrne, the Labour spokesman, to lay an Urgent Question and drag Iain to the Despatch Box. [95] Iain reasserted: "I have taken action on this particular programme. This programme will deliver on time and will deliver within budget."

Liam homed in on the timetable: "The NAO must agree its facts with the Department. Paragraph 13 of the NAO's report states: 'The Department is now reconsidering the timing of full rollout . . .'

"This morning the National Audit Office told me that the NAO and the Permanent Secretary have agreed that statement, yet it flatly contradicts what the Secretary of State has said to this House."

Iain's reply was robust, if wide of the point: "I must say that that was suitably pathetic, coming from the Right Honourable Gentleman."

I was relieved that on this occasion I did not face the same question in the Lords, where the tactic of harnessing cordial political abuse to get out of a tight spot was frowned upon.

The Prime Minister was a good deal more relaxed about the timetable than Iain. A week later he told Anne Begg's Committee: "My view is this is a good reform that will make work pay, that is widely supported across politics and other sectors. So we need to get it right. But we shouldn't be religious about timings." [96]

Howard was becoming increasingly sceptical about the Cabinet Office attacks on the work done by the contractors. Just before the NAO report was published he told me: "We're going through the work that has been done, with the PWC team. It's becoming clear that some of the work is good and usable. It would be most foolish and wasteful not to use what we can.

"I have been seeing the suppliers with the GDS people, including Tom Loosemore, and we have been going through it on a technical level, with a large amount of consensus. Also, there doesn't seem to be any evidence that the suppliers did things that we hadn't commissioned. I am going to see the Cabinet Office team to get them to accept that we will have to use this code and the suppliers for specific development. I'm not expecting it to be easy."

The disagreement broke into the open at the tetchy hearings on 11 September in front of the Public Accounts Committee. [97] Norma Wood, who had directed the original Major Projects review and designed the Blueprint, was asked whether or not a 'large chunk' of the IT just didn't work.

She confirmed: "It didn't work." Nor did she believe that the pathfinder technology could be scalable. As a result she believed that a 'significant chunk' of the IT expenditure would have to be written off. More positively she did, however, state: "I believe it is feasible to deliver this in the original time scales we talked about, so 2017 is still reasonable."

This set up the PAC nicely to excoriate the Departmental team, led by Robert Devereux, the Permanent Secretary.

As Robert tried to justify the pathfinder, a scornful Margaret Hodge, Chairman of the PAC, demanded: "So you think the pathfinder is fit for purpose to enable you to do a national roll-out of Universal Credit, as envisaged in the White Paper of the Act?"

Robert explained: "So the choice goes something like this: do we make sure that something is put into the field, so that we have some feedback about how people will respond to Universal Credit – how agents and staff will work – and learn from that, or do we simply do nothing at all?"

Margaret Hodge interjected: "I think something was put in the field to make everybody think that everything was all right but the thing that was put in the field was completely unfit for purpose."

Howard Shiplee made the main defence, bluntly contradicting Norma Wood. His early findings in his first 16 weeks in the job were: "There is substantial utility in what has been produced to date.

"On the basis of what I have been told and what I have seen so far, I believe that it has been demonstrated that the suppliers have got the capability to scale this up." He would be able to come to a formal position in four weeks' time.

When the PAC delivered its report two months later, in November, it was rather muted about the utility of the Pathfinder, although this did not stop Margaret Hodge declaring in her Press Release: "The pilot programme is not a proper pilot."

The Conservative Conference at the end of September was enlivened by Matthew d'Ancona's book *In It Together*, which captured George Osborne complaining that Iain had opposed every welfare cut and was 'not clever enough'. [98] It was followed by a reshuffle, in which Esther McVey was promoted to the role of the Employment Minister of State in place of Mark Hoban and the bluff Mike Penning was moved from Northern Ireland to take over the Disability role.

Back in the Department on 8 October, the first day after the recess, Howard briefed me on his conclusions. He was in quite a rage.

"We had the presentation of the GDS system last Thursday. It's good, like a Mercedes. It does exactly what we want. But when we asked when it would be ready they said it could be there by February 2015 but that was risky and the real date was November 2015. I checked back into the MPA report by Norma and found the phrase that the end-2014 date would be safe and secure.

"I've been checking through what the contractors built and found that it's good. I feel that I've been on a journey in someone's footsteps and found out the same thing, and that person was Philip Langsdale. We've just burned through nine months for nothing. The Treasury want an MPA review and I've told them that's fine, but it can't be run by the MPA, because with Norma at its head it is conflicted."

Two days later I popped in to see Philippa, who related: "Howard told Mike Bracken and Steve Kelly he never wanted to talk to them again. I had to go round to see Jeremy Heywood to sort it all out. I told him that the GDS solution doesn't deliver what we need politically. It's all agreed. We're going with a ramp up using existing technology to 200,000 before the election."

The Ministerial Oversight Group met in mid-October to review Howard's recommendation to expand the Pathfinder while continuing to build the new digital system in parallel. If approved in principle, he would then come back in a month's time with a fully worked up case. Meanwhile, he asked for a further £5 million to improve the efficiency of the pathfinder.

Howard briefly introduced the paper, taking a jab at the Cabinet Office. "The GDS system will not be ready till November 2015. I think it was brave and correct of them to give us that time-line."

As chairman, Iain tried to force the pace: "I've looked at this. My view is that I want to support Howard with this. That de-risks the pressure on Victoria Street. We need to come back in four weeks with a costed analysis of the business case."

Danny Alexander was now a strong supporter of the project. "I'm very happy to agree to that. It's sensible to take the extra four weeks. I'm not prepared to agree in principle before knowing the value for money and effectiveness of further options."

Francis Maude was still hostile to any expansion using the existing contractors.

"I don't have a problem with some very modest investment in the next four weeks and fixing some pathfinder technology," he stated. He jabbed back at Howard: "There are things that are not completely right in the paper. It is not the case that GDS think that the technology is reusable or that the ID Assurance programme won't be ready. It will be going live early next year. (The Cabinet Office had taken over responsibility for ID Assurance).

"My main concern is with using some of the same suppliers. There are lots of issues about the way it works. A team of 35 have produced a proof of concept that says this is the way it should be done. The previous team with 1,000 and £300 million have produced something not that great. The idea that we were using the same suppliers would invite a critical response from the media. I'm deeply sceptical about continuing to build with pathfinder technology. There's a question about whether they are able to be integrated together. It's a fundamentally different target model.

"I totally understand the desire to scale up. Can the expansion be done manually? We need to explore this. In other cases the technology has followed afterwards. We can prove the policy, which is already beginning to show benefits without the profound risks of throwing good money at suppliers who've failed."

Oliver Letwin, the Government fixer, said: "I don't believe in value for money studies. I think we'll be criticised if we spend large amounts of money but less if we spend less money. I'd like to see the costs of each of these. I feel very deprived of any piece of paper with timelines on it. I don't care when these things cover the bulk of people. This is one of the great changes in British welfare in the last sixty years. History will judge us on whether it works. It would be helpful to understand whether any hybrid could be supported."

It seemed to me that Jeremy Heywood was wavering, so I broke in: "We've been looking at this as a technology issue. It is much more than that, a major cultural change in the relationship between the state and the people it needs to support. I believe our focus should be on testing every aspect of the system before we go out in scale. That means different types; complicated cases and vulnerable people. We need to spend the next year or eighteen months testing UC so that we really understand these impacts."

It felt like a turning point. Jeremy Heywood summed up: "I'm very happy to support the SRO. We need to decide if there's still an objective to have 100,000 on UC before the election. If we are to have a dual track it's very important to understand how they interact."

Oliver asked: "What is the minimum we are trying to achieve by May 2015? We need to have tested that the system can be made to work for all the population, as David said. We'll have proved it works and it'll be up to the next Government to make it work."

Danny threw the weight of the Treasury behind the proposal: "I agree with Oliver's analysis. The task is to build a business case. I'm prepared to second someone to the Department to help."

This discussion set up – and pre-disposed – the Ministerial Oversight Group to take a definitive decision on whether to support the twin-track approach in the following month of November.

By now Robert Devereux was coming under intense pressure. Stories were circulating that he was being blamed for the problems at Universal Credit in hostile briefings by politicians. If there was little value in the existing code, and its cost had to be written off, it was difficult to see how he could avoid being dumped.

Mike Driver, the Finance Director, had spelled out the principles to the Board the day after the Ministerial Oversight Board.

"We've developed three hurdles. The first is to look at whether we've paid more than we should have. The analysis suggests we've paid what is reasonable.

"The second is whether there's ongoing utility. In my view there's ongoing utility on a permanent basis, till we know something else.

"The third test is whether there's ongoing use of the asset. At the moment our assumption is that the pathfinder has economic use. There are some areas we won't use, like the Informatic licences, which cost £4 million, so they'll have to be written down."

At the beginning of the following week Robert Devereux came in to see me to say: "I've been working for six or seven hours with a spread sheet over the weekend to show that if we can get some 150,000 onto UC early, say before the election, there is a positive NPV, which could be £70–£100 million or so, because of the very large benefits of the programme as a whole."

I was more interested in the value of testing early, an idea which had proved to have real cut-through at the previous Ministerial Oversight group. "The real gain will be from ramping it up faster once we get going because we will have tested it thoroughly," I argued. At a more formal meeting later that morning we continued to talk at cross purposes.

I repeated: "The one thing we can sell to the people who haven't already made up their minds is the concept of testing and it has much bigger values than a simple lump of volume brought forward, because it changes the whole trajectory of progress."

Unusually for a senior civil servant, Robert Devereux did understand how the numbers worked. He had taken his Masters at Edinburgh University in Statistics. By the next day he had worked through the trajectory concept. "Actually," he agreed, "the figures are much bigger if we can bring forward the migration profile. So maybe the story to the Treasury is a value of £100 million-plus if we bring forward 150,000 or so on the pathfinder technology and many millions more on a faster rollout, which we don't need to quantify precisely."

The meeting later in the day was much better, with everyone agreed on the testing concept, which we began to call 'Test and Learn'. Philippa warned: "That is absolutely not where Iain is. He wants to move ahead with the pathfinder technology as fast as possible. The GDS rollout is slowing down all the time."

At the internal planning update the next day Iain insisted on the need for a full plan to develop the pathfinder. "We need a series of pathways to cross over to the digital system, but they're moving back all the time."

I warned: "We need to be careful not to have Francis interpret that as a plan to dump Digital and go ahead with the old suppliers."

Iain replied smugly: "I'm talking to everyone and we don't have to worry about Francis." This was to prove unrealistic, although there were genuine signs that Francis had seriously overplayed his hand.

That weekend one of my team reported on the two-day planning meeting to set the direction for UC. "It was a bit of a disaster with 65 people sitting around and no real direction."

I phoned Robert, who told me: "I've drawn up three scenarios for them. It strikes me that in the third one - the hybrid - we should be looking at a region rather than going nationally initially."

By the end of the week we seemed to be getting close to building a case, although it extended out to the spring of 2019.

Iain pointed out: "We need to be able to claim that we'll complete this in 2017."

Robert argued: "We can see whether we can drop in all the people on tax credits in one go, which I think HMRC would like to do. Then we would do that in the last four months of 2017. But there's no way we can do all the people on the Employment and Support Allowance."

The hybrid version looked to expand the pathfinder approach through the North West, taking in couples as well as children from the autumn of 2014. Robert said on the phone call on the weekend. "I thought the costs were too large to justify doing children but the figures show a net present value of £73 million, so I think we should go for it."

I agreed: "It would mean constant trench warfare with the Cabinet Office if we need to look for another decision in a few months."

This approach would put about 100,000 onto the original service by March 2015. Meanwhile the Digital service would ramp up later, trialling with a handful of people from the summer of 2014 and scaling up to 10,000 households from November 2015. The approach increased the period of testing by between one and two years compared with a pure Digital route. It also meant that the pathfinder software had value and any write-offs would be significantly reduced.

By this stage Howard, Iain and Robert had lost confidence in the GDS model and were leaning heavily towards building out the pathfinder software. Howard's paper, heavily worked on by Robert, was quite explicit in its bias. I warned Robert: "You should tone down the stuff about de-risking the Digital and being able to further develop the supplier-led version. We don't need to mention it now and it'll just be sticking it into the eye of the Cabinet Office."

By now my view was that the security issues in the pathfinder version were unresolvable and that we would have to switch to the Digital version at some stage, even if it took longer to develop than the extravagant promises made by the Cabinet Office. At the same time I believed that if we did not keep rolling out Universal Credit in some form, it would be killed off. Sensitised by the debates in the House of Lords, I was also genuinely convinced that we would be able to introduce Universal Credit more effectively the longer we could test through all the processes. I started taking steps that week to ensure that we would operate 'Test and Learn' effectively.

Robert and I went round to brief Oliver Letwin on the plan on the first Monday in November, ahead of Howard's letter being sent. Oliver was positive: "I think I've got it. You'll do 100,000 or so for the cost of £90m and that will allow you to test it properly. I'll have lunch with Francis tomorrow to discuss it with him."

Robert concluded afterwards: "Well that went as well as could be expected."

Two days later the full contingent from the Cabinet Office arrived in Robert's office – Francis Maude, Stephen Kelly, Mike Bracken and Simone Finn (Francis' Special Adviser). I was not present as they squared up to Iain and Philippa. Afterwards I heard that there had been a lot of shouting. Simone told Francis: "You've got to face it, Francis, the GDS timetable takes too long for what Iain needs."

The next day Howard's formal proposal was issued. At the same time Margaret Hodge unleashed the PAC report condemning the "extraordinarily poor" management of the programme. Her Press Release stated: "£425 million has been spent so far on the programme. It is likely that much of this, including at least £140 million worth of IT assets, will now have to be written off." [99]

It had been a close-run thing for Robert Devereux and the attitude expressed towards him in the PAC report was clearly critical. In Margaret Hodge's account of her time as the Chairman of the Committee she wrote that Jeremy Heywood had rung her up "trying to make sure that I stayed out of that particular battle and did not use the report to undermine his staff." [100]

So, even though Margaret Hodge declared that Robert Devereux was "not my favourite witness", and that he was "ultimately responsible for the lax authorisation of expenditure," she decided "that did not mean that he alone should take the blame." She declared: "It was wrong for Ministers to try to influence a Parliamentary Committee and it was wrong for them to try to use us to dismiss a civil servant."

So the Committee was careful to avoid blaming Robert Devereux. It looked as if Jeremy Heywood's intervention had succeeded in saving the DWP Permanent Secretary. Jeremy Heywood was reported to have expressed his concern to the Prime Minister over the "concerted political briefing campaign". And that day a spokesman for Iain stated in the Press: "He has every confidence with the team now in place, and that team includes Robert Devereux."

When I caught up with Robert, he told me: "It's all sweetness and light. He told me he had never briefed against me at any stage. Whatever the truth of the story, Iain told me he wanted me to stay. It seems to have cleared the air."

Iain was in over-confident mood at our update meeting on UC on 11 November, at the beginning of the next week. It followed a good meeting between our officials and the Treasury team in the morning. The senior Treasury official, Sharon White, wanted more detail on the plan, particularly on 'Test and Learn'. However, she said they were disposed to get clearance of future steps back from the Cabinet Office to the Treasury.

Iain exuded confidence. "We'll get written clearance for the plan. It's not going to be a problem."

Nothing with Universal Credit had gone smoothly and I doubted that was about to change. I warned Iain: "I think the Cabinet Office will find it difficult to write a letter. They'll want a meeting so they can be forced into accepting the plan; then they can cavil continuously afterwards."

My main concern now was to ensure that we achieved the transfer of spending control away from the Cabinet Office to the Treasury. At the root of many of the accusations of financial mismanagement was a mismatch between the approvals process and the timing of development under the Agile approach. The Agile team would set its objectives for four-week periods, while the Cabinet Office clearance procedures took six weeks.

I went through the issue with Howard and his deputy, Ann Harris, later that day. Ann was a veteran of the Department and had been appointed as Programme Director on Howard's arrival.

I told them: "I'm really worried about the future ability of the Cabinet Office to slow us down. Our objective at the Ministerial Oversight meeting next week is to get clearance for a Governance structure that will allow us to proceed with this plan. If we have to get clearance for every step, we'll find ourselves hopelessly delayed. We need to make sure that the day-to-day control of spending decisions is taken from the Cabinet Office, otherwise they'll strangle us. Have we sorted out the discrepancy between the 4-week Agile period and the 6-week clearance procedure yet?"

Ann said: "No. Defra have got something for the Rural Payments Agency, but I'm not sure it really solves that."

I was right to be sceptical about Iain's proposal to clear the plan by correspondence. In the event Danny Alexander decided that an Oversight meeting would be appropriate, not least to reflect the PAC's recommendation for robust scrutiny. His official wrote that he "firmly supports Howard and the team's approach outlined." There was, inevitably, a price for Treasury support. With the Autumn Statement looming, the Chancellor insisted that to control costs the work disregards (or allowances) in UC would have to be frozen for three years.

By contrast, the Cabinet Office launched a full-scale assault on the 'twin-track' approach, arguing that expanding the pathfinder technology increased risk rather reduced it. Francis Maude wrote that he could not back Howard's approach. He forwarded a hostile letter from Norma Wood, in her position as Interim Director General of the Major Projects Authority. She wrote that the MPA could not support the investment to expand in the North West with couples and children. A memorandum from Mike Bracken, head of the Government Digital Service, stated that the 'twin-track' was at odds with the Government's agreed ICT strategy. Stephen Kelly, as the Government's Chief Operating Officer, warned in his note that it would not be sensible to keep skilled GDS resource on the project if DWP chose to pursue the twin-track.

The showdown took place in Iain's office on 20 November. I sat down at the end of his large table next to Sharon White. I knew her from my earlier stint at the Department in 2009, when she was Director of Welfare to Work and we sat at adjoining desks. Now she was at the Treasury, responsible for Public Spending, and was proving a key ally.

After Howard summarised the proposal, Danny Alexander declared: "I'm content with the vast majority of the plan. I've got some concerns I'd like to lay down. The digital solution makes sense. We should pursue the delivery of that. How do we make sure we're learning at each stage and that we're genuinely learning and the learning is being shared? I want to be clear that at each stage we need to have proper approvals. As for the framework for approval, I think that should be led by the Treasury, although the Cabinet Office has expertise it will call on. We've a good plan but at each stage we need decision points."

There was grudging support from Oliver Letwin: "I can't think of a better alternative."

Francis Maude launched an attack that followed the lines of his letter.

"I'm Cassandra on this. I can't support it. We've an obligation to listen to all the advice. We know that a lot of the big disasters in Government are when we insist on persevering with something that's gone wrong. We're in the position we're in, having to take a really uncomfortable position, because of the failure of the pathfinder programme. If we weren't facing an election we wouldn't have this imperative.

"There's a real problem in delivering any change programme. Now we're saying we can deliver two difficult programmes in parallel. The pathfinder technology is deeply flawed. You don't see large numbers coming into the system until just before the election. The financial risk is that all the estimates have been wrong up to now. That produces a pretty serious risk with the NAO and PAC. This is being promoted as a way of getting learning. I wonder how realistic that is. I'm not going to block it. But it would be wrong for us not to put very firmly on the record our concerns."

He closed by confirming that he would hand back the Cabinet Office spending controls to the Treasury as it made no sense to apply value for money controls to a programme that would not offer value for money. There would be an orderly transition in the digital build from GDS to the Department.

My contribution was to repeat the importance of testing the operating processes. I said: "We've been concentrating on the IT and while the IT is important, we have to recognise that this is a major change programme, both for our operational processes and for our client base. We need to test every aspect of it with great thoroughness and it doesn't really matter that some of the IT may be a bit clunky to start with during the testing phase. It's infinitely better than the experience claimants have today. I think this is a good plan and delivers what we need."

Iain stated: "We remain committed to the digital process. Kevin Cunnington believes that we can do this," he added, referring to our recently appointed Director General for Digital Transformation, who had an impressive track record. "We will get an orderly transition with GDS. We accept the approvals process."

Danny Alexander concluded: "This project is a priority for the whole of Government."

We were through and, most importantly, the Cabinet Office would no longer be part of the UC approvals process. Sharon White had carried through on her proposal to make the clearance process a sole Treasury responsibility. At the end of the meeting, I turned to her: "Thank you for all the help." She replied: "What you said was right. It's a major cultural change programme and that's the key point."

With the plan finally agreed, the Department was at last in a position to reach agreement on the appropriate software write-off with the National Audit Office and publish its annual accounts. The expansion of the pathfinder meant that only £41m had to be written off, although there would be accelerated amortisation of a further £91 million through the projected five-year life of the pathfinder technology. The National Audit Office took pains to spell all this out in great detail, but a £41 million immediate hit was a lot less dramatic than Margaret Hodge's predictions.

Department officials began to prepare a statement of the new plan in time for another appearance before Anne Begg's Work and Pensions Committee on 9 December.

If I had any illusions that we were through the worst, they were shattered a week later. When I caught up with Howard and Ann, they had shocking news on the Digital team.

"Their idea of an orderly transition is to pull everyone out," Howard told me. "Mike Bracken has said this is no longer an exemplar project. Kevin Cunnington has asked them all to stay, particularly the contractors, and they all say they don't want to. This is going to set us back by six months."

By early the next week, at the start of December, Howard was in despair. Fighting a terrible cold, he told me: "I don't know how people can get away with behaving like this but the result is that we're going to lose six months."

The DWP team leader in Victoria Street was the young, effective Lara Sampson. She told me: "The underlying issue is that we had formed a single team with the GDS people and this has broken that team up. We'll probably have to get our own people now."

Kevin Cunnington was a calming presence and, more importantly, had a long-standing relationship with Mike Bracken. I asked him: "Can you see if you can persuade him to slow this down."

"I'll see what I can do. I'm not sure that Mike is the one behind this."

He obviously had some effect, because the GDS team committed to restart the development Sprints in early January and cut back the period of delay to two months.

The statement on the new UC plan went out on 5 December 2013. [101] It admitted that new claims to existing benefits would be closed two years later in 2016 and that "most" – but not all – benefit claimants would be moved onto the system by the 2017 end date. It set us up for a relatively friendly session in front of the Work and Pensions Select Committee on the following Monday. Howard's cold had deteriorated still further, encouraging extreme brevity in his responses. I found it hard to keep a straight face when the Labour MP Debbie Abrahams asked if the cultural issues round leadership had been addressed.

"Yes," replied Howard. [102]

There was one more hurdle. The final publication of the annual report and accounts the next day, revealing the write-off, was another chance for Labour to hammer the project. Rachel Reeves had taken over the portfolio from Liam Byrne. Anticipating the large write-off predicted by Margaret Hodge, she was quick to lay down an Urgent Question. [103] This time it was repeated in the House of Lords. The contrast in the approach of the two Houses was stark.

Iain faced a deeply personal attack. Rachel Reeves was unphased by the relatively modest write-off of £41 million. She declared: "The Secretary of State is in denial. Doubtless, he will deny that he is in denial in a moment's time. But we all know that until he fesses up, no one will have any confidence in his management of this programme."

Anne Begg, so correct as Chair of the Select Committee, challenged: "Why should anyone believe him when he says that the delivery of Universal Credit is now on track?"

A Labour backbencher, Wayne David, demanded: "After today, does the Secretary of State honestly believe that he has any credibility left?"

In the light of this mauling, my session two and a half hours later was a model of decorum. [104] My new opposite number, Maeve Sherlock, wanted to know if it was true that 700,000 would still not be on UC by the end of 2017 and whether we were still on time and on budget.

I admitted to the shortfall: "We are planning to have all new claims for the six legacy benefits that UC replaces moved on in 2016. By 2017, we will take the remainder. An exception in the group is those currently on ESA, and the OBR estimates that 600,000 to 700,000 of them will be left on it.

"We think that it is much safer to deal with that group very carefully later; it is the most vulnerable group. I know that noble Lords in this Chamber have been extraordinarily concerned about this group and some of this reflects that concern."

There was much supportive nodding when I drew the contrast with the experience under the previous Government: "One thing that influenced us a lot was what happened with tax credits, which was why we took the decision to move in early and do this reset. Tax credits were announced in 2001 and rolled out from 2003. In the first three years of operations, £6 billion was overpaid and 400,000 claimants received their payments late; a third of cases monitored by Citizens Advice had their payments reduced below the poverty line; and IT systems were deemed unstable and not fit for purpose by the PAC.

"We have not done that. We have moved in early and made sure that we go safely and securely; and that when we introduce a system it is one that will not let people down."

Patricia Hollis said: "I hope very much that the Minister is right; we will be cheering him on if he is." I came back from the House feeling much more cheerful than Iain. Paul McComb told me: "He says that if he gets another experience like that he won't want to go on."

It wasn't just the turmoil in the digital team I had to face when I came back after the Christmas break. Ann Harris caught me after my first meeting: "Howard is pretty ill. The bronchitis turned into pneumonia and then he got Bell's palsy. He's meant to be coming back on Thursday but there's no way. His doctor has told him to take all of January off." The illness paralyses the muscles on one side of a sufferer's face and takes months to recover from.

Once again, Universal Credit was effectively leaderless.

PART VIII

WORTH

January 2014 – November 2014

CHAPTER 19

Yet Another Vacuum

The three priorities at the start of 2014 were daunting. We had to create a genuine process for 'Test and Learn': this was, after all, the key justification for rolling out the twin-track approach. We needed to build up the existing system – which we were now calling the Live Service – to cater for families. At the same time we had to create a brand new system – the Digital Service – which could safely allow online interaction.

The immediate news from the Digital team suggested that the concessions on staff by GDS were limited. Lara Sampson told me: "We're doing the Sprints, but the productivity is only 50 percent."

Kevin Cunnington prepared me a diagram of the times we could expect new recruits.

"We've got five now and are working on getting another four in the next couple of weeks. Then we can expect to get five more by mid-March."

This still left us looking at a delay. Firmly Lara said: "It's a question of making sure we get the right people. If they aren't, it takes us where we don't want to be." After the meeting, Kevin went back to Mike Bracken and managed to agree that another four of his GDS team would stay as long as we needed them.

The Sprints were similar to the design I was shown at Warrington for the original version. They were stages of build, often concentrated in a period of two to four weeks. The significant contrast was that the digital team's version of the Sprints included an in-house software build. At Warrington the team had sent the instructions for coding out to India.

It took another month to replace the 17-strong GDS team and inevitably this implied a delay to the programme. However, it alerted me to the need to plan for recruitment in this area. This was the first time a Government Department had tried to build a digital programme itself for a decade or more, ever since the strategy of outsourcing had been decided on. To resource fully, we would need to make a major effort to obtain these specialists and manage them successfully. By mid-March Kevin Cunnington had produced a plan for me that showed we would need to employ 250 people in the team within 15 months.

With great effort, the staff was assembled over the coming months. Most of the IT specialists in the team were hired on short-term contracts through the IT industry. However, despite a series of recruitment campaigns, it proved impossible to move significantly from this 'contingent' – and expensive – labour to staff we employed directly. This group of specialists seemed to find the prospect of a long-term career in the civil service antithetical to their working life-style.

In those early months I made a point of visiting the Victoria Street office on a regular basis. It was vital that a nascent team like this – and one which had suffered the body-blow of rejection by its GDS founder – felt supported from the centre.

In January I told the team: "The thing that most worried me about the process over the first couple of years was that no-one challenged us on some of the policy detail.

"The great thing about this team is that they are looking at the project as a whole and they are coming back with the hard issues. I'm not saying I enjoy revisiting these issues. They are head-bangingly difficult. But at least we now have a process for getting to grips with them. And you are leading that and that gives me a great deal of comfort."

The policy lead for working through the difficult issues was the dauntingly clever James Wolfe. In the months to come I would hold a series of 'Hard List' meetings to reach the many decisions needed. This was an extension of the 'Policy Solutions Group' which I had set up six months earlier.

In the midst of the turmoil over the hostile report from the National Audit Office, Stephen Brien's two-year period as expert adviser had come to term. I tried, and failed, to find a way to keep him on the project. One of my proposals was for him to lead the 'Test and Learn' initiative to which we were now committing ourselves. That didn't fly, but Robert told me he would put a strong performer in charge in the shape of John-Paul Marks – or JP – who had been Iain's original Principal Private Secretary.

My high opinion of JP tempered my disquiet at the loss of Stephen. And JP lived up to my expectations. I briefed him on the first day back from recess: "There are five issues. We need to have a proper overall governance structure. Our operational response when issues emerge has been too slow. We need to recognise a structural issue in a matter of weeks – not over six months. The labour market team is not adequately tied in, nor is the local support for the vulnerable. Finally, we need to make sure the econometric tests for the Treasury are properly based."

Within a few days he had produced a plan to test the extent to which UC outcomes matched our suppositions. This covered the various claimant groups to establish whether the numbers going into work would increase under UC and whether in-work earnings would rise.

He told me: "We've pulled in the labour market team to make sure this all fits together." He had also incorporated the team I had established to build a system of support among the Local Authorities for the most vulnerable.

A couple of days later he reported on a supportive meeting with his opposite number at the Treasury, Stuart Glassborow: "He's very keen on 'Test and Learn'. He told me George Osborne is agnostic about UC and if 'Test and Learn' can deliver scoreable gains with the Office for Budget Responsibility that's a big win for him."

Within a month he was telling me: "It's really a bit of a disgrace that we haven't got the labour market measures yet. The advisers don't know what they are targeting, so we don't know how to ramp the system up and down."

James Ross, the official responsible, told us: "We have three measures we think are right; job entry times, sustained jobs and progression."

I replied: "Within three weeks I would like to see a paper with the measures spelled out for my approval and in that time you will have checked that you can get the relevant management information for the comparable JSA group from HMRC's real-time pay feed."

Janice Hartley, who had successfully delivered the pathfinder, was in charge of making sure that the Live Service continued to roll out. Her immediate task was to widen the system so that it could take couples, with children to follow. She let me know her anxiety about hitting the June target for couples early in the year.

Mike Baker had been appointed the UC Operations Director in the early summer of 2013. Steadily he had built out the teams who were to introduce Universal Credit to claimants. I had made sure to visit all the new sites. Early on I visited the Bolton service centre where I sat with the official who had gone through the first data feeds from the PAYE system.

He pulled up one of the clients. "This guy made an application for UC but seems to have been working every week at an employment agency. It's enough to put him over the limit for UC. I phoned him up about it and he was pretty evasive."

I hypothesised: "Presumably under JSA he thought there was little chance of us catching him. Are you going to sanction him?"

"Well he clearly told lies. The team is working out what to do about him now."

Later in 2013 I had visited the Rugby and Inverness Jobcentres as they planned their Universal Credit openings. In the New Year it was the turn for the Bath Jobcentre and then Hammersmith. In each I would have a sit down session with the staff to find out what they had discovered. One of the most interesting findings came from the team of work coaches in Hammersmith.

They told me that the more intensive introductory interview with claimants was quite different to the approach they were accustomed to. "We're discovering the barriers people have and start working on them if they're not ready for work search yet."

Curiously I asked: "How many people do you think have mental health problems now?" This was an obsession of mine. I believed that mental health issues lay behind the inability of a sizeable minority of claimants to find work.

Without prompting, two of the work coaches replied: "Probably about 20 or 25 percent." This matched up with the figure suggested by national statistics, but it was one thing to compile generic statistics, another entirely to recognise a problem when it was in front of you. When I returned to the office, I challenged the Department to set up proper pathways for people where we recognised mental health issues.

With these different strands of work now in place, the Universal Credit team – more than 300-strong – filled the Methodist Hall for the kick-off meeting on 23 January 2014. It was an upbeat re-assertion of the determination of the Department to deliver this project now that the plan had been approved.

In Howard's absence I ran four break-out sessions at which I summarised the project and our objectives: "At the heart of what we are doing is combining in-work and out-of-work benefits. We're putting in a coherent financial incentive. Then we're adding on proper support – whether it's the claimant commitment for those we're helping to get to work or the Local Support Service for the vulnerable. Finally we're eliminating the discontinuities between the benefits, which I think will have a bigger impact on getting people into work than the pure financial incentive.

"It's not an IT project, although it uses IT. It's a business transformation; indeed, a cultural transformation. It changes how we interact with our claimants, our approach and the expectations that we have of them. It will encourage different behaviours among claimants. And we will have a far wider client base, whether it is the employed, self-employed or partners.

"The challenge to us is to think more widely. And that imperative underpins the new business plan. The Live service finds out what actually happens, and is underpinned by a sophisticated 'Test and Learn' process. The End-State team fits it all together conceptually. Whereas the existing legacy system is oriented to support the most vulnerable, UC aims to push as many people as possible towards independence. That's why the Local Support Service is key so that we do have the right support for the most vulnerable who can't handle the system, or need help to do so."

When I went on the platform to close the conference I simply said: "If I can be personal, I've worked in a whole range of contexts, from being a newspaperman to working with financiers and then the third sector. And what I can tell you is that this team is as good as any I have seen anywhere. With the right business plan, the right leadership, both of which we now have, I know you are able to deliver this cultural revolution."

By early February it was clear that Howard would remain absent for some time. Nor was he likely to return on a full-time basis. I met with Robert Devereux and Ann Harris to discuss what we should do.

Robert was concerned to prevent stories about losing another SRO, and argued that we could aim to manage with only minimal input from Howard until the Live Service launched for couples. "When you've got a running programme, the job of an SRO is to handle a lot of the external stakeholders, who want to meet with the senior man."

I told him: "But you need someone to constantly check the basic assumptions behind the plan to make sure they still stand as we roll it out. And that's a fairly disruptive process."

He suggested: "Well maybe for that role we could use you meeting with ET once a month to kick the tyres." ET was Robert's regular meeting of the senior executives in the Department – the Executive Team. Ann echoed: "That would be very helpful."

While I did meet with the senior team on a few occasions, this hardly proved a vehicle for driving the project forward. In practice, I found that I was the only senior figure with an institutional memory for the totality of what we were trying to do. Ann Harris was proving an effective Programme Director, who was able to knock the team into shape. She was buried in the day-by-day detail of keeping the show on the road.

I needed to stay on top of progress across the project as a whole. But in the vacuum, as Howard's absence stretched into months, I found myself concentrating on four main areas in a more executive way than suggested by Ministerial theory. The first was to find solutions for the problems we ran into as the Live service was rolled out in reasonable volume. Two issues quickly emerged. The number of sanctions imposed on people was much higher than it should be. More pressing still were difficulties in rental payments for housing.

My second task was to ensure that the detailed design of the new Digital service was specified in an optimal way. This 'Hard List' process was to prove complex and extended.

At the same time, I found my schedule of meetings with the key stakeholders was ramped up. These included employers and social landlords as well as the Local Authorities, where we worked out in some detail how they might support us in the roll-out of UC.

My final, self-imposed, task was to try to future-proof the project against problems that were likely to emerge. I was keen to see the error rate in the real-time PAYE system reduced before higher volumes started to make this a costly correction process. I also wanted to make sure that there were appropriate ways for benefit recipients to borrow on reasonable terms. I sponsored several teams to develop solutions in a number of areas outside the core UC project, with a view to re-absorbing them at the appropriate time.

This activity was not without its frictions, as I pushed for activity outside the conventional bounds of the project. Later Robert Devereux took me to task: "You were overloading the Department and distracting it from its core objectives."

Meanwhile, we were faced with yet another Review from the Major Projects Authority. It was a brief process. I told the team leader, Fiona Driscoll, when I had my formal interview with her: "We simply do not need a negative report after all the turmoil we've been through. I want the team to get a pat on the back. I want their tails up, good morale and an 'up and at them' attitude. So you can do this project a lot of harm if you are negative."

Fiona Driscoll, an experienced non-executive, sniffed slightly. It wasn't her job to worry about morale. Ominously she responded: "Well, we've got a lot of good things to say as well."

John-Paul Marks (JP) told me a little later: "It's ludicrous reviewing a programme in four days. They keep asking for the TOM (Target Operating Model) and they've got it on their desk but haven't opened it."

When the report arrived at the end of February the project scored Amber/Red, which was hardly a ringing endorsement. ('Successful delivery of the project is in doubt, with major risks or issues apparent in a number of key areas.')

Ann Harris confided: "The main problem is that we've got a muddled recommendation not to go ahead with the North West on the basis that we don't need the numbers."

I was infuriated: "That was agreed in the Ministerial Oversight Group. It's the Review team's job to say how well we are going in the plan, not to rewrite the agreed plan."

JP said: "I don't think they understand how many people you need to get some of these particular groups." It took a letter taking apart the figures and assumptions of the Review, sent by Robert to Sharon White, to keep the painfully-agreed plan on track.

Danny Alexander, who had taken over sole spending approval for the project, wrote in April to authorise the rollout in the Northwest of England to couples and families. However, the warnings in the MPA Review about critical gaps in the longer-term plans meant he was not yet prepared to clear the Strategic Outline Business Case. Supportively, however, he wrote that once the current work on these areas between the officials in the two Departments was completed, he would be content to sign the business case off.

The twin-track plan was holding but it was throwing up a seemingly endless stream of problems.

CHAPTER 20

Problems to Solve

As the team settled down in the spring of 2014, problems were emerging at a rapid pace – from each of the twin tracks. These ranged from the experience of running the Live Service, the detailed operational design of the Digital Service, to some of the knottiest issues surrounding support for the most vulnerable in society. The new design of UC was throwing up the shortcomings of the various legacy systems around it. Problems ranged from the sanctions regime, the security of our IT systems, housing, and controlling payday loan practices.

Sanctions
The most urgent issue thrown up in the roll-out of the Live Service was the level of sanctions. The figure was much higher in Universal Credit than in Jobseekers Allowance. This was an issue which had first emerged in November and the full analysis I commissioned was ready in March. I was shocked to see that the number of sanctions was almost as great as the number of people on Universal Credit.

The team explained: "We think it's because people find a job and don't tell us. On JSA they are automatically removed from the benefit five days after they miss interviews at the Jobcentre. In UC they get a sanction which rolls forward month by month until we get a real-time feed from the PAYE system. Others may have started their university course or gone abroad and then we may never find out."

I told them: "Well it seems pretty odd to sanction someone – even if they don't lose any money – when they have done the right thing and got a job. We've got to do something about our processes here and these figures. If they come out looking like this it'll kill UC stone-dead."

This set off months of work to establish a process in which we would only apply – and measure – sanctions for genuine reasons. It took more than a year but the end result was a sanction rate that was roughly comparable with the JSA equivalent.

Direct Payment of rent

Housing was another complicated issue, due to the way that the housing allowance was incorporated into the Universal Credit payment. This meant that social tenants would need to pay their landlords directly, reversing decades in which the social landlords had persuaded most of them to arrange for the Local Authorities to make the payment on their behalf.

We had set up the Direct Payment Demonstration Projects to find out the extent of the difficulties this would create. I was shown early results in mid-March. While the arrears rate deteriorated only modestly, the findings pointed up two distinct problems. It could take a significant minority of tenants up to three months to adapt to paying their own rent, in which time they built up arrears which were subsequently not tackled. It was also difficult to tell beforehand who could handle their finances and who could not. This would make it difficult to establish upfront which tenants should remain on 'managed' payments (i.e. state to landlord).

Some of the big social landlords were surprisingly positive about moving to direct payments by tenants. A few days later at a meeting with a group of landlords I urged them to start direct payments ahead of UC. I told them: "I'm prepared to explore the trusted landlord route in selecting who we should keep on managed payments, within bounds."

This was a scheme we were developing to let landlords decide which tenants could cope with direct payments and who should be left on managed payments.

Mark Rogers, Chief Executive of Circle Housing, was in favour of moving people early. More positive still was Neil Hadden, Chief Executive of Genesis Housing, who challenged David Orr. "Shouldn't the National Housing Federation be working to agree a strategy of switching over to direct payments?"

David Orr, the Chief Executive of the Federation, told him: "Those discussions are under way."

At the same time I was working on the design of recoveries, so that the social landlords would be able to get back any arrears that did build up within a year or so.

This somewhat leisurely progress was blown up by a report in May in

The Independent on Sunday, instigated by one of the housing associations in the Northwest, Golden Gates. It claimed that 94 percent of their tenants on UC were now in arrears.

I told the team: "This is really dangerous for us. The two main structural changes UC brings in are tax credits and housing. If it starts getting out that we are throwing housing associations into financial crisis we are going to have real problems rolling it out."

Mike Baker, the Operations Director, undertook a review of all of the Alternative Payment Arrangements or APAs, our jargon for managed payments and other non-standard payment support. At this early stage of the rollout there were only a handful.

The next day Mike reported that he had gone through all 62 APAs and, apart from three, they were working smoothly. Nearly half - 30 - were with Golden Gates' tenants and we arranged for him to talk to the company the next day.

He reported: "It was a good conversation. He said that he wanted everyone on APAs but I told him that this wasn't Government policy, which was trying to break down the barriers to work."

Later that week Mike told us: "We've managed to check about 60 of the non-APA housing and the error rate is higher - at about six so far. It takes an incredible amount of time. On one example we had to check through 200 different bits of information."

Iain laid on a display of theatrical fury that we had a problem on housing, although the performance was rather wasted because only JP turned up in person, with Mike on the phone.

"I don't understand. We knew this was a problem and nothing has been done. What's the problem? Are we short of people? Would more resource sort this out? If they've got arrears we can buy them out during the trial period. It's peanuts."

Within a month I was able to tell Iain that our tactical response on Direct Payments seemed to have got the position under control. His position had changed dramatically from the hard line he insisted on a couple of years earlier.

"We don't want to be too tough on this. I don't want to risk the introduction of UC just for this particular problem."

I replied: "For God's sake don't undermine my negotiating position by being too soft. The big social landlords are really getting on-board with the independence agenda. We can be reasonable with them, but only by starting off from a solid position."

The Hard List

The 'hard list' process stretched through the spring into the summer. Led by James Wolfe, we worked through the problems, issue by issue. In March we looked at how UC could be adjusted for unearned income like pensions, whose irregular pattern of disbursement distorted the UC payments. We worked out a system of smoothing it to avoid fluctuations.

In April we simplified the process for couples splitting and forming, so that they stayed on the same assessment period, or the earlier one in the case of two UC singles becoming a couple. In May we worked out a way of adjusting UC payments for people with irregular monthly payments. We also brought childcare reporting into line with other UC elements and decided on a generous treatment for the new tax-free Childcare Account.

In June we revisited the issues around couples where one was a pensioner and the other of working age. These couples would be on UC, rather than pension credit, but we decided that we would delay the introduction until the new higher state pension was in effect. The issues for July concerned our support for disabled people who were in work and ways to ensure they would receive the disability elements to which they were entitled. We also looked at how to end the anomaly of using the benefit system to provide support to students who were disabled or parents – an issue we failed to resolve.

IT Security

In March I was shocked by the announcement that our Chief Information Officer, Andy Nelson, was retiring. He had only been in post for a year. I asked Robert: "How have you managed to drive away our head of IT?"

He replied: "When you have someone used to spending big budgets and they are reduced to being the post-boy for youngsters who don't have a clue (in the Cabinet Office) and they have adequate means, why wouldn't they retire?" While UC had slipped Cabinet Office control, this did not apply to the main bulk of the Department's IT expenditure.

The security of our IT remained my paramount concern. Tom Loosemore had convinced me that the structure of the digital system was inherently safe and I arranged to have external verification for that claim at regular intervals. I was now concerned about the rest of our IT estate. At a workshop in June with the IT team they explained the series of security gateways that would be established in UC. I told them: "Once UC is in place we will become a more attractive target. My concern is that if a hacker does, somehow, get through our UC front door they can play merry hell with our legacy systems."

As a result, Kevin Cunnington set up a process to go through the whole of the Department's IT infrastructure to map out the weaknesses and establish a security masterplan.

Local Authorities: Support for the Vulnerable

I was anyway picking up a lot of the communication with our main stakeholders. As well as the social landlords, I made sure to see key employers. I told one group, organised by the Chartered Institute of Personnel and Development, "Universal Credit makes work pay and is helping to create a flexible workforce. Employers are absolutely vital to delivering this reform."

The Local Authorities were another critical group. The work on their pilots had begun to produce valuable insights about how best to help the most vulnerable. The 13 different piloting groups assembled in January to report their findings. There was surprising unanimity in their approach – from the big city environments like Birmingham to the rural areas of Lincolnshire. They favoured pulling public services, including the Jobcentre, into a single hub in at least one place in a locality. This was not simply for the convenience of the users but to allow the different services to understand how best to work together and avoid duplication of effort. The other consensus emerged around the need for an efficient method of triage – directing people to the right services.

When I met Merrick Cockell and his team from the Local Government Association in March, I told them: "The pilot teams were surprisingly unanimous in supporting the hub concept and that has got me thinking about co-locating our Jobcentres with the Local Authority services."

The Department was worried about me over-committing in this area. JP conceded: "We can probably assess about six." Merrick's team reverted: "It's vital that we do this in every region." To JP's consternation I cut in: "I'd be keen to see about 10."

In June 2014 I went to see the Local Authority team at Wigan, where Lord Peter Smith, leader of the council, expressed considerable anxiety about our plans to incorporate housing benefit into Universal Credit. The meeting turned much more positive when we spelled out all we were doing in this area, tactically and strategically.

Afterwards JP told me: "We need to get a regular newsletter out to the Local Authorities so they know what we are doing and don't feel their concerns drop into a black hole."

The co-operative background meant a warm reception when I addressed the Local Government Conference in July. Here I was able to announce a further round of 11 trials, which would explore how to promote financial and digital inclusion as well as the best way to triage the services.

One member of the audience declared that the various reforms – the Benefit Cap and the spare room policy – would have been a disaster if the LAs hadn't sorted the problems out. I replied: "That's exactly right and we are relying on LAs to manage local welfare provision."

Later that day I had a meeting with JP to agree the renaming of the Local Support Service Framework, or LSSF, as 'Universal Support . . . delivered locally'. We would announce the new snappier title formally when the pilots were launched in the autumn.

Real-Time PAYE

I was still worried about the accuracy of the information feed from HMRC. Peter Hopkins had led the original project to create a real-time PAYE system from within HMRC and he had transferred over to DWP to support our effort to use the information in UC. He had been monitoring the level of 'Late Missing and Incorrect' filings and told me: "The underlying level of inaccuracy is probably around 5 percent."

"That could be pretty expensive for us, given there's going to be seven or eight million returns a month," I observed. The 'interim' HMRC system relied on the information being supplied by employers. I was still strongly attracted to Vocalink's original proposal of monitoring the payments as they passed through the banking system. That way we would be able to pay people their UC based on the income they had actually received, not on what employers reported they had been paid.

My view that this was the right approach was encouraged by the

Payments Council, the organisation of financial institutions responsible for oversight of the UK's co-operative payment systems. They had told me in the previous autumn that they were working on an industry-wide solution called 'Extended Remittance Information'. They needed an indication from Government that this was a solution which it was interested in potentially adopting.

I assembled a cross-Government team of Ministers and officials in early February, with representation from the Treasury, Department for Business Innovation and Skills, Cabinet Office and even HMRC, in the shape of David Gauke. We were unanimous in wishing to see progress and I was able to write to the Payments Council afterwards that the Government wanted to push this further.

Within the Department I found an official prepared to promote the process in the shape of Mike Driver, the Finance Director.

My next step was to meet the big four banks. I made a veiled threat that we were prepared to by-pass them if they were unprepared to look for an industry-wide solution. I told them: "We had a strategic solution ready to go but we paused because HMRC were nervous about requiring too much from employers.

"We've waited to see if there's an industry solution but will have to go back to our original approach if that doesn't work." They undertook to support a two-month study, which would be organised by the leaders of the Payments Council, in the shape of Adrian Kamelard and Jeremy Wilson.

It was July when the banks assembled in my office again. By now the project had been renamed 'richer data'. There was clearly some momentum building behind it. One of the bankers pointed out: "There are a lot of initiatives which the Government is pushing on the industry at the moment and there may not be the bandwidth to do this one as well."

I pointed out: "You might find this one helps you with some of your other obligations, like the ones on reporting and money laundering. It will provide you with the information base from which to provide the reports." He looked a little more cheerful after that. It was another step in what was to prove a long journey.

Uncontrolled expenditure in housing

A category of housing called Supported Housing had costs well above normal social housing, since it was designed for the most vulnerable.

Because the costs could not easily be standardised, I had excluded the associated benefit payments from Universal Credit. Now I wanted to know how best to make sure we supported the vulnerable as efficiently as possible. I assembled the teams responsible from my own Department and the Department for Communities and Local Government. After 20 minutes I was little the wiser as to how this type of housing worked.

Feeling foolish that I had not probed the issue years earlier, I asked: "Well, how much are we spending on Supported Housing?"

"We don't know."

"Is it £100 million, or £500 million or £1.5 billion?"

"We don't know."

"Well, we shouldn't decide policy in an information vacuum. The smartest thing we can do is commission a piece of analysis to find out what's really happening."

It took a year-and-a-half to get the answer. In November 2016 the Government was able to issue a report that showed that Supported Housing accounted for no less than 17 percent of all housing expenditure at more than £4 billion. [105] It shocked me to discover that the Government had been completely in the dark over such a large piece of public expenditure.

Credit Unions and Payday Lenders

My support for the Credit Union industry meant we were working on an 'Expansion Project' to help them become financially viable. In the previous summer I had travelled down to Peckham to open an account at the London Mutual Credit Union.

When I visited the current account management team, I was shocked to learn about 'ransacking'. One of the team explained: "The payday lenders persuade clients to sign a continuous payment authority (CPA), so when their loan is not repaid they seize it from the account, together with interest and penalties."

"How much is this happening?" I asked

"Each of us get three or four of these a day." There were six in the department, making a daily total of around 20 for one credit union alone. They worked with their customers to reverse the CPAs, which stopped the ability of the payday lending industry to empty the accounts. I could see this was a deadly threat to Universal Credit, particularly if the payday lenders could intercept the funds which were due to landlords.

In July I attended a Ministerial Summit on High Cost Credit convened by the Liberal Democrat Consumer Minister, Jo Swinson. Martin Wheatley, Chief Executive of the new Financial Conduct Authority, described how they were planning to tighten up the rules. I concentrated my fire on CPAs both at the Summit and the following press conference.

I explained: "The practice of using continuous payment authorities to take UC funds which are designed for landlords and utility bills is something that we cannot tolerate as we pursue welfare reform."

It was a point which seemed to be accepted by Clive Maxwell, Chief Executive Officer of the Office of Fair Trading, when I lobbied him afterwards.

"At the moment they are not only charging high interest but also using CPAs to go to the top of the priority repayment list," he explained.

I replied: "They can do one or the other, but what they are doing is having their cake and eating it."

I held a meeting with both Martin Wheatley and Clive Maxwell later in the year to make sure my concerns were fed into the consultation that the FCA was holding. I was pleased to see that the FCA's new rules not only capped the amount the payday lenders could recoup but in July it introduced a rule stating: "High-cost short-term lenders are now limited to two unsuccessful attempts to use a CPA to take a repayment and cannot use a CPA to take a part-payment." [106] The effect of the FCA's rules was to shrink the industry considerably. Wonga, the flamboyant market leader, was to collapse into administration in August 2018.

CHAPTER 21

UC at Work

In early March, Howard Shiplee had recovered enough to come back to work. But he had clearly had enough. He told me: "I can do one day a week till June but no longer."

Robert told me: "Iain wants him back till August but that's not realistic. He might stay a little while out of loyalty but he's not the kind of man who would be happy to have his name above the door without doing anything."

When I caught up with Iain, he told me: "We just need him in place till the recess. Even if he doesn't have time to do much, he will remain an effective shield for us to get to the Northwest expansion. Without him we would never have got through the reset."

The steady improvement in the economy was now taking some of the sting out of the attacks from the Opposition. At the beginning of 2014 I took pleasure in responding to a question in the Chamber by pointing out: "The leader of the Labour Party said in 2010 that we had a programme that would lead to the loss of 1 million jobs. In fact, we have had a programme that has led to an increase of 1.2 million jobs." [107]

There was little let-up in the pressure on the UC programme, however. In May, *Computer Weekly* carried a story about Howard Shiplee's work schedule of one day a week and that we were looking for his successor. [108] "It's a malicious leak from the Cabinet Office," I was told.

Malicious or not, it set up Margaret Hodge, the Chairman of the Public Accounts Committee to give full vent to her scepticism over the UC programme at a hearing in early June. [109] The PAC was taking evidence from John Manzoni, the new - and effective - head of the Major Projects Authority. She announced: "Howard Shiplee has been away for three months; ill for three months. The head of IT is leaving in the summer." She concluded: "This is a programme in trouble."

She complained about the category of 'reset' which had been applied to UC in the latest Major Projects Authority assessment.

John Manzoni defended the approach. "It was a good thing for the project to give it time to get back on something of a front foot."

This renewed attack cast a pall over our announcement confirming that we were going ahead with the next phase of expansion in June. In late April I set out the plans to roll out UC from June across the Northwest of England. "In total 90 Jobcentres, or 1 in 8 Jobcentres in Britain, will offer the full Universal Credit once the Northwest expansion is completed."

I was also able to announce that we would be widening eligibility to couples. "During the summer the new benefit will also be made available for new claims from couples in a number of Jobcentres that already deliver the full Universal Credit, expanding to all the current live sites over time." We were not in a position to talk about our plans to take in children.

A few weeks later Janice Hartley outlined the challenge of getting the families with children on board.

"Guess what proportion of the build is for couples? It's 15 percent. Now guess what is required for families? Another 100 percent."

We were able to push the button on the expansion right at the end of June. However, we were having trouble getting approval from the Treasury for going ahead with children. This time the source of the problem was Danny Alexander, who normally was fully supportive of the project. Ann Harris told me: "The Treasury officials are fine and the Chancellor has cleared it. The costs are well below the original £35 million."

Danny was concerned whether it was necessary to use the Live Service to test family outcomes or whether the Digital Service would by then be providing such feedback. It took a major effort from Philippa and JP to lay out the arguments which convinced Danny to approve the step. His letter of approval arrived just in time to rescue us from another political row.

Margaret Hodge developed a new line of attack on UC. [110] At a hearing in early July on how the Centre of Government operated she again raised the topic of Universal Credit, demanding: "Have you signed off the business case? Have you signed it off yet?"

All projects go through phases of approval, starting with the outline strategic business case and later the full strategic business case. The reset process meant that the Treasury needed to approve a revised plan.

There was some classic flannelling from Nicholas Macpherson,

Permanent Secretary at the Treasury. To rescue him, Bob Kerslake, head of the civil service, stepped in: "I think we should not beat about the bush. It has not been signed off."

That set off another Urgent Question, for both Iain and I – with the traditional difference in atmosphere between the two Houses. The latest Opposition spokesman on welfare was Chris Bryant, who told Iain: "It feels as if this House has been misled by a Government engaged in a deliberate act of deception."

At this point the Speaker intervened to warn: "My judgment, having heard him out, was that he went beyond the line in making an accusation of deliberate deception against a group of Ministers." [111]

In the Lords I was able to explain: "On the apparent difference between my colleague, Esther McVey, and Bob Kerslake, they are both right, because they are answering slightly different questions. The first was about the strategic outline business case plans for 2013-14 and 2014-15. I went through in my Statement how they have been approved. Bob Kerslake was answering a question about the entire lifetime. As I said, that has not yet been approved, but we expect to have that cleared up and approved shortly." [112]

Our statement included the assurance that the Strategic Outline Business Case would be approved 'shortly' or, as Iain stated 'very soon', even though the Treasury had telephoned to cavil. In the event, it took more than two and a half months to get the sign-off, in late-September.

With the election now less than a year away, in mid-July the Prime Minister reshuffled the Cabinet for the second time. I was not expecting to be affected – an expectation that was to be upended.

It was no surprise when Esther McVey, who had been covering the Employment portfolio in the Department over the previous year, was called into No. 10 in the morning. As a former television presenter there had been rumours that David Cameron would want her representing the Government in the media across the board in the run-up to the election.

Paul came in to brief me about what happened.

"Esther was offered a general role, but she turned it down and was given Employment and Disability. But she doesn't want to do disability. Then apparently Mark Harper had a conversation where he was told he'd be responsible for implementing PIP, ESA and UC."

Mark Harper had obviously been lined up to replace Esther and her

248 · PART VIII: WORTH

rejection of the general role left the Prime Minister casting around on how to bulk up his portfolio.

"Well in that case I can stop doing this. I'm only here to do UC and if the PM doesn't want me to do it, I'm out of here."

I had spent four punishing years pushing through the reform programme and by now reluctantly accepted that it would take a couple of years more to see it through. Suddenly I had a vision of visiting the beach on the following afternoon. I phoned my wife, Cilla, to make arrangements for the trip and composed a resignation letter to the Prime Minister.

Iain came in: "It's all messed up but I can see a way through it. You need help with UC and it could work with Mark."

I got on well with Mark, but did not believe a job share could conceivably work. I told him: "I'm sorry to be rigid but I'm in a bit of a rage. I am only doing this to get the reform through and I am not prepared to have anyone else on a joint basis. I'm very happy to leave. You have my resignation in your back pocket."

Iain told me he phoned up Ed Llewellyn, the PM's chief of staff, to tell him he was about to lose one of his Ministers.

Ed replied: "Do not lose your Minister."

Iain asked: "Well, can I sort this out my way?"

After a couple of minutes Ed came back: "The boss says yes." So Iain left me with UC and built the disability portfolio round Mark. He told me later: "Your resignation threat was quite useful actually."

I cancelled the trip to the beach. Cilla texted: "What a shame."

I had been seriously concerned about the damage that could be done by another hostile report from the National Audit Office. In particular we were vulnerable over the disagreement with the Cabinet Office on the twin-track approach, which would be evident in the minutes of the Ministerial Oversight Group. Our public plan to complete the bulk of roll-out by 2017 looked undeliverable and the sanction volumes were uncomfortably high.

Ann suggested that the NAO could be contained by restricting their terms of reference, an idea which was dropped pretty rapidly. Robert Devereux pointed out: "I've never seen the terms of reference stop the NAO looking at anything they want."

On timing, JP warned: "HMRC will tell them they have simply not built the IT to do the transfer of tax credit cases in the final year."

By the time of the reshuffle Robert Devereux had come up with a handling strategy. He proposed: "We prepare our own document which goes out ahead of the NAO and which contains the new business plan and deals with all the issues in our own narrative."

I was impressed: "That's a really clever idea."

Robert was also working on the leadership of UC. As Programme Director, Ann had held UC together through the last nine months and had delayed her retirement plans to do so. She was finally leaving in October and her replacement would be Ian Wright, whom I thought was the best project manager in the Department. He had organised the introduction of the new Child Maintenance Service, which had gone remarkably smoothly.

In August Robert popped in to update me on the plans for Howard's successor as Senior Responsible Owner. Howard's extended period in the SRO role, despite its part-time nature, meant that Robert was now in a stronger position to promote from within rather than employ another big hitter from outside. "I've asked Neil Couling to do it. He's up to speed, so will be able to pick it up quickly." This was also good news. Neil had been head of working age benefits policy when I first arrived and had been a stalwart supporter of UC. He had spent the last two years running Jobcentre Plus (JCP), which had deepened his expertise still further. With Ian Wright alongside, we would now have a formidable team.

At the beginning of September Ann, with Ian Wright in tow for the first time, took me through the UC plan. It pushed out completion to the middle of 2019, with the migration of legacy recipients as the final stage.

With John Manzoni in charge of the Major Projects Authority, there was much more realism about the approvals process. The MPA would do a quick review of the new plans over the last three days of the week. The Strategic Outline Business Case would be updated with the specific changes but not rebuilt from scratch. By the end of the week, my Private Secretary Rob Cook let me know Manzoni had cleared the business case: "The MPA have given the UC plan a good review. Apparently there's absolutely no reason for HMT not to support the plan."

Ahead of Conference, we assembled in Iain's room in the House of Commons. He was planning to announce an acceleration in the UC roll out. There was absolutely no reference to the delay to migration – which was, after all the whole point of the revised plan.

I asked: "Do the team know what to say when someone asks about when migration will take place?"

Iain got angry with me: "No one is going to ask about that, only the geek on *Computer Weekly*. We'll just tell them that we'll start to close legacy benefits in 2016."

After this heroic display of wishful thinking I tried again: "Perhaps we can say we reset the programme in 2013 based on a 'Test and Learn' approach and we'll adjust the timetable based on our experience."

Iain practised: "We could go slower but also we could go faster."

Philippa pointed out quietly: "The new timetable will be laid out explicitly by the Office for Budget responsibility in December."

I managed to sit in the front row of the Conference Hall looking adoring as Iain declared: "I can announce that we are going to accelerate the delivery of Universal Credit from the New Year, bringing forward the national roll-out through 2015-16 to every community across Great Britain." In practice there was not much media pick-up.

In the event, Robert's strategy of pre-empting the NAO with our own report proved highly effective. I named it 'Universal Credit at Work' and it provided early evidence that people were making greater efforts to find work. [113] It spelled out how the 'Test and Learn' process was running.

In November 2014 we released the delayed 2019 end-date, firstly in the Commons and then in the Lords, where I answered a placed question by stating: "In the last strategic outline business case the costs of the programme to 2023-24 were £1.8 billion. That is down from the £2.4 billion figure that we had in 2011. Under that case, we anticipate that the bulk of the exercise to transfer people on to Universal Credit will be completed by 2019."

The next day, on 25 November, we finally announced the roll-out to families with children in the Northwest. This had the accidental effect of sparking a debate in the Commons, which pre-empted the NAO report, planned for a day later, much to Margaret Hodge's disgust. The NAO report, 'Universal credit: progress update' was anyway substantially muted compared to the previous one, and fell off the main story list in the media by lunch-time. [114]

However, before this engagement with the NAO could play itself out, I faced an entirely unexpected crisis.

CHAPTER 22

Ed Miliband Strikes

The worst week of my political life had its origins in an obscure meeting at the 2014 Conservative Conference. Dutifully, I had addressed the customary round of fringe meetings. On the last evening, on 30 September, I was on a panel which was discussing how to make Universal Credit work. [115] I had almost forgotten all about the event by the time it came back to maul me.

At the question and answer session a member of the audience, David Scott, a Councillor from Tunbridge Wells, said; "I have a number of mentally damaged individuals, who to be quite frank aren't worth the Minimum Wage, but want to work. And we have been trying to support them in work but you can't find the people who are willing to pay the Minimum Wage." He asked: "How do you deal with those sort of cases?"

This was the issue that I had tried to address three years earlier with Maria Miller. How could we help those people who had severe learning difficulties - with Down's syndrome or cerebral palsy - into mainstream activity? My attempt to introduce the Australian solution of Social Firms had got nowhere. I remembered the young woman at the Radar conference in 2008 who had demanded: "Will someone give me a job? I want a job." And I felt guilty that I had let the matter drop over recent years.

I admitted: "We have not got a system for, you know, kind of going below the Minimum Wage."[116] I explained that with Universal Credit, however, there was much more flexibility because the rate could move to reflect any level of earnings.

I picked up his language on the worth of these individuals in the labour market: "There is a group, and I know exactly who you mean, where actually as you say they're not worth the full wage; and actually I'm going to go and think about that particular issue, whether there is something we can do nationally and without distorting the whole thing... If someone wants to work for £2 an hour and it's working can we actually..."

David Scott was clearly appreciative that I would take the issue up. "Being employed in a job actually gives them so much self-esteem but nobody is willing to pay that Minimum Wage. And then we're supporting them massively financially but we also want them to work, for their own self-esteem and everything else."

One of the party whips, Damian Hinds, was listening in the audience in case anything dangerous or damaging was said. "I reported back that nothing came up," he told me later.

That was not the decision of the Labour team who were secretly recording the discussion. The Labour leader, Ed Miliband, had just suffered a terrible media drubbing at the Labour Conference. He had set about the bravura delivery of his Conference speech without notes and had forgotten to include the section on the country's deficit. Now there were rumours of last-minute coups against him in the short window before the imminence of the election ruled them out. He needed a powerful attack at the first Prime Minister's Questions since the Conference to demonstrate his authority and fend off the pressure until the window closed.

I was due to attend a meeting of the Conservative front-bench Peers in the Leader's office at the same time as Prime Minister's Questions. Just before I left my office, my Private Secretary, Rob Cook, alerted me: "There's a story doing the rounds that Miliband will launch an attack at PMQs on something you said about the disabled and the minimum wage."

I told him: "Yes, I answered a question from a councillor about what to do for people with severe learning difficulties." I cast my mind back: "I think it was the Resolution Foundation fringe meeting. I don't think I said anything particularly contentious. I just said I would think about the problem."

As I went into Leader's room, I got a text from the BBC's Nick Robinson just before midday. "Urgent watch *BBC2* Now. Ed Mil calling for you to resign on the basis of recorded comments re lower min wage for disabled. Need response asap."

Keeping to our standard approach I did not reply. Indecisively I went into the Leader's meeting before leaving to check what was happening. My team told me to hold tight and go to the car waiting in Speaker's Court to take Iain and I back to the office.

In the Chamber Ed Miliband was in the process of ambushing David Cameron: "Let me ask him about a very specific issue about disabled people and the minimum wage, which goes to the issue of living standards. In response to a question at the Conservative Party Conference, Lord Freud, the Welfare Reform Minister, said:

"'You make a really good point about the disabled . . . There is a group . . . where actually as you say they're not worth the full wage.'

"Is that the Prime Minister's view?" [117]

The Prime Minister was thrown back. It was clearly the first he had heard of the claims. This was not the easy post-Conference trouncing that he was planning. "No, absolutely not. Of course disabled people should be paid the minimum wage, and the minimum wage under this Government is going up, and going up in real terms."

Ed Miliband pushed home his advantage. He was happy to apply my remarks to all disabled people: "We need to be clear about what the Welfare Reform Minister said, because it is very serious. He did not just say that disabled people were 'not worth' the minimum wage. He went further and said that he was looking at 'whether there is something we can do . . . if someone wants to work for £2 an hour.'

"Surely someone holding those views cannot possibly stay in the right hon. Gentleman's Government?"

The Prime Minister did not quite disown me but his defence was less than robust. "Those are not the views of the Government. They are not the views of anyone in the Government. The minimum wage is paid to everybody, disabled people included."

He went on: "Let me tell you that I do not need lectures from anyone about looking after disabled people, so I do not want to hear any more of that. We pay the minimum wage, we are reforming disability benefits, we want to help disabled people in our country and we want to help more of them into work. Instead of casting aspersions, why does not the right hon. Gentleman get back to talking about the economy?"

Ed Miliband now delivered his punch-line, in which I was presented as the poster-child for vicious Conservatism. "If the Prime Minister wants to protect the rights of disabled people, I suggest that he reads very carefully what his Welfare Reform Minister has said, because they are not the words of someone who should be in charge of policy relating to disabled people. In the dog days of this Government, the Conservative Party is going back to its worst instincts: unfunded tax cuts, hitting the poorest hardest and now undermining the minimum wage. The nasty party is back."

When Iain came to the car, he told me: "This is very serious."

I replied: "I'm sorry. I've been a clot. If I have to resign, I am happy to do so."

Iain: "No, we carry our wounded home."

We were silent as we drove round Parliament Square, then: "How on earth could you say £2?"

I shook my head in embarrassment. I thought I had learned how to handle myself in public as a politician but I had let my guard down completely. I had committed three cardinal errors. I had accepted the language of the question, in using the word 'worth'. I had thought out loud. I had abandoned opaque language to be explicit, in using the example of £2.

After we checked that the coast was clear, the car drove into the basement garage at the Department. On the open-plan fourth floor all the television screens – set to the different news channels – were already showing various close-ups of my disgraced face. We went straight to Iain's office.

He declared: "Right, we need a statement in the next 20 minutes apologising." He sketched out the themes and gave them to Paul McComb to write up. After a little while Paul came in to say: "I'm sorry it's taking so long, the computer network's playing up." He had got the statement out to No. 10. "They're tweaking it a bit."

It was rushed out: "I would like to offer a full and unreserved apology. I was foolish to accept the premise of the question. To be clear, all disabled people should be paid at least the minimum wage, without exception, and I accept that it is offensive to suggest anything else.

"I care passionately about disabled people. I am proud to have played a full part in a Government which is fully committed to helping disabled people overcome the many barriers they face in finding employment. That is why, through Universal Credit – which I referred to in my response – we have increased overall spending on disabled households by £250m, offering the most generous work allowance ever, and increased the disability addition to over £310 per month.

"And I am profoundly sorry for any offence I have caused to disabled people."

Esther McVey was on the *Daily Politics* BBC programme to cover the employment figures as the story broke. She was rather less supportive than David Cameron. "I cannot justify those words, they were wrong," she said. "Those words will haunt him."

Iain was furious: "That's not what you say when a colleague's in trouble. She had plenty of time with Nick Robinson's pretty balanced introduction to think of a proper response.

"Pull her off the regional round this afternoon. The trouble is the story has now become Esther's disloyalty." He added: "Get the Department to start working on all the disability charities to explain what has happened."

When I saw Esther later she was unapologetic: "Well, this will haunt you. The disability lobby is the most vicious in the country."

I doubted very much whether I would survive this. I told Philippa: "Let No. 10 know that I am happy to resign the moment that they feel it is appropriate."

After the phone call to the Prime Minister's Chief of Staff, Ed Llewellyn, she told me: "He said that was really helpful; they have had real problems with Ministers on that in the past."

It was an inconvenient time to face a media storm. My wife, Cilla, had undergone a small eye operation on the previous evening and was travelling to and from Moorfields eye hospital for a check-up. Just before 2 pm I texted her: "I am in a little hot water at the moment, with attack by Miliband at PMQs. If journalists doorstep in the afternoon, don't open the door." *Sky News* came round even before she got home and left a card. I worried about how I could take care of her that evening.

My face was still on all the different channels as I walked across to my office to compose my resignation letter. It felt like being in the still centre of a hurricane.

The press office was working the phones. Lizzie Loudon, the Special Adviser responsible for media, came to offer reassurance in the mid-afternoon. By then the journalists had been able to read the verbatim version of my remarks. She reassured me: "They're all supportive on this. They feel Labour has manipulated what you meant. It's going to be all right."

The reaction was enough to ease the pressure for my immediate resignation at No. 10. After her latest conversation with Ed Llewellyn, Philippa told me: "No. 10 want you to go to ground for the next week. You can't go home. They're saying that if there's a picture of you anywhere you'll have to resign. We'll have to pull you off the oral question on credit unions and the debate on social justice tomorrow."

She explained: "There cannot be a picture of you anywhere because that just gives them the opportunity the run the story all over again."

She offered to shelter me that night at her west London home.

One of the TV screens was coincidentally showing a live picture of a car leaving the Department with darkened windows and claiming that I was in it. My new colleague Mark Harper, the Disabilities Minister, stood outside the Department to make a short, sharp statement of support.

Just after 4 pm Cilla texted that according to a neighbour: "They're all outside the house waiting for you to come home. I don't think it's safe to send a car for your things as they will only follow it."

I texted back: "I'll probably go back to Philippa's tonight and then see."

An hour later Cilla reported: "The rain has driven them away."

Robert Devereux offered me a glass of Prosecco, which became two in practice as we talked about progress in organising the Department. He said: "Well since I spent most of last year with people demanding that I be fired I know exactly how you feel. And I'm still here and so will you be."

Later, at 7 pm, Philippa's husband, David, came to the Department in his VW and we left for their house. They made sure I had a couple of glasses of wine with dinner and I took one of their son's P.G. Wodehouse books to bed to take my mind off the turmoil. The last message of the day came from Charlie Elphicke, Iain's Parliamentary Private Secretary and my local constituency MP. He reported: "In Commons have spoken to colleagues and made sure they understand what happened. They are understanding and supportive. Many have asked me to send you their best wishes and support."

With P.G. Wodehouse's help I managed to fall asleep but woke up very early with all the arguments running through my mind. I felt like I'd been physically hit. In the morning I mused to Philippa: "I realise why I got into trouble. It's using economic terms. When you get down to it, the problem was that I used the word 'worth' in its meaning of economic productivity to a commercial employer, and Miliband twisted it to mean human value."

Nick Clegg, the Deputy Prime Minister, certainly decided that my use of the word 'worth' was repugnant. In his *LBC* radio show that morning he declared: "He said, you know, some people with 'disabilities' weren't worth the minimum wage and that is what has quite rightly touched a raw nerve because it's kind of making a comment about someone's individual value, if you like 'worth'. And I think really, that was just so offensive to people." [118]

He must have been surprised when his two callers both came out in support of me. The first declared: "I'd like to have thought, naively, that if another political party had got a recording of it, which clearly they had, they would have used it as a positive slant to find a solution and not the negative slant to try to slay a head."

The second had an example of what happened before the minimum wage came in: "At this day centre they had a lovely time for I think a pound an hour just doing fairly menial tasks without in any way being offensive about it. And now they can't do that so they just sit and watch TV."

Later in the day his fellow Liberal Democrat, David Laws, rang up to say: "We looked at this in the morning and apart from some clumsy wording thought it was quite reasonable."

I spent the morning in Philippa's sitting room as messages poured in through the phone, text message service and email. Thanks to the hard work of the Departmental team, the reaction of the disability groups was moderated, with only a handful – including Mencap – coming out to demand my resignation. I made sure I answered all the messages that came through.

Philippa talked to Iain later in the morning. "He reckons that it will all die down by teatime today. So you may be able to go home to look after Cilla this evening."

We arranged for Tim Smith from Conservative Campaign Head-quarters to accompany me home at 8pm. He scouted out the locality to check whether there were any journalists lurking as I sat in the car at the end of the road.

"All clear."

I rushed into the house to greet my long-suffering wife, who was being looked after by our daughter, Juliet. Iain texted later that evening: "We managed a bit of a counter-attack on Labour as well which should get them off the case."

I tuned into the BBC political show *Question Time*.[119] The Health Secretary, Jeremy Hunt, was there to defend me on the last topic debated on the programme – whether I should resign. Nervously he pronounced: "I know it won't be popular but I think he should be given a second chance."

The Labour politician Angela Eagle had no doubts: "I do think he should resign. I think what he said was offensive. I think it's caused a great deal of offense to disabled people." Her own solution to the problem was "to go out and evangelise to employers about the benefits of employing people with disabilities."

Jeremy Hunt's face was a picture of delighted amazement as the Newbury audience turned on her. There was a round of applause when a member of audience accused of her being extremely disingenuous. "I think by the smirk on her face as she was saying it she realises it too."

Another asserted: "What you're doing is hypocritical political point-scoring and it's disgusting."

The original questioner summed up: "I just wanted to see if you would use that as a political football and you have done; thanks, Angela."

By next morning the right-wing political commentator Guido Fawkes summarised the debate under the headline 'Eagle Crash Landed'. "If Labour can't convince even the audience of *Question Time*, it suggests their attack on Freud may not have cut through as well as they'd hoped…" [120]

By Friday lunchtime the next day it was safe for me to leave for our place in East Kent. Philippa warned me that I would have to spend the day inside to avoid long-range camera lenses. That evening on the topical programme *Have I Got News for You* a mocking reference to my apology was met by dead silence and nervous glances from the panellists, who included Nick Robinson. By Sunday the pressure had come off enough for Philippa to declare that she was happy for me to risk a little gardening. It was a decision helped by an article in *The Sunday Times* by Dominic Lawson, who described how his younger daughter, who had Down's syndrome, delighted in her two hours a week unpaid work in a pub. [121]

On Monday, I abandoned my bicycle to travel into work in the Departmental Jaguar XL with darkened windows. My re-entry back into public life was due to take place on the following day when I was down to answer a question on sanctions for recipients of Jobseeker's allowance. I would need to apologise once again for my remarks.

I told the communications team that I wanted to say: "There is a particular group of very disabled people, with severe learning difficulties, for example, who face enormous challenges in their day to day life. Yet they want to work. They want to make their contribution to the economic life of the country. And our systems make it very hard for them do so. Surely in a compassionate society we could find a solution."

The team looked at me pityingly. Janine Lloyd-Jones, head of news, explained: "Then the newspapers will pick up the story and run it again. You cannot discuss this topic in public ever again. You have to stick with the words of your apology."

Obediently I stuck with the same form of words. Peers round the House were careful to concentrate the follow-up questions on the issue we were discussing. The apology got virtually no pick-up in the media.

Afterwards many Peers came up to me to say how disgraceful they found the entire episode. The former Labour Minister in the Department, Patricia Hollis, told me: "I've been making sure that none of the madness from the other end comes up here and is adopted by our Front Bench. I tried to do exactly what you were talking about when I was Minister. We called it therapeutic work."

At the Departmental Board dinner held coincidentally that evening I sat next to Esther, who apologised for her 'haunted' remark. "I'm just not that experienced. I picked up his expression and used it."

I replied: "Well, it would be hypocritical of me to complain about that, since that was exactly the thing that got me into trouble. Why didn't you get the Departmental briefing? Didn't your press officer know to push in before you were on air?"

Esther explained: "They tried, but they locked the door on them. It was a set up." We discussed the word 'worth'. Esther, whose Northwest constituency was Wirral West, told me: "Up in Liverpool it only means human value."

I said: "I think I've missed the way that word has changed. I blame L'Oreal with their tag line: 'Because you're worth it'."

The significance of Patricia's remark soon became apparent. Labour was planning to hold a vote of no confidence in me. However, this would not be held in the Lords, the body in which I was accountable, as one would expect. It would be held in the Commons, where I would not be present. Moreover, Rachel Reeves, who held the Opposition welfare portfolio, was not planning to lead the debate.

Outside the Chamber one of the Labour Peers, Michael Levy, pulled me aside. "I told Rachel that what is happening is a disgrace. You're a good guy. I told her you were a mensch. She told me she agreed." It was becoming clearer that Patricia meant that the Labour Peers had refused to do the vote of no confidence and now we began to wonder whether similar concerns might be the real reason Rachel was standing aside.

I was only able to watch the first half of the debate before leaving to answer a question in the Lords. It was led by Kate Green, the Under-Secretary on the Shadow team, who seemed genuinely bitter about me. She was supported by Steve Timms, who held the Shadow Employment portfolio. Mark Harper went through all the measures I had been organising to improve the lives of disabled and disadvantaged people. The no confidence vote was lost handsomely (243–302). Mark told me afterwards, "The debate was a disaster for them. Steve Timms hardly mentioned your name. He knew if he did, I would intervene to ask whether this was the same David Freud who had advised him in 2008."

It was also painful for Kate Green, who received a drubbing from Quentin Letts in the *Daily Mail* for her pains. He wrote: "By the end of her uncharacteristic, simplistic rant, Miss Green was red-eared. She looked sheepish. I don't think she believed a word she had said. The fool. She should have told those cowards Miliband, Eagle and Reeves to get stuffed and to do their own dirty work." [122]

Before the issue was finally put to bed there was one final spat in the following week between Rachel Reeves and Iain when he pointed out that she hadn't voted for the motion, or even signed it. She didn't specify her reason in the Chamber and left it to 'sources' to report in *The Daily Telegraph* later that she had been ill. "He does not know the reasons why I was not here, and I expect him to withdraw those comments," she retorted in the Chamber. [123]

It was left to the Prime Minister to sum it all up. In November he invited Cilla and me to join one of his evening receptions at Chequers. He told us: "You haven't become a proper politician until you've gone through one of these experiences."

The true price for Ed Miliband's diversionary attack was not paid by me. It forced me to break my promise to David Scott, the Councillor from Tunbridge Wells, to try to find a solution which would allow the inactive 94 percent of people with severe learning difficulties into the work-force. And it made the issue too politically dangerous for any politician to address.

PART IX

CUTS

January 2014 – March 2016

CHAPTER 23

The Pressure Mounts

At the beginning of 2014 George Osborne fired the starting pistol for the next election, due in less than a year-and-a-half. On the first Monday of the year he delivered a speech in the West Midlands in which he warned: "I can tell you today that on the Treasury's current forecasts, £12 billion of further welfare cuts are needed in the first two years of the next Parliament." [124]

He was immediately attacked by Nick Clegg for the "lopsided and unbalanced" focus on the working age poor. Iain let it be known in the media that he was alarmed by the proposal. His concerns were reflected in warnings from the Institute of Fiscal Studies that the cuts would be tough.

Iain told me the next day: "George did that without consulting us at all and now it's rebounded in his face. People don't like the cuts agenda, they like the reform agenda. We've been trying to get through to them but the barriers are up and they haven't been answering the phones all day. No. 10 have been apologising to us effusively."

The welfare spending record of the Coalition Government had been blurred by the intensely political arguments that enveloped the figures. Overall, in real terms, the welfare bill rose steadily through the five years - up nearly 12 percent in the period. ('Real terms' here reflects adjustment by the Consumer Price Index or CPI). Because the economy was growing, particularly in the latter part of the period, this meant that welfare costs fell as a proportion of GDP, from 11.7 percent in 2010 to 11 percent in 2015. This was a reversion from the previous trend; under the Labour Government, there had been a steady rise, with a sharp spike in the proportion of GDP taken up as the financial crisis of 2008 hit.

Within the Coalition's rising total, however, there was a division between the outcome for working age expenditure and for payments to pensioners. The latter increased to £116 billion in 2018-19 prices - up nearly 20 percent. By comparison the remainder, mainly working age benefits and tax credits, remained more or less flat in real terms to stand at £94 billion by 2015. So, as a proportion of GDP these working age benefits had declined from 5.6 percent to 4.9 percent. This brought it back into line with the levels in the early part of the Labour period. [125]

This underlying analysis was light years away from the political treatment of the topic. Here the key word was 'cuts', and these were a somewhat mythical concept. They were expressed as a reduction from previous projections – and these projections could be highly theoretical, particularly several years out. The Coalition claimed it had introduced £17 billion of cuts in real terms in working age expenditure over the period. However, in the event a substantial proportion of those reductions were undermined by faster than projected growth in various of the benefit payments. This was particularly the case for the disability and housing benefit streams.

Even though the cuts were partially offset, they were painful and difficult to implement. The two initial rounds represented the lion's share, taking place through 2010, in the second Budget of the year and the Autumn Statement, as described in Chapter 12. The Budget measures majored on the housing cuts, including the contentious removal of the spare room subsidy (or bedroom tax, as Labour dubbed it). It also exchanged the measure by which benefits were increased to account for inflation from the Retail Price Index to the – lower – Consumer Price Index. The Autumn Statement cut and localised council tax benefit (incidentally removing it from UC); time limited contributory Employment and Support Allowance and introduced the Benefit Cap. While we struggled to put through the legislation for these difficult changes, and then implement them, we continued to battle demands for further reductions.

We escaped relatively lightly through 2011. What measures there were focused on tax credits, within the Chancellor's own bailiwick. However, the pressure was back in the following year. In the autumn of 2012, we were presented with a long list of possible cuts, focused around housing and reduction in the child welfare elements. They were deeply unattractive and didn't save much money. Iain took the brunt of the pressure. At a Ministerial meeting in early November he told us: "We've been carving the measures away with analysis about how they don't work. Most of these ones left won't happen, so it's not worth getting too excited about them. I've told the Prime Minister that the best way to tackle this is with a single big cut that makes real money savings and that's got to be around a freeze."

The Liberal Democrat representative in the Department, Steve Webb, told us: "I've been talking to various of my colleagues and while there's not a single view, a lot of these housing cuts will not be supported. There might be something on reducing the uprating, although I'm not sure the party would stomach an outright freeze."

By the end of the month Iain was able to tell us: "It looks like some of the wilder stuff is out of the running. I've been telling them to go for one big thing, rather than all these silly bits and pieces which don't save any real money." A week later, the Chancellor announced an uprating of the main benefits, including the Local Housing allowance, of 1 percent in the following three years. This was intended to be a cut. However, in the event, the collapse of inflation in those years was to mean that the intended cut became a small real-terms increase.

The focus of battle switched in 2013. The initial internal briefing on the proposed Spending Review that spring was horrific, with a demand from the Treasury to cut the underlying Departmental Budget by 8 percent. I exploded at the meeting: "They can cut our DEL budget as much as they like, but what really matters is the impact on our AME welfare spending. If they want cuts like this we need to reshape Government rather than salami-slice. My vote would be to get rid of a big Department of State. Then we should stop the Triple Lock, which has cost us nearer £2.5 billion extra compared with the £0.5 billion estimated."

Iain said: "We've been incredibly lucky with the fuss about the spare room subsidy. Otherwise the other Ministers would be demanding lots more cuts, but they can see we're having trouble delivering the cuts which were baked in years ago."

When I saw Paul McComb later in the day, he told me: "We can't make these DEL cuts. The Treasury are probably only testing us. They just want a figure that the markets can believe."

Paul proved right about the Treasury tactics. The negotiation ended with a Spring Budget deal that allowed for a small increase in the Department's DEL spend.

Now that Universal Credit looked like becoming a reality, it moved into the Treasury firing line. The Autumn Statement in 2013 saw a three-year freeze in the UC work allowances. This meant that the amount that people could earn before seeing their benefit reduced would not go up with inflation. In the following Spring Budget the main feature was an increase in the UC subsidy for childcare spending – up from 70 percent to 85 percent. This restored a cut the Chancellor had imposed in 2010. The £400 million cost would come from within the UC funding envelope, although there was no precision as to how the money was to be found.

In the autumn of 2014 the focus was around a further freeze in working age benefits and tax credits. George Osborne announced at the Conference: "Even with the reforming decisions that Iain Duncan Smith and I have taken, benefits have risen more than earnings since Labour's great recession.

"That is not sustainable for any nation and it is not fair either. So I can tell you this today, working age benefits will have to be frozen for two years." [126] This would save £3 billion. It was, however, subject to a Conservative administration being in power after the election. In the Autumn Statement the UC work allowance took another hit, frozen for a further year.

This didn't stop the need to battle against wild proposals. That autumn Philippa rushed into my office to tell me: "They want to stop giving Jobseeker's Allowance to 18–21 year-olds."

I protested: "That's crazy. We'll just lose contact with them at the critical point."

Philippa replied: "Iain said we should destroy it. Can I say you are opposed?"

"Absolutely; stupid idea." The battle over this went on all week. On Friday Iain popped in to tell me: "I told No. 10 I was absolutely opposed and wanted to see the PM. At that point they caved."

The cuts agenda ran alongside the programme of long term, and fundamental, reform. Universal Credit was the central element. However, we were putting through a string of other programmes designed to transform the welfare system. There were two big changes to the support systems for disabled people. The Disability Living Allowance was being phased out in favour of the new Personal Independence Payment. At the same time the means-tested Employment and Support Allowance was being expanded.

There were major changes to the state pension. The age at which it was payable was being pushed back – to reflect greater longevity, as well as to make savings for the state. Steve Webb, the Pensions Minister, had brought in a major simplification of the cumbersome two-tier state pension system. He also oversaw the introduction of a new child support system, where couples had separated, to take over the ramshackle structures we had inherited. I had also redesigned bereavement benefits to reflect the introduction of Universal Credit and brought in a new state service to support people at risk of leaving the labour market through ill-health.

The line between reform and cuts was inevitably blurred. Some of the reforms naturally saved money. Universal Credit was far more efficient than the legacy systems and we estimated that, once fully operational, it would save the economy as a whole £7 billion every year. Part of those savings would go to the state.

Some of the measures sent a very clear message about the limits to welfare, even though the savings were relatively small. The Chancellor's Benefit Cap was the best example. It was estimated to save less than £300 million a year. However, it was designed in a way that incentivised people to enter the work-force (or, less desirably, to claim disability benefits).

The conflation of reform and cuts was promoted by politicians from both camps. The Chancellor sheltered his savings behind the genuine reforms. The Labour Opposition was happy to damn the reforms as cuts. In the midst of one of his rows with the Chancellor, Iain told me: "The party wouldn't have let him do all these cuts if we didn't have our reform agenda."

The context for this tension changed through the latter part of the Coalition period, as the labour market news became increasingly positive. By the end of 2014 employment was standing at an all-time high while the numbers on the key out of work benefits was down about 1 million to 3.9 million. There were signs that some of the structural unemployment and inactivity was being whittled away. The number of workless households in social housing – never lower than 46 percent even at the top of the business cycle – had now tumbled to below 40 percent.

Whatever the Government was doing – cuts, The Work Programme, reform or rhetoric – it seemed to be working. The falling welfare rolls generated, of course, significant savings for the Treasury.

The new team running Universal Credit were steadily taking control of the project. In November 2014, Ian Wright, the Programme Director, told me: "There are still elements of the programme that don't have clear reporting lines. I've spent this initial period just making sure we've got a proper governance structure so that all the activity can feed up into the main operating Board meeting."

In December the new digital system finally started operating, initially in Sutton with a handful of claimants. Iain and I went to see progress for ourselves in the New Year. The most unexpected finding was how the claimants had spontaneously started communicating with their work coaches through their shared online account. One of the coaches showed me the dialogue with a client. "He's been asking me about which of these jobs he should apply for and I've been able to tell him online. Normally I would only see him every fortnight. The account was never planned to work this way but it's incredibly effective."

In February 2015 we were in a position to report clear evidence of positive effects in the spring update of 'Universal Credit at Work'. [127] It found that people were more likely to be in work, would be in work longer and were earning more than comparable claimants on Jobseeker's Allowance.

The report also spelled out the plans for Universal Support. "For national expansion in 2015, DWP are putting in place funded delivery partnership agreements between JCP and Local Authorities. These will offer support for those needing extra help." This plan was built from the second set of trials with Local Authorities which began in the summer. They concentrated on the extra support people would need to handle their monthly budget and digital interaction with the UC system. However, it was becoming evident to me that this collaborative approach could easily be extended to help people with a range of problems.

That co-operation would be intensified if the services were co-located. In November 2014 I visited an operation in Wales where this had been done. In Flint, council services like housing were in the same room as Jobcentre staff. There had been a dramatic increase in productivity. The District Manager told me: "We closed one JCP with 16 people and relocated into two council properties with 10 people and provide a better service."

The main implication was the need for better sharing of information, whether or not the services were co-located. In December 2014 I was able to put out a set of regulations that allowed data-sharing for two specific requirements. The first was to work with landlords on rents. The second was to move information round the Universal Support network about vulnerable claimants. While the measure went through, there was some concern from stakeholders on the latter element. As a result I committed to consult on how the Department would apply the regulations when we had developed our plans in more detail.

I was also worried about how people would cope with switching over from a fortnightly payment in the legacy system to the monthly payment in Universal Credit. In practice they would have to wait for five weeks for the first payment, whereas the delay on JSA was, in theory, only two weeks.

As early as 2011 I had worked out that the Treasury should make a big one-off saving as we switched over. In a budgeting meeting I asked: "Have we accounted for the 4 percent that we save in the year we go from fortnightly to monthly and do the Treasury realise the impact?"

Sue Owen, then the overall head of strategy, said: "No, the Treasury haven't clocked it."

I responded: "Then we should devise a package that takes people from fortnightly to monthly over say three months, re-injecting the money the Treasury is taking from them."

This proved over-optimistic. The Treasury argued that because the claimants were being credited the funds over the monthly period, the accruals accounting methodology meant that the state did not see any gain from the switch. I simply did not believe this argument and sent the team back on a number of occasions to argue the case – to no avail. As a result, I developed a system of providing advances to new claimants who would be in difficulty because of the time gap. These advances could be paid back over six months.

Two years later, in the autumn of 2013, we were at our most defenceless – reliant on Treasury endorsement of the twin-track Universal Credit plan. They took advantage in the Autumn Statement by slipping in a delay before people were entitled to benefits, a measure which Neil Couling told me they had pushed for regularly. Seven days of so-called waiting days would apply to JSA, ESA and eventually Universal Credit. The adjustment would be made through regulations.

It was not till a year later, in November 2014, that I put through the first set of regulations in the House of Lords. These covered JSA and ESA and extended the number of waiting days from three to seven. I was given a rough ride in the Lords. The knowledgeable Liberal Democrat, Archy Kirkwood, pronounced: "These are savings dressed up. They are pretty mean-spirited and hit the most vulnerable." He went on to warn:

"A policy of this kind, if it were to be applied eventually to Universal Credit, would be much worse." [128]

With this warning about a likely vote against waiting days in Universal Credit, I read through the draft report by the Social Services Advisory Committee (SSAC) that weekend with mounting concern. It bluntly concluded: "The Committee's recommendation, based on the persuasive and compelling evidence presented to us, is that the proposal should not proceed." [129]

I wrote to the team: "I'm getting a bad feeling about this," and called an all-hands meeting to find a solution – not easy when annual savings of £200m were at stake.

Philippa stated: "We don't like this measure, so it would be wonderful if it was overturned in the Lords."

I replied: "It won't happen like that. It will end up being an attack on UC itself."

A couple of weeks later, in mid-December, I brought my solution to Iain. "Following the SSAC report we will inevitably be challenged on these regulations and that means we will be dragging the time delays in Universal Credit into the spotlight just before the election." I proposed that we should delay till the autumn at a cost of £15 million. Iain had already made up his mind: "Delay till July (at a cost of £5 million). I don't want to reopen it with the OBR at the Budget and £15 million is the kind of money that will alert them."

In mid-January 2015 I went through the time delay issue with Neil Couling, the Senior Responsible Owner of Universal Credit, in detail. He assured me that all the talk about accruals accounting losing the Treasury the gains from the switch to monthly payments was nonsense. "We'll be able to use it in the Budget negotiations."

I asked: "What about waiting days? Will you be able to kill it eventually?"

He laughed. "It's a rotten policy. They've tried to foist it on us for years and we had to accept it because we were weak. Now we're strong and we'll be able to get rid of it."

We let the interested parties know that we wouldn't be going ahead with UC waiting days before the election by sending a letter to SSAC, which they published. [130]

With the election looming, the process of assembling a Manifesto got under way in November. Jo Johnson, head of the Prime Minister's Policy Unit and brother of future Prime Minister Boris, was tasked with assembling the materials. Iain told me: "Jo is proposing to see all of the Ministers individually. I'm not having that. We'll gather the ideas ourselves and then give them to him."

I was very conscious of the importance of getting key policy proposals into the Manifesto. Once included, there became an imperative to implement, regardless of institutional opposition. This was how the DEL-AME switch was pushed through in 2010 despite Treasury resistance. Indeed, much of the work I completed in the *Get Britain Working* document of 2009 found itself in the Conservative Manifesto and then in the Coalition Agreement.

Philippa and I worked through a series of structural changes to take to Jo, whom we met in No. 10 later in November. I concentrated on the possibilities of expanding the concept of Universal Support so that a whole range of barriers that people faced could be coherently addressed. "We could move to working with Local Authorities right across the UK. We would provide the hard spine of a consistent benefit and conditionality structure, while they would be ensuring that the right services for their area were assembled round it. We could also co-locate many of the JCP offices with the Local Authority services."

I also suggested that we could make an announcement around supporting people with severe learning difficulties – the group over which I was attacked by Ed Miliband. Jo responded: "The Prime Minister will be very interested in that."

Philippa and I had completed a draft set of proposals for Jo by early December. It was a suite of measures aiming at full employment, with structural support for the most disadvantaged. Universal Credit was the centrepiece, and we would remodel the disability addition so that disabled people would not feel inhibited from working by financial considerations. We would expand Universal Support to provide a local safety net for the most vulnerable and widen the Work Programme to include the provision of skills and targeted health interventions. We included proposals for helping those with severe learning difficulties (a 'Long Term Apprenticeship' scheme); to ensure a world class payments system; to incorporate mental health provision into welfare to work; and the national roll-out of the Fit for Work service (support for the people in danger of leaving the labour market through illness.) The proposals were designed to reduce the welfare bill by moving as many people as possible into the work-place. The only overt cut was to switch the Support for Mortgage Interest system, or SMI, from outright grants towards loans repayable on sale of the recipient's home.

In the weeks before Parliament prorogued for the May election, I spent as much time as possible travelling to Jobcentres in the various regions as they took on Universal Credit. In January I managed Ashford, Newcastle, Port Talbot, Derby and Blackpool. In February I visited Birmingham, Daventry, Oxford and Abingdon; in March I was in Taunton, Grantham and Gainsborough. Across the country it was clear that the staff were genuinely excited to operate the integrated benefit. "This is the first time we have had a system we can work with, rather than battle against," one of them told me.

The Conservative Manifesto was published in mid-April, as the campaigning got under way. It was a bitter disappointment. Few of our proposals to support people into the workplace saw the light of day, in sharp contrast to my experience in 2010. There was a nod to Universal Credit, mental health and Fit for Work. However, George had not shifted from his determination to obtain a further £12 billion of welfare cuts. The Manifesto stated that the need to eliminate the deficit would "require a further £30 billion in fiscal consolidation over the next two years." [131]

It specified: "We will find £12 billion from welfare savings, on top of the £21 billion of savings delivered in this Parliament."

There was limited detail as to what the cuts might be. Working age benefits would be frozen for two years and the Benefit Cap on individuals would be lowered. 18-21 year-olds would see two restrictions: Jobseeker's Allowance would be replaced by a Youth allowance, time-limited to six months, and they would no longer have an automatic entitlement to housing benefit. These measures, which infuriated me by undermining the message of simplicity in Universal Credit, would raise only a fraction of the £12 billion.

I consoled myself by reflecting that – based on virtually all the polling – we would be back in Coalition with the Liberal Democrats, who would undoubtedly veto this hard-line Manifesto commitment. I was not alone in suspecting that this was what George Osborne thought too.

CHAPTER 24

Tax Credit Volte-face

To the consternation of the pollsters, the outcome of the May 2015 election was an outright victory for the Conservatives. They wiped out the Liberal Democrats in the West Country and gained a majority of 12 with 331 seats. Now there would be no excuses for failing to deliver the Manifesto commitments.

It took three days for Iain to be appointed. This compared with the re-appointment on the next day, Friday 8 May, for other major posts: George Osborne (Chancellor), Theresa May (Home Secretary), Michael Fallon (Defence Secretary) and Philip Hammond (Foreign Secretary).

Philippa told me: "There was a row all weekend. That's the third time Osborne has tried to get Iain out."

At the Monday morning meeting of the backbench MPs – the 1992 Committee – to which Peers were invited, David Cameron was jubilant. "I owe profound thanks to Andrea (Jenkyns) for defeating Ed Balls, which means I won't have to see" – he made a flat-lining motion – "all the time at the despatch box." Ed Balls was the Opposition Chancellor who had regularly signified poor economic growth with this gesture while David Cameron dealt with Prime Minister's questions.

Afterwards I caught up briefly with Iain. "I talked to the PM about you yesterday. You still want to do the job, don't you?"

I had already told him, and indeed Ed Llewellyn at No. 10, that I wanted to finish the job and it might take another year. But I was reluctant to continue taking the double load of the reform portfolio and handling all DWP business in the Lords on my own.

I re-affirmed: "Yes, subject to my conditions being met. I want some support in the Lords."

He re-assured: "We can do something there." Later in the day Ros

Altmann, a leading campaigner on pensions, was announced as Pensions Minister. She would be appointed to the House of Lords to take on the portfolio within the DWP. It was not in the way I expected, but my main condition had been met.

I was invited to No. 10 at midday on Tuesday. In his office David Cameron told me: "We'd like you to continue doing what you're doing on Universal Credit. The cuts will be vital and I want you to do more on housing benefit. You'll be Minister of State."

This was the level of seniority I had been promised in 2009, but they were hardly the marching orders I was looking for. I had a go selling him the concept of Universal Support. "It means that we can support the vulnerable jointly with the Local Authorities."

He asked: "But don't you have a problem sharing data?"

I told him: "We issued data sharing regulations a couple of months ago. People can now go into a hub providing services from us, Local Authorities and third sector organisations and be treated on a combined basis. I think it can be your compassion agenda."

He replied: "That is very exciting." We left it that I would forward a paper to him on the approach.

When the Ministerial team assembled on Wednesday, Iain laid out the problem we faced with the welfare cuts. "The trouble is that we have made so many promises during the campaign. I'm having a chart made up that shows that you start with £100 billion, you take off child benefit, then you take off disability and the total shrinks the whole time so that by the end the £12 billion is a very large proportion of what's left." We were planning two Welfare Bills, the first designed to quickly implement the cuts demanded by the Chancellor – cuts which now had the imprimatur of the Manifesto.

If we were to have cuts on this scale, I was determined that one of them should be focused on Support for Mortgage Interest (SMI). I wanted to turn it from an outright grant to a loan repayable once the recipient's home was sold – which could well be when the occupier died. SMI was paid to unemployed house-owners and poorer pensioners. It would be a cut in which no one's living standards would be directly affected.

Pete Searle, the head of working age strategy, told me it would have to go in the second Bill. "The first Bill is designed to be really straightforward and quick to deliver."

I insisted: "I want to see it in the first Bill we are working on, otherwise it will drift away." I went on pushing through the week, writing a letter to Iain, who agreed that SMI should go early.

This was by far the least contentious cut we were considering. I gave up early on reversing the introduction of waiting days for Universal Credit - a measure I had planned to kill after the election. There seemed little point in resisting in the context of £12 billion cuts, many of which would be more painful, since most of the people affected by waiting days would be coming from jobs.

Iain agreed: "We've got enough battles with the Treasury without this one," he declared. "We've got about four weeks to sort this all out. We're now working on a single Bill. It simply doesn't make sense to do it all twice."

By early June we were examining the impact of some of the proposals coming out of the Treasury. Pete Searle had developed a table of these - most of which were completely undeliverable. One of them was a big cut to child tax credit, which would throw nearly 1 million children into poverty and take £400 a week from some families.

Pete said: "They keep ruling out all the options and then saying: 'Bring us the nice cuts' - but there are no nice cuts."

Some of the proposals to reduce housing were equally undeliverable. I put my foot down on the idea for introducing a shared accommodation rate in social housing. This would force people to share their homes up to the age of 45 and even 65. I told Pete: "If they think the bedroom tax is bad, wait till people see this. I don't think the Government could get it through the Commons, let alone the Lords."

I was amused to see that Iain took an identical view a couple of days later. "It's the bedroom tax on steroids." It was becoming evident that the Treasury could not have £12 billion, if the time period was two years. On the more deliverable propositions we had been working on it could, conceivably, have the total if it was prepared to wait.

Philippa put her head round the door to ask if I would be prepared to resign if the Treasury raised the taper to 75 percent and dumped work allowances for childless couples and singles. I told her: "If they destroy the point of UC I'll leave because the only reason I'm staying on is to see this reform through."

The pressure mounted on work allowances in Universal Credit.

Philippa asked me: "Didn't you always want to remodel the work allow-ances? They want to cut them."

I explained: "They were only designed by Stephen Brien and Neil Couling to match the tax credits system. If they are cutting tax credits, we should be able to reduce the work allowances and still match. As you remembered, I was very concerned about the confusion of having so many different work allowances." We redesigned and simplified the work allowance structure.

Jeremy Moore, one of the senior officials in the Department, told me: "We're beginning to see a return to the conventional relationship between Prime Minister and Chancellor, where the Prime Minister worries about the impact of spending. That was all disguised when Clegg was holding the ring."

The news after the meeting with the Chancellor was that more was still wanted from work allowances, although the Prime Minister had got cold feet about some of the proposed cuts to tax credits.

Then Paul McComb and Philippa rang through. Philippa told me: "They want more out of UC." I replied: "We can't afford for any increase in the taper. That destroys the rationale for incremental increases in work. I'm adamant on this. We could look at the work allowances again."

I mulled over it overnight and rang back in the morning. "I'm genuinely prepared to resign on the taper. And I'm so angry right now I don't mind if you leak that to the papers."

Lizzie Loudon, our media Special Adviser, rang me back to say: "Iain doesn't want you to do any leaking. All that will happen is that they'll cut us out of the decision-making."

I came into work in the last week of June wondering whether this was the week I would actually resign. Philippa said: "If it all goes wrong, we'll send a message to No. 10 that you need to see the Prime Minister urgently."

I told her: "It may help the Department to defend UC when I've gone."

In the event I was not called on to visit the PM with my resignation. At the meeting with Iain, George Osborne acknowledged: "I understand the taper is one of the Department's red lines." This meant that the pres-sure reverted to further reductions in the work allowances – the amount of benefit people could keep regardless of their level of earnings.

At the meeting George revealed that he was planning a big reduction in tax credits, by reducing the thresholds (work allowances in UC-speak) and raising the taper, taking it above the level in Universal Credit. The relationship between the two systems was critical, since people would be transferring from tax credits to Universal Credit in the years to come and we didn't want there to be a substantial difference.

I asked the team to compare the tax credit and UC positions after all the proposed changes. The graphs showed they were similar and we did some fine tuning within the parameters.

George didn't get his £12 billion within two years. The package he announced in the Budget of early July produced reductions of just over £6 billion in 2017/18. However, five years out (in 2020/21) the total amounted to £13 billion. The big-ticket items were a four-year freeze in working age benefits; reductions in work allowances in Universal Credit and cuts to thresholds in tax credits, as well as a rise in the taper; the child element was limited to two children in both systems; social sector rents were cut by 1 percent for each of the following four years. In total these four measures produced the lion's share of the consolidation, at just over £10 billion five years out.

Even though we had seen off some of the most egregious proposals, there were a range of smaller items which would be painful both for welfare recipients and for the Department to implement. Among them, the Benefit Cap was lowered from a uniform £26,000 to £20,000 around the country and £23,000 in London. The disability payment for those able to undertake preparation for work was brought down to the basic rate for healthy jobseekers. Higher earners would be charged more for social housing and 18–21s would not be automatically entitled to housing benefit. Responsibility for the broadcasting licence subsidy for over-75s was handed over to the BBC.

There were some off-setting measures: a further increase in the threshold for income tax and higher levels of childcare subsidy. George had kept one surprise close to his chest. We had been recommending a big increase in the minimum wage. This would have the impact of switching support for low earners away from the benefit system towards employers. In the event, he went way above our £7.20-an-hour figure and introduced a National Living Wage which would reach £9-an-hour by 2020. The cameras were on Iain in the Chamber as he pumped both his fists in delight. It was an image that went viral on social media. The next day he was sitting in the restaurant in St James's Park when a party of school-girls walked past. "Hullo Iain," they called out, "Hullo Iain, Hullo Iain."

Rapidly, political pressure began to build against the changes to tax credits. I took a careful look at the overall impact, taking into account the changes to the National Living Wage, childcare and tax thresholds. In the first year there was an abrupt reduction in overall income; worse, the new higher taper rate in tax credits meant it could take six hours of extra work to make up the shortfall. However, as people moved across to the much more efficient Universal Credit the position eased and by 2020 the squeeze was much reduced.

Before this issue surfaced formally, I had to deal with the vexed issue of introducing an extra week's delay into the first payment of Universal Credit – the 'waiting days' measure I had hoped to kill.

It was not a surprise to be given a tough time in the House of Lords when I introduced the regulations in mid-July. I explained quite trans-parently: "It is a savings measure. It releases £130 million to £140 million in steady state. The blunt reality is that, in the present environment, if we did not find money here, we would have to find it somewhere else." I promised to keep a very close eye on the operation of the measure. I concluded, equivocally: "I have looked very long and hard at this and decided that, in this context, this change is appropriate and strikes the right balance. I will report back on whether that is the right judgment." [132]

The Lords let the regulation through. However, the mood was tough-ening up. Meanwhile, when we came back from the long recess in October, I found myself wrestling with the restrictions on housing benefit for 18-21 year-olds. The measure would support those who moved to take a job, but what about those who fled from an abusive step-parent, I wondered. When I met the team, I told them: "I want to kill the 18-21 housing change."

Pete Searle, in overall charge of working age policy, was unsym-pathetic. "Well good luck with that. It's in the Manifesto."

"It saves virtually no money and is much too complicated."

A few days later, by coincidence, I caught up with George as we both waited outside the Lords Chamber. It was the first time I had seen him face to face since we were in Opposition; at that period I had run in and out of his room on almost a daily basis. I told him: "The trouble with some of these changes is that they complicate Universal Credit, so people won't understand where they stand. And that stops them taking up opportunities."

George replied: "I buy that argument. What are the main problems?" I told him: "18–21 is bad and doesn't make us any money."

George replied sternly: "You should try to alert us early in the development of these policies." He had the good grace to falter when I looked at him incredulously. At least I now had an opportunity to re-open the issue with him, although in the event it was not till March 2018 that the Department succeeded in killing it.

Barely a fortnight later, the Government faced a revolt in the Lords over the tax credit cuts. Three motions were laid against the regulation, one of which – from the Liberal Democrats – would kill it stone dead. The other two would prevent it going ahead unless there was, in the second amendment from the Crossbencher Molly Meacher, an independent study of the impact and, in the third amendment from Patricia Hollis, full financial redress for those affected. Either of these would prevent the measure going ahead to time-table.

Since tax credits were a Treasury responsibility, the Department was out of the line of fire. The regulation was not even taken by the Treasury Minister in the Lords but by the Leader of the House, Tina Stowell, and her deputy, Freddie Howe. This was designed to change the terms of the debate from a dispute over welfare into a Constitutional issue.

In the Chamber, Tina argued that acceptance of any of the three amendments "would mean that this House has withheld its approval of the statutory instrument."

She went on: "That would stand in direct contrast to the elected House of Commons, which has not only approved the instrument but reaffirmed its view on Division only last week. It would have the practical effect of preventing the implementation of a policy that will deliver £4.4 billion of savings to the Exchequer next year – a central plank of the Government's fiscal policy as well as its welfare policy. It is a step that would challenge the primacy of the other place on financial matters." [133]

The Lords were unconvinced by the arcane debate of whether or not the Financial Privilege of the Commons over-rode the right of the Upper Chamber to reject – on rare occasions – secondary legislation. While the Liberal Democrat amendment was defeated, Molly Meacher's

won. She walked down the floor of the Chamber to bring the voting numbers to the Lord Speaker. It was a tight victory of 307 to 277. As the cheers went up from the Opposition, she awkwardly embraced Patricia Hollis, who was sitting en route. The Hollis amendment also prevailed, by 289 to 272.

Two days later Iain warned me: "They are coming after more cuts to Universal Credit to compensate for the erosion of tax credit gains. I'm beginning to think that these cuts are destroying the whole point of reforming the system. I may be going in the next few weeks."

I said: "Iain, I feel exactly the same. If you go, I'll resign with you."

At the meeting the next day the Chancellor kept up the pressure. Iain told me: "He's asked me to look at further savings in UC, maybe by kinking the taper. I told him I'd look at it, but there's no solution there."

By the next week, at the beginning of November, the Prime Minister was brought into play. Iain came into my room on Tuesday morning. "I've just come back from the PM. He summoned me in to complain that I was refusing to send the OBR (Office for Budget Responsibility) costing notes." After seeing the Chancellor, Iain had given instructions for the notes to be prepared but not sent to the Treasury until he had cleared them. The deadline for the OBR to receive the notes was three days ahead, in time for the Autumn Statement on 25 November.

"I categorically denied that we were withholding the notes. I told him: 'I promised the notes to the Chancellor. When have I ever not kept my word? Don't you trust me?' He looked shifty and said: 'Yes, yes, of course. But we are very interested in what a taper of 70 percent looks like.' I said: 'I have to tell you, Prime Minister, that whacking the people in Universal Credit harder when you have just lost a vote to whack them in tax credits doesn't make any sense at all.' Really, he is wetter than a duck's back. The way I feel now is that if they do move the taper that's it, I'm resigning."

I reassured him: "Iain, I am absolutely behind you on this. As far as I am concerned if they touch the taper I am out. You have my resignation in your back pocket. I will resign with you."

The Special Adviser working for Iain during this battle was Ed Boyd. As the struggle reached its peak, he checked on no fewer than three occasions that I was holding firm to my resignation threat. He told me: "The Treasury and No. 10 are in no doubt about Iain's and your determination.

If they lose the both of you it looks absolutely terrible for their welfare reform narrative."

In the afternoon, the Special Advisers from No. 10, Camilla Cavendish and Christian Guy, came over to assess the figures. They wanted to replace the missing £2 billion from tax credits by hitting Universal Credit.

Patiently Iain explained: "There's absolutely no reason to do that. It's an increase in debt, not in the running deficit they've got as a result of the defeat."

I pointed out: "The Chancellor has anyway got a problem if he softens the tax credits for too long. All that happens is that people lose more by switching over to Universal Credit and we will have to compensate with transitional protection. The two systems are connected and people will be moving from one to the other."

Camilla began to appreciate the point. "You're not the only Department to have this problem with the Treasury," she mulled. "The Home Office and Justice are also showing us how their approach doesn't add up."

By the evening Iain had gone on the offensive. The next morning the Centre for Social Justice, the think tank Iain had founded and which the newly ennobled Philippa Stroud was once again running, put out a note entitled *Reforming Tax Credits*. It concluded: "If the Government does seek to mitigate the costs of its new policy on tax credits it is essential that it does not do so by reducing the amount of money Universal Credit has at its disposal." [134]

Philippa told me: "It's very mild. I couldn't have been kinder to the Chancellor, though that's of course not how the media reported it."

By Thursday Iain was feeling pretty upbeat. He told me: "It's interesting how the Conservative Home poll shows a collapse in support for the Chancellor. These are the people whose support he needs. My feeling is that we have gone as far as we can. We've both been working for the last five years on changing the system to transform people's lives and these changes undo it all.

"At the same time we're putting in cuts in the Welfare Bill which I'm not particularly happy with and I know you aren't either. So I'm sending over those OBR notes that they want. They look pretty stupid, but in the end if they insist, I will simply not do them. I will resign rather than introduce them and you're telling me you'll go too."

I confirmed: "Absolutely. And if you want to use my earlier resignation tactically, I'm happy for you to do so."

Iain replied: "No, if we go, we go together. Anyway, I don't think it will come to that. I think they will back off.

The following day Fraser Nelson wrote a powerful piece in *The Daily Telegraph* which summarised the conundrum George Osborne faced. "He must now either abandon plans to find £12bn of savings by targeting the working poor – or stick to his guns and destroy the Conservatives' claim to being the new 'workers' party'." [135]

On Monday morning Iain popped into my office to say: "There's been a lot of good press last week, culminating with Fraser's piece which blows the whole thing open. The Treasury hasn't said a word in response. It's just radio silence over there. They pulled the shutters down. I'm seeing the Chancellor this evening and I'm going to tell him that if he wants to raid UC it won't be me that will do it and that my Welfare Reform Minister will be resigning too."

I was not at the meeting with the Chancellor. From the reports I got afterwards, Iain was at his most belligerent. The account went that at one point a member of the Chancellor's team suggested: "Maybe it would be appropriate to take a bit more off the work allowances?"

Iain lost his temper: "What do you know about what's appropriate? Who do you want to whack, the lone parents or the disabled, we've already taken them from everybody else?" He turned back towards the Chancellor. Iain recalled: "He looked at me quite frozen. I could tell he really thought I was going to hit him."

With growing concern evident from the Conservative back-benches, the pressure was off. By the weekend, *The Sunday Times* was writing: "Iain Duncan Smith has seen off an attempt by George Osborne to slash £2 billion from the budget for the Government's flagship welfare programme, after the Work and Pensions Secretary let it be known he was prepared to resign over the matter." [136]

Ten days later the Chancellor stood up to make his Autumn Statement. "I have had representations that the changes to tax credits should be phased in. I have listened to the concerns. I hear and understand them. Because I have been able to announce today an improvement in the public finances, the simplest thing to do is not to phase these changes in, but to avoid them altogether. Tax credits are being phased out anyway as we introduce Universal Credit." [137]

The cameras caught Iain's resigned, wry smile as this volte-face was announced. At our Ministerial away-day, two days later, I told my colleagues: "My number one concern is that we will have to recast the Universal Credit story. Rather than being the saviour coming round the corner, it carries the risk of being represented as the instrument of Government austerity." With tax credit thresholds unchanged and UC work allowances reduced, many people on Universal Credit would be less well off than if they were on tax credits. The inverse effect was that now UC was to do the heavy-lifting on cutting the cost of welfare, Treasury began to provide unqualified support.

I was already embarked on getting the Bill with the £12 billion cuts through the Lords. The Second Reading in mid-November had seen a sustained assault on the premise of the Bill. Crossbencher Colin Low, the former Chairman of the Royal National Institute of Blind People and blind himself, summarised: "Welfare can disincentivise work and keep people in a state of dependency, and that is rightly being tackled, but overwhelmingly, welfare benefits are paid to people in need and are the product of a society which increased prosperity and increased state provision has made increasingly civilised. The Bill legislates for a raft of cuts to meet the Government's target of cutting £12 billion from the welfare budget. That cannot but have a devastating impact on poor people who depend on benefits."

This was a far more contentious piece of legislation than the 2012 Welfare Reform Act. Bill McKenzie, for the Opposition, summed up the general view: "This is a wretched Bill. I am bound to say that it is the worst I have encountered in my time in the House." [138]

The convention that items specified in a Manifesto would be let through provided only limited protection; individual measures within the £12 billion figure could still be challenged. The only cut to receive general acceptance was the change to Support for Mortgage Interest (SMI), from which I took some private pleasure.

The first day of Committee was the most bad-tempered I had experienced. [139] We were not voting at this juncture; that would take place at the Report Stage. The initial discussion covered the two-child policy, where I had to hold firm, given the extent of the hostility. Maeve Sherlock, for the Opposition, opposed the whole proposal. "This measure will have all sorts of, presumably, unintended consequences: disincentivising kinship care and private fostering; disincentivising adoption; separating sibling groups; incentivising the break-up of larger families; and acting as a deterrent to the formation of step-families. It could require intrusive inquiries of women who have been raped and, of course, will take large amounts of money from families with children."

Archy Kirkwood, from the Liberal Democrats, talked about me "extending an olive branch" but that without it he would vote against the clause in its entirety. As I stuck carefully to the official line, Ruth Lister protested: "I was so disappointed with the Minister's responses to the olive branch that the noble Lord, Lord Kirkwood of Kirkhope, held out and the inflexibility in response to all the suggestions of how these clauses could be mitigated."

Afterwards I told Freddie Howe, the Deputy Leader: "It looks as if the Lords could be sending back as much as £12 billion of the Government's savings to the Commons. I can't see much point in offering the normal type of concessions at this stage. They'll just be swamped by the enormity of the amendments."

The mood improved as the Committee Stage progressed, although the attacks remained vigorous. Later in the first week Colin Low led an assault on the reduction in disability payments. By Monday Peers were talking about researching the impact of the sanctions regime and reversing the revised UC work allowance regulations, which had not been challenged in October. Later in December Molly Meacher argued convincingly that Carer's Allowance should not be subject to the new lower Benefit Cap. By the last Committee day in early January, the central issue was around how Supported Accommodation would be severely affected by the reductions in rents over the next four years. I was warned that the same sector would be badly hit by the overall cap on rents in social housing which the Chancellor had just announced in his Autumn Statement.

The impact on Supported Accommodation was the issue causing me greatest concern. This was a sub-group of the wider Supported Housing sector, providing specialist housing for the most vulnerable groups in society and which cost more than standard housing to operate. With all the battling over Universal Credit, I had not concentrated enough on this issue. I asked Neil Johnson, the head of housing benefit policy: "Did we know about this problem with Supported Accommodation?"

He confessed: "We knew it with the introduction of the cap but that's not due till 2018. We didn't know about the impact of rent cuts. The Treasury won't let us make concessions because, until we have the research, we won't know how much they will cost."

This was the research I had set in train when I discovered we knew next to nothing about how Supported Housing worked. However, it was proving slow to complete and would not be ready till the spring. I told Neil: "We need to sort this. We can't have refuges shutting down. My solution would be to hold these reductions in abeyance for a year while we look at the policy after the research is published. The cost has got to be within the 5 percent margin we've built in."

The Report Stage in late January was the time for concessions. Just in time I got clearance to exempt Carers from the Benefit Cap. It was enough to hold the losses on the first day to a single measure: a reporting obligation on child poverty from the Bishops. I promised the Carer's exemption, although Patricia Hollis took me aback with a well-argued case to also exempt those in receipt of an allowance to look after children, usually orphans, who were not their own: Guardian's Allowance.

The next day I told Iain: "I'd like to get rid of the Guardian's Allowance from the Benefit Cap, which should cost about £60,000." He told me (somewhat unrealistically): "Do it without telling anyone."

Just in time for the second sitting I got my concession on kinship carers in the two-child policy, although I failed to include those fleeing from domestic violence, as I wanted. It satisfied the Bishops, however, who withdrew their amendments to the two-child policy.

Colin Low was made of sterner stuff. He launched a fusillade against the reduction in disability payments. "Clauses 13 and 14 are all about making savings for the Treasury and have nothing to do with the interests of disabled people. They should be resisted," he declared. [140] He won his amendment convincingly (283-198).

The move to reverse the reduction in UC's work allowances failed, however, with the Liberal Democrats and Labour supporting different amendments. It was only left to wrap up the problem in Supported Housing where I was able to announce a deferral in the measure to reduce rents.

Iain was relieved that the attack on the work allowances in UC had failed. He told me: "That was the really valuable victory. I'm not sure I could have held our backbenchers on the work allowances, since they are spooked by the tax credits business."

With my hand considerably strengthened by the outcome, I set up a series of three concessions over the disability reduction, ready for the ping pong process between the Commons and the Lords. I also decided on full exemption from the Benefit Cap for recipients of the Guardian's Allowance.

The ping pong process in February was relatively straight-forward. The Commons sent back the two amendments, using Financial Privilege on the disability issue. I gave the Bishops statutory assurance that the main poverty figures would be published, with which they were satisfied. This left disability as the last issue. Here I offered my three concessions, which I had discussed beforehand with the Peers concerned. They were not enough for Colin Low, who called, and won, another vote (286-219).

The proposition, to delay the introduction of the measure, only persuaded one more backbench Conservative in the Commons, in the shape of Heidi Allen, to rebel - a total of three. In fact, the Government majority moved up appreciably this second time around.

I went to discuss strategy with John Taylor, the Government's chief whip in the Lords. I told him about a further potential concession I had up my sleeve.

John was a steady, calm operator, who had initially been my own whip. "We don't want a concession. We don't want to reward bad behaviour. The convention is that the Crossbenchers support the Government when it's Financial Privilege. You already split them in half first-time round."

I suggested: "Could you get the Labour and Lib Dem whips to put pressure on Colin? They may not want a constitutional crisis on this." John agreed with the strategy. And two days later I got a message from him: "Labour not voting Monday!"

When I went to see him, he told me: "Now that Labour has decided not to vote, they'll put pressure on Low not to put an amendment. They won't want to be seen abandoning the disability lobby."

Colin Low bowed to the inevitable and did not lay a further amendment. The final ping pong stage went through rapidly, although Colin was extremely bitter. "This is a black day for disabled people. The Commons have spoken decisively and we must bow to their wishes, but we do so under protest. Do not let anyone kid you that this is democracy in action."

He warned: "By this action, the Government have betrayed the trust of disabled people and they should not be surprised if they forfeit it for the rest of their time in office." [141]

Royal Assent to the Bill went through in the following week, in mid-March. I did not feel any sense of achievement.

In the latter stages of the Bill I was trying to sort out the problems created by the Chancellor's new cap on social rents. The cap was timed to come into effect in 2018, but would apply to new tenants from April. The landlords running Supported Accommodation warned me that new developments were now being abandoned as a direct result. I decided we needed to defer the April start date by a year. That would buy us time to work out what to do once we had the results from the research.

The Special Advisers and team working on the next Budget were reluctant to throw the £60 million required into the negotiations. I said: "This is not about politics. This is pure financial reality. No one will take on a permanent resident next financial year if they think the housing benefit will halve in 2018."

Pete Searle, leading the working age negotiations, suggested: "Well, wouldn't they be able to offer short-term tenancies?"

I demanded: "Are you expecting them to throw someone out in two years? How does that help them?"

When I saw Iain, he took the point straight away: "Well, of course we will have to do this. I don't really care about the £60 million. It's all up and down with the Treasury anyway. We'll throw it into the Budget negotiation. They want £1.2 billion for the OBR and are going for £1.8 billion because they think the OBR will throw out half. So I'm saying we've got you £1.4 billion and when we deal we'll throw this in. With luck that'll be next week."

By early March the deal was done and we had gained the one-year delay from the Treasury. When I saw David Orr, Chief Executive of the National Housing Federation, he told me: "This is a really bad mistake. People can't afford to run these places on these amounts and people will be badly hurt." I was utterly candid with him: "We got this wrong but it would be painful to undo it right now because we would simply lose all the money in OBR arithmetic terms and we can wait till we know what we are doing with the review."

There was one more major issue emerging from the Chancellor's cuts programme. Soon after the July 2015 Budget Neil Couling, now firmly in the saddle as Senior Responsible Owner of Universal Credit, explained: "These changes make it impossible to keep to our roll-out time-table. We can't introduce all the measures into Universal Credit without a delay. We don't even know what the exemptions in the two-child policy look like yet and they'll be very difficult to code."

He prepared various time-lines for consideration, which showed a substantial slow-down. Later in the autumn he told me: "The boss (Iain) won't even talk to me about it. He doesn't want to know." The issue, which we labelled 'contention', remained unaddressed as we swung out of the Autumn Statement review and headed for the next Budget in March 2016.

CHAPTER 25

An explosive resignation

Iain was now showing definite signs of cuts fatigue. He had taken the brunt of the pressure from Chancellor and Prime Minister for what was adding up to five separate 'fiscal events' within a 12-month period. We had faced a pre-election Budget in March 2015, albeit with minimal welfare changes. There was an in-year squeeze on Departmental spending of £105 million immediately after the May election. This was followed by the £12 billion of cuts in the July Budget. Hot on its heels came the Autumn Statement, with various smaller changes – including the problematic cap on social housing benefit payments. Now Iain was once again in battle. For the March 2016 Budget, the Chancellor and Prime Minister had the rapidly increasing claims on the Personal Independence Payment (PIP) in their sights.

In late February, as I was dealing with ping pong, Iain hurried into my room to update me on the PIP negotiations. He was scathing about both the Chancellor and the PM – who was, he told me, hard as nails. Iain's disenchantment with the Prime Minister was reinforced by the looming Brexit referendum campaign, where they would be on opposite sides, and which was due to begin in a matter of weeks.

The Department put out a response to a consultation on possible changes to PIP on Friday, 11 March.[142] It stated that applicants to the benefit should receive reduced points for difficulty with 'dressing and undressing' and 'managing toilet needs'. Justin Tomlinson, the effective and cheerful Disabilities Minister, justified the change in his Written Ministerial Statement: "PIP was introduced with the intent of supporting claimants with the greatest need to help them meet the extra costs arising from their disability or long-term health condition." However, the statement added: "Significant numbers of people who are likely to have low or minimal on-going extra costs are being awarded the daily living component of the benefit solely because they may benefit from the use of aids and appliances for certain activities." [143]

The weekend press carried a rather different slant, with an emphasis on the £1.2 billion savings that the move would generate and the headroom this would provide the Chancellor to raise the threshold at which the higher, 40 percent, level of tax was paid.

On Monday Iain expressed his anger when I talked to him: "I went into Downing Street to tell them they had screwed it up. You can get disability changes through – we do it all the time – but not like this. Not saying they're to pay for middle-class tax cuts. There's no way this is going through the Commons now. It won't even get to the Lords."

On Wednesday the Chancellor duly announced his Budget. He made no mention of the PIP changes in his speech, but he did lay out the tax reduction for better-off earners. He stated: "We made another commitment in our Manifesto and that was to increase the threshold at which people pay the higher rate of tax. That threshold stands at £42,385. I can tell the House that from April next year I'm going to increase the Higher Rate threshold to £45,000." The cost of this move was £600 million a year.

Iain was not in the Chamber for the statement, having gone to a funeral.

The next day I ran into Justin Tomlinson as he made his way back to the Commons from the Department. He had been dispatched to defend the policy. "I'm talking to all the MPs with the whips but they're not buying it. No. 10 say we should just tell them we were elected to do this, but I thought we were elected because people didn't fancy Ed Miliband and Nicola Sturgeon taking over. I'll talk to them as much as they want me to, but it won't make any difference. I wouldn't worry about PIP getting to the Lords. It'll be stopped by the Commons way before it gets to you."

With the rebellion growing, it was time for the blame game to begin. The briefings from the centre put out that Iain was responsible for the pre-Budget communications. "I could see the briefings getting more and more vicious," Iain told me later, "blaming the Department and me. George Osborne is completely without principle."

On Friday evening, David Cameron was on the phone to him trying to prevent his resignation, when Iain revealed: "It's too late. The announcement is on the screens." The Prime Minister reacted, Iain told me later, with a series of expletives.

Iain's resignation letter spelled out his growing exasperation with the cuts process. "I have for some time and rather reluctantly come to believe that the latest changes to benefits to the disabled and the context in which they've been made are a compromise too far. While they are defensible in narrow terms, given the continuing deficit, they are not defensible in the way they were placed within a Budget that benefits higher-earning taxpayers."

The frustration boiled over in the penultimate paragraph: "Too often my team and I have been pressured in the immediate run up to a Budget or fiscal event to deliver yet more reductions to the working age benefit bill. There has been too much emphasis on money saving exercises and not enough awareness from the Treasury, in particular, that the Government's vision of a new welfare-to-work system could not be repeatedly salami-sliced." [144]

The Prime Minister's response dodged the issue of who would take the blame. "We all agreed that the increased resources being spent on disabled people should be properly managed and focused on those who need it most.

"That is why we collectively agreed – you, No. 10 and the Treasury – proposals which you and your Department then announced a week ago. Today we agreed not to proceed with the policies in their current form and instead work together to get these policies right over the coming months.

"In the light of this, I am puzzled and disappointed that you have chosen to resign." [145]

The briefing blame game continued through Saturday. The Special Adviser at the Treasury, James Chapman, drafted a statement for my colleague Ros Altmann, the Pensions Minister, to put out attacking Iain. Her poor relationship with Iain made her susceptible to the proposal and in the afternoon of Saturday she tweeted out: "I simply cannot understand why he suddenly chose to quit like this when it was clear Number 10 and the Treasury had told him they were going to pause and rethink these measures. I'm particularly saddened that this really seems to be about the European referendum campaign rather than about DWP policy." The tweet emphasised: "He seems to want to do maximum damage to the party leadership in order to further his campaign to try to get Britain to leave the EU."

By Monday she was deeply regretting the statement. "I was set up," she told me. "I'm naïve."

Iain hit back with massive force. He went on *The Andrew Marr Show* on Sunday and spoke fluently and devastatingly about his motivation. "I care for one thing and one thing only. It is that the people that don't get the choices that my children get are left behind.

"I do not want them left behind. I want them given that opportunity and everything I've tried to do has been about that. Yes, we can debate some of those things that people didn't like because they're more about the deficit than about welfare reform, but over-archingly what I am passionate about is getting that reform done so society is reformed, so that we have more of those people who've been left behind brought back into the sphere and the arena where we play daily and they do not.

"That is what I am about and what I have been concerned about, and raised this time and again, is that we are beginning to lose that focus and I cannot do this from inside. That is my frustration. I believe I have to step out.

"It's not easy. It's painful to resign. I don't want to resign, but I'm resigning because I think it's the only way I can do this . . ." [146]

The performance stopped the attacks stone dead. By Monday *The Times* was carrying a story that David Cameron "blames George Osborne for the row over disability cuts". [147] My Ministerial colleagues, Justin Tomlinson, Priti Patel and Shailesh Vara, counter-tweeted their support for Iain against Ros Altmann.

I was paying little attention to the media storm. Iain's replacement was Stephen Crabb, the Welsh Secretary who grew up on a council estate. I had worked with him in the past, both when he was a whip for the Department and later when we were tackling the welfare reform programme as it applied to Wales. We had got on well. Now I joined him on his first afternoon in the office, on Sunday. It was a daunting promotion for him, as various officials briefed him on the main issues. Richard Caseby, Director for Communications, pointed out: "There are 50 people in the Communications team in head office alone. That's bigger than the entire Welsh Office."

As Robert Devereux stepped out to oversee the preparation of the statement on our PIP plans, I was left alone with Stephen for the first time. It suddenly occurred to me that we had a golden opportunity to use Iain's performance on *The Andrew Marr Show* to stop the Treasury salami-slicing.

I advised: "You should say in the statement 'no more welfare savings'. That will stop all the political wrangling stone dead. It's only recognising reality. Iain will be on the back benches with enough anti-cut MPs around him to put a stop to further cuts anyway." Unknown to me, Robert had already made this suggestion before I had arrived.

Stephen said: "You're right. There isn't a majority for welfare cuts in this Government anymore."

I added: "It will be a tremendous way for you to start as your own man. It's 50/50 whether you get it – but if you don't try you certainly won't get it. You will never be stronger than you are today."

Stephen went round to see George Osborne and Ed Lewellyn, the PM's chief of staff. Somewhat to my surprise, they agreed the phrase – 'no more welfare savings'.

By midday on Monday we were drafting the statement, joined by a couple of Treasury officials who seemed remarkably relaxed about the phrase. One of them took a phone call. We glanced at each other apprehensively. "They want to change the 'I' to a 'we'," he told us.

Robert Devereux observed drily: "We can live with that."

Then Mark Swindells, one of the private secretaries, hurried in. "That was Number 10. They say that the PM wants the sentence about no further savings taken out."

Robert sighed: "So it starts."

I said: "Just push back. Say we are not prepared to accept its removal."

Robert pointed out that it was unlikely to be a direct response from the Prime Minister, who was preparing for the European debate. "It's worth pushing back a few times."

As we broke up, Stephen's mobile rang. He held out against the pressure, pointing out: "This is what I agreed last night with George and Ed. There's not a Government majority for more welfare savings. This just acknowledges the fact." He agreed to make it clear that savings already agreed would go through. This did not undermine the story.

In line with convention, Stephen gave the statement first in the House of Commons – which I repeated in the Lords a little later, in the evening. He announced: "I can tell the House that we will not be going ahead with the changes to PIP that had been put forward."

He added "I can also confirm that after discussing this issue over the weekend with the Prime Minister and the Chancellor, we have no further plans to make welfare savings beyond the very substantial savings legislated for by Parliament two weeks ago, which we will focus on implementing."

As planned, the statement laboured the point: "I repeat that we have no further plans to make welfare savings beyond the very substantial savings legislated for by Parliament two weeks ago, which we will focus on implementing." [148]

The House gave him a relatively easy ride after that, particularly as he could duck anything complicated by responding along the lines: "My intention, very simply, is to look at all these questions with a fresh pair of eyes."

When I took it through the Lords, I was able to pay a tribute to Iain. "He was a remarkable champion for reform in the welfare state. I say with feeling that there is a reason why no one has transformed the system in the last 70 or 80 years and that is that it is very difficult to do. He had the political guts to get on and do it, and I am very proud to have supported him in getting the programme as far as it is. I think that he will go down in history for that achievement." [149]

The headlines the next day were as good as we could hope for. The *Financial Times*, in particular, summed up the position in its lead story. "Stephen Crabb, the new Work and Pensions Secretary, stunned MPs yesterday by suggesting a six-year crackdown on welfare spending was at an end as the Government fought to contain the damage caused by Iain Duncan Smith's resignation last week." [150]

We had managed to stop the desperate salami-slicing of the welfare budget – but it took Iain's resignation to achieve it.

PART X

VISION

May 2015 – December 2016

CHAPTER 26

Exit and Future

By the May 2015 election Universal Credit was making steady progress. It had been rolled out right across the 91 Jobcentres of the North West region for single people and families. The national roll-out programme for single people covered a further 160 sites. Some 50,000 people were receiving Universal Credit, which was available for people making fresh applications for benefit, and a third of Jobcentres were now operating the system. This was the original version of Universal Credit, the so-called 'Live Service', and we were on target to cover the whole country within a year.

The successor digital system – now renamed the Full Service – was operating in the Sutton Jobcentre and we planned to expand into one more office, in Croydon in South London, immediately after the election. The next step would be the central London office of London Bridge in November, followed by the conversion of 'Live Service' claimants in Hounslow to the Full Service early in 2016. This was much slower than the original projection of the Cabinet Office, which forecast a 'safe and secure' digital version by the end of 2014 – a figure later revised to November 2015. It would not be till the spring of 2016 that we would be in a position to start adding small numbers of Jobcentres to the Full Service offering. Nevertheless, the team was now quite clearly making steady progress, though not without a few glitches along the way.

One example was thrown up when I visited the benefit centre in Canterbury in October 2015. This was the first team to work behind the scenes on operating the full digital service. I held a round table discussion with about 30 of them to find out how it was going. One of them told me: "Unlike the Live Service we don't have a six-month run-on. So we had a case of a woman who was paid twice in a month, because the second was an early payment, and she was taken off Universal Credit."

I was genuinely shocked: "That is absolutely not what our policy intent is. It is vital that people can work less or more every month and not feel that they are risking their benefits." I had devised a process in the Live Service whereby people could go back smoothly onto their Universal Credit arrangement for six months after leaving the benefit – the six-month run-on.

Afterwards I reproached Neil Couling – who had taken over the job of SRO a year earlier – about the issue. He argued that I had approved the change on a temporary basis at a Hard List meeting. He added: "Fortuitously there is a proposal to address this coming up to the Design Authority next week." Later I looked through the meeting notes and failed to see any evidence of my approving the change. I let it ride for the time being. It was a prime example of how policy can be transformed by detailed operational fiddling.

It was also a good example of how difficult it can be to fix this kind of deviation. Exactly a year later, in October 2016, I discovered, to my surprise, that the six-month run-on had still not been re-instated. There was a testy stand-off about it in the meeting between two officials, one of whom insisted that I had cleared it.

I answered: "I cannot envisage clearing something like that, since it goes counter to the whole philosophy of Universal Credit, and even if I did it would have been a temporary expedient." There were mutterings about checking the paper trail, which never came to anything. A couple of days later Neil explained: "I told them to air the dispute in front of you; you being a lot calmer than I am. Someone took a decision and they forgot about it. I told them to fix it."

Together Neil Couling, Universal Credit's SRO, and Ian Wright, the Programme Director, took the operation steadily forward. By the spring of 2016 they were working on integrating the operational systems for staff with the core Universal Credit front end; the booking system needed to tie in with the availability of work coaches and drive the way they were managed. The system needed to be able to handle big volumes; the plan was to expand to 50 Jobcentres a month by early 2017. The data architecture remained secure, according to the outside assurances I made sure we obtained.

At the same time the central IT competence of the Department was being transformed following the appointment of Mayank Prakash as

Director General of Digital Technology. He joined from the investment bank Morgan Stanley at the end of 2014 and within months had developed a rigorous change programme. He planned to accelerate the insourcing of development expertise and infrastructure operations. He would remodel how we handled data and ensure that IT became integral to the Department's business processes.

The clear evidence that the reform programme was now coming under control meant I could look at a sensible departure date. I had committed to another year when I was re-appointed by David Cameron in May 2015. The sheer complexity of the programme to cut £12 billion inevitably put the date back. It also meant that I had a genuine value to contribute to the reform process in being able to threaten to resign – either with Iain or alone – if I saw measures that were too structurally damaging. I was concerned about the relative timing of my departure and Iain's. They needed to be asymmetrical so that we could transfer our knowledge to our successors. In the event the issue was solved by Iain's abrupt departure in March 2016. I judged that I could safely leave by the end of the year – which I told Stephen Crabb, the new Secretary of State, shortly after he took over. Later he asked me: "Are you sure about going at the end of the year? Can I say anything to get you to stay?"

"I'm sorry, Stephen. It'll be 10 years by then and I'm genuinely exhausted. My added-value is coming down now quite steeply. I know the task isn't over but my role in it is. I'm planning to use the period to pass on my knowledge to the new Ministerial team so they're on top of all the issues."

I was also acutely aware that the next phase of welfare reform would – or could – be just as monumental and time-consuming as the initial stage that was now established. Once Universal Credit was in place in the early 2020s, it would be possible to optimise our welfare system in a way that had not been feasible in the past. This was because Universal Credit is a coherent system where the elements are controlled and understood, unlike the legacy systems which mesh together poorly.

It will be for the reformers of the next decade to take advantage of the opportunities that will become available. As I tell the story of my last half-year in office, I will diverge to discuss the nature of those opportunities. Indeed, I aimed to set up some of those developments for the years to come while I was in office.

Perhaps the most important opportunity is to build our knowledge of the nature of an effective welfare system. Angela Merkel, the German Chancellor, affirmed in a *Financial Times* interview in late 2012: "If Europe today accounts for just over 7 percent of the world's population, produces around 25 percent of global GDP and has to finance 50 percent of global social spending, then it's obvious that it will have to work very hard to maintain its prosperity and way of life." [151]

The level of welfare support is central to a nation's culture. It has to balance two elements. The first is the safety net that people feel is appropriate; the second is the level of support that will continue to motivate recipients to take control of their own lives whenever possible. If too generous, it will leave the group next up in the hierarchy wondering why they are bothering to put in the effort for rewards barely, if at all, better than state dependency. That kind of concern will tend to drive up numbers, which will in turn enmesh another group in such disquiet.

However, the decision as to where to set the level of support has very little, if any, empirical research to guide it. George Osborne's decision to take £12 billion out of the system was an attempt to roll back the big increases seen in the tax credit bill since 2004. "These changes to Tax Credits are not easy but they are fair, and they return tax credit spending to the level it was in 2007–08 in real terms," he announced in his July 2015 Budget speech. [152]

With Universal Credit in place, those decisions can become more research-based. One of the measures I put into the 2013 Act was the ability to vary the key parameters of the benefit in trials. This is quite ground-breaking, and transcends the traditional approach of adopting national parameters in the welfare system. It means it will be possible for the DWP to test, for instance, what happens if the taper rate moves. It will be able to answer the question: "If the taper is reduced to, say, 55 percent, do overall costs to the Treasury move up as people receive more money or are recipients incentivised to work more, thereby reducing the total benefit bill?"

The same question can be asked of a hundred parameters: the level of work allowances; the benefits of another work allowance for a second earner in each household; variations in payments for disability. With a knowledge base like this it will be possible to optimise the Universal Credit system so that there is the maximum incentive to work balanced by the adequacy and cost of the safety net. It should also be possible to keep testing the key parameters as society and behavioural responses change in the decades ahead.

One other advantage of trials in Universal Credit is the availability of evidence. In the legacy system it is extremely expensive to collect the information on how people have responded to a particular change. In Universal Credit it should be possible to monitor quite cheaply any changes to earnings seen by people in a trial. This means that the Department can run an extensive programme of trials at reasonable cost.

The quality of the trials will be critical. Too often trials are run which do not produce definitive results. I spent considerable time with the strong team of analysts in the Department making sure that we were in a position to obtain results uncontaminated by wishful thinking and robust in terms of control. In my last months, Trevor Huddleston, the Chief Analyst, put together an excellent paper on how the Department would start to build the evidence base for Universal Credit. We reviewed it together and I told him: "It's good and I'm not surprised that the earliest you can start the trialling is 2019. I suspect, given the complexity, you will need all that time to set up a trial anyway."

The nature and level of support for people with disabilities is central to the benefit structure. Many, if not most, people with disabilities are able to work and, according to surveys, would prefer to do so. The legacy system was assembled in various elements and functioned by putting people into specific categories. So under the Employment and Support Allowance – or ESA – the disabled were actively prevented from working – or working very much – under the rules of their benefit. Widows and lone parents were examples of two other categories. This mono-centric view of human nature served to trap people in the welfare system.

Universal Credit undoes that trap. To take an example: a computer programmer might have an intermittent condition like Crohn's Disease. They could work for three months at a time and then the illness would return and render them unable to work for a period. Under the legacy system they would be wary of taking up the high-paying work in the first three months for fear of relapsing once they had lost their benefit arrangements. Under Universal Credit, the programmer could take on work secure in the knowledge that even if his earnings were very high for some months, his underlying right to Universal Credit would remain in place for half-a-year. In the current context, it is particularly suited to providing flexibility for the sufferers from long Covid.

There was, however, a problem which I wrestled with in my last years. This was the nature of the test to establish disability. The test, originally introduced in 2008 by the Labour Government, was called the Work Capability Assessment - or WCA. By definition, a person who scored under this test was being told they were not capable of working. If that was the message, the fact that Universal Credit did not erect financial barriers to working was of limited value. A person would be concerned that the next time they undertook the assessment, their work record would be taken as evidence of disentitlement to the disability element.

In January, before the 2015 election, I met with Mark Harper, the Disabilities Minister, to go through how we might transform disability benefits. I thought we should look at abandoning the WCA, which was anyway deeply unpopular, and simply use the same test as the new Personal Independence Payment - or PIP. This would have the virtue of halving the number of assessments and start to consolidate the two separate systems of support for disabled people.

I told Mark: "If we passport from PIP into Universal Credit we'll simplify the system but I don't think we understand what the differences between the ESA Support Group and the PIP group really are." We agreed to initiate a piece of primary research looking at the two benefit structures.

We discovered that significant numbers did not overlap in the two systems of support, making the option to move to a single assessment prohibitively expensive. When we re-assembled after the May election, we were no further forward in terms of a deliverable structure. Our internal debate had widened to take in how we would work with the NHS and whether we should beef up the Fit for Work service, which was now operating - although with disappointingly low referrals from GPs. In the context of our efforts to find £12 billion of cuts for the Chancellor Iain was worried that the Treasury would want to score any changes in the current spending round. "That would destroy any sense of reform," he pointed out.

To kick-start the process, he delivered a major speech two months later in August 2015. "ESA may have been designed with the right intentions, but at its heart lay a fundamental flaw. It is a system that decides that you are either capable of work or you are not. Two absolutes

EXIT AND FUTURE · 303

equating to one perverse incentive – a person has to be incapable of all work or available for all work.

"Surely, this needs to change. In the world beyond ESA, things are rarely that simplistic. Someone may be able to do some work for some hours, days or weeks, but not what they were doing previously. As ESA becomes part of Universal Credit, the two approaches seem at odds. We need to look at the system and in particular the assessment we use for ESA. The more personalised approach under Universal Credit sits alongside a Work Capability Assessment, which sets the wrong incentives.

"That's why I want to look at changing the system so that it comes into line with the positive functioning of Universal Credit." [153]

We had not got much further by the autumn. The stresses and strains of the cuts package were undermining any ability to drive through fundamental reform. Iain confessed: "I'm not sure that the centre will go for a big bill. What can we do with secondary legislation?"

I told him: "Well we might be able to do something. After all UC has got a route for tax credit people to be passported into disability from PIP, so we may be able to expand it. We'll look at two options, a full scale Bill and a smaller process."

I began to concentrate on whether we could replace the WCA with an assessment that looked at whether people were disadvantaged in the labour market. By the New Year the team were ready with a proposal. I pointed out: "It's no good having something that basically does what the WCA does. We might as well stay with the existing system."

Justin Russell, who was the Senior Responsible Owner for the reform process, explained: "The test says 'after a period we have established that people are disadvantaged in the labour market and therefore are due an income supplement'. We can focus the test on the key markers of labour disadvantage."

I asked: "So it won't be lost if people do a job?"

Justin: "Exactly. People will still register on an assessment of their disadvantage."

I concluded: "That satisfies me."

Later in the month I assured the Lords: "Halving the disability employment gap is a crucial part of achieving our full employment aspirations and a key priority for this Government in its own right." [154]

In practice, it proved difficult to achieve much progress as the change to the lower disability element in ESA was pushed through the Lords. The battle over the proposed changes to PIP, followed by Iain's explosive resignation, also dampened any momentum. Nevertheless, Stephen Crabb recommitted to the initiative to close the gap between the 50 percent rate of employment for disabled people compared with the 80 percent for the non-disabled. Soon after his appointment he said in a speech: "I think that gap is simply unacceptable." [155]

By October 2016 the Green Paper was finally released. [156] It treated the issues rather gingerly. It talked about reforming the WCA and updating the statutory sick pay system. In the Lords I confessed: "We all feel that this is taking a long time, but there is a good reason for it. We are transforming a system that put people in a silo of disability and did not let them back into work. Transforming that requires Universal Credit as a fundamental base where you do not just have those different groupings; you have everyone able to do what they want, with their pay adjusted accordingly." [157]

The options for the next decade in this area will be more wide-ranging. It would make most sense to integrate both the two assessments and the two different payments to disabled people. It may be attractive to treat the revised payments in the same way as those for Carers; part a non-means-tested allowance and part incorporated in Universal Credit and effectively means-tested.

One of the most important initiatives in the latter part of my period in office was to build a system of support for the most vulnerable, which we called Universal Support. I spelled out the approach early in 2015 to a Local Authority audience: "The roll out of Universal Credit is an opportunity to bring together many different agencies responsible for delivering the current multitude of benefits alongside other local support providers, like Local Authorities and charities. [158]

"Many of these services often work in isolation. Under Universal Support, these services will be brought together in a joined-up, potentially co-located way, based on local needs to provide whole person support; led by a partnership of the Local Authority and JCP, in the interests of both claimants and the taxpayer.

"Whilst we recognise the need to support vulnerable people we also recognise that, for many, vulnerability is not a permanent state but something that affects them temporarily. We also believe that, even for people with chronic problems, the role of support must be to maximise their life chances, help to move them towards full independence, work readiness (wherever appropriate) and social inclusion.

"Universal Support encourages that approach. This is why the strong integrated relationship between DWP, Local Authorities and third sector organisations are key in delivering this intent."

We had already created the Universal Support system as a way of handling two of the challenges thrown up for the vulnerable by Universal Credit in the shape of budgeting and digital capability. There was no reason that the system shouldn't be extended across a range of vulnerabilities; homelessness and other housing problems, banking services, training, even mental health support. It required a triage, or case worker, process as well as data sharing between the various agencies. Co-location, which several Local Authorities had already introduced, was also an effective ingredient. Nor was I looking for substantial extra funding. Many of the services were already in place; they were simply ineffective in transforming the situation of their clients on an isolated basis.

I had failed to insert the wider version of Universal Support into the Conservative Manifesto, but at least had a commitment from the Prime Minister to take a good look at it. I set about working with the welfare team at No. 10 on producing a paper on the way forward.

The initiative mirrored a major change in the way that Jobcentres operated over the 10-year period in which I had been involved. When I was researching my original paper, in 2007, the labour economics team described the exchange: "You get paid your benefit but the price you pay is to be nagged to get back to work. That's the effective driver in the process."

Two elements led to the change. Employment started to hit new peaks. Indeed, the rate kept on improving right up until the onset of Covid 19, peaking at 75.6 percent at the beginning of 2020. Once adjustment to the figures is made (reflecting the growth in student numbers, for example), this rate more or less matched the 80 percent aspiration which launched my own journey into welfare reform in 2006. Pre-Covid, those left with difficulty in the labour market were likely to be suffering from real barriers rather than experiencing the vicissitudes of the business cycle. At the same time, the changeover from personal advisers to work coaches triggered a real difference to the relationship between the claimant and the Jobcentre. The work coach was far more likely to spot the barriers and try to help the claimant to tackle them. The problem we faced was that there were too few tools to help the work coaches in managing those barriers. A close relationship with other agencies, possibly co-located with them in a hub, would increase the effectiveness of the process.

My plan to bring the Prime Minister on board with this initiative was overtaken by events. Nevertheless, with the narrow version of Universal Support in place, the groundwork for an expanded vehicle to help the most vulnerable tackle their problems in a coherent way represents a major opportunity in the decade to come. Already, as part of its response to the Covid pandemic in 2020, the Department used this approach in its introduction of Youth Hubs for those aged 18-24.

Iain's departure meant that Neil Couling could now raise the issue of 'contention' in the Universal Credit development plan. Iain had refused to acknowledge the issue, burned no doubt by the memory of past announcements about delay. "I spent 2013 hiding in this broom cupboard," he joked with a couple of us shortly before he left, as he opened a mysterious door at the back of his office.

The 'contention' issue was caused by the amount of extra work thrown up by the £12 billion of cuts. The Universal Credit IT build programme had to incorporate a large number of changes, some of which were reasonably straight-forward, like changing the work allowance rates and the level of the Benefit Cap. Others were proving much more complex. These included the change to disability rates and the removal of the automatic right to housing for 18-21 year-olds. Particularly problematic was the two-child policy with its complex exemptions for multiple births, rape victims and sibling groups. Neil also had to incorporate a so-called 'emergency brake' to stop new immigrants from other EU countries having access to Universal Credit. This was part of the deal David Cameron had agreed in February 2016 as he headed into the Brexit referendum. Incorporating these would inevitably lead to a delay in the roll-out plan for UC. Neil was working a difficult balancing act between the losses involved in delaying some of the changes with those created by delaying the introduction of Universal Credit. By mid-May the delay in UC was estimated at up to 12 months.

Shortly afterwards, Robert Devereux came into my office to tell me: "Right, I've got a solution. There's no iron rule about putting everyone on UC when we roll out, is there? If we exclude the families with three or more children and leave them on legacy, tax credits will handle them.

I've had a quick chat with HMRC and they say they can do this for us. What do you think?"

I said: "If it stops us having a bucket of pigswill thrown all over us, I'll go with it. We're only talking handfuls of people, aren't we?" It would still mean a slowdown in the delivery plan, but it was a big improvement. This was the option we worked up and presented to the Chancellor in mid-June.

By now the Brexit referendum was only days away and it was not until afterwards that George Osborne responded, accepting the proposal. By then the Prime Minister had announced his resignation, in light of the referendum decision to leave the European Union, and the race to succeed him had begun. The process was expected to stretch over the summer months. Among the contenders was Stephen Crabb, the new Secretary of State at the DWP. But the initial drama centred on two of the mainstream contenders who had supported Brexit, when Michael Gove failed to back Boris Johnson, who subsequently pulled out of the running. Two ballots among Conservative MPs selected Theresa May and Andrea Leadsom as the candidates for the party membership to choose between. Stephen Crabb withdrew ahead of the second ballot, and shortly afterwards was the subject of a story in *The Times* accusing him of sending suggestive texts to a woman. David Cameron, still Prime Minister till the campaign to succeed him was over, came to his defence: "He's a very effective Secretary of State for Work and Pensions and must continue with that work."

Amidst all the drama, we had assembled a statement dealing with the complex set of changes to the programme. The target date for the announcement was Monday 11 July. Over the weekend I discovered that No. 10 had pushed the date back three days, presumably to avoid the Prime Minister facing questions about it on Wednesday.

The timetable was overtaken almost immediately, when Andrea Leadsom abruptly pulled out of the race, damaged by a story in *The Times* about her alluding to Theresa May's childless state. Suddenly, Theresa was the only candidate standing and she took over as Prime Minister on Wednesday afternoon.

She set about a dramatic reshaping of her Cabinet, signalled by her ruthless firing of George Osborne as Chancellor. On Thursday morning I was in the Chamber doing a debate on poverty. My relatively young and enthusiastic whip, Natalie Evans, was sitting beside me. Early on she hurried out to respond to a phone call. She did not come back. I was keeping an eye on the news feed on my phone as the debate continued and was surprised to see the headline that she had been appointed the Leader of the House, replacing Tina Stowell. This was not the only distraction during the three-hour debate. Halfway through came the news that Stephen Crabb had resigned as Secretary of State to DWP. He had arrived at No. 10 clearly expecting to continue in the role and emerged after a long gap looking thunderous. The allegations about his texts had clearly had an impact and Theresa May proved less supportive than David Cameron.

When I rose to speak, I opened: "My Lords, I am responding to this debate in the most unusual circumstances imaginable. I started off with a Whip beside me; she disappeared after a few minutes and then popped up on my telephone screen as my new boss, the Leader of the House – the boss of all of us. So that is unusual. Later, I saw on the screen – I am sorry, I have not been quite as attentive as I normally am – to see that apparently my other boss, the Secretary of State, Stephen Crabb, has resigned." [159]

Stephen's replacement was announced later in the day. Damian Green had worked with Theresa May at the Home Office and was now recalled from the backbenches to the Cabinet. He had spent his early years as a business journalist and was a steady, thoughtful and unshowy politician.

The reshuffle process continued through Friday and the weekend. Ministers continue in post until they are told otherwise. I assumed, initially, that the new Prime Minister would want me to stay but that belief started to erode as the hours, and then days, ticked by without being called and the reshuffle proved far more radical than I expected.

At home on Friday, I watched the news as other long-standing Ministers in particular roles were either moved out or on. My colleague, Ros Altmann, left as Pensions Minister on Friday. She texted me the next day: "When I spoke to Theresa last night, she said you will now be the only DWP Lords Minister."

Despite this indication there was no contact through the morning and afternoon of Saturday. The Prime Minister fired two Ministers who had worked with me in her Shadow DWP team, in the shape of Mark Harper (chief whip) and Andrew Selous (Parliamentary Under-Secretary at the Ministry of Justice).

Finally, at around 6pm Natalie Evans, the new Leader of the House rang up. I told her: "Many congratulations. All my whips do well. That must have been a surprise."

"Telling me." She switched to the matter in hand. "Look, we want you to go on doing exactly what you're doing as Minister of State at the DWP."

I replied: "I'm happy to do it but you know I want to leave at Christmas. I wouldn't want to continue on a false prospectus."

"No, that's understood."

I added: "One other thing, I want the announcement to confirm me in role as Minister of State for Welfare Reform."

"They want to keep the portfolios flexible."

I insisted: "Could you just confirm formally that my title remains." I wanted (some) protection to keep doing Universal Credit. She came back five minutes later with the confirmation and the formal announcement included the title.

I was still in office and would need to spend my last months supporting an entirely new Ministerial team. The extensive nature of the reshuffle also meant there was no-one else in the Government with my durability in the same job – a point picked up later in the week in the Lords by the Liberal Democrat Archy Kirkwood.

He leapt up to ask: "Will the Minister confirm that, if my history is right, he is the single surviving Minister since 2010 holding down the same office in government, promoting the interests of Universal Credit? Is this because the subject area is so complicated, or maybe because he is unpaid? . . . I hope that the Minister will stay in his position for some time yet." [160]

With some pleasure I confirmed that I was the last man standing: "I thank the noble Lord. His sums on this are right, although, along with him, I am not sure whether that is a compliment or the opposite."

Damian Green had reworked the portfolios over the weekend. I kept Universal Credit and Universal Support, with the aim of moving Housing over to Caroline Nokes, one of the new arrivals who had joined the ministerial ranks for the first time. In the event, the complexity and contention of the housing issues meant that the handover was to be extended till my departure as I gradually transferred the portfolio to her.

The other elements of my portfolio would be inherited by Damian Hinds, the new Employment Minister, who had moved over from the Treasury, where he had been responsible for tax credits. I had worked with him extensively on the two-child policy and found him engaging and painstaking.

In retrospect, my efforts to hand over my portfolio to informed successors proved quixotic. Caroline Nokes and Damian Hinds were both gone within a bare 12 months of my departure, as indeed was Damian Green. The traditional merry-go-round for DWP Secretaries of State accelerated. There were no fewer than seven between 2015 and 2020.

Our first order of business was to deal with 'contention'. Damian Hinds joined my regular meeting with Neil Couling on Monday morning. As we got going, we were interrupted by the fire alarm so reconvened in the more relaxed surroundings of the Blue Boar café opposite the office. Neil told us: "We still haven't had clearance from No. 10 to release the Written Ministerial Statement. We have to do it by Wednesday, when I'm seeing the PAC."

I said to him: "Make sure you clean out all that crap about the four principles that Stephen Crabb put in. Just play it absolutely straight."

Finally, the statement was cleared for release and went out on Wednesday morning, 20 July. The Full Service (digital) version of Universal Credit, which covered almost all types of cases, would now continue to roll out at the pace of five Jobcentres a month till June, when it would accelerate to 30 and subsequently 55, completing the process in September 2018. (This compared with the commencement of the acceleration in February 2017 under the previous timetable and completion of the roll-out three months earlier in June 2018.) There would then be a contingency period till June 2019. Managed migration would start in July 2019 (a year later than the previous schedule) and finish nine months after the previous schedule in March 2022. New claims from families with more than two children would be excluded till November 2018, in line with Robert Devereux' solution. [161]

The statement was received rather quietly, with only a handful of news stories. At the Public Accounts Committee Neil justified the timetable change robustly. "It is a bit like you have asked me to build a house with three bedrooms in it and then halfway through, when I am laying brick, someone has said, 'Can you put another two bedrooms on it?' That is why I don't think it is a delay. It is actually an increase in scope – a change in design." [162]

The official PAC report, when it came out in November, brushed this argument aside and blandly condemned the team: "A flexible system should be able to cope with a degree of policy change." Given the ferocity of past excoriations from the Public Accounts Committee and National Audit Office this was, nevertheless, rather tame. [163]

The nature of my job was anyway changing in the last few months. The process of refining the specification of Universal Credit was now at an end as the ramp up in volume loomed. In the autumn, when I was looking at an area in which to make improvements, Neil told me: "We can't go on making changes now. I've got five teams building this out and I can't let even them make changes because they will inevitably interfere and undermine what the other teams are doing."

After my departure there was steady progress in undoing the complexity introduced by the cuts process. On departure, I was invited by Frank Field, the Chairman of the Work and Pensions Select Committee, to give evidence on my experience. [164] One of the blunter questions, from the Labour MP Neil Coyle, involved where I would prioritise extra money within Universal Credit if some became available.

I replied: "Universal Credit is oddly generous on the way out but not on the way in. I would look at two things to improve that. I think waiting days does not help in the introduction of Universal Credit. I also think you would look at a housing run-on for a fortnight, of housing rent in the old system, and that would start bridging that gap. Those wouldn't cost a lot of money."

This reflected my recommendations to Damian Green in the last months before I left, reflecting the emerging evidence that the wait for the first payment of Universal Credit was proving difficult for a proportion of claimants. I was surprised when the changes didn't go through in the next Spring Budget. In the event it took a damaging row for the changes to be made in the Autumn Statement of 2017.

In my retrospective I went on to discuss how to bring back more coherence to housing benefit payments: "The next area that I would work on, and this is more expensive, and it will have to be worked on at some stage, I think, is getting the payment system back to some coherence. It was meant to be set up on a 30th percentile and it is now slightly all over the place because of the restrictions. I think getting just a coherent, simple system back, which would cost some money, would be useful. Again, back into the simplicity." This concern reflected the fact that various rate freezes had undermined the Local Housing Allowance system and meant that in some areas there was virtually no private accommodation to rent at the prescribed housing rate. It took until 2020 for this reversion to be made as part of the emergency responses to Covid 19.

Finally, I went on to discuss how the Universal Credit system didn't work for short-term accommodation and other Supported Housing. This was a careful summation of the work to follow up the shocking discovery that we were spending more than £4 billion on Supported Housing and had only the loosest of controls on that expenditure. I had managed to get a consultation paper put out to tackle the issue. The solution I favoured was to pass the funds and control for all such accommodation to the Local Authorities. Such a system would have required the Local Authorities to have statutory responsibility for the defined vulnerable groups. It was not till I been retired for nearly a year that the rather tame outcome emerged. Short term housing, such as refuges, would be funded locally; sheltered housing would be funded under a formula rent scheme; however, DWP would go on funding the costs of longer term provision within Universal Credit.

I had emphasised the importance of simplicity when I gave evidence. Simplicity would mean that people would not worry about unforeseen consequences if they changed their work habits. Predictability would free people to work as much as they wanted and break the welfare trap. I did not spell out in detail the areas which would benefit from further simplification.

Any means-tested benefit should be incorporated into the UC system. Top of the list would be the council tax benefit, or rebate, which was kept out in 2011 in order to provide savings to the Treasury. The second area would be passported benefits, which are unusually extensive in the UK. As the SSAC report of 2012 pointed out, it should be possible to develop a way of incorporating these benefits, particularly school meals, into the UC system. Otherwise there will be particular earnings levels at which payments drop off abruptly and make people cautious about working more.

One of the anomalies in the system are the contributory benefits which lie alongside and in parallel with Universal Credit. Under current arrangements people who have paid enough National Insurance are entitled to six months of Jobseeker's Allowance and indefinite Employment and Support Allowance at the higher, support, level. Numbers are now relatively small and the cross-over with Universal Credit is highly complex. Sometimes Universal Credit will be worth considerably more to individuals, yet it may be worth sticking with the contributory payment because it is not income related. Cross-checking every month is an impossible task. The solution should be to close these contributory benefits to new applicants and run off the existing caseload.

A fully functioning Universal Credit would encourage reversal of some of George Osborne's more emblematic cuts. The Benefit Cap would lose its rough and ready justice in the context of the chaotic legacy system once Universal Credit built up a coherent entitlement for each citizen. Already in March 2018, the cut which treated 18-21's differently in the system, had been reversed.

One of the most significant implications of combining benefits and tax credits – the first for those out of work and the second to support those in work on low incomes – is the new relationship the Department will need to develop with the in-work population. This represents a fundamental change. When I first got to know JCP, its role was to cajole people into the workplace. Once a claimant got a job, the task was done. Under Universal Credit the relationship will be maintained while the claimant remains on low pay. A second objective has been introduced: to encourage working claimants to reduce their reliance on state funding. A series of trials have started testing the most effective way of doing this. Looking further ahead, however, it raises a fundamental issue about the relative importance of building and refreshing an individual's skills compared with the 'work first' strategy the Department has adopted – and found to be effective – for the out-of-work.

This goes to the heart of the low productivity puzzle which blights the UK. The country has a strong performance when it comes to tertiary education. It is far weaker than competitors like Canada or Germany when it comes to middle-ranking skills. So as the Department becomes concerned with raising earnings among the low paid, it will have to address the reality that working more hours is only a partial solution. The most efficient way to raise earnings on a sustained basis will be to encourage the acquisition of skills. The implication is that the Department will need to develop relationships with employers to encourage training and there may be substantial funding implications to realise the necessary investment. In a modest way I was able to initiate a skills acquisition strategy for benefit recipients in my last months. I ensured that lone parents with children between three and five could continue to receive their benefits if they went on a course, of up to a year, approved by their work coach.

Within the UK Government structure, the Department for Skills has been separated from the Department responsible for Employment since 2001. It has wandered around the bureaucracy from Education, then over to Business and, most recently, back to Education. There is a strong argument for tying Skills back with Employment and that argument is strengthened by the introduction of Universal Credit, where the Department will develop close relationships with low-paid employees who need to enhance their skills, as well as their employers.

The other relevant group is the self-employed. The rules within Universal Credit are stricter than those in tax credits (though tax credits have adopted some of the measures in Universal Credit). The most significant is the Minimum Income Floor, whereby the system assumes that the self-employed are earning at least the minimum wage after a period of building up their business. Early on I told the team: "If we are going to start having expectations of this group, we are going to need to find ways of supporting them in their businesses as well."

I summarised progress to Frank Field's Select Committee after I retired: "Self-employment in this area is something you do not get much help with under the tax credit system. You can go on earning miserly amounts without any support.

"One of the things I was trying to do is build a cadre of work coaches who understood small business. We had a group in, I forget the exact number, and they were spreading (expanding) that so there was someone in the Jobcentre who would specialise in the self-employed and supporting them in getting to that level if they are not earning enough.

"It is pulling in some of the New Enterprise Allowance and integrating that into Universal Credit. There is a lot of detailed work there. Getting a group in to help people in the self-employment space will be of huge value to the economy as a whole."

A central challenge for the Department is how it handles mental health. This is the largest single source of disability claims, accounting for around

40 percent of the total. The bulk represents mild to moderate conditions for which appropriate work can be a positive element in achieving recovery. With the Liberal Democrat Norman Lamb at the Department for Health I instituted a series of trials as to how support into work could best be organised for those with mental health conditions. While the findings were disappointingly limited, it remains likely that support at an early stage, together with close liaison with the health systems, could resolve much misery and lead to a more productive economy.

Disability and mental health require a complex organisational response. Many of the necessary elements are now moving into place. Under Universal Credit the financial disincentives to work are removed. A reformed assessment for disability would eliminate any bias in the system for people to think they are incapable of work. An early alert system in the shape of the Fit for Work service should allow intervention when people risk falling out of work rather than after a year or more of unsupported inactivity. Finally, a coherent package of measures could be put into place under an expanded system of Universal Support, in which the Department, Local Authorities, third sector companies and even the health service would work together. This structure is aimed at handling the various problems people face: very often someone with a mental health problem, for instance, may face further problems as well. Under an expanded Universal Support structure, a case worker would guide people to appropriate support and the various intermediaries would be able to share relevant data.

My first attempt to tackle these issues was through The Work Programme. This payment by results system encouraged the contractors to help the disabled back into work with payments as high as £13,000 per successful long-term job entry. The initial results, so far as the disabled were concerned, were disappointing. While they improved considerably, particularly for some of the contractors, it was clear that on its own The Work Programme would not solve the issue. The contractors were battling a benefit system which made taking up work risky and competing in a support environment which was highly fragmented.

In the autumn of 2015, I found myself at a disheartening research presentation on the impact of The Work Programme, which showed that it was not value for money. I protested: "But you've only looked out two years. The whole idea was to establish people in the world of work and effect a long-term transformation in their lives." The researchers shrugged sympathetically, pointing out that their terms of reference incorporated the two-year period. I could do little to save my creation (which was outside my Ministerial responsibility). Employment levels were nearing all-time highs, while the Department was determined to save as much of its own capacity as it could as the Treasury bore down on its operating budget. Instead, we launched the much smaller Work and Health Programme. I could console myself with the finding that The Work Programme was very considerably cheaper than previous programmes, saving the State some £500 million compared with previous funding arrangements.

It was only five years later that research established that The Work Programme, in the shape of one of its mainstream components, had indeed been value for money. A study of the group aged 25 or more found that, even within the two-year period, the programme had a positive economic impact for the participant, the DWP, the Exchequer and society. [165]

The Jobcentre work coaches have become key agents in finding and tackling the barriers that prevent people from working and, increasingly, earning more. We also found that they are well positioned to act as a conduit into Universal Support and, potentially, an expanded Universal Support system. However, they are provided with too few tools to help them in their task. In November 2016, just a month before my departure, I invited a group of high performing work coaches to a round table discussion.

I asked: "If you were in a complete fantasy world where you could have whatever support you wanted, what would you want to help with your clients?"

It was a pretty slow start. There were about eight work coaches and they were not used to being asked to think out loud with a Minister. I explained: "It's a waste of your time to have to go through all the information and education of your clients yourself. Wouldn't you want to send them to look through an app which was relevant and then you could talk with them about it in a fortnight's time. We've already developed one app for clients, on how to budget under Universal Credit."

After a bit they loosened up and the ideas began to flow.

"The apps have to be on the phone," they told me. "The claimants don't like computers."

We ended up with about 11 apps. Among the suggestions most enthusiastically promoted was an app to diagnose skills; another to establish the level of competence in English as a Second Language (Esol); a third would provide support for disabled people to get into work. Some of the tools would help the work coaches establish what help their clients needed. Others would give those clients the information or knowledge to tackle issues independently. It would appear self-evident that a modest investment in these tools would multiply the effectiveness of work coaches.

The Real Time Information system developed by the tax authorities is a major strategic advantage for the economy and one which, to date, has not been adequately exploited. It means that the Government receives details of employment and pay on a monthly basis. As such it has the potential to transform the statistical base of the nation. To take one example; the employment figures use a three-month rolling average which is woefully out of date. The RTI feed could supply up to date information within days of the end of each month and allow much more rapid responses to problems. Real-time earnings data, covering virtually all employees, could similarly accelerate the production of national statistics. It would offer a more sophisticated analysis of where support and intervention were required. It could provide a better calibrated support system for deprived schools than that provided by the crude measure of free school meals.

Many of these developments will lie years, if not decades in the future. I am convinced that Universal Credit will become a pattern that many countries round the world will want to imitate. On my last visit, in the summer of 2016, to one of the gatherings of European Ministers (the Employment, Social Policy, Health and Consumer Affairs Council), there was a clear indication that the EU trip I had initiated to see Universal Credit had made an impact. At a lunch to discuss the support systems for the self-employed, Marianne Thyssen, the European Commissioner for Employment, Social Affairs, Skills and Labour Mobility, said: "We have to ask the question whether we should move to single welfare systems, when there are so many grey areas between the systems targeted at particular groups." The remark suggested to me that she had accepted the UC concept. The political pressures now emerging around long Covid, with its intermittent impact on sufferers, is likely to reinforce the appeal of UC's flexibility round the world in the years to come.

My last fiscal event was the Autumn Statement, which took place on

23 November 2016. The run-up lacked the drama of previous occasions, thanks to our 'no more welfare savings' commitment. Damian Green, the new Secretary of State, confirmed at our first meeting to prepare: "I've told the Treasury that we are not going to make any welfare savings beyond those already agreed."

In fact, Theresa May's concerns about the group which she had dubbed 'just-about-managing' at the outset of her Government, meant we started looking at restoring some of the cuts to Universal Credit. The political embarrassment of reversing the work allowance cuts made a reduction in the taper rate more attractive. The country was already pretty close to cyclical full employment and changes to the taper would be reasonably efficient in encouraging people to work more.

If there was money available for Universal Credit, I also wanted some of it to be directed at easing the problem of the long wait before the first payment was received. In early November I held a meeting with Damian to argue for the elimination of waiting days and a two-week run-on of housing benefit. I told him: "This isn't about having a policy which looks good for the 'just-about-managing' group. This is about avoiding real problems as we roll out UC; the kind of problems which could derail the whole process."

Damian replied: "I completely agree with your point."

The Treasury was just as high-handed when it came to putting money back into the system as it was when it took it away. My warnings were disregarded and all the largesse was concentrated on a reduction in the taper from 65 percent to 63 percent, putting back £700 million a year into the system once approaching full roll out. The changes to waiting days and the housing run-on had to wait another year.

They were only the first of the reductions that were rolled back in the years after I left the Department. The blight on UC's reputation cast by the cuts agenda was slowly reversed with the departure of its author, George Osborne. Work allowances were boosted in 2018, and more legacy benefits were allowed to run on to close the gap before first payment.

The next year Amber Rudd, as Secretary of State, made a number of announcements about improving the system. These related to more flexible payment arrangements and a smoother way for social landlords to arrange direct payment of rent. In reality, most of these changes had been well in hand at the time of my departure.

It took the shocking advent of Covid 19 and the subsequent lockdown in March 2020 to mark a genuine turning point. Universal Credit received no fewer than 1.8m claims in a six week period – peaking at 135,000 over two days. The number of people on the system doubled over the year to nearly 6 million. The legacy system would have collapsed under this kind of pressure but Universal Credit was able to cope with the strain. And DWP was able to claim that 90 percent of those new claimants in the spring were receiving their funds on time and in full, a percentage that improved further through the year.

The political response was to boost the generosity of the system and its simplicity for claimants. An extra £20 a week pulled the underlying level of UC back to something like its original levels (and incidentally made it more generous than JSA and ESA). The increasingly ungainly support system for rents was restored to the system I had introduced in 2011, with recipients paid at the 30th percentile of the local rate. The restrictions on the self-employed were eased. Finally, also, my bugbear about allowing flexible earnings was satisfied by holding claims open for six months after earnings exceeded entitlement. While some of these changes were theoretically temporary, it would not be surprising if many of them stuck.

These changes substantially reduced the immediate problems facing UC recipients. Two further areas for improvement have been suggested by Nick Timmins, the former *Financial Times* correspondent who has followed the project closely. The first suggests curbing the aggressive method of recovering tax credits which the Treasury imposed on the system. The second is further amelioration of the initial five-week wait. [166]

All this lay far in the future as I organised my departure in 2016. My farewell seemed to extend across most of December. My retirement was announced at the beginning of the month and the Prime Minister kindly made No. 10 available for a retirement function a fortnight later. Here I was able to thank many of the people who had helped me over the 10 years since I first became involved in welfare. Damian Green summed up: "David has defied two common maxims: that businessmen always fall apart when they come into politics and that all political careers end in failure. He leaves at a time of his own choosing."

I felt more emotional on my penultimate day as I bade farewell to the officials in the Department, which I had grown to love over the decade.

"I have known so many of you over the 10 years and I have seen your careers progress and you developing and maturing. I'm leaving because you don't need me anymore . . ." at which point I found myself unable to finish the sentence.

The highlight took place on my last day, when John Taylor, the Chief Whip, had arranged a short debate on Universal Credit.[167] There were 21 speakers from all round the House; people I had debated with intensively over many years. As my opposite number on the Labour benches, Maeve Sherlock, generously put it: "The noble Lord, Lord Freud, has been unfailingly courteous to me and to all of us on these Benches. He has been generous in giving us access to his officials and he has done the House the courtesy of almost always coming here himself to defend his policies rather than sending a Whip.

"He usually seeks to defend his arguments by engaging with us and using evidence rather than just repeating the Government line. When we convinced him in debate, he would go back to his Department, push, and then sometimes return with real concessions. We may disagree on policy and I think that we will carry on doing so, but the noble Lord, Lord Freud, has been a loyal public servant of integrity."

Mike Farmer, the Conservative Lord who obtained the debate and who had organised highly effective support for the programme from the backbenches, concentrated his remarks on the lessons to be learned.

"There is no doubt that one major challenge to starting afresh with the benefits system, which caused previous Ministers to baulk – and understandably so, given the short-termism that plagues our political system – was the length of time that design and full rollout would require. The Minister has often talked about the 'Test and Learn' approach this Government has taken to welfare reform. I am encouraged, as a businessman who, like all of your Lordships, wants good government and sound management of the public finances, that an Agile approach to this very large project was adopted, albeit eventually. My impression is that we have learned invaluable lessons for future large-scale projects by taking the time to get this right."

When I responded I more or less ignored my notes. "My private office tells me that I have made 3,331 spoken contributions in my time as the Minister for Welfare Reform, and this is the last time that I will speak in that capacity. I thought that it would be most valuable if I concentrated on two things: the lessons we have learned from the process and what we can see for the future of welfare reform.

The first lesson concerned IT: "What I now think is that the change that Government as a whole went through in outsourcing its IT, which happened in the 1990s and early 2000s, was a fundamental mistake right across the whole of Government. I know that from the one example of the DWP.

"What it meant was that we lost control of our systems. People had been thinking about IT as a separate entity but it is not, it is part of the operation: lose control and an understanding of IT and one loses control of what one is trying to do. What we had to do was take our IT back in-house and to rebuild it, and the change has been quite dramatic. We have an integrated team of people on operations - coders, data architects and so on. It is one team; everybody has to be part of our team. I give your Lordships one of the most dramatic facts: for the first version of Universal Credit we used to have a release once every half year. We are now doing releases weekly. That is the difference."

I then went on to talk about the challenge of getting the operations team to feed back their experience: "The other thing - I was very conscious of this from my time as an adviser under the Labour Government - was that the operations people did not like to talk even to the policy people, let alone to the Ministers. I remember trying when I first came in to get the operations people to come back and complain when we stuck some structure down their throats. They would not. It has taken an awfully long time just to get the operations team to be the people who say what is working and what is not, and to turn it round."

I turned to the process of introducing a big change: "The other thing that is really interesting - this is across Government - is that an organisation of that size finds it impossible to deal with an abstract, conceptual notion. It cannot do it. Too many people have to have the same vision: you cannot get it when it is complicated. You have to get something on the ground that an organisation can shape itself round. It was an accident that we did it twin-track, but having that first track out so the organisation can get round something and start to get the lessons was, in practice, vital. This is the origin of what we have dubbed the 'Test and Learn' approach: get something out, find out how it works and iterate the whole time. I am pleased the Government has now announced, somewhat retrospectively, that this is Government policy. I can take pride in that one."

In discussing the future, I touched on the potential of Universal Support and the opportunity to use intensive trialling to optimise Universal Credit. I closed with an in-joke. When Ministers do not know the answer to a question, or when they have run out of time, the convention is that they offer up a letter which is made available generally to members in the Library. My last words as the Minister for Welfare Reform were: "I close by saying something I have always wanted to say. There have been a lot of questions I have not been able to answer today, but I will not write."

ADDENDUM *Governance*

Lessons for Government Projects

The birth of Universal Credit was traumatic. Some of the reasons were specific, while others mirrored the problems seen across Government projects more generally. Indeed, in the light of the long list of Government development disasters, it may well be that the most exceptional aspect of the Universal Credit experience was that the project managed to pull itself round successfully. Nevertheless, I came to the end of my 10-year spell in welfare reform with a belief that our governance structures are inadequate for implementing major change involving the central functions of the state. We are perfectly capable of commissioning a team to build the Olympic park and run a highly successful event. That capability seems much less evident when new structures are introduced at the heart of Government, whether they are a new electronic patient care record in the NHS (which was effectively abandoned) or a tax credits system to boost low incomes (which built up billions of uncollectable debt).

In this last chapter I will explore the lessons from Universal Credit and suggest a structure, or approach, for how we might organise the implementation of major heartland projects in future. There is an extensive literature on Civil Service reform, with a series of reports over recent decades making various recommendations on how to improve performance. However, the relationship between a permanent Civil Service and the political Ministers they serve is conceptually unchanged from its origins in the early Victorian era. In 1854 a report to Parliament by politician Sir Stafford Northcote and civil servant Sir Charles Trevelyan recommended public appointment on merit for an apolitical service. In particular they recommended that a career service should be established based on the recruitment of young men. "Our opinion is, that, as a general rule, it is decidedly best to train young men. Without laying too much stress on the experience which a long official life necessarily brings with it, we cannot but regard it an advantage of some importance. In many offices, moreover, it is found that the superior docility of young men renders it much easier to make valuable public servants of them, than of those more advanced in life." [168]

Most of the recent reports make recommendations on how to improve the Civil Service generally or make it more efficient. I will take a narrower focus here and concentrate on the problems – and potential improvements – to the delivery of major Government projects. In this context the concentrated focus on Civil Service reform seems over-narrow, since it takes too little account of the way that politicians are driven and behave. Worthwhile reform will probably require a hard look at our whole system of governance. When I retired, I gave evidence to Frank Field's Select Committee: "There is an odd structure, which I do not quite believe in anymore, which is the relationship between the politician and the Minister and the Civil Service, and the concept is the politicians decide what their objectives are and the Civil Service delivers it. I do not believe that you can divide policy and implementation in that way. That is a very big issue because our whole Government is built up with that concept and it has been for more than 100 years." [169]

It may well be that establishing the appropriate disciplines and governance for major heartland Government projects will allow a more sensible focus of where pure reforms to the Civil Service may be valuable.

At the heart of Universal Credit's troubles lay the capability of the Department in IT. It became evident that the commissioning out of IT a decade and more earlier had effectively removed any direct knowledge of how to build systems, or even monitor that the contractors were building those systems properly. This did not matter for smaller, discrete, pieces of software, where the Department had developed a good track record. Indeed, Joe Harley, Chief Information Officer for the Government, reassured me on the prospects for Universal Credit with the example of the successful recent implementation of the new Employment and Support Allowance.

This lack of competence meant that the Department did not recognise the scale of the system we wanted to build. We were still calling it "an IT development of moderate scale" in the White Paper and beyond. [170] There were two other errors at the outset. The Department did not realise the security issues involved in offering claimants an interactive system.

Too late, it attempted to address the challenge by retrofitting security into a legacy-style system, discovering the outcome to be hopelessly complicated for users. At the same time the first attempt to use the new Agile development techniques fell apart because the approach used – building up individual story lines – was highly inefficient. It was also badly undermined by its incompatibility with the central Government clearance timetable, leading to subsequent – misplaced – accusations of lack of financial control from the National Audit Office. The more rapid development schedule promised by Agile also allowed an accelerated timetable. The failure to achieve this schedule was to be the direct source of much of the public criticism of the project.

The initial timetable was simply unrealistic, given the scale of the challenge. The White Paper at the end of 2010 set out a start date of September 2013, with completion four years later in 2017. With the knowledge of hindsight, the earliest date that a working system could have started to take serious numbers of people into an interactive system would have been early 2016. This reflects a three-year build period from the completion of the regulations in early 2013. It assumes that the Department had built up its competence in Agile and created its own in-house development team and that there were no subsequent changes in welfare arrangements in the interim. On this more realistic timetable, completion of the full process could have been scheduled for 2020.

It is one of history's 'might-have-beens' as to whether the endeavour would have been given the go-ahead by the Prime Minister if the start date had stretched beyond the subsequent election. It would certainly have been all too easy to stop by a new Government. So the unrealistic time-table was of great value in getting the project underway. I am not conscious that Iain or I put pressure onto the Departmental team at the outset to get this time-table. It is likely that we did not need to, given the enthusiasm of the officials – both to please their new political masters and to dump the mess of legacy benefits – as well as the self-evident importance of producing outcomes within the electoral cycle.

In retrospect, the fundamental mistake was over-ambition, based on ignorance about the implications of an interactive system which the Department was simply not equipped to build. A more realistic objective would have been to build a legacy-style Universal Credit system, which would have delivered the bulk of the benefits of the new structure in an old-fashioned way.

Ironically, that was more or less the outcome of the desperate tussles of 2013. This incorporated the roll out of two distinct systems, dubbed the 'twin-track'. The first system was shaped like a standard legacy benefit, albeit one in which claimants could make an application online. Thereafter the interaction with the Department was through traditional post and telephone communication. Nevertheless, the Department learned how the key operational elements should function through this system, as well as the behavioural response from claimants to the new arrangements. Those findings helped shape the Full Service digital system which was developed and rolled out afterwards. It also maintained a sense of momentum at a critical time. Clearly, there were extra costs involved in this 'twin-track' approach, although they were offset by the gains involved in putting people on the system earlier. As is often the way in effective responses to crisis, however, the 'twin-track' approach may well have been the best way to introduce a complex new system. The early version acted as a pathfinder to inform the structure of the Full Service offering.

The response of the Department to this baptism of fire has been a wholesale restructuring of its IT capability, pulling development and maintenance of systems in-house and integrating its services more closely with operations. It has built a genuinely Agile capability in development. It has also given more authority to the operating teams, so that the detailed structuring of Universal Credit reflects the behavioural responses from the claimant base.

These changes represent a challenge to other Government Departments considering major developments. Purely in terms of IT, the lessons learned imply bringing development capability back in-house; building big integrated teams to adopt Agile technology; reversing a policy-led culture to one reliant on operational feedback.

One of the specific problems facing the Universal Credit team was the level of political commitment. In rhetoric it was described as a priority of the Coalition and subsequently the Conservative Government. In reality it proved anything but. This was because George Osborne, the Chancellor through virtually the whole period, had developed his own set of priorities round cost-cutting and bringing the nation's finances into balance. His austerity targets were narrowly drawn. Top of the list were working-age recipients of welfare. During the Coalition Government he claimed £21 billion of welfare cuts and he targeted a further £12 billion in the first year of the Conservative Government.

It is always difficult to cut pay-outs during a major structural reform, since it is politically compelling, and traditional, to compensate those who lose from any change. We did not have this luxury in the introduction of Universal Credit. Quite the reverse; we were managing substantial reductions in entitlement alongside the reform. Some of those reductions were entirely compatible with Universal Credit; to the extent that they focused people on work as a solution to their problems they supported a positive change in cultural attitudes in this period. However, the way that the cuts programme over-rode all the detailed adjustments necessary for a smooth introduction of Universal Credit was deeply counter-productive for a flagship programme. The row over waiting days which erupted after I retired was one entirely foreseeable – and foreseen – outcome.

The apparent agnosticism of the Chancellor towards the programme meant its survival was always fragile. That had the effect of putting further pressure on a team where morale was already hard-hit.

The interaction with the centre of Government was a major management task for the Department's officials. There was significant change in the process through the Coalition period. At the start David Cameron shrunk the operational base he inherited at No. 10 on the basis that his Ministers would design policy from within their Departments. Our ability to introduce Universal Credit in this early period can probably be attributed to this laissez-faire attitude. Subsequently the challenge of getting things through the centre became increasingly hard. The Prime Minister's approach changed dramatically after the problems Andrew Lansley, the Health Secretary, had getting his reforms through in 2011. At the same time other parts of central Government began to assemble their powers. Francis Maude, at the Cabinet Office, gathered authority in approving contracts, shaping the IT approach of Government Departments and developing a project oversight process with the Treasury. The Liberal Democrat junior partner in Government strengthened its position when the Deputy Prime Minister's office took shape. Nick Clegg's power base was the Home Affairs Committee, through which all new measures and most announcements needed to be cleared. The

Treasury ran a parallel – cuts-oriented – welfare strategy as well as disbursing spending on projects.

Other Departments developed their priorities as time went on, some of which would overlap with the changes we were making. However, there was no clear way of resolving clashing agendas through the centre. By the end of the Coalition the need to square off these four competing centres of power served to slow-down decision-making severely.

The involvement of the centre in Universal Credit represents a mixed picture. The newly-developed oversight process of the Major Projects Authority provided various warnings but demonstrated a scatter-gun approach. The short review times were inevitably antithetical to producing a coherent critique. The Government Digital Service developed a new data architecture that was secure, although it took far longer to build than envisaged. Their advice then became mired in internal politicking about the attribution of blame.

The new 'blueprint' master-minded by the head of the Major Projects Authority, David Pitchford, showed the difficulty for outsiders in assembling a fully coherent plan. The complexity and scale of the welfare system was severely under-estimated. The resulting proposals, undertaken under great time pressure, were a reflection of pre-conceived notions rather than detailed analysis. The Cabinet Office determination to stop the first 'Live' version of Universal Credit would probably have led to the abandonment of the whole programme, as the time-table for the digital version fell further and further behind.

Eventually the contract clearance process for which the Cabinet Office had responsibility was dumped when the Liberal Democrat Chief Secretary to the Treasury, Danny Alexander, cut the Gordian knot to allow the project to go ahead on a twin-track basis. This experience suggests that the route of outside review may not be the most effective way to ensure that a project is properly set up and functioning. Perhaps the most interesting observation about the review process came from John Manzoni, a former senior executive at BP, shortly after he was appointed the head of the Major Projects Authority. He told the Public Accounts Committee in 2014 that the team had benefited from having the pressure of categorisation removed. It gave it the space to get back on "something of a front foot."

If the internal oversight from the centre was less than helpful, the external review process was deeply damaging. The formal instrument was the National Audit Office, which reported through to the Public Accounts Committee of MPs, chaired through much of the period by the senior Labour politician Margaret Hodge. The tone from both bodies was highly hostile, which fed through to the unrelenting attacks on the project by the Labour Opposition. This politicisation should not have been surprising. By remaking the welfare system with the creation of Universal Credit, the Conservatives were threatening to take ownership of it from Labour. This was highly dangerous for a political party part of whose appeal was centred on its support for the less fortunate. Grudgingly Labour had claimed to support Universal Credit as a concept; project slippage and over-optimistic time-tables allowed it to attack the "chaos" of implementation by the Coalition Government.

Clearly the project warranted criticism. However, the most vehement public attacks on it took place after a much more realistic time-table was in place. There were savage complaints about the lack of transparency available to the various Select Committees. In the light of the way information was treated, it was difficult to disagree with Iain's caution about its early provision.

The politicisation of oversight did not take place in the Lords, where my experience was radically different to that of Iain in the Commons. In the Commons, Government and Opposition traded political abuse. The dynamic in the Lords discouraged such interchange. The Lords is structured so that the Government does not have an overall majority. Holding the balance of power is a group of Crossbench Peers, who effectively set the tone of debate. They support either the Government or Opposition on the strength of the arguments deployed. This allows quite rational discussion of the underlying issues involved in any topic. The emotional overlay typical in the Commons was actively discouraged by the suspicion of the Crossbenchers. My explanations of what had gone wrong with Universal Credit and what we were doing to put it right were received with both interest and even support in the Lords. I wanted to keep the Lords more informed than I did. However, Iain's concerns about the difficulties he would suffer in the Commons, if we embarked on the normal parallel process, somewhat reduced those ambitions.

The heightened political atmosphere round Universal Credit meant the hostile approach of the National Audit Office was counter-productive.

Its first report in September 2013, *Early Progress*, seemed to me to lean heavily on Cabinet Office sources, by then turning negative on the Department's plans.[171] It was brutally negative about the programme, while failing to isolate the central issue that had undermined progress. This was the inadequacy of the security design, which led to an inability to achieve a "detailed operating model". The tone changed markedly in the subsequent years. In May 2015 it produced a report that was far more nuanced and understanding of the challenges that the Department was facing. In 'Welfare reform – lessons learned' it allowed: "After a reset of the programme in 2013, the Department formed a more coherent plan of what it wanted to achieve and was better able to distinguish between necessary and desirable aspects of the programme."[172] Overall, it was cautiously supportive: "The Department has shown that it can introduce and adapt programmes flexibly in the face of uncertainty. And it has continued to make progress in difficult major programmes despite early failings." The reality was that much of what it reported on more favourably in 2015 was already moving into place in the autumn of 2013, when its ferocious findings served to undermine the Universal Credit programme.

The time horizons of a major programme of change fit remarkably poorly with the political cycle. It takes many years to effect major change, yet typically neither politicians nor civil servants are allowed the continuity required. In the 15 years since the Department was formed in 2001 until my retirement at the end of 2016 there were no fewer than 11 Secretaries of State. Iain's six-year tenure flatters the picture, bringing the average term of the rest down to less than a year. As I joked to David Cameron once: "You don't even have time to find the toilets."

The role of politicians has become increasingly difficult in recent decades. The unrelenting pressure of the 24 hour news cycle, the increasingly aggressive nature of the media – spurred on by the unforgiving disposition of social media – has made public discussion of difficult issues a high risk area. Senior politicians are an increasingly professional class as a result, trained to handle these pressures. The management of information and the media takes a disproportionate amount of their time and energy. The politically correct observations, the careful circumlocution of problem areas, the over-simplification and dogged sticking to the official line are the result. The public may not like this approach but the dangers for politicians of deviating can be terminal.

Few politicians have extensive experience in overseeing major projects. Nor do they have the expertise to take difficult decisions when there are hard choices to be made. Yet the Ministers, and particularly the Secretary of State, have full power to take decisions, even though they may be poorly equipped to reach them. They are driven by the agenda of the next three months or so, when political and media attention looms. A Secretary of State like Iain will have a vision of the changes he wants to see over a decade or more. Yet the relentless three-month horizon – in which presentational effort is rewarded – frequently overwhelms the two-to-three year horizon of detailed strategic planning necessary to effect any change at all.

One of Francis Maude's reforms in this space has made a substantial improvement to the ability of senior officials responsible for programmes to withstand political pressure. In October 2014, a new paragraph was introduced into *The Ministerial Code* which stated that Senior Responsible Owners "are expected to account to Parliament" for implementation. [173] As Neil Couling told me: "This has changed the power dynamic since your time. It has allowed me to give a voice to delivery issues and stand up to Ministers."

However, Neil Couling is a rare example of continuity. We have accidentally developed a vacuum in the two-to-three year planning horizon. Few politicians fill it, yet the Civil Service is also decreasingly well-equipped to provide continuity over this kind of period. This is because of the frequency with which the good officials tend to switch jobs. In part this is driven by an apparent policy to move people on regularly. However, the effective driver is pay. Civil Service pay has been frozen or constrained for most of the last two decades. This means promotion is often the only way for officials to see a pay rise. A prolonged period of constraint has now institutionalised a two-year promotion round for the best performers.

Bad luck and turmoil meant that there were no fewer than six Senior Responsible Owners and six Programme Directors in the first five years of building Universal Credit. This did little for continuity at the senior level. Less obvious, but equally problematic, was the high turnover down through the team. By the end of my tenure, I was seeing the third or even fourth generation of officials in various of the policy areas. It is one thing to possess limited corporate memory of events that happened

10 or 20 years ago; quite another to lose the rationale for decisions taken three or four years earlier. I found two of my key roles – unexpected at the outset – were to supply the medium-term corporate memory and to ensure we were consistently engaged in the two-to-three year strategic planning process.

A central deficiency of the UK governance structure is the separation of the public sector from the private sector. Other countries have developed ways to narrow the gap. The US separation of the executive from legislature means that the President can assemble a Cabinet made up largely of private sector executives, who in turn can build several senior ranks of support within their public sector Departments. France has less formal arrangements wherein senior executives pass back and forth between the public and private sectors, narrowing the cultural separation.

In the UK Civil Service, private sector executives find it difficult to establish themselves, with some notable exceptions such as John Manzoni, promoted to Chief Executive of the Civil Service in autumn 2014 and then in the following year Permanent Secretary for the Cabinet Office as well. Maintenance of the generalist Northcote-Trevelyan tradition has meant that the Civil Service is ill-equipped to deal with the corporate sector and its specialist staff.

As we built the Universal Credit team the Department could supply world-class expertise in some required areas. It had great operational expertise in the day to day management of welfare systems. It was able to create and draw up complex legislative instruments. Many of its high calibre staff had exceptional organisational skills. Its data analytics team were unmatched. However, it was short of key specialisations such as project management, contract management and, among several deficiencies in the IT sphere, data architects and security architects. Many of these are scarce resources in the economy as a whole and, as a result, pay expectations lie beyond the levels of the generalist Civil Service. It is not the overall quality of Civil Service staff that is the problem. It is the failure to build integrated teams that incorporate the relevant professional expertise. In Universal Credit the solution was to hire 'contingent labour', whereby key personnel were supplied through short-term contracts. This is an unsatisfactory and expensive way of proceeding and reflects the inflexibility of the generalist mono-culture.

Herein lies the main difference in the organisation of big projects between the private and public sectors. Private sector companies tend to build teams with great attention to getting the balance of expertise and personality right. The public sector tends not to value people on such an individual basis. Naturally there will be numerous exceptions to this distinction. But it is hardly surprising that the direct ownership devolved onto the leader of a project in the private sector concentrates his or her focus on the quality of the team rather than its cost. For the public sector team, with its high inbuilt turnover, this is a luxury that is hard to attain. Even so, IT projects fail in the private sector just as frequently as in the public sector; they simply don't have the same level of unrelenting media attention directed at them.

The classic division of roles between Civil Service and politicians, when it comes to major heartland projects like Universal Credit, seems to me unreal, as I observed to Frank Field's Select Committee. The Northcote-Trevelyan tradition was built on in 1918, when the Viscount Haldane chaired a Committee to report on the machinery of Government. This was in response to the growth of large executive Ministries in the First World War.

It established a civil service role for "the organised acquisition of facts and information, and for the systematic application of thought, as preliminary to the settlement of policy and its subsequent administration." [174] However, Ministers would retain full responsibility to Parliament for those decisions and administration. This inter-dependent relationship has remained essentially unchanged over nearly a century, although there has been substantial tinkering to improve efficiency. The concept of ultimate ministerial responsibility for administration has also been eroded, reflecting the reality that Secretaries of State in post for a matter of months can hardly be genuinely at fault for maladministration in a branch of their Department they have never heard of.

The Haldane settlement, as it applies to major heartland projects, means that the Civil Service provides policy advice for Ministerial decision and then goes ahead with the implementation of the project, reporting back to Ministers on key developments. The shortcoming of this structure is that in practice there are a whole raft of secondary decisions which are closely tied into the implementation process. Many of those decisions are deeply political in nature, requiring almost constant oversight and leadership. The Civil Service implementation executive then runs down a parallel, rather than an integrated, track. In the case study of Universal Credit, the roles of Minister and Civil Servant became deeply inter-twined in a way that was quite outside the Haldane norms. However, as Ministers, neither Iain nor I had formal authority over the implementation team, whether in their selection, their reward or their promotion.

If the Haldane settlement is not up to the job of safely steering heartland projects, what structure would do better? Any set of proposals would need to work broadly within the Constitution as it stands. A switch to the US system of Government, dividing executive and legislature, for example, is hardly a realistic proposition.

Any adjustment should aim at achieving a number of objectives. A reduction in the level of political heat would be desirable for long-term projects. However, it would remain important that the leadership of the project remained publicly answerable, preferably to Parliament. This would ensure that there was an effective dialogue over the many decisions affecting citizens' lives. It would be a dialogue that would allow the leadership to provide the critical role of user specification with authority.

Continuity of leadership and the team as a whole would be a central requirement. Such plans can always be confounded by bad luck but they should not be affected by a systemic bias in favour of high turnover.

Almost by definition the team would need to function within the relevant Department. Some projects, such as the Olympics, can function perfectly well as stand-alone organisations. Heartland projects like Universal Credit cut across central Government functions and cannot be successful from outside the system. Likewise, the team needs to be integrated within the Department responsible for operating the new system long term. An externally created system with inadequate feedback from operators would suffer from a high risk of rejection.

At the same time there has to be a way of bringing world-class expertise into the team in the specialisms it does not have, nor indeed needed to have before the new project. This will often imply the effective integration of private sector expertise and a better mix of generalist and specialist capability.

This is a long and somewhat idealised list of requirements, which I will attempt to deliver in this preliminary sketch of a structure.

Firstly, the country needs to recognise that there is a limit to the number of major heartland projects it can undertake successfully at any one time. There is a scarcity of skills which need to be focused. For arguments sake we might restrict the number to three at any one time. Examples of what they might be include: achievement of the 2050 net zero carbon goal; levelling up of the North/South divide; an educational recovery programme after the Covid 19 pandemic.

There should be a legislative process denominating these as 'Priority Projects'. One of the benefits of such categorisation would be to provide a measure of protection from the clashing agendas of other Departments. The process would also have demonstrative force as to what a Government's major priorities really were. In addition, it might be possible to obtain cross-party support through this device. While this would not be a necessary feature, such agreement would reinforce the prospects for long-term continuity.

The next objective is to create a world-class team integrated into the relevant Department. The first step is to select the best possible leader. He, or she, will probably come from the world of business, with experience of establishing major projects. He should be recruited for the role of 'Implementation Minister' within the Department. Building on my own experience in Universal Credit, they would sit on the Front Bench of the House of Lords. It would be absolutely clear that the new Minister was expected to see the project to effective completion in this position. Early departure would be seen as a sign of failure.

The position in the House of Lords would provide a forum in which the Minister could be publicly answerable. Arrangements could be made for the Minister to update the Lords on a regular basis in a process that was not paralleled in the Commons. This forum would be less politicised than we have seen in the Commons and there would be an opportunity for intensive probing of developments. The current responsibilities to appear before the various Commons Select Committees would also be in force.

Where the proposition diverges from my own experience is that the Implementation Minister would be given direct powers to build a team to achieve the project. The Minister could select and balance his senior team and be given the powers to pay the market rate for the key specialisations. There is a delicate balancing act here. The Minister is responsible for implementation of the project within the overall ministerial team and would work for the Secretary of State of his Department. He is also likely to have direct contact with senior members of the Cabinet, including the Prime Minister and Chancellor. At the same time, he will have to ensure that his team is built in a way that can deliver the project but integrates effectively with the rest of the Department.

The dividing line between detailed policy design and implementation would be rubbed out with this appointment. The overall objective would be set in the 'Priority Project' legislation. The detail, the team and the timetable would be the responsibility of the Implementation Minister. One sensitive area is likely to be the arrangements for interaction with the Treasury, accustomed to micro-managing projects through drip-feeding funds stage by stage.

Such a structure would require detailed work to establish. Nevertheless, it would provide a reformed model of governance for heartland projects without turning UK constitutional arrangements upside down.

ACKNOWLEDGEMENTS

I am grateful for all the support from politicians and civil servants, as well as outsiders, in helping interpret this complicated story. I am particularly indebted to my early readers, who tightened up the draft and make it more comprehensible. These include Stephen Brien, Robert Devereux, Iain Duncan Smith and Philippa Stroud. Nick Timmins was indefatigable in going through the book on two occasions, commenting in detail and with precision. My son-in-law, Dan Savidge, cast a particularly valuable eye on the text as a music impresario, with no direct experience of the world described. Tristan Pedelty shepherded the text through the Cabinet Office process.

From those who were working within the civil service at the time, my thanks go (in alphabetical order) to Mike Bracken, Neil Couling, Kevin Cunnington, Ann Harris, Stephen Kelly, Leigh Lewis, John-Paul Marks, Liam Maxwell, Paul McComb, Sue Moore, Sue Owen, Lara Sampson, Pete Searle, Howard Shiplee, Isobel Stephen, Mark Swindells, Sharon White, Malcolm Whitehouse and Jessica Yuille.

From outside the civil service, I received invaluable support from Simone Finn, David Gauke, John Hutton, Francis Maude, James Purnell, John Williams, Shriti Vadera and Steve Webb. At the Institute of Fiscal Studies, Robert Joyce kindly checked through the figures for benefit cuts in Chapter 23.

In the House of Lords, my colleagues generously gave their time. My thanks go to Ros Altmann, Joyce Anelay, Richard Best, Edward Garnier, Bill McKenzie, Norman Fowler, Michael Levy, Tom Strathclyde and John Taylor.

I have been well served by my editor, Alan Ogden, who was meticulous in ensuring that my meaning was clear, while William Winter did an excellent job of checking through the text. My daughter-in-law, Anna Freud, kindly took my photograph for the back flap, while Lyn Davies was a formidable designer and typesetter, and Auriol Griffith-Jones was diligent in her indexing. Anthony Weldon was, again, an inspiring publisher.

Sadly, five of the characters in the story have since died, in the shape of Alan Cave, Jeremy Heywood, Patricia Hollis, Philip Langsdale and Tony Newton. Each was a major figure in the story of welfare reform and they are missed by many.

DRAMATIS PERSONÆ*

Danny Alexander Liberal Democrat politician. Chief Secretary to the Treasury 2010-15.

Ros Altmann Conservative Peer. Minister of State for Pensions at DWP 2015-16.

Joyce Anelay Conservative Peer. Chief Whip 2010-14.

Mike Baker DWP official. UC Operations Director 2012-16.

Anne Begg Labour politician. Chair of Work and Pensions Select Committee 2010-15.

James Bell Bishop of Ripon and Leeds 2004-17. Ex officio Member House of Lords.

Richard Best Crossbench Peer. President of the Local Government Association 2007-16.

Tony Blair Labour politician. Prime Minister 1997-2007.

Mike Bracken Head of the Government Digital Service (GDS) 2011-15.

Stephen Brien Consultant at Oliver Wyman 2009-10. Expert Adviser on UC at DWP 2011-13. Deputy UC SRO 2012-13.

Gordon Brown Labour politician. Chancellor 1997-2007. Prime Minister 2007-10.

Liam Byrne Labour politician. Chief Secretary to the Treasury 2009-10. Shadow Sec. of State for Work and Pensions 2011-13.

David Cameron Conservative politician. Leader of the Opposition 2005-10. Prime Minister 2010-16.

Alan Cave DWP official. Delivery Director 2007-12.

Nick Clegg Liberal Democrat politician. Deputy Prime Minister 2010-15.

Merrick Cockell Chairman of the Local Government Association 2011-14.

Rob Cook DWP official. My Private Secretary in 2014.

Neil Couling DWP official. Director of Working Age Benefits 2010-12. Work Services Director 2012-14. UC SRO from 2014.

Stephen Crabb Conservative politician. Secretary of State at DWP 2016.

Kevin Cunnington DWP official. Director General for Business Transformation 2013-16.

Gareth Davies Senior policy adviser to Tony Blair on welfare. Later head of the Prime Minister's Strategy Unit 2009-10.

Robert Devereux DWP official. Permanent Secretary 2011-18.

Steve Dover DWP official. Director for Major Programmes and UC's Deputy Programme Director 2011-12.

Jeannie Drake Labour Peer. Pensions specialist.

Mike Driver DWP official. Chief Financial Officer 2012-16.

Iain Duncan Smith (IDS) Conservative politician. Secretary of State at DWP 2010-16. Former Leader of the Conservative Party 2001-03. Founder of thinktank Centre for Social Justice 2004.

Angela Eagle Labour politician. Shadow Leader of the House of Commons 2011-15.

* Multiple references only.

Charlie Elphicke Conservative politician. MP for Dover 2010-19. Parliamentary Private Secretary to IDS 2014.

Natalie Evans Conservative politician. My Ministerial whip 2015-16. Leader of the House from 2016.

David Gauke Conservative politician. Shadow Treasury Minister 2007-10. Exchequer Secretary to the Treasury 2010-14. Financial Secretary to the Treasury 2014-16. Later DWP Secretary of State 2017-18.

Chris Grayling Conservative politician. Shadow Secretary of State for Work and Pensions 2007-09. Minister of State for Employment at DWP 2010-12.

Damian Green Conservative politician. Secretary of State at DWP 2016-17.

Sally Greengross Crossbench Peer. Specialist in issues of ageing.

William Hague Conservative politician. Leader of team negotiating Coalition 2010. Chair of Government cyber strategy group as Foreign Secretary 2010-14. Former Leader of the Conservative Party 1997-2001.

Peter Hain Labour politician: Succeeded John Hutton as DWP Secretary of State in 2007.

Philip Hammond Conservative politician. Shadow welfare spokesman in 2005-07. Then Shadow Chief Secretary to the Treasury in 2007-10. Later he was Chancellor 2016-19.

Matt Hancock Conservative politician. Chief of Staff to Shadow Chancellor George Osborne 2005-10.

Joe Harley DWP official. Chief Information Officer 2004-12. Also Government CIO 2011-12.

Mark Harper Conservative politician. Shadow Minister for Disabled People 2007-10. Minister of State for Disabled People at DWP 2014-15.

Rupert Harrison Chief Econ. Advis to Geo. Osborne and David Cameron 2006-10. Chief of Staff to the Chancellor 2010-15.

Janice Hartley DWP official. Director of delivery for UC pathfinder 2012-13, then Director for Delivery of the Live Service 2013-16.

Ann Harris DWP official. UC Programme Director 2013-14.

Ron Haskins One of the principal Republican architects of US welfare reform under President Bill Clinton in 1996.

Chris Hayes DWP official. First UC Programme Director 2010-11.

Caroline Haynes DWP official. My Departmental aide in 2008-9. Left DWP to become part of Shadow team preparing *Get Britain Working* 2009-10.

Jeremy Heywood Permanent Secretary to Downing Street 2010-12. Cabinet Secretary 2012-18.

Steve Hilton David Cameron's Director of Strategy in Opposition 2009 and in office 2010-12.

Damian Hinds Conservative politician. Assistant whip 2014-15. Minister of Employment at DWP 2016-18.

Margaret Hodge Labour politician. Chairman of the Public Accounts Select Committee 2010-15.

Patricia Hollis Labour Peer. Lords Minister at Social Security/Work and Pensions 1997-2005.

Freddie Howe Conservative Earl. Deputy Leader of the House of Lords from 2015.

Trevor Huddleston DWP official. Strategy director in 2010. Chief Analyst and Chief Scientific Adviser 2016.

John Hutton Labour politician. Secretary of State at DWP 2005-2008, moving to Business, Enterprise and Regulatory Reform 2008 under Gordon Brown. He became a Peer in 2010.

Stephen Kelly Cabinet Office official. Government's Chief Operating Officer and in charge of the CO's Efficiency and Reform Group.

Archy Kirkwood Liberal Democrat Peer. Former MP and Chairman of the Parliamentary Select Committee on Work and Pensions 1997-2005.

Steve Lamey HMRC official. Director General of Benefits and Credits 2008-12.

Martha Lane Fox UK Digital champion. Author of *DirectGov Strategic Review* 2010. Former joint owner of *lastminute.com*.

Philip Langsdale DWP official. Head of IT and SRO of UC in 2012.

David Laws Liberal Democrat politician, Shadow Work and Pensions spokesman in 2007. Minister of State for Schools 2012-15.

Oliver Letwin Conservative politician. Policy review role in Opposition 2009-10. Minister of State for Government Policy in the Cabinet Office 2010-16.

Leigh Lewis DWP official. Permanent Secretary 2005-11.

Ruth Lister Labour Peer. Specialist in benefit system. Former Director of the Child Poverty Action Group 1979-87.

Ed Llewellyn Downing Street Chief of Staff 2010-2016.

Tom Loosemore Cabinet Office official. Helped write Martha Lane Fox's 2010 report. Deputy Director of Government Digital Service (GDS) 2010-15.

Lizzie Loudon Special Adviser on media at DWP 2014-15.

Bob Lovett DWP official: Head of UC security 2011-12.

Colin Low Crossbench Peer. Former Chairman of the Royal National Institute of Blind People.

James Mackay Conservative peer. Former Lord Chancellor in Thatcher and Major Governments 1987-97.

John Manzoni Former oil industry executive. Chief Executive of the Major Projects Authority 2014. Later Chief Executive of the Civil Service 2014-20.

John-Paul (JP) Marks DWP official. Principal Private Secretary to IDS 2010-11. UC Strategic Design and Planning Director 2014-16.

Francis Maude Conservative politician. Minister for the Cabinet Office 2010-2015.

Theresa May Conservative politician. Shadow Secretary of State for Work and Pensions 2009-10. Prime Minister 2016-19.

Liam Maxwell Cabinet Office official. Deputy Government Chief Information Officer 2012. UK Chief Technology Officer 2012-16.

Paul McComb DWP official. Deputy Director, Welfare Policy 2011. Principal Private Secretary to IDS 2011-16.

Bill McKenzie Labour Peer. Parliamentary Under-Secretary of State for Work and Pensions 2007-10. Opposition welfare spokesman in the Lords 2010-16.

Esther McVey Conservative politician. Parliamentary Under-Secretary of State for Disabled People at DWP 2012-13. Minister for Employment at DWP 2013-15.

Molly Meacher Crossbench Peer. Active interest in welfare issues.

Maria Miller Conservative politician. Parliamentary Under-Secretary of State for Disabled People at DWP 2010-2012.

Ed Miliband Labour politician. Leader of the Opposition 2010-15.

Sue Moore DWP official. Project leader on the Integrated Risk and Intelligence Service (IRIS) 2012. Director for Delivery of the second phase of the UC Live Service 2012-13.

Terry Moran DWP official. UC SRO 2010-2012.

Jim Murphy Labour politician. Minister of State for Employment and Welfare Reform at DWP 2006-07.

Karolin Nakonz UC Deputy Programme Director 2012.

Andy Nelson DWP official. Chief Information Officer 2013-2014.

Fraser Nelson Editor of *The Spectator* from 2009.

Tony Newton Conservative Peer. Former Secretary of State for Social Security 1989-92.

David Orr CEO of the National Housing Association.

George Osborne Conservative politician. Shadow Chancellor 2005-10. Chancellor 2010-16.

Sue Owen DWP official. Director General of Welfare and Wellbeing 2009-11. Director General of Strategy 2011-13.

Eric Pickles Conservative politician. Secretary of State for Communities and Local Government 2010-15.

David Pitchford Cabinet Office official. Chief Executive of the Major Projects Authority 2011-13. UC Chief Executive and SRO 2013.

James Purnell Labour politician. Secretary of State for DWP 2008-9.

Hilary Reynolds DWP official. UC Programme Director 2012-13.

Lara Sampson DWP official. Deputy Director, UC Service Design 2010-13. Product Director, UC from 2013.

David Scott Conservative councillor from Tunbridge Wells.

Pete Searle DWP official. Worked on my 2007 report. Working Age Benefits Policy Director 2012-19.

Peter Seymour Head of Government and Public Service at Vocalink, which ran the banks' automated clearing system.

Maeve Sherlock Labour Peer. Former Special Adviser to Gordon Brown as Chancellor covering child poverty and welfare. Opposition welfare spokesman 2013-16.

Howard Shiplee DWP official recruited from construction industry. UC Chief Executive and SRO 2013-14.

Isobel Stephen DWP official. Team leader for my 2007 report 2006-07.

Tim Stone KPMG consultant. Chair of Global Infrastructure and Projects Group 1995-2011. Former colleague at S.G. Warburg/UBS.

Tina Stowell Conservative Peer. My Ministerial whip 2012-13. Leader of the House 2014-16.

Tom Strathclyde Conservative Peer. Shadow Leader of the House of Lords 1998-2010, then Leader of the House 2010-13.

Philippa Stroud Executive Director of think-tank Centre for Social Justice 2004-2010 and 2015-16. Special Adviser to IDS at DWP 2010-15.

John Taylor Conservative Peer. My first Ministerial whip in 2010-11. Chief Whip in the Lords 2014-19.

Nick Timmins Public Policy Editor at the Financial Times 1996-2011. Author of *The Five Giants*.

Steve Timms Labour politician. Minister for Employment and Welfare Reform at DWP 2008. Shadow Minister for Employment 2010-15.

Justin Tomlinson Conservative politician. Parliamentary Under-Secretary of State for Disabled People at DWP 2015-16.

Shriti Vadera Special Adviser on private sector and international finance to Chancellor Gordon Brown 1999-2007. Former colleague at S.G. Warburg/UBS.

Ian Watmore Cabinet Office official. Chief Operating Officer 2010-11. Permanent Secretary 2012.

Steve Webb Liberal Democrat politician. Minister of State for Pensions at DWP 2010-2015.

Phill Wells DWP official. Analyst for my 2007 report 2006-07. Bill captain on 2012 Welfare Act.

Sharon White DWP then Treasury official. Director of Welfare to Work at DWP 2009. Director General for Public Spending at the Treasury 2012-13, Second Permanent Secretary 2013-15.

342 · CLASHING AGENDAS

Malcolm Whitehouse DWP official. Deputy IT Director 2010. UC Director of IT 2010-11. UC Programme Director 2011-12.

David Willetts Conservative politician. Shad. Min. for Innovation, Universities and Skills 2007-10. Former Paymaster General 1996.

John Williams Special Adviser to John Hutton, Secretary of State at DWP, 2005-07.

Tony Wilson DWP official. Team member for my 2007 report 2006-07.

Norma Wood Lead reviewer of UC for the Major Projects Authority 2013. UC Transformation Director 2013. Director General of the Major Projects Authority 2013-14.

Ian Wright DWP official. UC Programme Director from 2014.

Jessica Yuille DWP official. My first Private Secretary 2010-13

GLOSSARY OF TERMS

ALMP, *Active Labour Market Policies*:
Government programmes to help the
unemployed find work, often described
as 'welfare-to-work'.

APAs, *Alternative Payment Arrangements*:
Alternatives to the standard monthly
payment of UC, comprising 1) direct
(or managed) payment of the housing
element to landlords; 2) shorter payment
periods and; 3) the division of payments
within a household.

AME, *Annually Managed Expenditure*:
Treasury category of spending of which
the largest component is payment of
welfare, which is effectively demand-led.

Bedroom Tax: The name Labour dubbed
the withholding of some housing benefit
from people with surplus bedroom space,
introduced in April 2013. Otherwise known
as the 'Social Sector Size Criteria', the 'Removal of the Spare Room Subsidy' and the
'Under-occupancy Charge'. (See RSRS)

Benefit Cap: A limit on the total amount of
benefit working-age people can claim,
introduced from April 2013.

CO, *Cabinet Office*: One of the central Departments of Government, alongside the
Treasury, No. 10 and (during the Coalition
Government) the Home Affairs Committee chaired by the Liberal Democrat
leader Nick Clegg. The Cabinet Office
took direct oversight of Government
procurement and project management
in this period.

Cerberus, An early plan to retrofit security
into the UC software through a major contract with the IT suppliers. It was named after
the three-headed dog guarding the underworld in Greek mythology.

Cobra, *Cabinet Office Briefing Room A*:
where Government crisis response meetings
take place – as well as standard meetings
at other times.

CBI, *Confederation of British Industry*:
The main lobbying organisation for
business in the UK.

CPI, *Consumer Price Index*: A measure of
changes in consumer purchasing power.
It takes price-induced adjustments in
purchasing patterns into account and
tends to grow less rapidly than the Retail
Prices Index, which it replaced as the
main inflation measure in 2010.

CPA, *Continuous Payment Authority*:
Permission given by a borrower to allow
money to be taken from an account whenever the lender deems funds are due. Used
by payday lenders to increase the likelihood
of repayment.

Contributory benefits, Paid as of right to
people who lose their jobs or become
disabled on the basis of their past National
Insurance contributions. The interplay
with UC proved highly complex.

CSJ, *Centre for Social Justice*: A think-tank
founded by Iain Duncan Smith in 2004 to
make policy recommendations on how to
tackle poverty. Its *Dynamic Benefits* report

of 2009 was a key inspiration for UC. (See *Dynamic Benefits*)

Child Benefit: Traditionally paid tax-free to all families on a four-weekly basis, reflecting the number of children in the household. Payments were tapered away from 2013 for households where one adult was taxed at the higher threshold.

CTB, *Council Tax Benefit*: Payment by the state of recipients' council tax. The benefit was replaced by Council Tax Reduction in 2013, a system under which each Local Authority decided on the level of support to provide for benefit recipients.

CTR, *Council Tax Reduction*: See above

CU, *Credit Unions*: Community-focused, and non-profit making, savings and loans institutions. They remain a small part of the UK financial system, although Government encouraged their growth with the Credit Union Expansion Project.

CIS, *Customer Information System*: Computerised data base at DWP storing basic identifying information on claimants such as name, date of birth, address and national insurance number as well as some short-term information on claims history.

DEL, *Departmental Expenditure Limit*: The main operating budget for Government Departments, including all expenditure which that Department is expected to control, in contrast to Annually Managed Expenditure. (See AME)

DCLG, *Department for Communities and Local Government*: Responsible for managing Local Authorities and housing, this Department interacted closely, and sometimes acrimoniously, with DWP.

Defra, *Department for Environment, Food and Rural Affairs*: The Department's 'Rural Payments Agency' digital service, introduced from 2014, was dogged by similar problems to UC. (See UC)

DWP, *Department for Work and Pensions*: Responsible for the largest Departmental budget, with approaching 100,000 employees, DWP administers the state pension system, most welfare payments (excluding Tax Credits, which are now being subsumed in UC), Child maintenance and the state employment operation, Jobcentre Plus. (See JCP and UC)

DPDP, *Direct Payment Demonstration Projects*: Set of six pilots to discover the consequences for tenants and landlords of introducing direct payments in UC for social housing rent. (See UC)

Disability benefits: Portmanteau term for Disability Living Allowance and its replacement, the Personal Independence Payment. Neither is means-tested. Attendance Allowance is the equivalent benefit for pensioners. (See DLA and PIP)

DLA, *Disability Living Allowance*: Established in 1992, DLA was a tax-free, non-means tested and non-contributory benefit with two components, each set at three rates, for personal care and for mobility. It was replaced by the Personal Independence Payment for adults from 2013. (See PIP)

Dynamic Benefits: Policy Report from the CSJ produced by Stephen Brien which analysed the way to combine all welfare benefits into two components, a Universal Work Credit and a Universal Life Credit. (See CSJ)

ERC, *Economic Recovery Committee*: A business group set up by David Cameron in 2009 to advise the Conservative Party in opposition how best to tackle the economic aftermath of the 2008 financial crash.

ESA, *Employment and Support Allowance*: A means-tested payment for incapacity which replaced Incapacity Benefit from 2008. The gateway to the benefit was a medical assessment called the Work Capability Assessment. (See IB and WCA)

FCA, *Financial Conduct Authority*:

Regulator of the financial services sector, with the objective of protecting consumers, promoting competition within the sector and safeguarding financial markets. Alongside the banks, building societies, insurers and major investment firms it directly regulates, it is also responsible for the credit union movement.

FND, *Flexible New Deal*: Revamp of the Labour Government's New Deal programme in 2009. It was contracted out, covering roughly half the country on launch, and was replaced by The Work Programme in 2011. (See New Deal and TWP)

GCHQ, *Government Communications Headquarters*: Based in Cheltenham, this Intelligence and Security Agency monitors signals and information from the internet. It is a key player in cyber security for the Government and country as a whole.

GDS, *Government Digital Service*: Established within the Cabinet Office in 2011 to drive service delivery to digital across Government as well as providing support for Departments as they introduced the digital approach. Public funding for its directly-managed cross-Government project – Verify – to build common identity assurance was cut off in 2018.

GDP, *Gross Domestic Product*: A measure of total economic activity in a country.

HMRC, *Her Majesty's Revenue and Customs*: Responsible for collecting all taxes, customs duties and National Insurance, as well as paying out Child Benefit & Tax Credits. Within income tax, it operates the Pay-As-You-Earn system. (See PAYE)

HMT, *Her Majesty's Treasury*: The powerful overseer of the economic direction of the country and its public finances. It controls public spending, particularly the budgets of other Government Departments; the delivery of public sector infrastructure projects; and financial services policy. It

maintains oversight of the UK tax system.

IB, *Incapacity Benefit*: The precursor of ESA, introduced in 1995, which included a test for claimants. Between 2011 and 2016 virtually all claimants were reassessed and, where considered appropriate, transferred onto ESA. (See ESA)

Incapacity benefits: Portmanteau term for payments of ESA, Incapacity Benefit, Severe Disablement Allowance and Income Support on the grounds of incapacity. (See ESA, IB and disability benefits)

ICT, *Information and Communications Technology*: Updated expression for Information Technology (IT) which captures the concept of combining telecommunications with computer networks. (See IT)

IT, *Information Technology*: Use of computers to manage information. Subset of ICT. (See ICT)

IRIS, *Integrated Risk and Intelligence Service*: Plan developed in 2011 to detect UC fraud by creating a central hub to gather and analyse claimant data. The project was abandoned after the Cabinet Office refused funding.

JCP, *Jobcentre Plus*: Combination of the state-run Jobcentre employment offices with the Benefits Agency in 2002-2008. It allowed the more efficient reinforcement of work obligations as a condition of receiving benefit. In 2002-2011 it was an executive agency reporting to the Minister for Employment within the Department, before being absorbed back into DWP.

JSA, *Jobseeker's Allowance*: Basic unemployment benefit for those who worked less than 16 hours a week. It was paid as of right to those having made adequate National Insurance contributions (typically for two-years) and on the basis of need for others. All claimants had to demonstrate they were actively seeking work. The benefit was incorporated into UC. (See UC)

Leap: A phase in which the Agile software was designed in the first 'Live' iteration of UC. These took place over a matter of months initially. The Leaps were made up of Sprints.

LPs, *Lone Parents*: Single parents with a dependent child under the age of 16. The relevant benefit was Income Support, which had no work obligations attached till 2008. By 2012 LPs whose children were aged five or over were eligible for JSA when making a new claim, with attendant work obligations.

MPA, *Major Projects Authority*: Established as a joint venture between the Cabinet Office and the Treasury in 2011 to monitor the progress of major projects. It also aimed to support Departments in developing project management capability. In 2016 it was merged with Infrastructure UK to form the Infrastructure and Projects Authority.

MCDG, *Ministerial Change and Delivery Group*: Weekly internal briefing in SoS's office by officials on the implementation of key programmes. The regular Ministerial attendees were the SoS and Minister for Welfare Reform, while senior officials included the Permanent Secretary, Finance Director and Chief Information Officer. (See SoS)

MOG, *Ministerial Oversight Group*: Cross-Departmental group of Ministers – from the Cabinet Office, Treasury and DWP – to oversee the reset of UC in 2013. (See UC)

MoS, *Minister of State:* Second Ministerial tier behind Secretary of State. Usually a member of the House of Commons.

NAO, *National Audit Office*: An institution under the control of the House of Commons in the shape of the Public Accounts Committee. It scrutinises public spending and audits central Government Departments and other public bodies, reporting the results to the Parliament. (See PAC)

New Deal: A Welfare-to-Work programme introduced by the Labour Government in 1998. It was divided into a number of separate elements such as the New Deal for Young People and the New Deal 25+. The Employment Zone initiative within the programme was the inspiration for The Work Programme. (See TWP)

NICE, *National Institute for Health and Care Excellence*: A Non Departmental Public Body providing guidance and advice on improving health and social care.

OBR, *Office for Budget Responsibility*: Established by the incoming Conservative Government in 2010 to provide an analysis independent of the Treasury as to the current and projected state of the economy and public finances, as well as the budgetary impact of Government programmes.

OJEU, *Official Journal of the European Union*: The publication in which all tenders for the public sector above a financial threshold must be published. It aims to create a more level playing field for companies across the European Union.

PUS, *Parliamentary Undersecretary of State*: Third and most junior Ministerial tier, behind Secretary of State and Minister of State. (See MoS and SoS)

PAYE, *Pay-As-You-Earn*: A system for deducting income tax at source introduced in 1944. The tax authorities provided employers with a tax code to indicate the correct proportion of income to be deducted. Designed in an era of life-time employment, the system was coming under strain in an era of multiple jobs.

PAYE2, *Pay-As-You-Earn2*: A reform designed by Vocalink to track wage payments in real time as they went through the banking system.

Permanent Secretary: The senior civil servant in a Government Department, responsible for its running and making sure that the SoS is supported. The Permanent Secretary is the accounting officer of the Department, responsible to Parliament for its performance. (See SoS)

PIP, *Personal Independence Payment*: A tax-free, non-means tested and non-contributory benefit for working age adults replacing DLA from 2013 intended to help with the extra costs of living with a disability or long-term health condition. The two components, daily living and mobility, are each paid at standard or enhanced rates. (See DLA)

PS, *Private Secretary*: A civil servant responsible for managing the working life of a Government minister.

Programme Director: Official responsible for the day by day running of a project. Works in tandem with the SRO. (See SRO)

PAC, *Public Accounts Committee*: A select committee of the Commons responsible for overseeing Government expenditure, established in 1861. It is supported by the NAO. (See NAO)

The Quad: Regular meetings of four senior ministers from the two sides of the Coalition Government in the shape of the Prime Minister (David Cameron) and Chancellor (George Osborne) for the Conservatives and the Deputy Prime Minister (Nick Clegg) and Chief Secretary to the Treasury (Danny Alexander) for the Liberal Democrats. These would decide major matters of policy.

RTI, *Real Time Information:* From 2012 HMRC started modernising the system of PAYE so that employers transmitted information to Government about tax and other deductions each time they paid an employee. This allowed an up-to-date monthly calculation as to an individual's UC entitlement reflecting current need, as well as accurate withholding of income tax. (See PAYE and PAYE2)

RSRS, *Removal of the Spare Room Subsidy*: The Government name for the withholding

of some housing benefit from people with surplus bedroom space, introduced in April 2013. Otherwise known as the 'Bedroom Tax', the 'Social Sector Size Criteria', and the 'Under-occupancy Charge'.

RPI, *Retail Prices Index*: A long-standing measure of consumer price changes. It usually registers a larger rise than the Consumer Price Index, which replaced it as the main measure of inflation from 2010. It lost its status as a national statistic in 2013. (See CPI)

SoS, *Secretary of State*: Senior Minister, responsible for a Department and member of Cabinet.

SRO, *Senior Responsible Owner*: Person with responsibility for ensuring that a project meets its overall objectives. In 2014 SROs were made directly accountable to Parliament for the implementation of their projects.

SSAC, *Social Security Advisory Committee*: Independent statutory body which advises on welfare issues and scrutinises secondary legislation, making public recommendations to which the DWP must respond. (See DWP)

SpAd, *Special Adviser*: Political appointee by senior Ministers to provide them with advice and support. Media handling is often a key role.

Spending Review: Typically a five-year review of the Government's spending plans, covering the budgets of all Government Departments.

Sprints: A short intensive phase of development, typically lasting two weeks. In the digital version it was aimed at delivering working software code. The Sprints involved the whole team, from programmers to operators of the business. (See Leaps)

SI, *Statutory Instrument*: The most common form of secondary legislation, which contains the detailed provisions of a law.

It is only rarely rejected by Parliament. Depending on the form set out in the primary legislation, it can be presented through a negative resolution (which presumes its passage unless challenged) or through an affirmative resolution (requiring positive approval).

Supported Accommodation (or Housing): Housing schemes which integrate support and sometimes care services. They include homeless hostels, refuges and sheltered housing. Some were categorised as 'exempt' which allowed higher rents to be supported by housing benefit. This was widened in 2014 by the introduction of yet another category called 'specified accommodation'. Annual rents for supported accommodation exceed £4 billion.

SMI, *Support for Mortgage Interest*: A scheme in which the jobless and poorer pensioners were entitled to a benefit to help pay their monthly mortgage bills. This was changed to a loan in April 2018.

Support Group: The higher category of disability within ESA which deems people to have a limited capability for both work and work-related activity. The UC category matches this with a definition of 'limited capability for work-related activity' (LCWRA). There are no work requirements placed on individuals. (See ESA and UC)

The Taper: The rate at which UC is reduced as earnings increase. It was set at 65 percent at the outset, so that for every extra pound earned, the benefit was cut by 65 p, leaving 35 p. The rate was improved to 63 percent in 2016. (See UC)

TOM, *Target Operating Model*: The shape an organisation needs to become in order to achieve its strategy.

Tax Credits: Support for the less well off in the shape of Working Tax Credit, for the low-paid, and Child Tax Credit for both the low paid and those on benefit. Introduced by Gordon Brown at the turn of the century, the Conservatives made much of the administrative problems.

TWP, *The Work Programme*: Flagship welfare-to-work scheme of Coalition Government, introduced in 2011 and replacing the previous New Deal and Flexible New Deal programmes. With employment at record levels, it ended in 2017 and was replaced by a much smaller programme called the Work and Health Programme. (See FND and New Deal)

Third Sector Taskforce: A investigation into the role of the voluntary sector in welfare-to-work programmes, chaired by Tony Hawkhead of Groundwork UK and reporting to the DWP. (See DWP)

Train to Gain: Labour Government programme introduced in 2006 to deliver vocational training to employees. It was replaced by the Conservative apprenticeship programme in 2010.

Work Allowances: The amount people in UC can earn before their benefit starts to shrink. This threshold varies for households in different circumstances and was sharply reduced in 2015. (See UC)

WCA, *Work Capability Assessment*: The medical assessment to determine whether claimants are entitled to either of the two categories of ESA, or the equivalent categories in UC. The WCA process, introduced in 2008, was contracted out. (See ESA, WRAG and Support Group)

WMS, *Written Ministerial Statement*: Announcement putting every-day Government business on the record.

WRAG, *Work Related Activity Group*: The lesser category of disability within ESA which deems people capable of work at some time in the future and are capable of taking steps immediately towards moving into work. In the UC equivalent, claimants are categorised as having 'limited capability for work' and are placed in the 'work preparation group'. (see ESA and UC)

UC, *Universal Credit*: The replacement for six main working age benefits – Income-based Jobseeker's Allowance, Income-based Employment and Support Allowance, Child Tax Credit, Working Tax Credit, Housing Benefit and Income Support.

USdl, *Universal Support delivered locally*: Co-operation between DWP and Local Authorities to provide transitional support for UC claimants who may need help over budgeting or to handle their claim on-line. (See DWP and UC)

UQ, *Urgent Question*: Commons procedure in which MPs can apply to the Speaker for a same-day appearance by a Government Minister at the despatch box to answer questions on a matter of urgency or importance.

NOTES

1. Department for Work and Pensions: Reducing dependency, increasing opportunity: options for the future of welfare to work by David Freud. HMSO, March 2007.
2. Nicholas Timmins (2016) *UC: From Disaster to Recovery?* Institute for Government.
3. *Financial Times*: Britain's changing pattern of poverty by David Freud, 19 June 1979.
4. Anthony Seldon with Peter Snowdon and Daniel Collings (2007) *Blair Unbound*, Simon & Schuster, pp501-50.
5. Department for Work and Pensions: The introduction of Jobcentre Plus: An evaluation of labour market impacts by Rebecca Riley, Helen Bewley, Simon Kirby, Ana Rincon-Aznar and Anitha George, Research Report No. 781, 2011.
6. Ron Haskins (2006) *Work over Welfare. The Inside Story of the 1996 Welfare Reform Law,* The Brookings Institution .
7. The Stationery Office: *Is Work Good For Your Health and Well-being?*, by Gordon Waddell and A Kim Burton, pviii, 2006.
8. Depart. for Work and Pensions: Evaluation of Employment Zones: Report on a Cohort Survey of Long-Term Unemployed People in the Zones and a Matched Set of Comparison Areas, National Centre for Social Research by J. Hales, R. Taylor, W. Mandy, and M Miller, Research Report No 176, p139, 2003.
9. John Hutton, speech: Welfare Reform: 10 years on, 10 years ahead, 18 December 2006.
10. HM Treasury: Prosperity for all in the global economy – world class skills, Leitch Review of Skills Final Report, by Alexander Leitch, December 2006 .
11. *Financial Times*: Brown to press on with welfare reforms, by James Blitz and Ben Hall, 2 March 2007.
12. Institute for Government: Making policy in opposition: The Work Programme, 2007-2010 by Catherine Haddon, November 2012.
13. John Hutton, speech: Welfare to Work Convention in Birmingham, 20 June 2007.
14. Nicholas Timmins (1995. Edition 3, 2017) *The Five Giants* originally published by William Collins.
15. *Financial Times:* Dozen big contractors could take welfare role, by Andrew Taylor, Ben Hall and Nicholas Timmins, 6 March 2007.
16. Department for Work and Pensions: In work, better off: next steps to full employment, Green Paper, 18 July, 2007.
17. *Financial Times:* Welfare Reform Green Paper Published by Nicholas Timmins, p3, 19 July 2007.
18. *Financial Times:* Hain cool on private sector job contracts by Nicholas Timmins, p1, 31 July 2007.
19. *Financial Times:* CBI fears for private sector after Hain remarks by Nicholas Timmins, p3, John Cridland, CBI deputy director-general, quoted, 1 August 2007.
20. *Financial Times:* Welfare-to-work plans watered down by Nicholas Timmins, p2, 6 August 2007.
21. *Financial Times:* Hain changes welfare-to-work tone by Alex Barker, p3, 13 Sept. 2007.

22. *The Daily Telegraph*: Will it be grumpy Gordon or Father Brown by Rachel Sylvester and Alice Thompson, 12 June 2007.

23. Chris Grayling, speech: No one benefits from being on benefits. At Policy Exchange, 12 December 2007.

24. Conservative Policy Green Paper No 3: Work for Welfare: REAL welfare reform to help make British poverty history, 8 Jan. 2008.

25. *Financial Times:* Tories vow overhaul of benefits by Alex Barker, p2, 9 January 2008.

26. *Financial Times:* Freud appointment sends signal on welfare-to-work by Nicholas Timmins and Jim Pickard, p4, 28 Jan 2008.

27. *The Daily Telegraph:* 1.9m on benefit 'should go back to work' by Alice Thomson and Rachel Sylvester, p1, 2 February 2008 .

28. *The Daily Telegraph:* Welfare? It's a mess that no one can manage by Rachel Sylvester and Alice Thomson, p16, 2 February 2008.

29. Department for Work and Pensions: No one written off: reforming welfare to reward responsibility. Public Consultation, July 2008.

30. The Third Sector Taskforce: Welfare to Work reform: the third sector's role, Final Report, 4 February 2009.

31. *The Sunday Times:* Tories steal welfare guru from Brown by Jonathan Oliver and David Smith, p1, 15 February 2009.

32. *The Sunday Telegraph:* David Cameron recruits Labour adviser to Conservatives by James Kirkup, p1, 25 February 2009.

33. *The Times:* Even Labour MPs are short-selling bust PM by Rachel Sylvester, p23, 17 February 2017.

34. *Evening Standard:* Gordon's on the Orient Express – with an awful lot of suspects by Anne McElvoy, p15, 18 February 2009.

35. *Hansard* HL Deb. Vol. 713, cols 834-44, 29 October 2009.

36. *Hansard* HL Deb. Vol 716, cols 23-24, 5 January 2010.

37. Social Justice Policy Group: Volume 2: Breakthrough Britain. Ending the costs of social breakdown. Policy recommendations to the Conservative Party, July 2007.

38. The Centre for Social Justice: Dynamic Benefits: Towards welfare that works. A policy report from the Economic Dependency Working Group chaired by Dr Stephen Brien, September 2009.

39. David Cameron, speech: At Conservative Conference in Manchester, 8 October 2009.

40. Samuel Britain (1995) *Capitalism With A Human Face,* Edward Elgar Publishing.

41. Vocalink: Creating the Single Account Tax and Benefit System, a briefing paper for Lord Freud, 10 March 2010.

42. Conservative Party: Conservatives welcome support for 'Service Academy for unemployed, 15 March 2010' .

43. Conservative Party: Invitation to Join the Government of Britain, The Conservative Manifesto, 13 April 2010.

44. *The Daily Telegraph:* The Tories have just the man to find more jobs for British workers by Fraser Nelson, 8 April 2010.

45. Institute for Fiscal Studies: Post-Budget Presentations: Opening Remarks by Robert Chote, Director, 23 June 2010.

46. *The Mail on Sunday:* Revealed: The blazing row between Iain Duncan Smith and George Osborne by Brendan Carlin, 22 August 2010.

47. Department for Work and Pensions: 21st Century Welfare, Cm 7913, pp24,25, July 2010.

48. *The Times:* Deal Struck for £9bn Bonfire of the Benefits by Rosemary Bennett and Roland Watson, p1, 1 October 2010 .

49. George Osborne, speech: At Conservative Conference, Conservative Party Speeches, 4 October 2010.

50. *Hansard* HL Deb. Vol 721, col 373, 11 October 2010.

51. Department for Work and Pensions: Universal Credit: welfare that works, Cm 7957, November 2010.

52. *Hansard* HL Deb. Vol 722, col 325, 11 November 2010.

53. *Hansard* HL Deb. Vol 722, col 329, 11 November 2010.

54. *Hansard* HL Deb. Vol 725, col 1518, 8 March 2011.

55. *Hansard* HL Deb. Vol 725, col 1608, 9 March 2011.

56. Work and Pensions Committee, Examinations of Witnesses, Questions 97-197, 3 November 2010.

57. *Hansard* HL Deb. Vol 724, cols 744-780, 24 January 2011.

58. *Hansard* HL Deb. Vol 725, col 589, 15 February 2011.

59. *Hansard* HL Deb. Vol 726, cols 1250-94, 30 March 2011.

60. *Hansard* HL Deb. Vol 731, cols 981-82, 31 October 2011.

61. Department for Work and Pensions: Working for a healthier tomorrow: work and health in Britain by Dame Carol Black, 17 March 2008.

62. *Hansard* HC Deb. Vol 524, col 934, 9 March 2011.

63. *Hansard* HC Deb. Public Bill Committee, Session 2010-11, col 171, 29 March 2011.

64. *Hansard* HC Deb. Vol 524, col 883, 15 June 2011.

65. *Hansard* HL Deb. Vol 730, cols 628-742, 13 September 2011.

66. *Hansard* HL Deb. Vol 730, cols GC323-4, 4 October 2011.

67. *Hansard* HL Deb. Vol 730, cols GC369-73, 6 October 2011.

68. *Hansard* HL Deb. Vol 731, cols GC160-72, 20 October 2011.

69. *Hansard* HL Deb. Vol 732, cols 183-84, 14 November 2011.

70. *Hansard* HL Deb. Vol 730, cols GC349-361, 6 October 2011.

71. *Hansard* HL Deb. Vol 732, cols GC5-50, 8 November 2011.

72. *Hansard* HL Deb. Vol 732, col GC407, 23 November 2011.

73. *Hansard* HL Deb. Vol 733, cols GC74, 28 November 2011.

74. *Hansard* HL Deb. Vol 734, col 1099, 25 January 2012.

75. *Hansard* HL Deb. Vol 735, cols 681-780, 14 February 2012.

76. Department for Work and Pensions: 21st Century Welfare, Cmnd 7913, p33, par5, July 2010.

77. Department for Work and Pensions: Universal Credit: welfare that works, White Paper Cmnd 7957, p32, November 2010.

78. Transform Innovation: Directgov Strategic Review – Executive Summary by Martha Lane Fox, p4, 23 November 2010.

79. Cabinet Office: Digital by Default proposed for Government Service, press release, 23 November 2010.

80. CIO UK: Profile: DWP and UK Government CIO Joe Harley brings a boardroom ethos to public-sector IT by Graham Jarvis, 23 June 2011.

81. Department for Work and Pensions: Universal Credit internal report – now published, by Tony Collins, Campaign4Change, 20 October 2016.

82. David Freud (2006): *Freud in the City*. Bene Factum Publishing, 2006, p20.

83. Francis Maude, speech: At Conservative Conference, 3 October 2010.

84. Francis Maude, speech: At supplier summit, 1 December 2010.

85. Cabinet Office: One Year On: Implementing the Government ICT Strategy, May 2012.

86. *Hansard* HL Deb. Vol 733, col 1011, 12 December 2011.

87. *The Spectator*: The Universal Credit crunch, p3, 15 September 2012.

88. *The Guardian*: Time to Talk by Terry Moran, 4 February 2016.

89. *The Independent on Sunday:* Benefits reform under threat after IT glitch by James Cusick, 11 Nov 2012.

90. Social Security Advisory Committee: Passporting to the Future, Cmnd 8332, February 2012.

91. Francis Maude, Speaker's Lecture: The Future of the Civil Service, 13 September 2017.

92. Work and Pensions Committee, Universal Credit, Q9-10, Q33, Q38 oral evidence, HC, 10 July 2013.

93. National Audit Office: Universal Credit: early progress, HC 621, 5 September 2013.

94. *BBC Breakfast:* Interview with Iain Duncan Smith, 5 September 2013.

95. *Hansard* HC Deb. Vol 567, cols 467-69, 5 September 2013.

96. Work and Pensions Committee: Oral evidence from David Cameron, 10 Sept.2013.

97. Public Accounts Committee: Oral Evidence on 11 September 2013, Q74, 82, 96-7, 118, 135. HC619, published 7 November 2013.

98. Matthew d'Ancona (2013*): In it Together: The Inside Story of the Coalition Government*, Viking.

99. Public Accounts Committee: Universal Credit: early progress, HC Thirtieth Report, 4 November 2013.

100. Margaret Hodge (2016) *Called to Account, How Governments and Vested Interests Combine to Waste Our Money*, Little, Brown pp262-4.

101. *Hansard* HC Deb. Vol 571, 65-6 WS, 5 December 2013.

102. Work and Pensions Committee: Oral evidence on Universal Credit and DWP Stats, Q91, HC867, 9 December 2013.

103. *Hansard* HC Deb. Vol 572, cols 133-45, 10 December 2013.

104. *Hansard* HL Deb. Vol 750, cols 723-7, 10 December 2013.

105. The Department for Work and Pensions and the Department for Communities and Local Government: Supported Accommodation Review. The scale, scope and cost of the supported housing sector by Ipsos MORI, Imogen Blood and Associates and Housing and Support Partnership, Research Report No 927, November 2016 .

106. The Financial Conduct Authority: Tougher rules for payday lenders take effect, 1 July 2014, .

107. *Hansard* HL Deb. Vol 751, col 228, 15 January 2014.

108. *Computer Weekly Editors Blog:* Is DWP looking for yet another new chief for Universal Credit by Bryan Glick, 29 April 2014.

109. Public Accounts Committee: Oral evidence on Major Projects Authority from John Manzoni Q1-82, 5 June 2014, 10th Report published 16 July 2014.

110. Public Accounts Committee: Oral evidence on Centre of Government, 19th Report, 7 July 2014.

111. *Hansard* HC Deb. Vol 584, cols 293-5, 5 July 2014.

112. *Hansard* HL Deb. Vol 755, col 221, 5 July 2014.

113. Department for Work and Pensions: Universal Credit at Work, 22 October 2014 .

114. National Audit Office: Universal Credit: progress update, 26 November 2014 .

115. Resolution Foundation, forum: Universal Credit – how do we make it work?, with Lord Freud, Julian McCrae (Institute for Government), Julia Unwin (Joseph Rowntree Foundation), Vidhya Alakeson (Resolution Foundation) and Anuhska Asthana (Sky News – chair), 30 September 2014 .

116. *www.politicshome.com/uk/article/ 106453/fresh freudian_slip percent3F.html.*

117. *Hansard* HC Deb. Vol 600, cols 292-3, 15 October 2014.

118. *LBC:* Call Clegg, 9am 16 October 2014.

119. *Question Time:* BBC1, 16 October 2014.

120. *Guido Fawkes*: Eagle Crash Landed. Watch Question Time Audience turn on Labour over Freud, 17 Oct 2014.

121. *The Sunday Times:* Lord Freud's slip I don't mind, but the confected outrage disgusts me by Dominic Lawson, 19 Oct 2014.

122. *Daily Mail:* Labour's voice of equality? I don't think she believed a single shrill word she said by Quentin Letts, Yesterday in Parliament, p26, 29 October 2014.

123. *Hansard* HC Deb. Vol 587, col 540, 3 November 2014.

124. George Osborne, New Year Economy Speech: at Sertec. Treasury, Gov.uk, 6 January 2014.

125. I am indebted to Robert Joyce of the Institute for Fiscal Studies for reviewing these figures.

126. George Osborne speech: At Conservative Conf. in Birmingham, 29 September 2014.

127. Department for Work and Pensions: Universal Credit at Work – Spring 2015, 15 February 2015.

128. *Hansard* HL Deb. Vol 757, cols GC160-2, 19 November 2014.

129. Social Security Advisory Committee: The Universal Credit (Waiting Days) (Amendment) Regulations 2015 (S.I 2015 No. 1362), p4, June 2015.

130. Social Security Advisory Committee and Department for Work and Pensions: Universal Credit waiting days: statement from Paul Gray, 19 March 2015.

131. Conservative Party: Manifesto 2015, p8, 14 April 2015.

132. *Hansard* HL Deb. Vol 764, col 432, 13 July 2015.

133. *Hansard* HL Deb. Vol 765, col 979, 26 October 2105.

134. The Centre for Social Justice: Reforming Tax Credits. A short Note, November 2015.

135. *The Daily Telegraph:* It's not too late for Mr Osborne to show he's on the side of the strivers by Fraser Nelson, 6 November 2015.

136. *The Sunday Times:* IDS quit threat foils Osborne's benefits raid by Tim Shipman, 15 November 2015.

137. *Hansard* HC Deb. Vol 602, col 1360, 25 November 2015.

138. *Hansard* HL Deb. Vol 767, cols 118-9, 17 November 2015.

139. *Hansard* HL Deb. Vol 767, cols 1362-83 and 1399-1430, 7 December 2015.

140. *Hansard* HL Deb. Vol 768, cols 1299-1302, 27 January 2016.

141. *Hansard* HL Deb. Vol 769, cols 1073-4, 7 March 2016.

142. Department for Work and Pensions: The Government Response to the consultation on aids and appliances and the daily living component of the Personal Independence Payment, Cmnd 9194, 11 March 2016.

143. *Hansard* HC Deb. Vol 607, col 32WS, 11 March 2016.

144. Iain Duncan Smith resignation letter: In full on *BBC news website*, 18 March 2016.

145. Letter from Prime Min. to Rt Hon Iain Duncan Smith MP, Gov.uk, 19 March 2016.

146. *The Andrew Marr Show*, BBC1, 20 March 2016.

147. *The Times:* Cameron: I blame Osborne by Sam Coates and Matt Chorley, p1, 21 March 2016.

148. *Hansard* HC Deb. Vol 607, cols 1268-9, 21 March 2016.

149. *Hansard* HL Deb. Vol 769, col 2135, 21 March 2016.

150. *Financial Times:* Tories signal end to welfare cuts in bid to end turmoil by George Parker, Kate Allen and Jim Pickard, p1, 22 March 2016.

151. *Financial Times:* Merkel warns on cost of welfare by Quentin Peel, 16 December 2012.

152. *Hansard* HC Deb. Vol 598, col 335, 8 July 2015.

153. Iain Duncan Smith, speech: Work, health and disability at event hosted by Barclays and Reform, Gov.uk, 24 August 2015.

154. *Hansard* HL Deb. Vol 768, col 1041, 25 January, 2016.

155. Stephen Crabb, speech: Transforming Lives Through Welfare and Work, 12 April 2016.

156. Department of Work and Pensions and Department of Health: The Work, Health and Disability Green Paper, 31 October 2016.

157. *Hansard* HL Deb. Vol 775, col 485, 31 October, 2016.

158. David Freud, speech: At the Local Government Association (LGA) about Universal Credit and Universal Support, 12 January 2015.

159. *Hansard* HL Deb. Vol 774, col 371 14 July 2016.

160. *Hansard* HL Deb. Vol 774, col 522, 19 July 2016.

161. Department for Work and Pensions: Statement made on 20 July 2016, UIN HCWS96.

162. Public Accounts Committee: Oral Evidence: Universal Credit: progress review, Question 15, HC489, 20 July 2016.

163. Public Accounts Committee: Universal Credit and fraud and error: progress review, HC489. 4 November 2016.

164. David Freud oral evidence to Work and Pensions Committee, HC 898, 8 February 2017.

165. Department for Work and Pensions: The Work Programme: A quantitative impact assessment by Jeraldine Kay and Simon Marlow, p 15, 24 November 2020.

166. Nicholas Timmins (2020) *Universal Credit: Getting it to Work Better*. Institute for Government.

167. *Hansard* HL Deb. Vol 777, cols 1696-1720, 21 December 2016.

168. Stafford H Northcote and C.E. Trevelyan (1853): *Report on the Organisation of the Permanent Civil Service*. Presented to both Houses of Parliament in 1854.

169. David Freud oral evidence to Work and Pensions Committee, HC 898, 8 February 2017.

170. Department for Work and Pensions: Universal Credit: welfare that works, White Paper Cmnd 7957, p4, November 2010.

171. National Audit Office: Universal Credit: early progress, HC 621, 5 September 2013.

172. National Audit Office: Welfare reform – lessons learned, par 2.6 and Summary 16, HC77, Session 2015-16, 29 May 2015.

173. Cabinet Office: Ministerial Code, Paragraph 5.6, October 2015.

174. Ministry of Reconstruction: Report of the Machinery of Government Committee, Part 1, par 12, 1918

INDEX

NOTE   Page numbers in *italic* refer to entries in the Dramatis Personae

Agile IT developers, Warrington 158-9, 161-2, 167, 180, 212, 221-2, 325
Alexander, Danny 134, 199, 216, 222-3, *338*
  and spending control 235, 328
Alexander, Douglas 118
Allen, Heidi 286
Alternative Payment Arrangements (APA) 238
Altmann, Ros, Baroness 291-2, 308, *338*
  as Pensions Minister 273-4
Andrew Marr Show 292
Anelay, Joyce, Conservative chief whip in Lords 74, *338*
Annually Managed Expenditure (AME) 17-18, 21, 30, 34, 265
Antonovski, Aaron 130
Appeal Court, and improper sanctions on claimants 206
apprenticeships 63
apps, phone 316-17
Ashton under Lyne, UC pathfinder launch in 202-3
Australia, Social Firms model 131, 251

BACS
  and benefit payment system 82-3, 99-100
  see also Vocalink
Baker, Mike, UC Operations Director 231-2, 238, *338*
banking system, bailout 52

banks, and real-time PAYE 242
Bath Jobcentre 211, 232
Begg, Anne, Work and Pensions Select Committee 211-12, 213-14, 224, 225, *338*
Bell, James, Bishop of Ripon and Leeds 147-8, 150, 152-3, *338*
Benefit Cap 117, 118, 139, 146, 147-8, 149, 152
  exemptions 285
  introduction 205-6
  Osborne and 267, 272, 277, 313
benefits
  and behavioural changes 120
  claims process 50, 101
  and earnings thresholds 194, 195-6
  fraud and error in system 96
  frequency of payment 133-4, 269-70
  high marginal rates of withdrawal 77, 78, 102-3, 112
  payment delays 177
  payment system 82-3, 99-100, 113
  rising expenditure on 264
  working age 272
  see also Benefit Cap; Universal Credit
Benefits Agency 12
Bennett, Rosie, *Times* social affairs 116
Bernanke, Ben, Federal Reserve 51
Berridge, Elizabeth, Baroness 148
Best, Richard, Baron 126-7, 142-3, 147, 150-1, 153, 204, *338*
Black, Carol, mental health report 130-1
Blair, Tony *338*
  resignation 38

rivalry with Gordon Brown 2, 29, 45
and welfare reform report (2007) 10, 22,
24–5, 31, 33, 34
Boles, Nick 63
Bolton service centre 232
Boswell, Tim, Baron 149, 153
Boyd, Ed, Special Adviser 280–1
Bracken, Mike, Government Digital Service
173–4, 196, 197, 204, 208, 215, 338
and four critical roles 210
and Kevin Cunnington 225, 229
and twin track approach 222
Breakthrough Britain report 76
Brexit referendum 306, 307
Brien, Stephen 76–7, 99, 200, 338
and Agile 163, 172, 183
and death of Langsdale 190
and development of Universal Credit 161,
164–5, 173, 182–3, 186–7
secondment to DWP 111–12, 230
Bright Ideas Trust 66
Britain, Samuel, *Capitalism with a Human
Face* (1995) 80
Brown, Gordon 338
and New Deal programmes 15, 48
as Prime Minister 38, 39, 48, 52, 57–8
and proposals for single benefit 50
rivalry with Tony Blair 2, 29
and tax credits 77–8
and welfare reform report (2007) 25–7,
29–30, 32
windfall tax 15
Browne, Anthony 66
Bryant, Chris 247
Burns, Harry, Chief Medical Officer,
Scotland 130
Burstow, Paul 91
Byrne, Liam 135–6, 189, 213, 225, 338

Cabinet Office 174, 184, 196–8, 201, 204, 327–8
and contract clearance 328

and spending controls 222, 223
and twin track approach 222–4, 328
and UC pathfinder 209
see also Maude, Francis
Cameron, David 205, 338
and 2007 report launch conference 44–5
and 2015 election 273
and Big Society concept 64
and Coalition benefit reform group 102–3,
104
and Coalition government 89–90
and DF's comment on Minimum Wage
252–3, 260
and IDS 78–9
offer of job to DF 1, 3, 92–3
and Policy Board review 64–5
relations with Treasury 110
resignation (2016) 307
and resignation of IDS 290–1
on welfare benefits 144
Campbell, Jane, Baroness 140
cancer sufferers, and Employment and
Support Allowance 140, 145, 150
Canterbury, benefit centre 297–8
Capgemini, technology consulting firm 182
carers
and Personal Independence Payment (PIP)
143, 146
and Universal Credit 133–4
Carer's Allowance 284, 285
Carter, Stephen, Baron 54
Caseby, Richard 292
Cave, Alan 48, 104, 338
Cavendish, Camilla, Special Adviser 281
Centre for Social Justice 76, 80, 281
Channel 4 News 47
Chapman, James, Treasury 291
Charlesworth, Ian, Shaw Trust 20
child benefit 114
excluded from Universal Credit plan 103,
146

child maintenance system 139-40, 148, 149, 150, 153, 206
Child Poverty Bill (Labour 2009) 74-5
child support system, new 267
childcare, funding 135, 143
Childcare Account 239
Citizen's Advice 96
Civil Service
  history of reforms 323-4, 333-4
  lack of continuity 331-2
  lack of specialist expertise 332
  relations with politicians and Ministers 324
claimants
  and Alternative Payment Arrangements (APA) 238
  couples 231, 233, 239, 310
  families with children 246, 250
  see also disability; lone parents; mental health; vulnerable
Clarke, Ken 67
Clegg, Nick 89, 338
  and DF's comment on Minimum Wage 256-7
  Home Affairs Committee 327
  and policy paper 104
  and Universal Credit White Paper 118
Clinton-Davis, Stanley, Baron 123-4
Coalition government (from 2010) 1, 89-92
  benefit reform group 102-4
  cabinet reshuffle (2012) 185
  and digital technology 157-8
  and Emergency Budget (2010) 94, 107-9
  employment programmes 104
  Spending Review process 109, 111, 117, 265
  welfare spending 263-4
Cockell, Merrick 179-80, 240, 338
College of Arms 70-1
companies, and support for Get Britain Working programme 83-4
Computer Weekly 245, 250
Conservative government (from 2015) 273-4
  'fiscal events' 289
  rebellion on welfare cuts 290-4

see also Osborne, George
Conservative party
  conference (2009 Manchester) 67-8, 78
  conference (2010 Birmingham) 116-17
  conference (2013) 215
  conference (2014) 249-50, 251-3
  and Economic Recovery Committee 54
  and Get Britain Working programme 63-9
  leadership contenders (2016) 307
  Manifesto 85
  and opinion polls (2009-10) 84, 86
  in opposition 61-9
  Policy Board review (2009) 64
  and welfare reform 42-3
  Work Programme 63, 65-9, 95-6
Conservative-Liberal coalition see Coalition government
Consumer Price Index, and welfare inflation index 109, 263, 264
contributory benefits, and Universal Credit 172, 177, 210, 312-13
Cook, Rob, Private Secretary to DF 249, 252, 338
Couling, Neil
  DWP 100, 101, 114, 133-4, 338
  as head of benefits policy 167, 180
  and pathfinder launch 202
  and roll-out timetable 298, 310-11
  as Senior Responsible Officer of UC 249, 287-8, 331
  and time delays 270
council tax benefit 114, 118, 134, 139, 312
couples 239
  UC Live Service launch 231, 233, 310
Courtney, Katherine 180
Covid-19 pandemic 319
  and employment 305
  Long Covid 301
Coyle, Neil 311
Crabb, Stephen, Work and Pensions Secretary 299, 338
  and disability employment gap 304

as leadership contender 307
resignation 308
succession to IDS 292, 293-4
credit, Ministerial Summit on High Cost
Credit 244
Credit Union movement 131-2
and payday lenders 243-4
Cunnington, Kevin, GDS 224-5, 229-30,
240, 338
cyber-fraud 158, 163, 170-1, 183

Daily Mail 260
The Daily Telegraph 42, 85-6, 260, 282, 341
DF's interview 46-7
d'Ancona, Matthew, *In It Together* 215
Dannatt, Gen Sir Richard 56
data-sharing 268-9, 274
David, Wayne 225
Davies, Gareth, policy adviser to Blair 13, 21-
2, 24-5, 29-30, 46, 338
de Mauley, Rupert, Baron 146
Department for Skills 314
Department of Work and Pensions 49-51,
93-8
accounts 209, 210-11
and budget cuts 106-9, 265
and IT development 103, 110, 115
Labour Markets team 48
and lack of continuity 331-2
lack of specialist expertise 324-5, 332
media handling 96-7
Ministerial Change and Delivery Group
(MCDG) 186, 189-90
Ministerial team 96-7
and preparations for Universal Credit 95-8
relations with Cabinet Office 174, 184, 196-
8, 201, 204, 327-8
relations with Treasury 110-11, 113-16, 328
restructuring of IT competence 298-9, 326
turnover of ministers 54, 310, 330
Departmental Expenditure Limit (DEL)
17-18, 21, 30, 34, 265

Devereux, Robert, Permanent Secretary at
DWP 160, 182, 186, 256, 338
and Cabinet Office 196, 197-8, 209
and Langsdale 193
and Margaret Hodge 220-1
and National Audit Office 248-9, 250
and organisation of the project 164, 165,
170, 175, 233-4
and PIP plans 292-3
and Public Accounts Committee 214
and security problems 184
and twin track approach 217-18, 219-20
and UC delays 306-7
digital technology
and cyber-fraud 158
need for new system 216-20, 222-3
new system in operation 268
UC Full Service 297, 310, 326
see also Government Digital Service; IT
development
disability
and barriers to work 19
and employment gap 302-4
and reassessment of Incapacity Benefit
44, 50-1
UC support for 144-5, 301-4
see also mental health; Personal
Independence Payment, Employment and
Support Allowance
Disability Living Allowance 80, 103
for children 148, 150
medical reassessment 109, 114-15
replacement by Personal Independence
Payment (PIP) 140, 266
Donaghy, Rita, Baroness 144
Dover, Steve, Agile Director 162, 174, 180,
338
Drake, Jeannie, Baroness 127-8, 144, 338
Driscoll, Fiona, MPA 235
Driver, Mike, DWP Finance Director 186,
208-9, 217-18, 242, 338
Duncan Smith, Iain (IDS) 1, 3-4, 76-81, 95, 338

and Andrew Marr Show 292
and budget cuts 264-5
Centre for Social Justice 76
and concessions on Welfare Reform Bill 149
and Conservative conference (2014) 249-50
and DF's comment on Minimum Wage 254, 255
and housing benefit cuts 107-8
and invocation of Financial Privilege 148
and MPA review 209
and NAO report 213
and organisation of Universal Credit project 166-7
and pathfinder technology 218-19
and PAYE2 system 83, 84
and PIP changes 289-90, 292
and progress on Universal Credit 181-2, 194-5
and raising of pension age 128, 129
relations with Cabinet Office 197-8
relations with Treasury 109-10
resignation (2016) 289-94
role in Shadow Cabinet 78-9
as Secretary of State for Work and Pensions 90, 104, 185, 273-4
and tax credits 94-5
threat of resignation 280-3
and Universal Credit White Paper 118
and Welfare Reform and Work bill 285-6
and Work and Pensions Select Committee 211
Dykes, Richard 163-4
Dynamic Benefits report 76-7, 78, 79, 110
as model for Universal Credit 103, 112
Dyson, James 68

Eagle, Angela 257-8, *338*
Economic Recovery Committee (Conservative party) 54
election (2010) 89-90
Conservative Manifesto 85

formation of Coalition 89-92
election (2015)
Conservative Manifesto 270-2
new Cabinet 273-4
Elphicke, Charles, MP 56, 256, *339*
employment, rising rate of 267, 305
Employment and Support Allowance (ESA) 18, 52, 114, 140, 266, 302-3
Support Group 150, 152
tiers 145, 147, 150
time-limiting 152
WRAG (Work-Related Activity Group) 145, 147
see also Personal Independence Payment
Employment Zones 16
Enterprise Allowance Scheme 63
Evans, Natalie, Baroness 308-9, *339*
external review process 329-30
see also National Audit Office; Public Accounts Committee

Farmer, Mike, Baron 320
Fawkes, Guido, political commentator 258
Field, Frank, Work and Pensions Select Committee 311, 314, 324, 333
Financial Conduct Authority 244
financial crisis (2008) 2, 51-2
Financial Times 46, 294
1979 article by DF 9
Fisher, Mark 193
Fit for Work service 271, 302, 315
Flexible New Deal (Labour) 48, 49
cancellation of contracts 104-5
contracts for 67, 68
Foulkes, George, Baron 141-2
Fowler, Norman, Baron 149
France, public and private sectors 332
free school meals 135, 194, 312
Freud, Cilla, Lady 55, 248, 255
Freud, David (DF)
and 2015 election Manifesto 270-2

and comment on Minimum Wage for those with severe learning difficulties 251-60
Daily Telegraph interview (2008) 46-7
departure (2016) 299, 319-22
and Economic Recovery Committee 54-7
and European Ministers 317
and *Get Britain Working* programme 63, 65-9
in House of Lords 2, 97, 123-7
ill-health 154
and launch of 2007 welfare report 31-2
as Minister for Welfare Reform 1, 2, 3, 91-3, 96-8
and Osborne 278-9
peerage 54-5, 56, 70-1
previous career 3, 11-12
re-appointment (2015) 274
relations with Theresa May 65-6, 67, 68-9
threats of resignation 197-8, 248
Times interview (2010) 116
see also Reducing dependency report
The Full Monty (film) 16
Future Jobs Fund 52

Garel-Jones, Tristan, Baron 71
Gauke, David 339
and costings for Universal Credit 108, 119
and HMRC 242
and PAYE2 system 84-5, 100, 113
and pilot scheme 178-9
and tax credits 102
GCHQ, Cheltenham, and cyber security 174-5
Get Britain Working programme 63-9
and Conservative Manifesto 85
costings for 82, 115-16
Service Academy 83
'Work Pairing' 116
Gibbon, Gary, *Channel 4 News* 32
Glasgow, Easterhouse estate 76

Glassborow, Stuart, Treasury 231
Gove, Michael 194, 195, 196, 307
governance
and Government projects 323-36
heartland project requirements 333-6
need for 'Priority Projects' 335
role for Implementation Minister 335-6
separation of public and private sectors 332-3, 334
Government Digital Service (GDS) 173-4, 208
and new system 223-5, 229-30
problems with 215, 216-20
Gray, Paul 178
Grayling, Chris 58, 135, 185, 339
as Minister of State for Employment 90, 91, 92, 96
and welfare reform 43-4, 50
and Work Programme 105, 115-16, 132
Greater Manchester, UC pathfinder 180-1
Green, Damian, Work and Pensions Secretary 308, 309, 310, 318, 319, 339
Green, Kate 260
Greengross, Sally, Baroness 128, 129, 339
Greening, Justine 108
Groundwork UK charity 52
Guardian's Allowance 285
Guy, Christian, Special Adviser 281
Gwynne-Jones, Peter, Garter Principal King of Arms 70-1

Hadden, Neil, Genesis Housing 237
Hague, William 89-90, 171, 339
Hain, Peter, Secretary of State for Work and Pensions 39, 40, 45, 339
DF and 41-2
Haldane, Viscount, Civil Service reforms 333-4
Hammersmith Jobcentre 211, 232
Hammond, Philip 42, 339
and 2007 welfare reform report 33
and costings for *Get Britain Working* 82

Hancock, Matt, as adviser to Osborne 54, 61, 339
Harley, Joe, IT 115, 159, 164, 175, 324, 339
Harper, Mark 247-8, 308, 339
  Disabilities Minister 256, 260, 302
Harris, Ann 221-2, 226, 233, 235, 246, 249, 339
Harris, Hugh 146-7
Harrison, Rupert, adviser to Cameron 54, 57, 102, 111, 117, 339
Harrogate Jobcentre 211
Hartley, Janice 188, 198, 231, 246, 339
Haskins, Ron, and US welfare reform 13-14, 38, 339
Have I Got News for You 258
Hawkhead, Tony, Groundwork UK 52
Hawkins, Antony 61, 62
Hayes, Chris, DWP 160, 164, 339
Haynes, Caroline 51, 55, 61, 62, 83-4, 339
health
  and work 14, 96, 130-1
  see also cancer sufferers; disability; mental health
Heywood, Jeremy, Downing Street Permanent Secretary 102, 110, 217, 339
  and Devereux 220, 221
  and IDS 185-6
Hilton, Steve, Director of Strategy to Cameron 63-5, 68, 339
  work with DF 79-81, 82-3
Hinds, Damian 252, 339
  as Employment Minister 309-10
HMRC
  and PAYE2 scheme 85, 100, 113
  and tax credits 9, 78, 90-1, 94
  see also PAYE
Hoban, Mark 185, 215
Hodge, Margaret, Public Accounts Committee 214-15, 220-1, 225, 245-7, 329, 339
Hollis, Patricia, Baroness 73, 138-9, 226, 339
  on council tax benefit 142
  DF and 143-4, 146-7

and DF's comment on Minimum Wage 259-60
on disability allowance 143
and tax credits 279, 280
Hopkins, Peter 241
House of Commons
  Fatal Motion (on housing regulations) 126-7
  reception of 2007 welfare reform report 33-4
  and UC Strategic Outline Business Case 247-8
  Welfare Reform Bill (2012) 136
  and Welfare Reform and Work bill 286
  Work and Pensions Select Committee 124-5, 211-12, 213-14, 224, 225-6
House of Lords 2, 75, 329
  DF's final speech as Minister 319-22
  DF's introduction and maiden speech 71
  Oral Questions 97, 123-4
  passage of legislation 72-4
  reform of 151-2
  revolt over tax credit cuts 279-80
  UC regulations 269-70
  and Welfare Reform Bill (2012) 126-9, 137-41
  Welfare Reform and Work Act (2016) 283-7
housing
  Affordable Rent project 134-5
  sheltered 312
  short-term 312
  Supported Accommodation 284, 287
  Supported Housing expenditure 242-3, 284, 312
housing benefit 311-12
  for 18-21 year olds 277, 278-9
  and 'bedroom tax' 107-8, 118, 147, 150-1, 153, 204-5, 264
  cuts (2010) 106-7
  payment to tenants 134-5, 142-3, 147, 166, 237-9
  reductions for private tenants 124-5, 126-7
Howe, Freddie, Earl 279, 284, 339
HS2 rail project 53

Huddleston, Trevor, DWP 100, 301, 339
Hunt, Jeremy, Health Secretary 257-8
Hutton, John, Secretary of State for Work
  and Pensions 10, 11, 29-30, 39, 339
  and 2007 report 30, 31, 37, 38
  and New Deal 15-16
Hyman, Chris, Serco 20-1

identity assurance 169-70, 174, 216
'Implementation Minister', role for 335-6
Incapacity Benefit 16, 18, 22
  and JSA 19
  review of 44, 50-1
  see also Employment and Support
  Allowance (ESA)
Income Support 18
The Independent on Sunday 189, 238
inflation, and real-terms benefits increase 265
Institute of Fiscal Studies 263
Institute for Government 34
Integrated Risk and Intelligence Service
  (IRIS) 170, 175-6
intermittent earnings, adjustment for 210
Inverness Jobcentre 211, 232
IT development (for Universal Credit) 103,
  110, 115, 321
  Agile 158-9, 325
  budget write-down 208-9, 224
  and cyber-fraud 158, 163, 170-1, 183
  data links 163-4
  development Sprints 162, 225, 229-30
  and government suppliers 159, 169, 216-18
  and identity assurance 169-70, 174, 216
  lack of Departmental capability 324-5
  need for new system (2013) 203-4, 208-9
  Oracle Policy Modelling system 200
  problems with 182-4, 188, 196, 214-15, 324-6
  system security 173-7, 182-4, 208, 239-40,
    324-5, 330
    Cerberus retro-fit 171, 183-4
  see also digital technology

Jackson, Glenda 125
Jobcentre Plus (JCP) 12, 16, 272, 313
  co-location with local authorities 268, 305
  problems of benefits delivery 49-50
  and proposed single benefit 20-1
  and Universal Support 304-6
  work coaches 305-6, 316-17
Jobseekers Allowance (JSA) 18, 19
  cuts 266
  sanctions 236
  and Youth allowance 272
Johnson, Boris 307
  as Mayor of London 66
Johnson, Jo, and election Manifesto 270-1
Johnson, Neil, housing policy 284-5
Johnson, Richard, Serco 132

Kamelard, Adrian 242
Kelly, Stephen 197, 200-1, 215, 222, 339
Kerslake, Bob 247
Khoo, Daniel 80
Kirkwood, Archie, Baron 128, 139, 269-70,
  284, 309, 340
Knight, James, Baron 127

Labour government (from 1997)
  and Flexible New Deal 48, 49
  New Deal programmes 15
  see also Blair, Tony; Brown, Gordon
labour markets 231-2
  rising employment 267
Labour Party (in Opposition), and UC 245, 329
Lamb, Norman, mental health support 315
Lamey, Stephen 102, 113, 340
Lane Fox, Martha 158, 173-4, 340
Langsdale, Philip, IT 186, 187-90, 340
  death 190, 193
Lansley, Andrew, Health Secretary 327
Laws, David 340
  and 2007 welfare reform report 33
  and DF's comment on Minimum Wage 257
  and Universal Credit 194-5, 196

Lawson, Dominic 258
LBC, Nick Clegg's radio show 256-7
Leadsom, Andrea 307
Leakey, David, Black Rod 123
learning difficulties, adults with 131
legislation
    invocation of Financial Privilege 148-9, 151
    passage through Lords 72-4
    primary 124
    secondary 124, 135
Lehman Brothers, collapse 51
Letts, Quentin, Daily Mail 260
Letwin, Oliver 79, 110-11, 217, 340
    and Universal Credit 194-5, 199, 220
Levy, Ian, GCHQ 196
Levy, Michael, Baron 259
Lewis, Leigh, Permanent Secretary at DWP
    11-12, 22-3, 25, 47, 93, 340
    and Coalition benefit reform group 102
    and design of single benefit 19-20
    retirement 160
    and tax credits 94
Liberal Democrats
    and Coalition benefit reform group 102, 104
    and Welfare Reform Bill (2009) 73-4
    see also Coalition government
Lister, Ruth, Baroness 144, 146, 152, 284, 340
Livermore, Spencer, Treasury 27-8
Llewellyn, Ed, Downing Street head of staff
    90, 248, 255, 293, 340
Lloyd, Stephen 124
Lloyd-Jones, Janine 259
Lobban, Iain 175
Local Authorities
    co-location with Jobcentres 268, 305
    and support for the vulnerable 240-1, 268,
    304-6
Local Government Association 179-80
London, and cycling 66
lone parents 16
    and age of youngest child before taking
    work 15, 22, 28, 32-3, 37, 40, 72-3

Long Covid 301, 317
'Long Term Apprenticeship' 271
Loosemore, Tom 201, 204, 208, 210, 239-40,
    340
Loudon, Lizzie 255, 276, 340
Lovett, Bob, head of UC security 170, 182,
    183-4, 340
Low, Colin, Baron 140, 283, 284, 285-6, 340

McAvoy, Tommy, Baron 123, 142
McComb, Paul 165, 170, 196, 202, 204, 226,
    254, 340
    and budget cuts 265
    and MPA review 209
McElvoy, Anne, Evening Standard 57
Mackay, James, Baron 139-40, 146, 148, 153,
    340
McKenzie, Bill, Baron 73, 118, 128-9, 144, 340
    and Benefit Cap 140, 152-3
    and Welfare Reform Bill (2012) 137-8, 145,
    150
    and Welfare Reform and Work bill 283
McKinsey consultants 161
Macpherson, Nicholas, Treasury 246-7
McVey, Esther 215, 247-8, 259, 340
    and DF's comment on Minimum Wage
    254-5
The Mail on Sunday 109
Major Projects Authority 167-70, 182, 196, 328
    reviews 197-8, 207, 209-10, 235
Mandelson, Peter, Baron 54
Manzoni, John, MPA 245-6, 249, 328, 332,
    340
Marks, John-Paul, PPS to Duncan-Smith
    170, 340
    secondment to UC 230-1, 235, 240-1, 248
Martin, Paul 180
Maude, Francis, Minister for the Cabinet
    Office 158, 201, 340
    and cyber fraud 171
    and Government Digital Service 174, 201,
    327

and IT suppliers 216
and Major Projects Authority 168-9, 197,
  209-10
relations with Devereux 197-8, 207
on Senior Responsible Owners 331
and twin track approach 219, 222
Maxwell, Clive, OFT 244
Maxwell, Liam 196, *340*
IT 'Futures' 174, 176, 184
May, Theresa 74-5, 85-6, 94, *340*
and *Dynamic Benefits* report 78, 79
and *Get Britain Working* programme
  65-6, 67, 68-9, 83-4
as Home Secretary 90
as Prime Minister 307-9, 318
Shadow Work and Pensions Secretary 58,
  61-3, 65-6
Meacher, Molly, Baroness 148, 150, 152, *340*
and Carer's Allowance 284
and tax credits 279-80
means-tested benefits 114, 129, 260
and poverty trap 9
UC and 77, 80, 304, 312
media
and 2007 welfare reform report 33
and pressure on politicians 330-1
Mencap 257
mental health
and disability benefits 130-1, 314-15
and UC claimants 232, 271
see also disability; vulnerable
mesothelioma scandal 131
Miliband, Ed 205, *340*
and DF's comment on Minimum Wage
  252-3, 260
Miller, Maria 96, 131, 149, 185, *340*
and Committee stage of Welfare Reform
  bill 136
Minimum Wage
and National Living Wage 277-8
and people with severe learning difficulties
  251-60

Ministerial Code 331
Ministerial Oversight Group 199, 200, 201,
  202, 208
and twin track approach 216, 217-18
Moore, Jeremy 276
Moore, Sue, IRIS 176, 188, 190, *340*
Moran, Terry, as Senior Responsible Owner
  for Universal Credit 160-1, *340*
and organisation of the project 164-6, 167,
  170
withdrawal 186-7
Morgan, Delyth, Baroness, Breast Cancer
  campaign 145
Murphy, Jim 37, *340*
Myners, Paul, Baron 54

Nakonz, Karolin 176-7, 182, *340*
National Audit Office 329-30
and DWP accounts 209, 224, 248-9, 250, 325
Early Progress report 212-13, 330
National Housing Federation 96
National Living Wage 277-8
Nelson, Andy 193, 239, *340*
Nelson, Fraser
Daily Telegraph 85-6, 282, *341*
The Spectator 185-6
Newton, Tony, Baron 142, 149, *341*
Nice (National Institute for Health and Care
  Excellence) 130
Nokes, Caroline 309, 310
North West
pathfinder expansion in 219, 246
UC roll-out 297
Northcote, Sir Stafford 323-4

Oakley, Matt, Treasury 102
Office for Budget Responsibility, UC
costing notes 270, 280, 281
Oliver, Craig 213
Oliver, John, PPS 30
Oliver Wyman management consultancy
  76, 80, 161

Orr, David, National Housing Federation 204-5, 237, 287, 341

Osborne, George, Chancellor of the Exchequer 4, 307, 341
2015 Autumn Statement 282
2015 budget 277-8
2016 budget 290
and benefit reform 102, 103-4, 119
and Budget cuts 106-20, 263, 264-5, 266, 272, 274-7, 289
DF and 42, 43, 53, 54-7
and disability benefits 289-90
and *Dynamic Benefits* programme 79
and Emergency Budget (2010) 94, 108-9
and National Living Wage 277-8
and PAYE2 system 83, 84-5
relations with Theresa May 68-9
and Spending Review (2010) 117
and tax credit reductions 276-9, 282-3
and welfare cuts 293-4, 326-7

Owen, Sue, DWP 100, 101, 269, 341

Pannick, David, Baron 206
Parliamentary Voting System and Constituencies Bill (2011) 129
Patel, Narendra, Baron 140, 145, 150, 152
Patel, Priti 292
pathfinder (UC) 178, 180-1, 184, 198, 199
expansion 209, 211, 216, 246
launch 202-3
technology 218-19
payday lenders, use of continuous payment authority (CPA) 243-4
PAYE
and integration with benefits and tax credits 99-100
need for updating 81, 82, 85
and PAYE2 82-3, 84-5, 113
real-time error rate 234, 241-2
payment of benefits 82-3, 99-100, 113, 238
delays 177
frequency 133-4, 269-70

housing benefits 134-5, 142-3, 147, 166, 237-9
waiting days 275, 278, 311
Payments Council 242
Penn, Joanna 65
Penning, Mike 185, 215
pensions
raising of age 266-7
rising expenditure on 263-4
triple lock 265
People1st 66
Personal Independence Payment (PIP) 140, 143, 145, 147, 266, 302
budget threats to 289-94
see also Employment and Support Allowance (ESA)
Pickles, Eric 341
and localism 119, 134, 138-9
Pitchford, David 168, 193, 197-8, 328, 341
Chief Executive of UC 198-9, 201-4, 207
politicians
lack of expertise 331
and media 330
professional 331
Portland Trust 9, 39
Prakash, Mayank, DWP Digital Technology 299
private contractors
proposed role in 2007 welfare reforms 16, 18, 20-1, 23, 40-2, 48-9
and Work Programme 115-16, 132, 315
private sector
relations with public sector 331-2
team-building 333
productivity 313-14
Public Accounts Committee 211, 214, 220-1, 310-11, 329
Purnell, James 2, 57, 341
and Gordon Brown 57-8
and implementation of 2007 reforms 46, 47-9, 50, 52

Question Time and DF's comment on Minimum Wage 257-8

Radar, disability network 51, 131
Real Time Information system 241-2, 317
Reducing dependency, increasing opportunity options for the future of welfare to work (2007 report) 2
  conference 37-8, 42-5
  Conservative view of 43-5
  Consultation Paper 51
  cost/benefit estimates 26-7
  DEL-AME switch 17-18, 22-3, 30, 34
  design of single benefit 19-20
  DF and 11-12
  draft report 18-23
  Green Paper on 37, 39-40
  Hain and 41-2
  launch 30-4
  modifications 24-30
  presentation to Blair 22-3
  and private contractors 16, 18, 20-1, 23, 40-2, 48-9
Reeves, Rachel 225, 259-60
Renewal UK 63
Reynolds, Hilary, UC Programme Director 188, 189, 193, 341
  resignation 199-200
Ripon and Leeds, Bishop of *see* Bell, James
Robinson, Nick, BBC 252, 255
Rogers, Mark, Circle Housing 237
Ross, James 231
Roycroft, Bee 65
Rudd, Amber, Secretary for Work and Pensions 318
Ruddle, Paul 132
Ruffley, David 42-3
Rugby Jobcentre 211, 232
Russell, Justin 303

Sainsbury, Roy, York University 19
Sampson, Lara 224-5, 229, 341

sanctions 206, 234, 236-7
Scott, David, Tunbridge Wells 251, 252, 260, 341
Searle, Pete 13, 341
  and working age policy 274-5, 278, 287
self-employment, and Universal Credit 135, 314
Selous, Andrew 308
Senior Responsible Owners 331
Serco 20, 132
Seymour, Peter, Vocalink 82-3, 178-9, 341
Shapps, Grant, Housing Minister 134
Sharples, Adam 48
Shaw Trust 20
Sherlock, Maeve, Baroness 225, 283-4, 320, 341
Shield, John 211
Shiplee, Howard, Chief Executive of UC 203, 204, 207, 245, 341
  and expansion of pathfinder 209
  and GDS 224-5, 226
  illness 224, 225, 226, 233, 234
  and Public Accounts Committee 215
  and twin track approach 216, 219-20
  and Work and Pensions Select Committee 211
Shotton Jobcentre 211
skills, and productivity 313-14
Skillsmart Retail 66
Sky News 255
Smith, Peter, Baron, Wigan 241
Smith, Tim 257
Social Security Advisory Committee 178, 270
state pension, raising age of 127-30
Stephen, Isobel 38, 341
  team leader on 2007 report 13, 14, 15, 19, 21, 28
Sterling, Jeffrey, Baron 71
Stone, Tim 9, 90, 341
Stowell, Tina, Baroness 279, 308, 341
Strategic Outline Business Case 235, 246-7

Strathclyde, Tom, Baron 74, 92, 151-2, 341
Strathie, Lesley, HMRC 85
Stroud, Philippa, Baroness 84, 90-1, 186, 341
    and Cabinet Office 209
    and Coalition benefit reform group 102
    CSJ 78, 91
    and DF's comment on Minimum Wage
        255-6, 257
    and Major Projects Authority reviews 168,
        182, 197
    Reforming Tax Credits 281
    and relations with Treasury 108, 111, 146-7,
        275-6
The Sunday Telegraph, on DF's move to
    Conservatives 57
Sunday Times 57, 258, 282
Support for Mortgage Interest system 272
    from grant to loan 274-5
Supported Accommodation 284
    landlords 287
Sutton, UC digital system 268, 297
Swindells, Mark 293
Swinson, Jo, and Ministerial Summit on
    High Cost Credit 244
Sylvester, Rachel
    DF's interview with 46-7
    on DF's move to Conservatives 57

tax credits 77, 94-5, 109, 226
    and benefits 313
    HMRC and 78, 90-1
    IT development 103
    taper 275-7, 278, 280-1, 318
tax threshold, higher rate rise 290
Taylor, John, chief whip in Lords 286, 320, 341
team-building
    need for, in major government projects
        335-6
    private sector expertise 333
    and role of Implementation Minister 335-6
Third Sector Taskforce 54
Thomson, Alice, DF's interview with 46-7

Thyssen, Marianne, EU Commissioner for
    Employment 317
The Times 116, 292
Timmins, Nick, Financial Times 39, 319, 341
    coverage of 2007 report 39-42
    The Five Giants 39
Timms, Steve 51, 260, 341
Tomlinson, Justin 292, 341
    Disabilities Minister 289-90, 292
training programmes 63
Treasury 10
    and 2007 welfare reform report 34, 42
    and budget cuts (2010) 107, 109-10
    DF's view of 120, 318
    and integrated benefit system 99-100, 111,
        269
    and UC spending controls 223
    see also Vadera, Shriti
Trevelyan, Sir Charles 323-4
trials, value of 300-1
21st Century Welfare, Green Paper 110-12

UK Uncut protest group 205
unemployment
    effect of financial crisis on 51, 63
    reduction 267, 305
    youth 52
United States
    separation of powers 332
    welfare reform 13-14
Universal Credit (UC) 80
    and Alternative Payment Arrangements 238
    application process 162-3
    budgeting
        and budget cuts 265-6, 273-88
        costings 108, 119, 152, 166
        expenditure write-down 210-11, 224, 225-6
        projected savings 108, 119-20, 267
    'contention' issue 306-7, 310-11
    and earnings thresholds 194, 195-6
    and frequency of payment 133-4, 269-70
    future options for 304

'Hard List' process 230, 239
implementation
   expansion 109, 246–9
   Live Service roll-out 231–2, 233, 297–8
   national roll-out 297–8
improvements 318, 319
IT development 103, 110, 115, 306
   digital Full Service system 297, 310, 326
   digital platform 157–8, 216
January 2014 conference 232–3
labour market measures 231–2
leadership 249–50
legislative process
   Green Paper (*21st Century Welfare*)
     110–12
   policy paper 99–102
   and political commitment 326–8
   regulations 177, 269–70, 278
   Welfare Reform White Paper (2010)
     111, 117–19, 157
Minimum Income Floor 314
and passporting 135, 146–7, 194
Policy Solutions Group 210, 230
preparations for 95–6, 111–17
problems 133, 236–44
   with design 112–13
   fundamental 324–6
   project organisation problems 164–7,
     171–2, 188–90
Programme Board 164–5
publicity plan 110–13
review process
   external 329–30
   Major Projects Authority reviews
     167–70, 182, 189
   and Ministerial Oversight Group 199,
     200, 201, 202, 208
   Red Team reviews 181–2, 183, 184–5
Steady State Blueprint 199, 207–8
Strategic Outline Business Case 235, 246–7
and 'Test and Learn' 218–19, 220, 229, 230–1,
   250, 320, 321–2

timetable 159–60, 173–90, 202–3, 250, 288,
   306–7, 310–11
   unrealistic 325
twin track development 216, 217–18, 219–24,
   235, 326, 328
waiting days for 275, 278, 311
work allowances 275–6, 285–6, 318
see also IT development; pathfinder;
   Universal Support Service; Welfare
   Reform Bill (2012)
'Universal Credit at Work' report (2014)
   250, 268
Universal Life Credit 77
Universal Support Service 233, 268, 271, 304–6
   and mental health 315
Universal Work Credit 77

Vadera, Shriti, Treasury 56, 341
   and 2007 welfare reform report 24–9
Vara, Shailesh 292
Vocalink (BACS) 84, 94
   and benefit payment system 82–3, 99–100, 113
   and real-time PAYE 241–2
vocational training 66
vulnerable, local authority support for 240–1,
   268, 304–6

Waddell, Gordon, and Kim Burton, *Is Work
Good For Your Health and Wellbeing?* 14
Walker, Professor Janet 193–4
WASPI (Women against State Pension
   Inequality) 129
Watmore, Ian 171, 208, 341
Webb, Steve 96, 205, 265, 341
   Pensions Minister 128, 129, 267
welfare
   budget cuts (2010) 109
   budget cuts (2015) 274–7
   Coalition spending on 263–4
   end to budget cuts 293–4
   and proposals for single benefit 19–20, 50
   see also benefits; Universal Credit

Welfare Reform Act (2012) 127-36, 165, 173
  Committee stage 136, 141-6
  concessions 149-53
  invocation of Financial Privilege 148-9, 151
  and passporting 135, 146-7
  Report stage 147-8
  Royal assent 153-4
  secondary legislation 198
  Statutory Instrument (for pathfinder launch) 202
Welfare Reform Bill (2009) 72-4
Welfare Reform White Paper (2010) 111, 117-19
Welfare Reform and Work Act (2016) 283-7
  Report Stage 285-6
'Welfare Reforms' conference (2007) 42-5
welfare system
  future opportunities 300-1
  research-based decisions 300-1
welfare trap 9
  and disincentives 18
Wells, Phill, data analyst 13, 18, 21-2, 142, 341
Wheatley, Martin, Financial Conduct Authority 244
White, Sharon, Treasury 221, 224, 341
Whitehouse, Malcolm, DWP 100, 186, 187, 342
  IT director 158, 161-2
  Programme Director 164, 167, 171-2
Wigan, Local Authority 241

Willetts, David 63, 342
Williams, John, Special Adviser at DWP 10-11, 13, 56, 342
Wilson, Jeremy 242
Wilson, Tony, work on 2007 report 13, 19, 342
Wolfe, James 230, 239
women
  and raising of state pension age 128-9
  see also lone parents
Wonga, collapse 244
Wood, Dr Norma 196, 197, 198-9, 201, 203, 222, 342
Work Capability Assessment (WCA) 50, 302, 303
Work and Health Programme 316
Work Programme 63, 65-9, 95-6, 104-5, 267, 315-16
  private contractors and 115-16, 132, 315
Working Rite 66
working tax credit, childcare subsidy 135
Wright, Ian, UC Programme Director 249, 267-8, 298, 342

YouGov 84
Youth Hubs 306
youth unemployment schemes 52
Yuille, Jessica, Private Secretary to DF 93, 94, 96, 97-8, 195, 342

FREUD
IN THE CITY
by *David Freud*

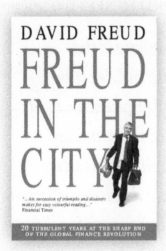

'The revolution
started here . . .
Twenty years on from
Big Bang, David Freud
looks back at an era of
far-reaching change
and outrageous salaries.'
The Observer

Battered and bemused – that's how David Freud emerged from 20 years at the sharp end of the financial revolution that shook the City of London after Big Bang. In *Freud In The City* he tells the inside story of how he accidentally moved from the world of journalism to being one of the leading and most respected investment bankers of his generation . . . and yet it all ended rather messily in a wastepaper basket.

Written with insight, pace and wit David Freud's account of his work and life is as accessible to interested outsiders as it is to those who have worked in the City of London and has been acclaimed by press and readers alike.

'*A gift for storytelling makes this autobiography of an investment banker both amusing and insightful.*' **The Financial Times**

'*The book that everybody in the Square Mile is talking about . . . a rip-roaring account of his 20 years in the City . . .*' **The Daily Telegraph**

'*A fascinating book from one who was in the thick of it.*'
Evening Standard

Hbk | 216 × 138 mm | 418 pages | ISBN 978-1-903071-19-9 £12.99   Ebk | ISBN 978-1-910533-39-0 £4.99

SEND FOR LEVENE

by Peter Levene

With a foreword by RT HON THE LORD HESELTINE CH PC

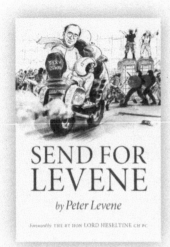

'Peter Levene is the ultimate insider who has somehow managed to retain the outsider's perspective. This story of his life is wise, surprising and often funny too.'

Daniel Finkelstein

Send for Levene records the author's remarkable career from his early days in private enterprise, his sudden transformation into a senior civil servant as Chief of Defence Procurement at the invitation Michael Heseltine, his move into investment banking and unexpected appointments to act as Prime Minister John Major's Efficiency Advisor.

In parallel, he worked his way up the City of London's civic hierarchy, becoming Lord Mayor of London which gave him the opportunity to promote the image and services of the City across the globe.

'Peter Levene gives fixers a good name. This book is full of fascination and insight.'
The Lord Hennessy of Nympsfield

'Peter Levene played a major role in winning the Cold War. he enabled Britain to build, train and deploy forces that were among the best in the world. His memoir is a page-turner and a timely cook book for our current security challenges.'
John Lehman, US Secretary of the Navy, 1981-87

Hardback | 234 × 156 mm | 256 pages | 16-page picture section | ISBN 978-1-910533-42-0   £20.00

SPOILS OF WAR

by CHRISTOPHER JOLL

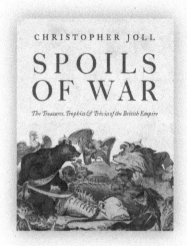

'*Each of these trophies of victory, ranging from the priceless to the valueless, has a story which Joll recounts – and sometimes debunks – with style, humour and insight*'

Michael Portillo

Over the last seven hundred years the United Kingdom has acquired a staggering array of treasures as a direct result of its military activities – from Joan of Arc's ring to the Rock of Gibraltar to Hitler's desk. *Spoils of War* describes these spoils and how they came to be acquired as well as telling the tales of some of the extraordinary (and extraordinarily incompetent) men and women, now mostly forgotten, who had a hand in the rise and fall of the British Empire. Along the way the book debunks a significant number of myths, exposes a major fraud perpetrated on a leading London museum, reveals previously unknown spoils of war and casts light on some very dark corners of Britain's military history

'*Christopher Joll has a magpie's eye for a story, combined with the dogged research skills to sniff out and solve mysteries. No one is better equipped to ignite history in this tangible and novel way.*'

Philip Mould, presenter, *Antiques Roadshow* and *Fake or Fortune*?

Hardback | 246 × 189 mm | 320 pages | Illustrated throughout | ISBN 978-1-910533-46-8   £25.00

www.nineelmsbooks.co.uk

The DRUM HORSE in the FOUNTAIN

& Other Tales of Heroes and Rogues in the Guards

CHRISTOPHER JOLL & ANTHONY WELDON

'To *dip in and out of this book is immensely enjoyable.*'

The Daily Telegraph

Co-authors Christopher Joll and Anthony Weldon capture the careers, accomplishments, follies and the occasional crimes of over three hundred of the officers and men, many of whom have been forgotten or overlooked, who, since King Charles II, have served in the seven Regiments of the Guards.

They have earned forty-four Victoria Crosses, founded the SAS, led the WW2 development of the Commandos and acted as spies, double agents and spy masters. Also included are extraordinary cast of characters such as the preferred candidate for the throne of Albani, one UK and two N Ireland Prime Ministers, plus a whole host of Cabinet Ministers, and an Archbishop of Canterbury, known as 'Killer', with an MC.

In other spheres, there have been championship boxers, footballers and Olympic medallists; best-selling authors, playwrights and composers; singing sensations, international musicians in the fields of pop, jazz, light and classical music as well as comedians, artists, and two Oscar-winning film stars.

Hbk | 234 × 156 mm | 314 pages | ISBN 978-1-910533-40-6 £20.00   Ebk | ISBN 978-1-910533-41-3 £4.99

www.nineelmsbooks.co.uk